William Henry Giles Kingston

The albatross

Or, Voices from the ocean

William Henry Giles Kingston

The albatross
Or, Voices from the ocean

ISBN/EAN: 9783337071653

Printed in Europe, USA, Canada, Australia, Japan

Cover: Foto ©ninafisch / pixelio.de

More available books at **www.hansebooks.com**

THE ALBATROSS

OR

VOICES FROM THE OCEAN

A Tale of the Sea

BY

WILLIAM H. G. KINGSTON

AUTHOR OF "DIGBY HEATHCOTE"

LONDON
GEORGE ROUTLEDGE AND SONS
THE BROADWAY, LUDGATE
NEW YORK: 416 BROOME STREET
1877

LONDON:
SAVILL, EDWARDS AND CO., PRINTERS, CHANDOS STREET,
COVENT GARDEN.

TO THE

RIGHT HON. EARL NELSON.

MY DEAR LORD,

THE most valuable privilege of an author being the opportunity he enjoys of dedicating his works to those whom he highly esteems, I have the gratification, although conscious that the following trifling pages of a sea story are scarcely worthy of your Lordship's acceptance, to offer them to you, both as one ever foremost to promote every noble and virtuous object, and as the energetic champion, in the Senate, of that glorious service in which your great relative fought and died, and to which all wise men still must look in time of need, as the firm bulwark of our beloved country.

I have the honour to be,

My dear Lord,

Very faithfully and respectfully yours,

WILLIAM H. G. KINGSTON.

THE ALBATROSS:

OR,

VOICES FROM THE OCEAN.

CHAPTER I.

LEAVING HOME.

"HOME, home, sweet, sweet home, there's no place like home!" so I sing, and so every honest man will sing, who is blest with one, and knows what it is to be sent roving round the world for years at a stretch, without one glimpse of those dear familiar faces that one has known from childhood: a mother's fond glance, a father's kind smile, and the affectionate embraces of half-a-dozen laughing blue-eyed sisters and noisy brothers, not to speak of one other with whom one has ventured to exchange tokens, which one cherishes as the apple of one's eye, amid the raging storm, the shipwreck, and the fight; but I must not touch on that subject, or I shall be apt to grow sentimental and bothersome, for however agreeable and delightful it may be for oneself to contemplate, the hard-hearted public do not care one straw about it. Many are the long weary months one has to pass without getting a line from them, to say whether they are alive or dead, what new ones are born, and who is married. What a yearning springs up in the heart to see them all again; with what trembling eagerness does one tear open the long-looked-for letter from home; how breathlessly does one read on to see that all are well. Oh, "you gentlemen of England who stay at home at ease," if you think lightly of these things, just go away from all you love, wrench asunder all your ties to earth, and if your hearts are not withered like parched peas or blighted apples, you will understand the feelings of seamen, and know how to appreciate their sacrifices and their hardships. "Ah! little do you think upon the dangers of the seas."

"Mary, my dear, another cup of tea—Carry, hand mamma the cream jug—Come, Johnny, get through with that slice of bread and butter, and run up and finish your sum—Fanny, it's your turn to butter papa's toast—How's Pop this morning, Frank?—Oh, he'll keep up with Trumpeter, if papa ride him,—Robert, send me over the eggs, I'm sharp set this morning." Such were the sounds flying round the breakfast table, when the servant placed the post bag in due form in my father's hands. Its contents were drawn forth, when a long official-looking letter made its appearance. "On Her Majesty's Service," was printed on the left-hand upper corner, and the superscription was to Lieutenant Walter Fairfield, R.N., so and so, near so and so, Hants, being to no less a personage than my humble self. "His promotion," exclaimed one. "How nice, to have him made a captain," cried another. "Not very likely," I answered; and if for a moment such a vain idea did cross my mind, it speedily vanished. "Miracles have long since ceased." I tore open the envelope. "Appointed to Her Majesty's brig, Albatross, as second lieutenant," I exclaimed. "She'll be ready for sea in three or four weeks; she's a beautiful craft, just the one I should have chosen." In the thoughts of active service, so pleasant to a seaman, I confess that I forgot for the moment from whom I must part.

"Why, Walter, the Albatross; she's fitting for the Coast of Africa," exclaimed Frank, who knew the name of every ship in commission, with all their officers, and longed to follow my footsteps on the sea.

"Are you certain, boy?" asked my father, half angrily, as if the youngster had been the means of sending her there, for the name sounded ominous in his ears.

"Oh, positive!" answered Frank. "It's in last Sunday's paper."

I knew he was right, but did not like to say so. The paper, however, was produced by the thoughtless boy, and his assertion found to be correct.

"My dear child, how dreadful," exclaimed my mother, the tears coming into her eyes. "That horrid coast! I wish it had never been discovered."

"Never mind, mother," I answered, laughing. "The devil, you know, isn't half as black as he is painted, and one only has to take care of oneself, not to sleep on shore, drink brandy, or be swallowed up by sharks or crocodiles, to find it a perfect paradise. Just think of the lots of things I'll bring you home. Elephants' teeth, bags of gold-dust, and jars of palm oil, or, if you like it better, a tame alligator, or a live elephant. Think how interesting it would be, to have them running about on the lawn. Tim and Pop will be delighted to have such nice playmates, wont they, Fanny?"

"How can you joke about such dreadful things, my poor boy?" answered my mother, fairly weeping. "May Heaven in its mercy preserve you; but you are so careless and thoughtless, you'll never take care of yourself."

"Ah! mother," I replied, softened, "but you know there's 'a sweet little cherub who sits up aloft, to take care of the life of poor Jack.' He'll watch over me, mother, and if I didn't value my own life, I know there are those who would mourn were I to slip my cable, so rather than grieve their hearts, I promise I'll do my best to bring myself back safe in limb and constitution. What more can I do? Where I'm ordered, there I must go. It would never do, if every officer in Her Majesty's service were to look out for a soft plank for himself."

That day was a melancholy one in my family—every member of

it had conjured up in their mind's eye pictures of damp fogs, burning suns, yellow fever, noisome marshes, sharks, alligators, pirates, and slavers, till they believed it was scarcely possible for human beings to escape from their united attacks. It was some time before they got at all reconciled to the thoughts of my departure, and every time I met my mother she had tears in her eyes. Oh! what a boundless sea of love there must be in a mother's heart, thus to feel for one son out of many, and he not more loved than the rest. My sisters were more affectionate than usual, and the boys were ready to do everything I asked them.

That evening found me walking in a green shady lane which led between my father's house and the vicarage. It was little frequented except by the two families, who were on terms of friendly intimacy. I was not alone, and though my companion wore a straw bonnet and a shawl, she was not my sister. The blue laughing sea was visible in the far distance beneath the overhanging trees; green meadows, and yellow fields of corn, with waving woods, and many a neat cheerful cottage, a village church spire, and a stately mansion surrounded by beautiful gardens, filled up the interval. It was a lovely view, such as England only can furnish, and eyes looked on it then, than which brighter shone not in the world; the breath of heaven never fanned softer or more sunny curls from a fairer brow; redder lips never parted with a sweeter smile, to disclose more pearl-like teeth, or a voice more melodious uttered words more pleasing to the lover's ear. It was the voice, that estimable thing in woman, which did the work, after all, I believe. The fact was—there is no use longer concealing it—I was over head and ears in love with the most beautiful and charming girl in the neighbourhood, and—however, I have no business to say how she felt towards me. If her eyes sparkled with pleasure when I first sang,

> "I'm a brisk and sprightly lad,
> Just come home from sea, sir;
> Of all the lives I ever led,
> A sailor's life for me, sir, &c. &c."

so did those of my sisters and mother and half-a-dozen she cousins besides. We sat down on a green bank to look at the view, and somehow or other her hand was in mine and she forgot to withdraw it. It is a way young people have of establishing an electric telegraph in aid of conversation, and for the life of me I could never see any objection in it. We were far from loquacious, though we had much to say. We looked at the view, and drank in its beauties.

"I shall often think of this evening, Edith, when I am far away," I whispered. "It will be a sunny spot in memory to light up the picture of life, though all around is dark and gloomy."

She did not answer. There was a pearly drop on her fair cheek, and a slight sob told plainly that feelings which made my breast even then thrill with delight, had overpowered her—feelings which, had it not been for my contemplated departure, she would have scarcely owned even to herself. Truly the sweets of life are sent to soften the bitterest potions it is our lot to drink. Sunshine and clouds are kindly mingled by our beneficent Ruler. What could I do but draw her unresistingly to my heart, to kiss away those precious tears? Oh, that evening lives ever, and will ever remain the bright oasis in my life's rugged desert. Edith, I did not speak false, when I told you so.

I was proud, very proud. I had won the love of a peerless girl. What matters it to the public how I had done so—and why she preferred me to a number of soldier-officers, sedate clergymen, and elder sons with large fortunes? Perhaps it was that I was a bold, harum-scarum, fearless youth, with a countenance somewhat like mahogany—a contrast to her own fair cheeks. Perhaps because I told her of my voyages and hair-breadth escapes, the tempests and fights I had encountered. Perhaps because I had given her an honest, guileless heart, and had told her how fondly, how devotedly I loved her.

The tears had ceased to flow, and smiles had taken their place, and there was a rich glow upon her cheek.

"Oh, Walter, Walter!" she whispered, "I ought not to have confessed to you as I have done, but I was taken by surprise; indeed, indeed it was the thought that you were going away, that I might see you no more, that made me say what I did."

"For worlds, dearest, I would not have it unsaid," I replied. "Edith, you have made me more happy than I can express."

But avast, here am I running on against all my previous intentions, and telling the world little bits of my own private history, which, however sweet and delightful to myself, the said busy world no more cares for than it does for the proceedings of the man in the moon or the Khan of Tartary. The sun went down into the purple sea in a way it seldom condescends to do on the shores of England; the rooks flew home over our heads with loud caws to their long-inhabited domains; the cottage chimneys sent up curling wreaths of smoke, as the good wives were cooking their husbands' suppers; and the twilight, that blessing of a northern clime, grew less and less, and still we sat on, forgetful of the coming night. So it is in life—another of the immeasurable blessings showered on the heads of those who do not carry thick umbrellas to guard them; we are able to enjoy the present sunshine without thinking of the dark clouds in store for us. Suddenly we were reminded of the realities of the world by feeling a pair of arms with dirty hands thrown round our necks, and the rosy face of my young monkey of a brother Frank shoved in, grinning, between ours.

"Where have you two been all this time?" he exclaimed. "Why there's the tea-urn has been hissing away on the table this half hour, and every one thought you were lost. Edith, I shall take precious good care you don't go out walking with that young *ossifer*, except you have a sage old man like me to look after you."

The sly rogue, he had the impertinence to steal a kiss while he was speaking. Edith and I did, I'm afraid, look very conscious, when we walked into the drawing-room, and all my brothers and sisters would have guessed what had happened, even if that young mischief-maker, Frank, hadn't taken good care to enlighten them. Everything must have an end, and so had that blessed day, and the few other days I could call my own.

CHAPTER II.

A LIFE ON THE OCEAN WAVE.

At length I trod the deck of Her Majesty's brig Albatross as her second lieutenant. When I joined her, she was still alongside the old Topaze, in Portsmouth harbour; and every one who has fitted out a ship knows the contrast she must have offered to the cheerful quiet of our country home. Instead of the soft voices of my laughing sisters and the sweet tones of their music, the sound of the boatswain's whistle, and the hoarse bawling of his mates, were continually in my ears—sounds then little consonant to my feelings. Though other ships fitting out for southern stations at the same time were short of men, we had little difficulty in making up our complement. Jack, as long as he gets a ship he likes, and a good captain, cares little where he goes. The risk of death by yellow fever and cannon shot never comes within his calculations.

With the two first most certainly no fault could be found. Our ship was a model of nautical beauty and sea-worthy qualities. With great beam, and consequent stability, she had sharp bows and a clean run; nor did she afterwards belie her appearance. Her captain was every inch a sailor, of the rough-and-ready school, yet withal of very gentlemanly manners, of bravery oft-tried, and honour as keen as his sword. Though he had been all his life at sea, he had managed to become the father of a large family, but I can answer that the service lost nothing on that account. He wanted interest, however, though not merit, and was now, at the age of sixty or upwards, sent as a commander to the coast of Africa, either to gain his promotion, and a few hundred pounds prize money, or to make way for younger men. I will describe my other shipmates by and by. The week after I joined we cast off from the hulk, and went out to Spithead, where we took our powder on board, and hoisted the Blue Peter; the men were paid their wages in advance, all visitors were sent on shore, and in two days more we were running out at the Needles with a north-easterly breeze, which carried us clear of the Channel. Here was I once more fairly afloat, and happily on such occasions one hasn't much time for thought, or it might be too painful to bear. There is so much bustle and hurry, and too much to do, for a moment's idleness. Everything is at bottom and nothing at top, and everything has to be stowed in its proper place; and when below, everybody has something to say—to ask who one knows, and where one has been, and with whom one has sailed; all of which questions must be answered and asked in return; and the sea air and the fatigue of one's duty make sleep easily gained; and as thought is painful, one tries not to think. I speak from my own feelings, and I believe others will agree with me.

We soon had still more occupation, for a gale sprung up from the south-west, which drove us nearly back into the chops of the Channel, and kicked up such a sea, that the weatherly qualities of the craft were well tried, as was the seamanship of her officers, and the stomachs of the youngsters and landsmen. For three days and nights we were hove-to, tumbling about and pitching our bows into the sea, but not a drop of water did she make below, and scarcely a spray broke on deck, and on the fourth day, escaping all danger, we again made sail to the southward.

The first land we sighted was the snow-capped Peak of Teneriffe, which, when one of the youngsters saw somewhere about thirty miles off, he took to be an iceberg taking a summer cruize; and was much surprised at the time we were getting up to it, and more so when, instead of a lump of ice, he beheld a black rugged mountain, twelve thousand feet high, rising like a vast burnt-up cinder from out of the blue ocean, the brightness of the sun glancing on its lava-coloured sides, making it look as if it had rushed up red-hot from some mighty furnace within the far-down bowels of the earth—nor could one suppose that anything with animal or vegetable life could inhabit it, except the fire-loving salamander. It has, however, human beings, and fruit trees, and vineyards, and a town, yclept Santa Cruz, containing a church, which boasts not of saintly relics—St. Anthony's toe, or St. Barnabas's wig—but of trophies which are to be seen in very few other places: namely, two British Union Jacks, taken from us on the night when Nelson lost his arm, and very nearly his life. We can well afford to let them remain, for neither Nelson's memory nor British honour suffers thereby, I opine.

The next place we brought up in was Porto Praya, in St. Jago, one of the Cape de Verde Islands, that our captain might pay a visit to the governor, who resides at Praya, in order to gain his assistance in procuring information as to where we might fall in with the slavers.

The town of Praya is one of the most unattractive-looking places I ever saw. It stands on a slight elevation above the sea, at the head of a shallow bay, bounded on either side by marshy swamps, which do not make it one of the most healthy places in the world. It is guarded by a battery of guns which have seen better days, and are now more likely to injure those who attempt to fire them off than an enemy.

I accompanied the captain in his visit to the governor. We disembarked at a most primitive landing-place on the rough rocks, from whence a road—but little indebted to art—conducted up to the town. Dirt is the characteristic of the place. Sights unwonted in northern climes met our eyes at every turn. Black children, of all ages and sizes, without a rag of clothing, rolling with friendly pigs in the mud; animals of various sorts, donkeys and swine, goats and dogs, wandering about in and out of the houses in unrestrained freedom.

The house of the governor is the best in this most delectable place. A black soldier, in a ragged uniform, with his toes through his shoes, was doing duty as guard at the gates, and presented arms as we passed into a court-yard strewed with rotting straw, and filled with asses, goats, poultry, hogs, and dogs, who seemed very little inclined to make way for us, as we endeavoured to wade up to the entrance door. This even was not accomplished without a desperate encounter with a large baboon, the guardian spirit of the place, who, as soon as he caught sight of us, flew at us with grinning teeth, and loud chattering, but was fortunately brought up by a chain, which tethered him to the ground, before he had committed any mischief; then commenced a concert of all the other animals, ducks quacking, geese cackling, donkeys braying, pigs grunting, and dogs barking; in the midst of which we were ushered into the state apartment of Senhor Capitao Diego Bravo de Castro Montero, or some other similarly long name, who received us with due politeness, and offered for our accommodation two of the six chairs which composed his furniture.

While he was doing the polite to the captain, one of his officers attended to me, though as he spoke only a very few words of English, and I not one of Portuguese, we did not very clearly comprehend each other. The conversation, however, lasted for some time, but we went away about as wise as we arrived. Of course his excellency was entirely ignorant of any slaving transactions—poor innocent man—and would not say a word on the subject, but he acknowledged that not long before our arrival, a large armed schooner had put in there under French colours; that she had a numerous motley crew, who spent their money freely; and that she did not appear to be fitted as a slaver, and certainly not as a merchantman. Gaining full particulars respecting the appearance of this vessel, we took our departure the same evening, and made sail for the island of Boa Vista, passing several others of the same group on our way.

The Portuguese government agent in this place is a notorious slave dealer, although a very polished gentleman in his manners. Scarcely had our anchors' reached the bottom, than he came on board, accompanied by a present of coffee, fruit, and vegetables, and attended by two soldiers as a body guard. Both were negroes armed with rusty muskets, the head of one covered with an old straw-hat, that of the other with a battered shako—their jackets were made for men of smaller dimensions, and were now out at elbows—yellow cross belts, and trowsers which once were white, with the legs in tatters, exhibiting their shoeless black feet and ankles below, completed their costume. But such things were trifles to this citizen of the world. His aim was to keep us there if he could, or to learn our intended proceedings. He was very ready to give us every possible information which might mislead us. We here, however, gained further intelligence of the strange schooner, and from all we heard there was little doubt that she was a pirate. Several vessels which had called off here had been chased by a craft answering her description, and one which was expected some weeks before had never been heard of.

Boa Vista is a miserable-looking place, composed of some fifty or sixty huts; and we were not sorry to get free of it and its slave-dealing governor.

CHAPTER III.

A MAN OVERBOARD.

A FINE breeze carried us clear of Boa Vista, its dirt, its rags, and slave dealers, as we sailed on our way towards the delectable coast of Africa, to endeavour to capture, sink, or destroy, all vessels engaged in the nefarious traffic in human flesh. Englishmen are ever ready to expend their lives and their gold in a good cause—and what more noble one is there than the abolition of slavery? But it is sad to think how inadequate our success has been to our exertions, and how much extra misery the unfortunate captives suffer in consequence. It is in vain, however, to hope to put a stop to the trade, while the Brazilians and other Americans, as well as the Portuguese, do all in their power to protect the wretches engaged in it. I have known over and over again, vessels fitted out in the Tagus, the Douro, and at Rio, expressly for the purpose, the money being supplied by merchants, who having by the same means amassed large fortunes, were considered by their countrymen as of great credit and respectability. It is no wonder such countries do not flourish—the withering curse of God must hang over them while they are guilty of such crimes. But I have got a long way out of my course. I was going to describe a sad accident which happened the day after we lost sight of the islands. It was the forenoon watch, and I was walking the quarter-deck with Upton, our first lieutenant, with whom I was earnestly discussing our future prospects, and the best method of performing the onerous duties imposed upon us by our country. There was not much sea running, though it was blowing pretty fresh from the north-west, and we were bowling along at the rate of some eight knots an hour. I had just turned at the break of the quarter-deck, after having looked up to see how our canvass stood, and observed a top-man going out to the fore-topsail yard-arm, when, before we had scarcely made two paces, the startling cry of a man overboard sounded in our ears. I ran to the side—it was no false alarm—and within a few feet of the ship I saw a poor fellow struggling in the waves, and turning an imploring glance at us for assistance. I hove a rope, which was at hand, to him, but at that moment a wave coming rolling down and breaking over his head, it missed his eager grasp, and his fingers clutched the air. The effort was almost fatal to him, for he could swim but little, and his strength was soon exhausted. When I saw him miss the rope, which I had hove with almost supernatural strength, without waiting to see what became of him, or attempting to heave it again, for I knew it would be useless to do so, I rushed aft to the life-buoy, and pulling the lanyard which secured it to the taffrail, let it fall into the water. The performance of what I have been describing did not occupy thirty seconds—Lieutenant Upton was issuing the necessary orders to heave the ship to.

"Let fly the fore-topmast studding-sail sheets," he exclaimed, in a clear, steady tone, which did not betray the slightest quiver of excitement. "Port the helm—jam it down—brace up the main yard—man the starboard head braces—rise the fore-tack—square the head-yards. Be smart about it. Run away with the starboard braces, my lads—belay all that."

The men needed no words of encouragement, for every one felt that the life of a fellow-creature depended on the exertions. As it happened, unfortunately, not one of the watch on deck were good swimmers, and although I was perfectly at home in the water, an accident a few days before, which had lamed my arm, would have made it madness in me to leap overboard to the poor fellow's rescue. While the ship was being brought up to the wind, Green, the master, who had that instant come on deck, called the crew of the larboard quarter boat, and running to the falls, made preparation to lower her into the water as soon as it could be done with safety. When I had let go the life-buoy, I watched the poor fellow carefully that I might direct the boat in what course to steer. Everything, on such occasions, depends on each officer performing his especial duty, that two may not be engaged in doing one thing, while some other essential point is neglected. I regretted to see that the man could not reach the life-buoy, though he kept himself well above water, by paddling with his hands, and treading with his feet. I shouted to him, and pointed to the life-buoy, for if he could once have got hold of it he would have been safe enough, but he could neither hear nor see me, and I suspect was so frightened, poor fellow, that he scarcely knew what he was about. It was sad to see his head now rising on the top of a wave, now sinking again, and to feel that before human aid could reach him, he might go down into the profound depths of the ocean, and be no more seen by his fellow-men. Already he seemed almost cut off from us—an inhabitant of another world. The ship was quickly brought to, the gig was lowered, and Green, with five men, leaped into her, and guided by me as I stood in the main-rigging, pulled in the direction of the drowning man. He was now, from the change in the position of the ship, on the starboard beam. The men bent to their oars with every nerve strained to the utmost, to the no little risk of swamping the boat, for there was so much sea running, that much exertion was required in keeping her head to it, when the heavier waves broke. Several times I thought she would have filled, when the lives of all would, too probably, have been sacrificed. The brave fellows, however, thought not of the danger to themselves, but dashed onward. I waved them on. I saw the man's head for a moment on the summit of a foaming wave. I looked eagerly, with beating heart, for his reappearance. Seconds flew by—on such occasions, moments are like hours, of ordinary life—sea after sea rose and fell without a speck to be seen amid these foaming crests. In vain I looked—the boat reached the spot where he had been—she pulled to it—I threw up my hand to shew that I could no longer see him; I perceived by her wide steering that the people in her were equally unsuccessful in finding him. They persevered, however, for some minutes in the search, and I trusted at one time that they had got hold of him, but it was only his hat.

"He's gone," exclaimed several voices near me, in sorrowful tones. "Honest Jack Power; poor, poor fellow!—

> "'He'll ne'er hear more the tempest howling,
> For death has broached him to.'"

He was a fine active young fellow, and no one could account for the cause of his falling from aloft, except, as it was supposed, that he must have been seized with some sudden fit or dizziness, and lost his hold. Green evidently did not like to come on board without the man, for he continued the search long after all hope must have fled. Seeing this, Captain Dainmore ordered the signal to recall the boat to be hoisted. Observing it, the master pulled for the life-buoy, which he towed alongside. With sorrowful faces, the boat's crew came on deck, the boat was hoisted up, so was the life-buoy, and replaced in its proper position, the sails were again filled, and the ship was kept away on her former course. In a few more minutes everything was as before, and the proper inquiries having been made as to the accident, Upton and I resumed our walk on the quarter-deck, as if nothing had happened out of the usual course, though naturally our conversation referred to the event which had occurred.

That day at the gun-room dinner it was also the subject of conversation. Captain Dainmore happened to be dining with us, which he did frequently, to our very great benefit, for his conversation was not only agreeable and sensible, but he contrived to throw in so much good advice, without appearing to be giving it, that no one could fail of profiting by it. I need not say that he was loved and respected by us all.

Upton, our first lieutenant, was a fine gentlemanly fellow, without any interest, or he would have been a post captain before that. He was tall, and remarkably good-looking, though his countenance was somewhat weather-beaten and sun-burnt, in the tropical climes and icy regions in which he had spent the flower of his youth. He did not repine at his lot; I never heard him grumble during all the time we were together, or abuse the powers that be, because he had not received the due reward of his merits. In general society he was inclined to be silent, for he was of a retiring, modest disposition, but he could talk well, and even on sufficient occasion would be very eloquent; indeed, at such times, he had full command of language, for his soul was in what he said. His mind was philosophical, but he was not at all deficient in quick humour, and of his power of narrating a story, I will leave others to judge. I will not further sound his panegyric than by saying, that he was every inch a sailor, and a polished gentleman, a good Christian, and a first-rate officer. Of the second lieutenant of the Albatross, Walter Fairfield, it becomes me not to speak, further than to say, that he hoped he possessed some good qualities, that most assuredly he was not without faults, that he earnestly wished they were fewer, and that he endeavoured to correct them. If, however, his character must be published to the world, he would rather it were one drawn by Miss Edith Mowbray, than a portrait taken by any other hand. Yet he has a shrewd suspicion that were he to give it in these pages, not only would he be accused of a piece of absurd vanity, but the world would insist, that if it were a likeness at all, it was wonderfully overdrawn. All he can say is, that he wishes he was like the picture, and that if he has since grown more similar to it, it was thy gentle hand, sweet girl, which, with consummate art, moulded his rough form into the shape thy pure fancy had first conceived it. But avast, avast! how egotistical is man's nature, so I will not say another word about myself.

The name of the master was, as I have said, Green. He was as excellent a fellow as ever stepped; not very polished, and not highly educated certainly, but he was essentially a gentleman, that is to say, he would never do an act a gentleman need be ashamed of, and had done many things the proudest noble in the land might well be vain of doing. He was married, and was very fond of his wife, though he had no children. I never saw his good woman as he called her, but from all I could hear, she was a very amiable person, well suited to add to his happiness, during the short time he was able to remain at home with her. I see his round, good-natured countenance before me as visibly as if we had just parted, and hear his joyous ringing laughter even now in my ears, such as he indulged in as he listened to some facetious story, or told some of his own amusing adventures.

Haggis was our surgeon, a clever man in his profession, and a sensible, kind-hearted person. He was a Scotchman, and had most of the peculiarities of his countrymen—peculiarities, by-the-by, which often enable them to triumph over difficulties which would have turned back the people of any other nation. He had seen a good deal of service, had visited many different countries, had much observation, and consequently possessed a fund of valuable information, by which we, his shipmates, much benefited.

Our purser was called Sleepwell. He was a very good sort of man—he was not either particularly liked or disliked; he was not stupid, but certainly not witty; if he didn't do much good, he was never accused of committing a bad action, and we might easily have got a worse purser. He might have been said to be a single-minded man, for he never allowed a conversation to continue any length of time, without introducing the interesting and edifying subject of the purser's accounts. He did so most ingeniously, and might have been compared to a practised Indian hunter waiting for his prey, so dexterously did he throw in the dart as the quarry passed by. It proved what an excellent purser he was, and how closely he attended to his studies. To him the subject was the most interesting and absorbing in the world, and it did not occur to his mind that others would not take so much interest in it.

The senior mate was Henry Seaton, a gentlemanly, highly-educated young man, slightly inclined to be sentimental, but an excellent officer and a brave fellow. He had plighted his troth to a fair girl, the last time he was on shore, and I, of all people in the world, had no right to find fault with him for so doing. The tenant of the midshipman's berth next in rank to him was Hawkins, a strong, active, good-tempered young man, very steady, and fond of his profession. However, I do not intend to give a catalogue *raisonné* of the officers and crew of Her Majesty's ship Albatross, and will therefore wait to describe their characteristics as they come before me in the course of my narrative. As it is, I am afraid that I may be considered by the world to have given too partial and favourable an account of my shipmates, and that the ill-natured will exclaim, " I dare say you were all a very stupid, good set of fellows, from whom not a particle of fun is to be expected. Except Sleepwell, there was not a single character worth a line of description, and he, after all, was merely the common type of pursers, or indeed of small-minded men of any other profession in the world."

If such be said, my reply is, that my readers must find fault with the Admiralty. I did not appoint the officers to the Albatross. I was myself merely one of the appointed. Had I, however, been allowed to choose a set of fellows, who were likely to pull well together, I can truly say, I could not have made a better selection, for the Albatross was, in every respect, a happy ship. The captain regarded his officers and crew as his children, and they loved and revered him in return.

I must not forget another inhabitant of the gun-room, who was not borne on the ship's books. Frank Marsden had come out from England with us as a passenger for the benefit of his health. It may seem strange, that he should have selected the coast of Africa for that purpose, but he was advised to cure a desperate ill by a desperate remedy. His malady was supposed to be consumption, and it was hoped that a tropical climate might ward off the voracious tyrant. Poor fellow! we all liked him exceedingly—he was so amiable, so gentlemanly, so talented. He was distantly related to Captain Dainmore, and also to Upton, and hence it was that he became our guest. Very glad, indeed, were we to have him, and he certainly contrived to raise our intellectual faculties far higher than they would have probably soared without his example.

The wind had gone down since the morning, and so had the sea, and with the skylight off, we were seated in the gun-room, the cloth being removed after dinner, sipping our wine. As I said, the conversation turned on the accident which had occurred in the morning, and Captain Dainmore impressed upon us the importance of being always prepared for such an emergency.

" How many a melancholy catastrophe might have been prevented by proper precautions," he observed. " The boats' falls should always be kept clear, and the life-buoy trimmed, and ready to let go in a moment. I feel sure, Mr. Upton, such is always the case on board this ship."

" I trust so, sir," answered Upton. " Indeed, of the importance of what you say, I have had too many convincing evidences not to make me feel that I should be very culpable were I to neglect to see to that matter. I remember, in particular, an incident which occurred a few years ago, respecting a poor lad, in whom I felt considerable interest, and as my story will not take long to tell, you shall hear it, sir, if you please, before we go on deck."

" Gladly," answered Captain Dainmore; and we all responding to the same sentiment, Upton began in his fluent, yet quiet way, the following tale. I suspect that he was rather proud of his peculiar powers of narrating a story. It might have been supposed that he was all the time reading what he had previously carefully written. He shared in the extraordinary talent possessed by that refined and delightful novelist, Mr. G. P. R. James, whose language, when he speaks or dictates to his amanuensis, is as flowing and harmonious as his works appear when printed. Those who have heard him converse, will support the very inadequate praise I can bestow. Upton's tale will, I hope, be considered worthy of the separate chapter which I have devoted to it.

CHAPTER IV.

THE FIRST LIEUTENANT'S YARN.—POOR TOM BUNT.

BEAULIEU River, though little known to fame, possesses beauties of no ordinary kind, and yet I suspect that not ten of the many thousand persons who have passed through the Needles have ever floated on its tranquil waters, or wandered along its fertile banks. I may venture, therefore, to describe it. It is a stream whose embouchure is on the coast of Hampshire, opposite the Isle of Wight, and about midway between Southampton and the pretty little town and port of Lymington. It takes its rise amid the sunny glades and green slopes, the majestic time-worn oaks, and dense groves of the far-famed New Forest, now the largest which merry England boasts. After winding its way slowly onward for some miles beneath the umbrageous shelter of the forest trees, with many a deep pool where the fat tench delight to live, it hurries through a wild open heath till it passes beneath the walls of the old Manor House, then through the arches of a long and low bridge, when it expands into a broad and beautiful piece of water (at least, when the tide is in), its banks on either side broken into little points and bays, thickly covered with trees of many varied tints and graceful forms. Thus it runs on, more like an inland lake than a salt water river, till, gradually widening and deepening, it finds its way into the broad expanse of the Solent sea. On the west bank of the river stand some hoary ruins, the remains of the beautiful abode of the pious and wealthy monks of Beaulieu, till they were driven forth to wander exiles in strange lands, while their property was confiscated by the eighth Henry of England. A few gable ends and crumbling walls, used to support cow-sheds, and certain underground chambers, unknown to the public, are all that remain of the venerable pile. Changed indeed is Beaulieu.

Within the memory of many of the tenants of the neighbouring farm-houses, it boasted of a royal dockyard, where several noble ships of war, which afterwards carried the victorious banner of England into strange seas, were built; but now not the sound of a solitary carpenter's saw or hammer is heard, except for constructing a pig-shed, or repairing a fishing-boat, and a lobster dredger or a smuggling cutter are the only vessels one meets. Some years ago,

B

a pretty neat little cottage stood not far from the water's edge, inhabited by an old woman and her grand-niece.

Betsy Turner was one of the prettiest girls I ever saw, that is to say, a perfect rural beauty of the true Norman race, who abound in that part of Hampshire, nut-brown maids, with dark flashing eyes, and rich ruby lips; and she was as good and modest, too, as she was handsome, though she did not pride herself on being either one or the other. Now Betsy had a lover, in which she was perfectly right, as he was a fine, dashing, good-looking young fellow, and few would think the worse of her for it, however much the girls might envy her. Tom Bunt loved Betsy with all his heart, and she had given him hers in return. He was a sailor, and a good one, too; the most active aloft, the first to go to the weather earing in a squall, the most fearless in danger. Tom had made several voyages before he lost his heart, and had brought home plenty of the rhino, but he was open-handed and the greater part of it soon went, till somehow or other Betsy and he found themselves, one fine Sunday afternoon, walking home together through a quiet green lane.

Tom told his love, and took Betsy's hand in his, and his heart almost jumped up his throat when she did not withdraw it; and when he afterwards ventured on a kiss, though she blushed, she did not grow angry, but rather the contrary. Thus Tom Bunt and Betsy Turner plighted their troth. Then it was Tom first began to regret he had not saved his money. The little he had remaining would scarcely support him and his wife for a few months in the way he thought she deserved. Betsy's aunt, too, would not hear of her marrying a man who had not money to keep her as she had been accustomed.

"No, her niece should never marry a sailor, who would go and leave her a widow, or as good as one, and perhaps never come back again."

This made poor Tom very sad. In this humour, as he was walking home by himself, after a severe lecture from the old lady, he met an acquaintance, Dick Dounton by name, the owner of a fast-sailing lugger, long well known to the revenue cruisers. In fact, Dounton was one of the most daring smugglers about the island. The king's cutter had watched for him year after year in vain; he was so sharp a fellow, and had so many artful dodges, that they could never catch him.

"Well, messmate, Tom Bunt, ho, ho!—where away now?—why so downcast, man?" he sung out, as Tom was about to pass him with a slight salutation.

Tom knew that Dounton was a freetrader, yet, though he had never done anything in the smuggling line, it could not be expected that he should look on it as a very heavy offence. Tom could not do less than heave to, and shake Dounton by the hand.

"Oh—nothing, nothing," he answered: "one can't always be singing, you know."

"Oh, come now, you can't deceive me by hoisting false lights," replied Dounton; "you've got a sweetheart, man, and she hasn't been kind to you."

"No, no, not so bad as that neither; she loves me more than I deserve, but it's the want of the rhino that bothers me. I wish I knew how I could double my gold as the merchants do, to satisfy the old lady."

"Oh, is that it?" exclaimed Dounton, with a whistle; "come into the 'Jolly Rover,' and we'll talk the matter over with a pipe and a glass of ale."

Into the bar of the "Jolly Rover" they went, and Tom opened his heart to Dounton, and Dounton told Tom how he might not only double his fortune, but make it ten times as large in a few weeks with only a little trouble and danger. The proposal seemed so tempting to the lover's imagination, that before they parted Tom had engaged to embark all the money he had saved in a smuggling speculation with Dounton. One trip across the channel would do the job, and he would then forswear smuggling, marry Betsy, and live quietly at home attending to their farm and his fishing-boat. He forgot the old saying, "that there's many a slip between the cup and the lip."

Betsy was surprised to see him come back in such high glee the next morning. When, however, he told her of his plan, she looked grave, and endeavoured to dissuade him from it, but his arguments were so powerful that at last love triumphed, and she consented to let him go. She also had been taught to look upon smuggling as a very venial offence; everybody, more or less, around her, was engaged in it; and small was the quantity of liquor in any of the neighbouring farm-houses or pot-houses which had ever paid duty.

Behold Tom Bunt, then, on board the Skittish Kitty lugger, Richard Dounton, master, on his way across channel to Cherbourg. Dounton, it must be known, was not a man of capital, or he would long since have made his fortune. He was employed by the great London house of Sneak, Cheat, and Chouse, who took the shark's portion of the profits; he got the minnow's, and, as ill-luck would have it, whenever he had saved up a little money, and made a venture of his own, he was unfortunate, and had to throw his cargo overboard to avoid the risk of being condemned. His employers also always kept him deep in their books. He was a useful man to them.

On her passage across, the Skittish Kitty was chased by a cutter, but as she had nothing in her, Dick hove her to, that he might have the pleasure of giving the king's officer the trouble of going on board.

"What, after your old tricks again, Master Dounton," said the mate of the cutter, as he stepped on board, for they had often met with the same sort of feelings with which the cat encounters the cur who lives in the neighbouring house.

"I don't know what you means by my old tricks, sir," answered Dick, looking as innocent as a Quakeress, "I'm out piloting, as lawful a calling as dodging after smugglers, I take it."

The officer having satisfied himself that there was nothing to warrant him in stopping the Skittish Kitty, allowed her to proceed on her voyage.

The Skittish Kitty had her cargo on board in a few hours,

consisting chiefly of tubs of spirits, and bales of silk, with her crew considerably increased by a number of Frenchmen, who were engaged to assist in working the goods. Dounton was too knowing a hand to take the same course he had made in going, so he kept away to the westward, intending to come in through the Needles with the first of the flood, which would make about nine in the evening. It was late in the autumn, and the days were getting short.

The first part of the time during the run across the weather was fine, but as the day drew on, dark clouds gathered up from the south-west, and it came on to blow great guns and small arms. They made the land about Portland early in the day, so that it was agreed that it would be expedient to heave the lugger to, and wait till it grew darker before they attempted to run in at the Needles.

"Just the weather one wishes for, Tom. You're in luck, man," said Dounton, as the boat pitched her bows into the foaming seas, "only I wish there was a little less wind, and it was rather darker. Howsomdever, if it comes on to rain hard we shall do well."

The lugger, it must be understood, was hove to under her small mizen and jib, with her head to the southward of west. She was just outside the Race, with Portland Head on her lee-bow, and the Shambles, a dangerous ledge of rocks, over her quarter, while astern, lighted up by the rays of the setting sun, as it shone for an instant beneath a bank of heavy clouds, could be seen in the far distance the lofty snow-coloured cliffs of the Isle of Wight. Portland and Weymouth Roads were thus just open on her beam, as she lay a little to the southward of the clear way between the Shambles, of which I have been speaking, and the Race, though well outside and clear of both dangers.

"We did'nt heave to a bit too soon, Tom," said Dounton, addressing his mate, as he held on by the mizen rigging.

"Old Davy has sent a fresh hand to the bellows, and we are going to have a rough night of it."

"So I think," answered Tom, who was, however, thinking much more of his Betsy, and the happiness of seeing her, after he had landed his cargo safe. "We've a light boat and plenty of sea room, howsomdever, so except luck's cruelly against us, we shall have nothing to complain of."

"It's very dirty up to windward, though," observed Dounton, "Look out, my lads—here comes some fresh salt for your jackets."

As he spoke, a heavier sea than usual came tumbling towards them, and though the little vessel rose bravely over the bulk of it, the spray flew on board, drenching their pea-jackets thoroughly. The sun went down, and the gale blew stronger than ever, the clouds grew thicker, the rain came down in torrents, and the night became darker and darker, till it was impossible to see beyond the end of the lugger's little stump of a bowsprit. The crew were all on deck, for it was not a time for any one to remain below, and they were endeavouring to shelter themselves from the spray and pelting rain by crouching under the weather bulwarks of the little vessel.

Some of the best eyes on board were employed in looking out to see if possible where they were driving, or to give notice, so as to avoid any vessel coming up channel.

At last the waning moon arose, and as she broke through the clouds her light fell on the canvass of a large cutter close aboard them.

"The Stag, and no mistake!" exclaimed Dounton. "Up with the helm, there's a lull now; let draw the mizen sheet. Stand by to hoist the fore-sail! ready with the main halliards there! It's better to run her under water than to be taken. Huzza, my boys, she's away before it!"

With such exclamations he encouraged his crew, who, backed by Tom, flew to obey his orders.

In the heavy sea there was then running, the risk of keeping away was very great. A tremendous wave came rolling towards the vessel as her broadside was exposed to it, and even the bold smugglers held their breath. It rose above the bulwarks, and like a victorious foe scaling the walls of a beleaguered city, rushed along the decks.

"Hold on! for your lives, hold on!" shrieked Dounton.

The men seized whatever was nearest to them to secure themselves. Two were not in time, and the furious waters carried them over the lee bulwarks.

"There goes poor Tom Bunt!" exclaimed the skipper; but another wave rising at the instant, dashed up the lee side of the vessel, and washed one of the men back again. The hatches were battened down and the scuppers open, or it would have been all up with the Skittish Kitty. She was now before the wind with the dark-white crested seas toppling up astern and ready to break over her poop.

"Hoist away the mainsail!" sung out Dounton.

"Ay, ay, up with it, my boys," answered a seaman, swaying on to the halliards with a will.

It was the voice of Poor Tom Bunt. The sea had washed him on board again.

The king's cutter, which, when first seen was with close reefed mainsail and storm jib, evidently running into Portland Roads for shelter, was now seen dead before the wind with square-sail set, in eager chase. Neither pursuers nor pursued thought of danger; one thought only of making a rich prize, the other of saving their property and escaping, or of being sent to serve on board of a man-of-war.

As soon as the cutter had made all the sail she could venture to carry, she got a gun forward and began firing at the lugger; but she might as well have attempted to hit the moon in that heavy sea, for the shot fell now into the waves, now on one side, now on the other, and sometimes flew high over their heads.

"She's determined to shew us where she is, at all events," said Dounton, laughing; "but if any on us is hurt, her skipper will have to pay for it. How does he know that we've got any contraband on board?"

Tom was a brave fellow, but as he stood leaning against the thick mainmast to shelter himself from the rain, and thought of his own Betsy, of the dreadful death he had just escaped, heard the roaring of the angry waves around him, and saw the flashes of the cutter's guns, the first time he ever had guns with the flag of England flying over them turned against him, he repented of having engaged in the unlawful undertaking. He felt that he was on the wrong side, and he vowed never again to have anything more to do with smuggling. It was too late, however, now to recede, and he must take the consequences.

Away the two vessels tore through the foaming sea, and as the rain ceased and the atmosphere became more clear, the Needles' lights were seen shining brightly over the lee bow. Dounton and his crew considered that their best chance of safety was to keep the open sea. Something might carry away a spar on board the cutter, or perhaps her mast, while if they once got inside the Wight, other cruisers might be brought down upon them. Few even of the oldest sailors on board the lugger had passed a night of more anxiety and danger.

The Stag was one of the fastest and finest cutters in the service, and though on a wind the Skittish Kitty would have beaten her in her long tacks, before it they were nearly equal.

As the night drew on, the wind fell considerably and the sea went down, thus lessening the smugglers' chance of escape. The morning broke just as they had opened the Nab light and Dunnose had risen over their quarter.

"Never say die while a shot remains in the locker!" was Dounton's motto, and he stuck to it, and though the Stag continued blazing away at him, he did not dream of giving in. With daylight, however, her aim was more certain and her shots came nearer and nearer the mark; one came right through the mainsail, another struck her quarter, on which the French part of the crew, who, if they were taken, had few disagreeable consequences to expect, began swearing, and crying, and tearing their hair in evident trepidation, exclaiming that they must give in, and shewing other signs of mutiny.

"Hold your jaw, you jabbering monkeys, and go down below!" exclaimed Dounton, in a rage; "but if you talk of giving in while we've a plank to stand on, I'll send every one of you to blazes, I will."

The Frenchmen, though not understanding the whole of this elegant harangue, comprehended its tenor, and were soon under hatches. Dounton was at the helm, Tom tended the main halliards, in case it were necessary to lower their mainsail, the rest of the Englishmen bestowed themselves as well as they could out of harm's way. Dounton had been turning many an anxious glance over his shoulder as the cutter grew more distinct, through the gray light of morning, but yet it was impossible for the people in one vessel to distinguish what was going forward in the other. He now called Tom aft.

"Tom," said he, "it's no use, we haven't a chance of escaping. The game's all on their side, do ye see. If we might give 'em shot for shot, it would be different, so before it's light enough for 'em to make out what we're about, we must have the goods up and heave 'em overboard. There's no help for it."

Poor Tom heard this decision with a heavy heart, but he saw the necessity and the alternative of being sent to sea, and losing his property at all events.

The matter once decided on, there was no time to be lost, so all hands set to work, and got the cargo up. Cases of silk, bales of tobacco, kegs of brandy, all went overboard into the greedy sea. Daylight, however, was rapidly advancing on them as the work proceeded, and the clouds breaking away, objects became more distinct than was altogether agreeable. Lightened of her cargo, however, the little vessel flew faster than ever before the breeze, but so, unfortunately for them, did a shot from the cutter, which carried away their main halliards, and their main yard came tumbling down on deck. The smugglers hurried to repair the damage, but the accident gave an immense advantage to the cutter, and another shot coming on board, wounded a Frenchman.

This was more than his compatriots bargained for, and making a rush aft, they put down the helm, notwithstanding Dounton's efforts to prevent them, and luffed the vessel up into the wind.

All chance of escape was now gone, though if the mainsail had been ready to hoist, they might have gone off in the wind's eye. With many a curse on the heads of the Frenchmen, they hove the lugger to as a sign they had given in.

The cutter accordingly sent a boat's crew on board, under the command of the mate, who immediately set to work to splice the main halliards.

"Hoist away the mainsail!" sung out the officer, while one of the revenue men went to the helm.

"I don't exactly know why you comes on board my vessel, Mr. Hicks," said Dounton, "but take care with that mainsail, them luggers is ticklish craft."

"I'll tell you what I'm about, Mr. Dounton; I'm going to pick up some of those tubs we saw you heave overboard not ten minutes ago," answered the officer.

"You must have sharp eyes, then, to see what never happened," answered Dick, boldly.

The officer, who had been long in the service, and knew all the smuggler's tricks, cocked his eye at him and laughed.

"You mistake me for Mr. Green, my man, but you are wrong," he observed. "Look out for that tub there—there's another one."

Several were got on board. The cutter was equally successful in her search, and in a short time both vessels were running past St. Helen's on their way to Portsmouth.

Dounton had been several times before in prison, but poor Tom felt deeply his loss of character, his loss of fortune, and, more than all, his loss of Betsy, from whom he knew, if the vessel were condemned, he must be long separated, if he did not lose her altogether.

At length the trial came on before the inspecting commander of the district. Several of the cutter's crew swore positively that they had seen the tubs thrown overboard, and never lost sight of them till they were picked up, while Dounton declared as boldly on his oath that not a tub or a bale had ever been on board his craft since he last left Beaulieu river, all his crew corroborating his statement with the exception of one. He, moreover, asserted, that he had gone out piloting, that he had fallen in with an American ship, and piloted her into Cherbourg, and that he had taken the Frenchmen on board to assist him in navigating his vessel. Nobody, however, in court believed him.

The only man who refused to swear falsely was Tom, and nothing could induce him to say a word till the Skittish Kitty and her crew were condemned; he then acknowledged the justice of his sentence, and, by the advice of his counsel, threw himself on the mercy of the court.

The president was a young officer, who was himself just about to marry a very charming girl, and he knew poor Tom's history. Every body was interested in his favour.

"It was his only fault," said his counsel. "He was enticed by the false representations of that notorious smuggler, Dounton; and think of the grief, the misery of the poor girl to whom he was about to be united, when he is torn from her." Stern justice, however, triumphed over all the softer sympathies of the judge, and Poor Tom Bunt was condemned to serve his majesty afloat.

Tom behaved like a man. "I've served his majesty before, and I'm ready to serve him again, and to do my duty too," he observed, turning to his judge, "and I am grateful to those who have spoken kindly in my favour."

The —— frigate was then ready for sea, and Tom was drafted on board her. The day following she went out to Spithead, with the Blue Peter flying at the masthead.

I had been ordered a passage in the —— frigate out to Malta, and I soon recognised among the seamen my friend, Tom Bunt, whom I had known at Beaulieu. A day or two before we sailed, Tom was doing some duty or other aloft, when a wherry with two women in her came alongside. One was very old and ugly, the other young and very pretty, and they inquired for Tom Bunt.

Tom's name was passed along the decks, from thence into the tops, and at last he heard himself called. A glance below told him who was there, for the eye of true love is keen of sight; and his duty being concluded, down he came by the main topmast back stay, quick as lightning, upon the deck. Betsy thought not of the officers in their cocked hats, their gold epaulettes and swords, of the marines in their red coats, of the numbers of seamen standing round, but rushing forward to meet him, threw her arms round his neck, and burst into tears. Tom, too, forgot where he was, in the pleasure of meeting her and at this mark of her affection, and he endeavoured to soothe her to the best of his abilities, and at length succeeded.

"We must part, Betsy, dear; but time slips by, you know, as a ship glides through the water before a stiff breeze, and I shall soon be back again."

"May heaven preserve you, Tom, for if you were to die my heart would break," sighed Betsy.

"Never fear, my girl, never fear," answered Tom. "Remember

Betsy, 'there's a sweet little cherub who sits up aloft, to take care of the life of poor Jack.' He'll watch over me and bring me back to you."

"And you will not forget your Betsy, Tom?"

"Forget you, Betsy!" exclaimed Tom, in a tone almost of reproach. "No, my girl, a sailor's heart is soft, they say, but depend on it, it takes many a salt sea to wash away from it the picture of the girl he loves. In the battle or the gale, on land or on shore, in sunshine and calm, I'll not forget you, Betsy."

"Nor I you, Tom."

And thus they parted, for it was time for Betsy and her aunt to return to the shore.

The following day we sailed, and had a fine run as far as Gibraltar. Tom Bunt proved himself one of the best men in the ship; the most active aloft, the most fearless in danger, he was the favourite of all his messmates, and esteemed by his officers. After we passed through the Gut, the fine weather forsook us, and a heavy gale came on which blew away most of our sails out of the bolt-ropes. The sea had been calm and shining as glass, and not a cloud was to be seen in the clear, deep-blue sky, when suddenly a small dark cloud arose down to leeward in the south-east, every instant growing bigger and bigger, till it formed a thick black bank which rolled on towards us. The third-lieutenant, the officer of the watch, was not so wide awake as he might have been or he would have been prepared. The sun had just set, and darkness was coming on. Fortunately the captain came on deck to take a look at the weather

"Why, what is that, Mr. ——? What have you been about not to call me!" he exclaimed. "Turn the hands up and shorten sail! —rouse up, my men, rouse up, we have not a moment to lose." The men flew aloft.

"Stand by tacks and sheets, let fly, clue up, haul down! Be smart about it, my lads!"

Such were the orders which issued from the voices of the officers as they hurried forward to their stations.

The captain prognosticated the truth. Not a moment had we to spare; indeed, as it was, we were too late to save the sails. Suddenly the atmosphere became dark as ink, except when the white glistening foam was seen driving along the surface of the troubled sea. Waves, as if by some sudden impulse of their own, rose up in a mad dance. The roaring of the unseen blast was heard. It struck the noble ship. Her tall masts quivered and bent, and, unable to stand its fury, she went over before it on her beam ends.

"Up with the helm," shouted the captain. "Let fly everything aft. Brail up the spanker. Now she feels it."

The pressure of the after canvass being taken off, her head slowly turned from the wind, and, righting herself, away she flew before it, a sad contrast to the neat and gallant ship she had a few moments before appeared. Her main-topmast was gone, and her fore and mizen top-gallant masts had also been carried away, while her canvass streamed in ribbons from the yards, and her running rigging was flying out, and lashing the shrouds and masts in fury.

As the frigate righted herself, that dreadful cry arose, and was passed from mouth to mouth, "A man overboard! a man overboard!"

"Lower away the starboard quarter boat!" sung out one of the officers, and numbers of volunteers rushed to the falls.

"Hold fast!" cried the captain. "No boat can live in this sea Let go the life-buoy!"

"It's gone!" exclaimed a midshipman, who had wisely not waited for orders; and as I looked over the taffrail, I saw the bright light shedding its beams around through the darkness, and I fancied that I saw a human figure hanging to it. How dreadful must be the fate of that unfortunate wretch, I thought. It were far better had he sunk at once amid the boiling surges than to linger on, as he probably will do, till he wastes away with hunger and thirst—a speck on the ocean. How can it be expected that any ship will pass near him till too late to bring him assistance! "Man, man," a voice borne on the tempest's blast seemed to whisper in my ear, "never mistrust the mercy of Providence,— a swallow falls not to the ground without the will of God."

Away we flew before the squall; the voices of the officers and men blending with the whistling of the wind, the lashing of the waves, the flapping of the torn canvass and slackened ropes, to create a tumult, the like of which my ears had never heard.

"Who saw the man go?" asked the captain, after the ship had been got somewhat to rights.

"I did, sir," answered a main-topman. "He was on the main-topsail yard-arm, and was shaken off by the sail when the topmast went."

"Who was he?" asked the captain.

No one was able to answer.

"Call the names of the main-topmen over," said the captain.

The men were all at their stations. Several answered to their names, but when that of Tom Bunt was called, no one answered. Tom never shirks his duty. Alas! alas! it must have been he. Such was the fate of POOR TOM BUNT.

The gale lasted all that night, but towards evening it moderated, and by the end of the forenoon watch the sea was as calm, and the sky as clear, as it had been before the squall. The temper of the weather harmonizes well with that of the inhabitants of those southern climes. Before we reached Malta, we contrived to repair damages, to rig a new topmast, and to put all ataunto, so that, when we entered the harbour, no one would have suspected the disaster we had encountered. I spent two years in that little military hot-house, and then returned to England. I had got several small things which were found in poor Tom's kit, and which I had claimed that I might preserve them to give to Betsy when I got home. I accordingly took an early opportunity to start off on a fishing excursion to Beaulieu, that I might offer this slight consolation to the poor girl.

I had no difficulty in finding the cottage where she dwelt, for I remembered it well, but it struck me that a wing had been added to it since I was last there. There was a little flower-garden in front of the cottage, and I stood at the wicket, irresolute how I should commence talking on the painful subject to the unhappy girl. While thus meditating, the door of the cottage opened, and a fine, buxom young woman, with a curly-headed, laughing infant in her arms, advanced towards me.

I regarded her earnestly—I rubbed my eyes, for I could scarcely believe my senses, for there stood Betsy, a smiling matron, before me. That curly-headed boy, too : there was no mistaking whose child he was, for he was her very image, and, as I live, there was another on the stocks ready to be launched.

"Oh, woman! woman!" I exclaimed to myself, "this is your boasted constancy. Why the poor fellow could not have slept in his ocean grave many months before she had forgotten all about him. Well, well," I thought, I always knew the sex,—false, fickle, changeable! high or low, rich or poor, it is always the same. Talk of rural virtue, it does not exist, and the vices of the city are only made coarser and more disgusting."

"Please, sir, what do you require?" asked Betsy, hearing me speak, and not recognising me.

I was inclined to turn away, but I did not.

"Oh, you don't know me, Betsy; some people's memory is very short," I answered gruffly.

On this she drew nearer, and opening the wicket, looked me in the face.

"Oh dear, sir, I beg pardon, sir, I did not see it was you. Pray come in and rest yourself—my good man will be so happy to see you."

On this, dancing the little curly-headed boy in her arms, she led the way into the cottage.

"Here, Tom—Tom!" she exclaimed, speaking to some one in another room; "here, here, there's Mr. Upton come to see us."

"Well, she's faithful to the name, however," I thought; "I suppose she made that her excuse."

Just then the door opened; I started back at the sight of an apparition, for there stood before me the full-sized ghost of poor Tom Bunt.

"Well, he's made a pretty tolerable husband for a ghost," was the thought which passed through my mind. I, however, instinctively held out my hand, and an honest, hard palm, which had nothing of the phantom about it, was respectfully pressed to mine.

"Speak, Tom, is it you, or your ghost, or anybody else, I see before me?" I exclaimed.

"Why, sir, Betsy thinks it's me, and I'm pretty certain it's not my ghost, though I was near dying, and I'm still more certain it's not anybody else, because I don't think she'd love anybody else as she loves me, so I can't but help thinking it is myself, sir."

On this Betsy laughed and Tom laughed, and I laughed, and the curly-headed boy set up a huge crow of delight, though it was not likely he understood his father's wit.

"It's him, sir, I'm pretty certain of it now, sir," put in Betsy, "but when I first saw him, I took him for a ghost too."

"Till he convinced you he was not," I added.

"Yes, sir," she answered, blushing, and looking at him affectionately, "he took good care to shew me he wasn't."

"So I should think. But tell me, Tom, by what miracle you

were saved from the dreadful death to which I fancied you were consigned."

"Why, sir, it's a long story, but I'll make it as short as I can,' replied Tom. "You must know, sir, when the ship was hove on her beam-ends, and I was washed off the lee main-topsail yard-arm, I thought it was all over with me, for I knew no boat could be lowered in that sea to pick me up, when suddenly I saw a bright light burst out just before me, and I found that some one had let go the life-buoy. I swam up to it, and easily contrived to secure myself to it. I did, however, feel forlorn, for away flew the ship through the darkness, leaving me alone on the dark, stormy sea. At first I expected nothing but death, and thought I might as well let go at once as hang on there till I died by inches, but then I recollected that a brave man never gives in while there is life; besides, even then, it was pleasant to think of Betsy, and her love for me; so I made myself fast to the life buoy, and determined to hope for the best. Before the light of morning broke, the squall had blown over, and the sea had gone down, so having nothing else to do, I went to sleep. I awoke much refreshed, and rubbing my eyes looked about me, for I could not tell exactly where I was and how I had got there. When I remembered, I cast my eyes in every direction, in hopes of seeing land, but there was nothing but water and sky, for as you know, sitting as I was, with my head only a couple of feet above the water, I could not see very far.

"At last the sun came out and dried my clothes, but I was very hungry, and would have given any thing for a mug of water. As, however, I was feeling in the pocket of my jacket, I found the best part of a biscuit which I had stowed in at supper-time, and two quids of tobacco. This made me thankful, for I knew this would keep body and soul together for a day or two at least, and I thought too, sir, of the old song—

"'There's a sweet little cherub who sits up aloft,
To take care of the life of poor Jack.'

"Several times during the day I fell asleep and dreamt sweet dreams of Betsy and my home, and of the green fields and woods of Beaulieu, and when I awoke I felt quite happy, and began to wonder when the ship would appear which was to pick me up, for I made as certain that she would come as if I had chartered her. However, the sun went down again; I was still alone, so I munched a bit of biscuit, and took half of my last quid, and made myself fast to pass another night. It was the longest I ever spent. The silence was the most awful part of it. The sea was as smooth as glass, and the life-buoy floated without making a ripple in the water, so that my own breathing sounded quite loud to my ears. I was half asleep and half awake the best part of the time, and I cannot tell you now the strange thoughts which came into my head, and the stranger sights I saw, and the sounds too I heard. Betsy says it was all fancy, and because I'd an empty stomach, and perhaps she's right. At last the morning came again, and the sun rose, and I finished my last bit of biscuit, and put my remaining quid into my mouth. The sun rose higher and higher, and with the sun, fortunately, a breeze sprung up, for which I was thankful, as I knew no vessel was likely to fall in with me while the calm lasted. It was about the end of the forenoon watch, as far as I could judge by the sun, when as I was looking round to see if I could make out a sail, I spied the royals of a brig just rising above the horizon.

"I kept my eyes fixed on her, to make sure she was standing my way. The wind was from the eastward, and she was running right before it, with studden sails alow and aloft. The top-gallant sails and topsails next appeared, and on they came till I could see down to the foot of her courses. Now was the time I felt the most anxious lest the people on board shouldn't see me, because I was so low in the water. I hailed as loud as I could, but there was so much noise on board that they couldn't hear me, though I could almost hear them speaking to each other.

"I took off my hat, with my handkerchief made fast to it, and waved it in the air, shouting at the top of my voice. No one saw me, and she flew by me. I thought all was over with me, when I saw her studden sails taken in, royals and top-gallant sails furled, and her main-topsail laid to the mast, and a boat lowered from her quarter. Then my heart did jump into my mouth, and I felt as if I was going off into a swoon. I and my life-buoy were soon on board, and in a few hours I was myself again.

"Do you know, sir, a little child was the only living being who saw me on board the brig, and he took me for some odd fish floating on the waves, and pointed me out to his father. The brig, was a fine Liverpool merchantman, homeward bound, and had on board a gentleman and his lady, and the little boy I spoke of, their only child. The gentleman was a lord, and they were very great people, with heaps of money, and had the cabins all to themselves. The lady was beautiful, and good, and kind; it was like having an angel on board to see her, and her boy was a fine, manly little fellow, just as Tommy there will be some day. She loved her child a hundred times more than herself, and would any day have died for him, I am sure.

"Well, after we got outside the Straits, and had shaped our course for England, it happened that Master Adolphus and his mother were on deck while my lord was below, when he sent for his lady to look at some curiosity he had been examining in the cabin. Though it was blowing fresh, and there was a good deal of sea on, we were making fine weather of it, by running before the wind with everything set alow and aloft.

"What does the youngster do, however, when he saw no one watching him, but try to climb up into the main rigging. Just then my lady comes again on deck, when the boy, knowing he was doing what he ought not, got frightened, and letting go his hold, fell right back into the sea. Never shall I forget the scream of terror the poor lady gave, and if some one hadn't prevented her, she would have jumped in after her child. I was forward at the time, and was just going aft to take care of the boy; so when I saw what had happened, of course overboard I went after him. I had my shoes and jacket off, so I swam easily, and watching for the poor child, as he should appear above the waves, I got hold of him before he sank, for his petticoats kept him afloat. I kept the child' head above water as well as I could, but was wishing for my lifebuoy, when, to my joy, I saw some one heave it to me over the taffrail. I managed to get hold of it, and climbing on it with the child, I held the little fellow up to his mother, who was looking at us and wringing her hands in despair. When she saw that her boy was safe she fell back into her husband's arms and fainted. They were some time heaving the brig to and lowering a boat, but at last the boy and I got safe on board again, and it was a pleasant thing to give him back into his mother's arms.

"Well, to make a long story short, my lord and lady were very kind to me, and called me the preserver of their child, and said it was a blessed day when I and my life-buoy came on board, and that the hand of Providence was in it, though of course, as you know, sir, I would have done the same for any human being who had gone overboard, even for the black cook's nigger boy—and as to the hand of Providence being in it, I never could make out where the hand of Providence is not. I said something of this sort to my lord, just to shew him that I didn't think I had done anything out of the common way, so as not to impose on him, you know, sir. He, howsomdever, smiled, and said he wished the world acted as I did; and when we reached England he got me regularly discharged from the service, and told me to go down to Beaulieu to see Betsy, for he knew about her, as he had managed to worm all my story out of me, even all about my smuggling trip, and how I was sent to sea when I was taken and parted from her.

"Well you may be sure I was glad enough to go down to Beaulieu, and gladder still when I found my Betsy as fond and pretty as ever; for the news of my going overboard not having reached England, she was spared the misery of believing I was lost. She was looking out for me too, and so was her aunt, for some one had prepared them, it appeared, for my coming, which was strange, but what I thought stranger still was, that Betsy told me, that two days before, a gentleman had come down and asked her name and learned all about her, and then told her that the day she married me she was to have fifty pounds a year; so, sir, as there was nothing now to prevent it, we were spliced three weeks afterwards. We often heard, too, from my lady, who once came over from the island, where she was staying, to see Betsy, and proud we were to receive her. She smiled and talked, and when she looked at Betsy, told me I wasn't too flattering a painter; and when Tommy there was born she sent a parcel for him, with fifty pounds in it, to his mother, and told her it was to begin his fortune.

"I now, sir, with Betsy's aid, have taken to farming, and succeed very well; and I amuse myself by taking a trip now and then over to the island and fishing a little, but never as long as I live, will I ever have anything to do with smuggling.

"Dounton, you know, sir, deserted from his ship and took to the old trade again; his cutter was last winter run down in the channel, in a gale of wind, it is supposed, for neither she nor any of her crew have since been heard of."

With a very different feeling did I return home to that which led me to Beaulieu to console Betsy for the loss of POOR TOM BUNT.

CHAPTER V.

AN IMPORTANT SUBJECT.

ALL his auditors expressed themselves highly pleased with Upton's story, and whatever were its merits, it certainly owed not a little to his manner of telling it. I had been busily engaged all the time in taking it down in shorthand, an art I had learned during a spell I once enjoyed on shore.

"Thank you, Upton, thank you!" exclaimed every one, in a breath. "Capital! excellent! we must have some more of your yarns."

"They are as good as printed stories," said the purser, "and would be almost as interesting to look over, if they were written down, as my accounts."

"They are better by far than anything I ever saw in print, because they are true, which is more than can be said of all one sees in black and white," observed Green. "At least, Upton, I never heard you say anything that I was not certain you believed as firmly as the Gospel."

"Thank you for the compliment, master," answered Upton, smiling. "I'll rummage out my brains and try if I can get some more stories ready to launch on another afternoon."

"I wish that you would, Upton," said I; "and to be honest with you, I intend to log them down, and get you to touch them up afterwards. I am certain that Poor Tom Bunt will read well in print, and if you can give me any others like him, I will make a collection of them, and send them forth into the world when we get home again."

"Oh, you may make what use you like of all the yarns I can spin, provided you do not insist upon my fathering the bantlings."

"I will be answerable for all their faults, provided I may enjoy the credit they gain from their readers," I replied. "But I give you fair warning, I shall not only book your tales, but every yarn which is spun in my hearing on board. I have long been wishing to make a collection of sea stories, and now I am determined to begin."

"Well, heave ahead, messmate," exclaimed Green; "you'll pick up plenty before the cruise is over."

"Yes, but I want to settle a very important point," I observed: "it is one which takes as much consideration as does the composition of a whole volume. I want to find a title for my work!"

"Oh, call it Stray leaves from Lieut. Fairfield's Log," said Upton, laughing.

"I want something newer than that," answered I.

"The Cruise of the Albatross," suggested Green.

"There would be rank plagiarism in that, and a comparison might be drawn which would assuredly gain me but little credit," I replied. "That will never do."

"The Fairfield Account Book wouldn't be a bad title, I think," put in the purser. "It would look like business."

The observation produced a general laugh. "Bravo, purser, every man should stick up for his trade as you do!" exclaimed Green.

"Thank you, Sleepwell; but I fear that would not be an attractive title to general readers," said I.

"What then do you think of the Fairfield Memoirs?" asked our good medico, Haggis. "There is weight and dignity in the name, you must allow."

I scarcely knew whether he was laughing at me or not.

"No, no, I want something more poetical and attractive—something suited to the subjects. Cannot you help me, Marsden?" I asked, turning to our young passenger.

"I have been thinking of a name for you," he replied, "and several have suggested themselves. What say you to Voices from the Ocean? The title will, I think, prove attractive, and it is certainly appropriate. It is better, at all events, than the old fangled titles for books, compounded of 'yarns' and 'logs,' which denote that the interior has something more or less remotely connected with the sea."

I was meditating on the title he had suggested, while he continued speaking. "Excellent! capital!" I exclaimed, jumping up and seizing him by the hand. "My dear Marsden, you have relieved my mind of a weight of care—you have, indeed, I can assure you. Nothing I can think of will, I am certain, suit as well—'Voices from the Ocean,'—I see, I see. Whatever is said on board is a voice from the ocean, although it may never reach the shore; but if we write what we say and hear, and our pages reach our friends at home, they will most justly be called 'Voices from the Ocean.' I am deeply indebted to you. If you knew how much trouble an author takes to find a good title for his book, you would enter into my feelings, and more highly value the assistance you have afforded me."

He smiled as I spoke, and I afterwards found that he had already gained far more credit as an author than I could ever hope to enjoy.

"Come, Marsden," said Upton, "I saw you engaged this morning in writing what I took to be poetry, and must beg you to read it for the benefit of the mess. I hold that every man is bound to contribute his talents to the general amusement. I have set the example, and I think that you will follow it."

"Very gladly," answered Marsden; "but I fear the trifle is scarcely worthy of notice. I have called it the 'Wreck.' The subject was suggested by a story I was reading this morning." Saying this, he produced his pocket-book, and read the following lines:—

"THE WRECK.

"See where the sturdy watcher o'er the deep,
High on the wave-worn cliffs undaunted stands;
His night-glass sweeps the sea around;
'Tis darkness all—he hears no sound,
His weary eyelids close in sleep.

> Hark, hark to the distant cry,
> Startling the slumb'ring guard,
> 'Midst the thunder's crash,
> And the lightning's flash,
> And the whirlwind raging high.
>
> Say, is it the cry of the wild sea-bird,
> Or the tempest's rushing sound?
> Or is it alone the billows' roar
> 'Mid the rocky caves of that iron shore,
> In solemn midnight heard.
>
> No; rising, borne o'er a mountain wave,
> With foaming crest, see a shattered bark:
> A flash illumes the abyss profound—
> 'Tis the pallid seamen's shrieks resound,
> As they gaze below on their yawning grave.
>
> Hark! hark! far above the billows' roar,
> Or the shriek of the ocean bird,
> Are the echoes shrill of that piercing cry,
> As the seamen are hurled in agony
> On the cavern'd rocks of that rugged shore."

"Thank you, Frank," said Captain Dainmore, when Marsden ceased. "I am not a judge of the poetic art, but at all events, these lines paint a picture a seaman can understand. I never could bear your sentimental ditties about sighing plough-boys and shady groves, and lilies and daisies. Give me something with pith and marrow, like 'Ye Mariners of England,' by Thomas Campbell, or 'Rule Britannia,' or like some of old Charlie Dibdin's songs. Now I like this poetry of yours, Marsden, because I know what it's about. One hears the raging of the tempest, the faint cry of the seamen rising from below the lofty cliff. There is a flash of lightning which reveals for one instant the shattered ship. There is no need of seeing more to foretell the inevitable result. Every soul on board a vessel cast on those rocks must perish. One piercing cry announces the moment of the dreadful catastrophe."

"I am glad you like my poetry, sir," said Marsden. "And though I cannot spin a yarn off the reel like Mr. Upton, or Mr. Green either—who, let me tell you, is a great adept in the art of story-telling, I will endeavour to write out some for the general amusement, on another afternoon."

"We shall keep you to your promise, Frank," said the captain. "And remember, Mr. Green, we shall put your abilities to the test on the first opportunity; but I believe, gentlemen, our duties now require some of us on deck."

At this hint our party broke up, and so well did the idea I had proposed take, that all hands promised to exert themselves to contribute to my "Voices from the Ocean."

CHAPTER VI.

THE BURNING SHIP.

THOSE who have been alone accustomed to the quick changes of a northern clime, the seldom-failing breeze, the heat and cold, the clouds and sunshine, which harden and invigorate the frames of Englishmen, can scarcely picture to themselves the lassitude of mind and body, and the weariness of one whose eye rests from day to day on the same unchanging expanse of the ever-shining and boundless sea, and the blue, cloudless sky. For some days we lay almost like a log on the water, without life or animation, when even a gale of wind and a black canopy of clouds with deluges of rain, would have been welcomed as a change. At last, towards evening, a breeze sprang up, and carried us along in our course, at a somewhat faster rate than we had for some time past moved.

I had the first watch that night, and somewhere about seven bells I was walking the quarter-deck with the mate of my watch, Henry Seaton, as gentlemanly, open-hearted, and fine a youngster as ever stepped.

"It is a strange part of the world we are bound for," he observed. (I had before discovered that he was fond of moralizing.) "Even the profusion of nature's bounties become curses, and man adds his own worst passions to turn the paradise into a pandemonium. What might not Africa become if the inhabitants were civilized?"

"And the marshes drained," I added, laughing.

"And why not?" he asked. "Surely equal labours have been performed by mankind, and if all were to put their shoulders to the work, even Africa might become an Arcadia."

"You are in a poetical mood to-night, Seaton," I observed.

"I believe I am, sir. It is a night to make every one fanciful."

He spoke the truth. The wind was still so light that it had scarcely raised a ripple on the glass-like surface of the ocean, on which the myriads of stars which dotted the dark arc of heaven were reflected as in a gigantic looking-glass, except where the young pale moon, just sinking in the sky, cast a line of light like chased silver upon the water. A thin, transparent mist filled the atmosphere, in which one almost expected to see floating things of another world, the guardian spirits of the calm, with snow-white wings and crowns of pearls, and to hear the soft music of their voices. Not a sound met the ear except the gentle ripple of the water against the vessel's bows, as she clove her onward way, and the occasional flap of some finny inhabitant of the deep, as, after rising above the surface, it fell again into its native element. There are seasons when, from some peculiarity in the atmosphere, or from the scenery, the *genius loci*, or from one's own internal sensations, one feels more inclined to give way to superstitious feelings. This was one of them.

"Do you know, sir, that I feel that I shall not enjoy many more nights like this," continued my companion. "Something tells me that my days are numbered. You will laugh at me, sir, when I tell you, that just now, as I stood looking over the taffrail, I distinctly saw a figure, dressed in shining white robes, rise out of the sea, and with a look of deep grief beckon me towards her. The features became gradually like those of my sainted mother, now in heaven, and I heard a strain of music like that which strikes the ear as one perchance passes at a little distance from a church where mass is performing. I felt a strong inclination to follow the blessed vision, but it faded gradually from my sight the moment I heard your voice calling me. Depend upon it, sir, we shall have a hurricane or something peculiar before long."

"The vision, if vision it were, more probably was sent to assure us of safety," I answered gravely, for I saw that the lad was not in a mood to be laughed at. "More probably it was the work of your own imagination."

"With due respect to you, sir, I think not," he answered, calmly; "I was never of an imaginative turn till now, though my fancy, I confess, has run rather wild lately. Ah, sir, I thought I was right!" he exclaimed, suddenly pointing to the south-east, nearly ahead of our course. "Look, sir, look at that red glow which has just lighted up the eastern sky. It cannot be the sun rising some hours before his time."

I gazed in the direction he pointed. At first I thought it was some phenomenon like the aurora borealis, but it gradually grew redder and redder, till it was of a far deeper hue than that ever assumes. We watched it attentively, and as we advanced in our course it appeared to extend more widely over the sky, and to radiate from a centre below the horizon.

"Go aloft, Mr. Seaton, and see if you can make out what it is, before we are relieved," I said.

He sprung into the fore-rigging, and in a few minutes was again by my side.

"A burning mountain, or a ship on fire, sir. I fear the latter; for I fancied that I could see her masts amid the flames."

"I agree with you, Seaton: I fear that this strange light proceeds from a burning ship. How's her head?"

"East-south-east, sir," he replied. "We are standing directly for the light."

"Keep her so, and we shall soon solve the mystery."

The master soon after came on deck to relieve me, but I was far too interested to turn in; so I continued pacing the deck with my brother officer. Our master was a character in his way, and a very pleasant one, for he was one of those happy fellows who are never put out of temper. He knew everybody in the service and out of the service, and everybody knew him, and there was not a corner of the world where he hadn't friends. He used to declare that whenever he fell he always tumbled on his legs; that he was once blown off the foreyard-arm in a gale of wind into a boiling sea, but that, managing to get hold of a rope towing overboard, he worked himself on deck again; that he was once hung by mistake for another person, but that the rope broke, and that his supposed corpse being left alone, he came to himself, and quietly walked away; and that another time he was left floating by himself in an empty cask for a whole week, in the middle of the Atlantic, with only a bundle of cigars and a bottle of rum to support life, by which he argued that he was born neither to be hanged nor drowned. In stature he was short and broad, with a round head and ruddy countenance.

As the morning drew on the breeze freshened up a little, but not enough to satisfy our impatience, when we discovered, as we soon did, to a certainty, that a large vessel was burning ahead of us, and that every moment's delay might consign some of our fellow-beings to the most dreadful of deaths. The captain, according to his standing orders, when anything unusual occurred, was called, and as soon as he came on deck, he ordered every stitch of canvass the brig could carry to be set. The seamen flew with alacrity to the work, and very soon every soul in the ship, except a few inveterate sleepers, were on the alert.

As we approached the burning ship the sight was awful, and at the same time beautiful. The whole sea seemed on fire with the reflection of the bright flames, which towered up in wreathy columns around the tall masts towards the sky, and cast their ruddy glow on our wide spread of canvass; but when still too distant to render assistance, the masts, one after another, were seen to shoot upwards and then to fall—we almost fancied we could hear them hiss—into the water, and after that the flames rushed forth from stem to stern, still brighter and more fiercely, till it was clear that not a human being could be existing on board. She was burning rapidly to the water's edge. We still persisted in nearing her, for it was probable the whole or part of the crew might have escaped in the boats. Our glasses were employed in looking for them, but none could be seen. We, however, fired several guns, in case any people remained afloat, to warn them of our approach to their assistance. The fire was still burning as fiercely as ever, when, as we were gazing at it, the whole mass seemed to oscillate for a moment, and then we were left in sombre darkness. The wreck had sunk beneath the waves. What had become of the human beings who lately peopled her, was the question? We shortened sail, and lay to near the spot, firing guns at intervals, while the boats were got into the water and pulled about in every direction, in case any one should be still floating alive on rafts and spars, though our hope of finding them was faint indeed. I was in the gig, and had taken rather a longer sweep than before, when a man I had placed in the bows to look out, exclaimed—

"Starboard, sir, starboard! There's something, I see, away on our larboard bow—steady, so."

On standing up in the stern-sheets, I could perceive a long dark object floating on the water, to which I could not help fancying I saw several human beings clinging. We hailed, but there was no answer. The men gave way with all their might, and we were soon up to a topmast or the bowsprit of the burnt ship, and as we pulled along it, we perceived the head of a man resting on the jib-boom end, while his body was supported by a grating, which he had contrived to lash to it, and which had saved him from the sharks, who had been attracted to the spot.

At first we thought he was dead, but on getting him into the boat, we poured a few drops of spirits into his mouth from a flask I had, by the doctor's advice, taken with me, when he gave signs of returning animation. Our further search proved unavailing, and at length we returned to the ship, with the only man saved from the wreck. He was a negro, but dressed in an English seaman's jacket and trowsers. For some time the surgeon's exertions to recall him to his senses were unavailing, and when he opened his eyes and looked about him, he evidently thought some grievous personal injury was about to be inflicted on him.

"Oh, massa, no cut throat! Let lilly bit child live! Oh, de poor young missie! Pirate kill all, all, all. Oh, massa, pirate no kill. All de blood, de blood! run like big river. Oh, oh, oh!"

These broken exclamations were the first intimation we had of a dreadful tragedy, which had been enacted the previous evening near the spot on which we now floated. The black, it appeared, had belonged to a large ship, the Anna, which had touched at the Cape, on her way from the Mauritius, and taken several passengers on board, so that she mustered in all between fifty and sixty souls fore and aft. Unsuspicious of evil, she was approached by a schooner under British colours, who hailed her to know the longitude, and to ask her for water. The crew and passengers of the ship were looking at the strangers, who, after speaking them, had gone a little distance from them, when they observed two boats shove off from her side, but they thought nothing of this, as they fancied the people were in a hurry to quench their thirst. As the boats pulled up on one side, the schooner went about and ranged up on the other, when a tarpaulin, which had concealed some men in the bottom of the boats, was thrown off, and before a gun could be brought to bear from the ship, or the crew could seize their arms, thirty desperadoes were on their decks, cutting and slashing right and left, and killing every one they met without mercy. Their aim was evidently to leave no one alive to tell tales. All the men, who offered any resistance, were cut down at once, but the women, the negro fancied, had been carried on board the schooner. The pirates then set to work to rifle the ship, and to transfer everything they considered of value to their own vessel. The negro had escaped forward, when he saw that they were overpowered, and had remained clinging to the bight of a rope, hung overboard under the bows.

On seeing the pirate sheer off, he had returned on deck, when, to his horror, he found that the miscreants had set the ship on fire in several places, leaving the crew, whom they had bound hand and foot, so that they could not free themselves, and the wounded and dying, to this terrible fate. He liberated those he could reach, but all their exertions could not quench the flames, which now raged furiously. His companions had made a rush aft to lower away one of the quarter-boats, but the fire overtook them before they could accomplish their object. He had climbed out to the end of the bowsprit, where, as the ship came up head to wind, he remained till the heel being burnt almost through, it was carried away by the falling masts. He knew very little more of what happened till we picked him up.

Returning daylight enabled us to ascertain that there was no boat or any other floating thing upon the world of waters; but good look-outs were sent aloft to watch for any sail we might sight. After the dreadful account we had heard, every man in the ship was eager to come up with the pirate; indeed there was little fear of his escaping notice, should he come within the range of vision, for every instant men were going to the top-gallant-mast-head to watch for him.

Thus passed the greater part of the day, without a sail appearing to break the dark line of the horizon. About the middle of the afternoon watch, my young friend Seaton had gone aloft to take a look round, when I heard him shout out, "A sail in sight on the starboard bow!"

"Port the helm," I cried.

"Port it is," was the answer.

"Steady—how does she go now, Mr. Seaton?"

"Right for it, sir," he answered, from his lofty perch.

"Get a pull on the larboard braces," I cried. "That will do."

The wind was now on our starboard quarter, and with studden sails set alow and aloft, away we bowled after the stranger.

CHAPTER VII.

THE PIRATE.

THE freshening breeze carried us bravely along over the laughing blue waves, the foam flew from our bows, and the white sails strained and pulled like impatient spirits, eager to drag onwards their bodies of grosser mould. Thus we rapidly approached the stranger; for instead of flying from us she was standing towards us, on a bow-line, under easy sail.

"I fear she is not the craft we are in search of," said the captain to me, "or she would not stand on so close to us in that bold way."

"I do not know that, sir," I replied; "she may mistake us at the distance she is still from us, for a merchantman. Many of the Liverpool traders are fine vessels, and the Portuguese and Spaniards often carry a broad spread of canvass. Perhaps she may find that she has caught a tartar."

"I hope you are right, Mr. Fairfield," replied the captain. "If she prove the slaver we'll make her pay for her last night's work. What do you make her out to be, Mr. Green?"

"A large square topsail schooner, sir," replied the master, who was addressed. "She has a wicked look about her which sadly belies her if she is honest."

"I do not think there is much of that commodity on board yonder craft," I observed. "Wait a bit, and as soon as she makes out what we are, depend on it, she'll turn tail at a great rate."

"Beat to quarters," exclaimed the captain; "we'll at all events make the fellow show himself as soon as we come up to him"

Still the schooner approached till we thought it scarcely possible she should not discover that we were a man-of-war, for though our ports were closed, no pains had been taken to disguise ourselves. Through our glasses we could perceive that she was a long low vessel, with ten guns on a side, and a long one amidships, not to speak of sundry brass swivels which graced her quarters. In fact she was one of the most rakish looking crafts I ever saw.

"If they are pirates, they are bold fellows to beard a British man-of-war in that way," I observed to Seaton, who was standing near me.

"There seems something strange about the craft altogether, sir," he replied. "Who would suppose that yon beautiful fabric was employed as an instrument of evil? yet, I feel certain that, notwithstanding her behaviour, she is the pirate which destroyed the ship last night. And do you know that even now I fancy she is destined to work us some evil."

"Why, Seaton, you are growing fanciful," I replied, laughing. "At night the imagination may be excused if it ramble a little, but in the day-time you ought to keep it within bounds."

While we were speaking, whiz—bang—went a shot across our fore foot, and up went the flag of Spain to the peak of the schooner. Our captain laughed outright.

"The fellow is determined to be beforehand with us at all events," he exclaimed. "Hoist our colours, and run out the guns to show him that we have teeth as well as he, and can bite as hard when we have a mind for it."

"Shorten sail, Mr. Upton," to the first lieutenant, "and be ready to tack ship, for as soon as the fellow discovers his mistake he'll be off in the wind's eye, and be a mile to windward of us while we are taking in our flying kites."

Not a bit of it—the stranger came on, and passing close to us on the other tack, hailed in Spanish to know what ship we were. In answer to the same question put by us, he said he was bound to Cadiz, from some port the name of which we could not make out.

"Heave to, then, and send a boat on board us!" exclaimed the captain; but the stranger did not, or would not, comprehend the order.

"Give the fellow a shot then, across his bows," continued the captain; "he must be taught manners if he does not know them."

No sooner, however, was the shot fired, than he backed his foretop-sail and remained stationary on the waters, the sharp bow of the vessel rising and falling gracefully in the swelling wave—but he did not send a boat on board as he was ordered to do. Accordingly, we hove about and ran down to him, asking him why he did not do as desired.

"Non tengo, senores," answered a man standing in the main chains. "They have all been lost or disabled, and we have none which can swim."

The truth of this assertion might have been doubted, for a dingy, —a small boat,—in very good condition, apparently, was hanging over her stern, and her starboard quarter-boat appeared uninjured, though the larboard one looked as if it had had a shot through the bows.

The captain, however, did not seem to have any suspicions as to her character, as he answered that he would send a boat on board, and ordered me to go in the gig and overhaul his papers. A boat was immediately manned, and I jumped into her. As I pulled alongside I observed a number of villanous-looking countenances peering down upon me, and being fully impressed with the idea that the men among whom I was about to venture, were a set of daring cut-throats, I should not have been at all surprised, had I been knocked on the head as I stepped on board. With this impression, I ordered the men on no account to be tempted up the side, or to answer any questions put to them, but if they saw any thing suspicious, to shove off at once, for I thought there was no reason why the poor fellows should be sacrificed, even if I were. As my boat touched the schooner's side, I cast one glance at the Albatross, my last link, I felt, to earth, for I had a feeling almost unaccountable, very similar to that experienced by the Weird Sisters on the approach of the regicide Macbeth, when they exclaim—

"By the pricking of my thumbs,
Something evil this way comes,"

that there was a great deal of evil where I was about to go.

I was therefore somewhat surprised when a pair of unexceptionable white side-ropes were handed to me through the gangway, and I found the sides manned man-of-war fashion; more so still, when I was received on the quarter-deck by a fine, gentlemanly man, in a sort of undress naval uniform, who politely bowed to me, welcomed me on board the Spanish schooner, Esperanza, belonging to the Port of Cadiz, and lately from Havannah, having been driven somewhat to the southward of her course by a gale she encountered ten days before.

"A very probable account," I thought. "But, Senor, may I beg to know if you are the captain of this ship?"

"I have the honour to command her," was the answer.

"And your name, Senor?"

"Don Diego Lopez de Mendoza, at your service, Senor," he replied, with another of his inimitable bows.

"Then, Senor Don Diego de Mendoza, I must trouble you to show your papers."

"Con mucho gusto, Senor," he answered, smiling blandly. "Will you step down below into my humble cabin, and I will show them to you?"

I bowed, and prepared to follow him, casting a look, as I got to the head of the companion ladder, towards my own ship; she was well to windward, and kept the schooner completely under her guns. I was scarcely prepared for the luxury displayed in the cabin, the damask hangings and coverings to the sofas and chairs, the profusion of plate and glass, and the quantity of weapons of various manufacture, swords and fire-arms, arranged against the bulk-head. The cabin was right aft, and the stern windows were open, admitting the fresh breeze—a box of cigars was on the table. After placing me on a luxurious sofa he politely handed me the box with a lighted match, observing, "We ought always to make the most of life, and do as many things as we can at a time; we cannot tell how soon it may be brought to a close. We can smoke while you look over the papers."

I took the proffered cigar; it would have been an affront, or would have shown suspicion had I refused it, and employed myself in lighting it while he produced his papers from a handsome escritoire, inlaid with ivory. As he turned sharply round he caught my eyes fixed on the array of weapons.

"Ah mio amigo, I have a few pretty little pieces there, and some honest toledos, which have seen some service in their day. I keep them as curiosities to ornament my cabin, though, as a peaceful sugar carrier, I have little use for them."

"And your guns on deck are——"

"Chiefly for ornament also," he answered, finishing my sentence, " that is, at present, for the fact is, this vessel was a slaver, captured and condemned at St. Jago de Cuba, where I bought her, and as I thought it more than probable that I should fall in with her old owners, who would be likely to consider that they can show a better right to her than I have, I judged it prudent to keep the means on board of defending my property."

"Besides, there are pirates still among the West Indian Islands, and even in other seas, who might find a fast sailing craft, like yours, very serviceable," I observed, and was about to tell him of the discovery we made last night, but thought it more prudent to say nothing about it. I then looked over his papers; they were in every respect perfectly correct. He smiled blandly as he received them back from me, observing,

"It must be disagreeable to you, Senor, thus to suspect every stranger you meet on the high seas, but we caballeros understand these matters between each other You would wish, I presume, to look over the ship."

I signified that such was part of my duty, and accordingly, he leading the way, I looked into some other cabins and over the hold, which had far from a full cargo. There were, however, neither slave decks nor shackles to be seen, nor anything which would authorize us to detain her, though I confess I remember seeing a very miscellaneous collection of goods stowed below. Our eyes often rest on objects with little or no attention, but afterwards, when removed from them, they come vividly before us, and we are surprised that we did not remark them more minutely at the time —and so it was with me. I did, however, observe the villanous countenances of her crew, who accompanied their captain below and watched me most suspiciously, while, as I passed along the lower deck which was free from cargo, several others who were lying or sitting about, merely lifted up their heads as I passed, and I caught some of them making, as I afterwards thought, very significant gestures at each other. I was not sorry, I must own, when I was able to breathe the free air on the upper deck. The captain of the Esperanza accompanied me to the gangway, and insisted on shaking hands with me as I descended to my boat. At that instant I fancied I heard a faint cry as if from a female voice, within the vessel, but it was not repeated, and the next moment I believed it was merely a sound of my own imagination.

"Shove off," I sang out, and the men gave way with a will, for as the coxswain, Bill Leadline, observed, "he didn't like the cut of that chap's jib."

I saw Don Diego Lopez de Mendoza waving his hat to me as I pulled under the stern of his vessel to return to my own. Again, when some distance from the schooner, the stroke oar observed, that there was for a moment some one beckoning to us, from the cabin windows, but none of the other men saw any one, so I believed he was mistaken as I had before been.

My brother officers received me with congratulations as I stepped on deck. "We have all been insisting that the fellow is a pirate, and fully expected to see you run up to the yard-arm."

"Yes, and Seaton,"—(he was the senior mate, and would have stepped into my shoes,)—"was going to make a bid for your uniform," observed the purser.

"Yes, and Haggis, our medico, was thinking of begging your body of the miscreants, to be able to give an anatomical lecture to the ship's company, with a real subject," said our first, laughing.

"Ye may laugh as much as ye please, sirs," exclaimed the surgeon, "but let me tell ye, the men might be less profitably employed than in listening to one of my discourses; and I may as well observe that before long, if report speak true of the climate, I shall have as many corpses as I desire."

"Well, Medico, I will and bequeath to you this mortal husk of mine when its spirit has departed, to do with as you list, on one condition, that you do not poison me to get hold of it sooner," cried the master, who had a mortal aversion to physic, as have sailors and other men also, if they are wise.

While we were thus running on, the schooner had again filled her topsail, and was standing on in a course which would quickly have brought her to windward of us. She had already made some way when the negro whom we had saved from the wreck was brought on deck, as the surgeon thought some fresh air would do him good.

No sooner did his eye fall on the white sails of the receding schooner than it became fixed and dilated, as if he had seen a spirit of another world,—his thick lips parted asunder, exposing his white grinning teeth, his black, woolly hair almost uncurled and stood on end, as he started up from his seat on the booms where he had been placed, pointing towards her with his outstretched arm.

"What is dat—what is dat I see?" he screamed out. "De schooner, de cursed schooner, dat rob and murder all my shipmates. For what he come here—for what he go away?"

"What is that you are speaking about?" I asked, attracted towards the poor fellow by his extraordinary attitude and exclamations.

"De schooner—de pirate, sare—de d—d pirate, sare! Me know she well by de tree new cloths in de mainsail; she big villain, massa."

"Are you certain she is the pirate that attacked you?" asked I, his words confirming the suspicions I had begun to entertain about her.

"O, certain, sure, massa; me sabe that scoundrel if me meet her in one hundred years," answered the black, positively.

"In that case we ought to be after her without delay," I exclaimed, as I hurried off to the captain.

"All hands wear ship," he exclaimed, in a sharp, animated tone without waiting to ask further questions. The men flew to their stations, and the brig's head came rapidly round in chase of the supposed pirate. "Beat to quarters, Mr. Upton," he added, addressing the first lieutenant, for the guns had again been secured on my returning on board. The people of the schooner were not long, as may be supposed, in perceiving our change of course, nor were they evidently ignorant of the reason for it, for they instantly packed on every stitch of sail she could carry, and luffed up sufficiently near the wind to carry her well to windward of us. The heads of both vessels were now about north-north-east, except that the schooner could lay rather closer to the wind than we were able to do. As we were still somewhat to windward of her, we were able to fire our foremost guns without keeping away. A single shot was first sent wide of her, as a signal for her to lay to, but she took no notice of it. Another was then pointed at her, and it took effect on her counter, for we could see the white splinters glance off from the wounded wood—but she no more heeded it than the first.

"Now, my men, take good aim, and fire steadily. We must knock away some of her spars, to make sure of catching her, for she's a clipper, depend on it, and will otherwise walk away from us."

This was uttered by our gallant first lieutenant, in general a most silent man, but on exciting occasions he became absolutely loquacious. The men cheered and worked away with a will, and it is extraordinary with what rapidity the bow guns were loaded and fired.

At last Don Diego Lopez de Mendoza seemed to think that we had the game too much on our side, and while we were congratulating ourselves on seeing his peak halliards shot away, bang—a shot went through our fore-topsail, and two guns he had got run out at his stern ports began blazing away at us, though without doing us any injury which we could not immediately repair. The two vessels sailed very equally, though the enemy fore-reached on us; but then, again, the time he took to bend on new peak halliards and reset his mainsail, enabled us to regain the distance we had lost. The Don evidently did not wish to fight, though, as he had more guns and men, he might have had a chance of victory; yet, as he had everything to lose and nothing to gain, he wisely determined to avoid falling into our clutches by running away. Night also was approaching, which made his chances of escaping greater, should he manage to run us out of sight, as also making it more difficult for us to hit him, particularly as thick clouds, gathering rapidly, threatened to obscure the sky. The wind, too, had become more variable than before, which might or might not be in his favour, according as it shifted. Everything, therefore, combined to make us anxious to clip the fellow's wings in time.

"Come, Mr. Thompson," I said to the gunner, who was considered the crack shot in the ship, "see what you can do for us, in the matter of knocking away some of the fellow's spars."

"I'll try, for the honour of the service," answered the gunner, glancing his bright eye along the sight of the gun, and slapping the breach. "Now do your duty, old Bess." He fired. "I thought as how I'd done it," he exclaimed, jumping up, and down came tumbling on the deck of the schooner her main-top-gallant mast and its spar.

"Bravo!" exclaimed several voices. "Try again, Mr. Thompson." The second shot he fired missed; but the third hit, and badly wounded the main-topmast.

"Capital! A few more shots like that and we shall have the fellow snugly under our lee to handle as we like," I cried, with the greatest glee, entirely forgetting that lives were at stake in the game we were playing. The men worked with a will, and handled the guns as if they had been toys. For some time no other damage was done on either side, though occasionally one of the pirate's shots would go through our sails, and would cut in two a rope which was speedily again spliced. The sun, just sinking beneath a heavy canopy of dark clouds in a mass of red mist, threw a ruddy tinge on the canvass of the schooner, and the crested tops of the waves now fast rising with the increasing breeze.

"Come, my men, we must hit him before he sneaks away in the dark," exclaimed the first lieutenant, coming forward. "Here, let me try." He fired, and a shout escaped the crew at his success, for the main-topsail-yard of the schooner was evidently wounded, for we could see her people mounting aloft to secure it with battens. Before, however, they could succeed in doing so a stronger gust of wind struck the vessel, the yard bent forward, and away it went, shaking several of the hands on the outer part into the sea. The poor wretches had no chance of help from their own comrades, and we could not bear down to pick them up, so they were left to perish miserably.

This accident, of course, prevented the schooner from keeping so close to the wind, but the advantage we gained was somewhat counterbalanced by the increasing gale which compelled us to hand our lighter canvass. We, however, drew nearer to her, and our shot hulled her several times through the bright copper which caught the hot glow of the sky as she heeled over with the strength of the blast. Thus closed the day, the darkness gradually increasing till the dim outline of her form only was seen. Another sun had set ere retributive justice had overtaken her; was it to rise again and find her still unscathed?

A sharp look-out was kept to watch every movement the schooner might make, as, should we once lose sight of her, she would have altered her course, and her chances of escape would have much increased.

The master, Green, and I, with two midshipmen and old Thompson the gunner, were standing on the top-gallant forecastle, where we got our jackets well drenched from the heavy spray which flew in showers over the vessel, endeavouring to make out the effect our shot, which we still continued to send after her from our bow-chaser, had on her, when a ball from one of her stern guns, directed more by chance than with an aim, struck our fore-topmast just above the cap, and down it came, carrying away the jib-boom as it fell aft into the sea. We fancied we could hear the shouts of satisfaction raised by the pirates, at the success of their fire—and they again went on blazing away, in the hopes evidently of creating still further mischief.

While all hands were busy in repairing damages as well as circumstances would admit, I continued looking-out forward. The schooner had ceased firing, and did not draw ahead of us as fast as might have been expected, so I concluded that some of the last shots we had fired had done her more harm than appeared; she was, however, distancing us. As we were watching her we observed a flash as if from a pistol, though we could not hear the report.

"What is that?" I observed; "the fellows do not think that they are within pistol-shot of us."

"Probably some one was looking to his arms, and it went off by chance," answered the master. "By jingo! one ought to have a sharp pair of eyes to see in such a night as this. Mine are growing dim, I believe. Where the d—l has the chase got to?"

"Where!" I exclaimed. "Why—hang me if I can see her either. Can you see her, Jenkins?" I asked of the midshipman standing by me.

"No, sir, she's just gone into that thick wall of mist there," answered the youngster. "There—I see her again!"

"That's more than I do," observed the gunner. "At first I thought as how she'd tacked to weather on us; but I don't see her anywhere away ahead, where she would be if she'd done so. I can't make it out rightly."

"How does the chase bear now?" cried the captain through his speaking trumpet. I sent Mr. Jenkins aft to tell him.

We watched and watched in vain the best part of an hour, the pirate did not again appear. We still, however, held the same course, for it was considered likely that she would also do so on the chance of our tacking or bearing up. Thus the night wore on. We managed to clear away the wreck of the topmast, and made preparations for sending up a jury topmast at daybreak, for it was impossible, in the heavy sea there was then running, and in the dark, further to repair our damages.

Such are some of the scenes in a sailor's life.

CHAPTER VIII.

THE NIGHT ENGAGEMENT.

THE ship had been made snug, the guns secured, and the watch below had gone to their hammocks, an example I was meditating following, when, as I cast my eyes to windward, I fancied I saw a towering mass looming through the darkness.

"What is that away there?" I asked of the master, who had relieved my watch. I pointed to the spot indicated; he looked earnestly.

"A vessel, by Jupiter!" he exclaimed. "The pirate as I live! All hands on deck; call the captain; beat to quarters."

"He's standing towards us," I observed.

"Ay, and will be right down upon us, too," answered Green.

The captain and first lieutenant were on deck in an instant. They looked at the advancing vessel, now growing every instan more distinct.

"Run out the guns and give him a broadside," shouted the captain through his speaking trumpet.

"He intends to pass under our stern and rake us in passing, I think, sir," observed the first lieutenant.

"We'll give him our larboard guns and then keep away," replied the captain. "By heavens! no; he's rounding to, and will be on board us. Larboard guns—fire, men—now fire!"

Our whole broadside was discharged into the approaching stranger within pistol-shot of him. The fire blazed forth, and the loud crashing of the shot was heard as it tore through the planks and timbers of the enemy. Loud shrieks and cries then arose high above the howling of the blast, but still the stranger came on.

"Boarders, be prepared to repel boarders!" shouted our commander, ere the terrific tumult had ceased. The seamen rushed for their cutlasses. Crippled as we were, it was difficult to avoid a collision whenever the enemy chose to board us.

The towering mass approached; a tremendous crash was heard; the sides of the two vessels ground together; grappling irons were hove on board us, and a hundred fierce countenances appeared in the nettings and lower rigging, lighted up by the flashes of pistols and swivel guns, with which they endeavoured to cover their attempt to board. They were to be met, however, by British seamen—fellows not easily daunted by the ugliest visages under the sun.

"Boarders, follow me!" shouted our first lieutenant, flourishing his cutlass and leaping into the main rigging. He was there met by so strong a party of pirates that he was thrown back on the deck with a number of our men, and full fifty of the enemy leaped after him with the wildest shrieks fury could call forth.

Our marines, meantime, who were stationed on the poop, were clearing the after part of the pirate vessel, while our two foremost guns were blazing away into her bow and knocking the foremost ports into one.

On seeing the fall of our first lieutenant, I hurried to his assistance with the men nearest to me. He was uninjured, and was up in a moment, and laying about him with such right good will—an example well imitated by our people—that half the miscreants were cut to pieces on the deck, and the remainder were either driven back into their own vessel or overboard, where they were crushed between the sides or perished miserably in the boiling sea.

Never have I heard a more infernal din—the crashing of the bulwarks of the two vessels as they ground together—the tearing and rending of the shot as they went through the pirate's bows—

the thunder of the guns, and the sharp report of the muskets and pistols—the howling of the storm—the lashing of the waves—the wild shrieks and hoarse shouts of the combatants—the cries of despair and agony—mingled in one deafening and terrific discord.

As my post was forward I had no opportunity of boarding, but the first lieutenant, backed by the master, after defeating the attempt of the pirates to board, succeeded in getting on the decks of the schooner, when they were met by my amigo, Don Diego Lopez de Mendoza, who, to do him justice, pirate as he was, behaved like a brave man. He fought desperately for some time, till at last Green gave him a blow on the head which brought him to the deck; and some of our fellows who had been of the boat's crew, and recognised him as captain, got hold of him and hauled him on board as a prisoner.

While Upton was carrying the fore-part of the schooner, Green fought his way aft, where a strong stand was made against him. As we could no longer fire our guns without a risk of injuring our own people, I led the remainder of our boarders on to the deck of the pirate, when, seeing Green hard pressed, I hurried to assist him, and, with this additional strength, we soon drove most of those who were opposing us, overboard. Others jumped down below, where Green and I followed them. A lamp, suspended from a beam, was burning in the centre of the cabin, its light shedding a lustre on the silver utensils, the jewelled arms, the glass mirrors, and the rich damask coverings of the furniture. In an instant after, it was obscured by smoke, the mirrors were shivered by the bullets, and the furniture deeply stained with the blood of the combatants. The pirates, driven to desperation, fought with the fury of demons; they felt that they could expect no mercy, and sought for none. But our brave fellows were more than a match for them, and few escaped the sturdy blows of their cutlasses. Many stood still at bay, when I heard Green's voice above the din, exclaim—

"Back, men, back to the brig for our lives; she's on fire and sinking."

I repeated the orders to our people, and as I was making my way up the companion-ladder, I saw Green carrying a young girl in his arms, followed by two men, bearing between them a female form. There was no time for explanation; as we reached the deck, in the darkness of night, the scene appeared doubly terrific, and for a moment the horrid thought appeared to me that the two vessels had separated. It was not the case, they still were fast by the main chains; and our people were rushing to regain the brig, followed by the pirates, some fighting, others with the idea of prolonging their lives for a short time.

The last of our men who had been below had just reached the deck, when a bright flame burst up from the main hatch of the schooner with a loud explosion. I had reached the main rigging of my own vessel, my men had followed me, and two of the pirates attempted to leap after us. One was shot dead by one of our men, who turned round and fired deliberately at him. The other leaped, but the vessels were parting, his hand missed his grasp, and, as he fell back with a shriek of agony into the dark gulf below, the glare fell on his distorted countenance, his long hair streaming in the blast, his eyes starting from their sockets, his mouth wide open, and his neck bent back, while his sword still waved idly in the air. I shall never forget the horrors of that dreadful picture. It seems to this day more vivid than any of the scenes of that terrific night.

"Cut away everything—get clear of the schooner—up with the helm!" shouted the captain. "Square away the mainyard—ease away the larboard braces!"

The brig paid off before the wind. The men flew to cut away the lashings which held the dangerous foe to us.

"Huzza! we are clear," shouted our crew, as we tore away from the schooner.

Then ascended a cry of agony, despair, and horror, from the survivors of the pirates, as they stood on the deck of their fated vessel. They knew no mortal power could save them, and they had provoked alone the vengeance of heaven. The explosion had been only partial, for the magazine was drowned; but the schooner was on fire fore and aft, and sinking. One or the other of two dreadful deaths was to be the lot of all who remained on board. It was literally a struggle between the two elements, which should obtain the prey. The flames burned up brightly and fiercely, while the raging seas rose high above her sides and swept over her decks with terrific fury. The waves were to be triumphant! On a sudden a vast flame ascended as it were to the sky, and some declared, though it must have been the work of the imagination, that they heard shrieks, and groans, and cries, with shouts of mocking laughter, uttered by no earthly voices. Then there was total darkness, and the waves danced up where the ship had been.

The pirate schooner had sunk. We afterwards had reason to know that the pirates had run us on board, in consequence of finding their vessel in a sinking condition from the holes our shot had made. It was their only resource; they thought that they might take us by surprise, and perhaps capture us. At all events, they expected to have their revenge, by destroying us with themselves.

The events I have been describing took place in the course of a few minutes. How short the lapse of time since I had seen the pirate schooner, like an evil spirit stalking through the night, approaching to destroy us—and now, a blackened hulk, she was many fathoms down in the depths of the ocean.

I do not mean to say I made these reflections at the moment, for my energies and those of all on board were required to repair our own damages. They were considerable; our larboard bulwarks and main chains were torn away, while the quarter was much stove in; and had the two vessels remained much longer together, I verily believe our sides would have been ground down to the water. However, she still remained tight. We secured the guns, got up temporary bulwarks, and secured the main rigging. The brig had, on getting free from the enemy, been kept away on our proper course to the southward, nearly before the wind.

CHAPTER IX

THE PRISONERS.

WE were hard at work all night long, and when day broke and the sun rose, he shone aslant decks still slippery with human gore, and a ship almost a wreck. The wind and sea had fortunately gone down, so that our work proceeded with less difficulty. When the crew were mustered, five were found missing, who must have been killed by the pirates, or fallen overboard in attempting to leap into the schooner. Two were killed on our own decks, and nine wounded, so that our loss was severe, and shows the desperation with which the enemy fought.

Eight bells in the morning watch had struck before I knocked off work to go below and recruit with breakfast; and I then, and only then, remembered the females I had seen Green engaged in preserving. Without speaking a word to any one, I jumped down below, and opened the door of my cabin. I stood transfixed with amazement, for there I saw—her head on my pillow—an infantine face so perfectly beautiful, so angelic in its expression, that I thought for an instant I beheld a being of another and a better world. She slept soundly the sleep of innocence, for my entrance did not awake her. Her long dark eye-lashes marked distinctly on her almost alabaster skin, though her hair, which floated in ringlets round her neck, was of a golden hue. One fair arm was stretched out instinctively, as if to steady herself on her couch, while the other was placed beneath her head. How can so bright a flower bloom amid scenes thus stormy and wild?

Green just then poked his head into the gun-room. "Hillo, master," I exclaimed, "some visitor from a better world than ours has taken possession of my cabin, so I'll e'en go and wash my foul, blood-stained hands in yours."

"Oh! mine's occupied too," he answered. "Try the purser's; he's snoring there himself, and won't awake in a hurry; but bear a hand about it, and come and sit down to discuss breakfast, and I will tell you how it all happened."

We were soon assisted by the surgeon in doing ample justice to a substantial breakfast, in which we were afterwards joined by the first lieutenant, the deck being left in charge of the senior mate. Upton had received an ugly cut across the left arm, but he had it bound up, and, like a gallant fellow, refused to neglect his duty. Neither Green nor I had received a scratch. The captain had, I found, been slightly wounded by a musket-ball in the side, and one of the midshipmen very severely by a cannon-ball, while the purser, Mr. Sleepwell, had received a shot through his hat which spoilt its beauty. These were the only injuries received by the quarter-deck officers. Upton, as he took his seat at the table, looked sick and faint, but his thoughts were with others.

"How are our poor fellows going on, Haggis?" he asked. "They tell me John Smith is likely to slip his cable."

"Weel there's gude chance o' that in the climate we're ganging to; but if we could put him on board a homeward bound ship, should he survive two or three days, he may yet escape; but I would wish you, Upton, to take more care o' yourself mon—your life's o' value to many, and ye must na be playing ducks and drakes with it."

"Thank you, Haggis, I shall do well enough. I am only a little fagged," replied Upton.

"Then take a little breakfast and turn in, and I will just put some cooling stuff on your arm, or it may prevent ye sleeping."

"Thank you, doctor, thank you," said Upton. "Well, master, how do your protégés get on? I hear, like a knight of old, you saved two demoiselles of beauty rare, from the power of the robbers."

"I know very little more than any one else," answered Green. "While I was between decks in the schooner, I followed two or three of the pirates, whom I suspected were going to try and blow up the vessel with us and themselves into the air, and had just knocked them on the head, before they had time to accomplish their kind intentions, when I fancied that I heard a scream from a cabin built up in the hold. I forced open the door, and found a female on her knees with a chain round her waist, and a child clinging to her neck. The lady shrieked still louder as we appeared, and told us, in English, to kill her at once, rather than prolong her misery. We knocked off the shackles in a moment: and we could not make her comprehend we were friends, though the little girl perceived that we were, and came with me willingly, and we had just time to reach the deck, when some of the villains who had got down forward, managed partially to blow up the vessel. I fear the poor lady—for a lady she is, from her appearance and way of speaking—is out of her mind—mad, quite mad."

"Ay, ye may well say that the poor thing is demented—there canna be a doubt o' it," said Haggis.

"The horrors she must have undergone on board that schooner, were enough to make her so," I observed. "Does any body know if she were one of the passengers in the ill-fated ship, which suffered from the pirates' handy-work?"

"Little doubt about it," answered Green. "Has the negro we picked up yesterday, seen her?"

"No, poor fellow, he was knocked over with an ugly wound from one of the first shots the pirates fired, and has ever since been in his hammock," answered the surgeon.

"Ye have the prisoners, though, whom ye may examine. Your friend, the Spanish Captain, may say something."

"My friend! What, has that scoundrel lived to be hung?" I exclaimed. "I doubt, however, if you will get much information out of him."

"You are right," observed Upton, "he has not spoken a word since he came on board, and, by his looks, will die game: but, surely, the little girl will be able to tell us her history."

"When she awakes and is somewhat recovered, we will ask her," said Green. "But, poor little thing, she was so agitated, that I would not tease her with questions : and scarcely had I placed her on-the bed, than she was fast asleep."

By the time breakfast was over, we had learned all that each other had to communicate; and I was then not sorry to throw myself on the deck, in the corner of the gun-room ; notwithstanding the rolls and pitches the vessel made, I enjoyed two hours' sound sleep and forgetfulness of the rough present, for my dreams were of home and its dear faces, the green lane, and my own Edith.

When I awoke the sun was shining down through the cabin skylight,—(at first I thought its beams came through the window of my snug little room in my father's house,)—the sea had gone down, and the brig was making her way calmly and quickly onward.

When I went on deck I found the captain, who told me to go down below with the corporal of marines, and endeavour to elicit some information from the pirate captain, as to the history of the lady and the child we had saved, as I was the only officer who could speak or understand Spanish, a necessary qualification for holding communication, which had been before overlooked.

On going below I found my friend, Don Diego Lopez de Mendoza, seated on the deck, within a screen in the forehold, and heavily manacled. His head was bent down between his knees, his dress was torn and besmeared with blood, and his hair hung lank and clotted with the same ruddy stream, over his shoulders. As the light of the lantern, carried by the corporal, fell on his countenance, his eye glanced up with the glare of a tiger, as if he would spring and destroy the person who came to disturb him. He probably fancied that we were come to drag him forth and run him up to the yard-arm, according to his own system of justice. When his eyes were accustomed to the glare of the lantern, he recognised me immediately.

"Ah! I thought you had been killed, from not seeing you," he observed. "I am glad you escaped, for you understand my language, and I wish to have some one to speak to."

"The man has something of humanity in him at all events," I thought.

"Things have changed with me since yesterday morning," he continued ; " and I must observe, your barbarous shipmates do not treat me as if I were a gentleman."

" Deliciously cool of the murderous ruffian," I thought.

"You will have more courtesy, and will explain to your captain, that as an Hidalgo, I ought not to be treated in this unbecoming manner—as a mere robber. But, tell me, how was it you attacked me after letting my vessel go free? I shall complain to my government, and they will insist on compensation."

" You are mistaken, Senor, in supposing that we do not know the character of your vessel," I replied.

" Why, what do you take me for ?" he asked, with the most inimitable coolness.

"A pirate!" I replied. " It were wrong to deceive you, and as such you must prepare to meet death."

" I, a pirate, indeed !" he exclaimed. "You are the pirate rather :—I was quietly sailing on, when you fired into me, and thinking you were a pirate, I endeavoured to escape, till you reduced my vessel to a sinking condition.,'

"You cannot deceive us," I answered; "several witnesses will appear against you; a lady and her child were saved, and we, yesterday morning, rescued a black from the wreck of the ship you burned, who immediately recognised you."

He started, and his countenance grew pale, I thought. He seemed to be mastering himself.

"That comes of not carefully destroying every human being on board," he observed, in an every-day tone, as if he spoke of a matter of indifference. "I said such foolish mercy would lead to our destruction. Well, at all events, if die I must, let it be like a caballero, and not as a common thief, by the *garrotto*" (the gibbet).

I told him in reply, that we should have no voice in the matter, that he would be tried by the laws of our country at Sierra Leone, and if found guilty of piracy, that no distinction would be made between him and his companions. I then asked him if he would give me any information about the unhappy lady we had rescued from his vessel.

"What, a lady and her child?" he asked. "I know which you mean. There were several others on board, for we are far too gallant to injure any ladies we capture. They are somewhat scarce on the high seas; but they were forward, I suppose, and went down with the vessel. About this lady, though I know no more than you do, she came on board my schooner because her ship was on fire. Cannot she give an account of herself?"

I told him that she was mad.

"Oh, then she cannot appear against me," he replied, laughing.

"There may be quite sufficient evidence to hang you," I observed, irritated at his heartlessness.

"There is many a slip between the cup and the lip," was his reply, or, at least, he made use of a similar Spanish proverb: "The flax is not yet grown which is to hang me."

"Be not so sure of that," I answered; "we treat pirates with scant ceremony."

"Pirates! yes, but I am no pirate," he exclaimed, as if a new plan of defence had occurred to him. "What I have said to you in joke, you, as a caballero, are not to bring against me."

Of course I promised him nothing, and disgusted at his audacity, and despairing of getting any of the information I required, I left him. I heard him, as I turned my back, uttering a deep oath, accompanied with an expression far from complimentary to the officers and ship's company.

From the other three prisoners, who were fierce ruffians of the lowest order, I could not gain any information, so we were compelled to wait, as must my readers, for another day, to satisfy our curiosity respecting our unfortunate passengers.

CHAPTER X.

A DEATH BED.

"LAND ahead!" sounded in my ears as I awoke out of a deep sleep into which the unremitting exertions of the last two days had thrown me. I jumped up, my head still confused with the scenes I had witnessed: of the ship on fire, the night engagement, the storm, and the subsequent events, and for the first few moments I could not tell whether I was returning to the shores of my native land, or was still outward-bound. I had been dreaming of that land—of the loved ones there—of her I loved more than all; and my imagination half deceived me into the hope that my time of banishment was ended, and that the well-known cliffs of Albion was the land in sight. Vain delusion! it was soon dispelled by the voices of my messmates.

"Whereabouts are we, master?" asked the purser, who, with some other person, was in the gun-room, while Green was busying himself in examining the chart.

"Not a hundred miles north or south of Sierra Leone; but we shall soon see when we get on shore," was the master's rather vague answer.

"I'll go on deck and have a look at the place, and see if it be as bad as people say," observed Sleepwell, as he ascended to the deck.

The third voice I heard was soft and low—how strange it sounded among those of the rougher beings on board!—it was that of the little rescued stranger. I was not long in slipping on my habiliments, and preparing to go on deck. As I stepped out of my cabin I stood for a moment to watch Green and his little charge. She was looking up confidingly and affectionately in his face, while he guided her soft little fair hand over the chart, to give her a lesson in geography.

"Oh, how nice it is to be near the land, Massa Green! and shall I be able to go and run about, and to pick flowers for poor mamma, as I have often before? It is so pleasant to run about in the shade, under the green trees! You must come too, dear massa, and so must dear mamma; it will do her good to sit under the trees, and listen to the birdies singing. We will all go—will we not, massa?"

A tear came into Green's eye as the child spoke, and I saw it running down his well-bronzed cheek. Poor child! she little knew that the days of her only parent were already numbered. As I went into the gun-room from one side, the doctor entered from the other, and though we tried to entice the little girl to come with us on deck, she would not quit Green, but kept fast hold of his hand till he led her there himself. I then asked Haggis how the unfortunate lady we had rescued was getting on. He shook his head as he answered,—

"Oh, puir leddie! she ne'er will tread the green earth again, nor sit under the green trees, as the little lassie was saying. She canna last till to-morrow's sundown, I am thinking."

"Poor thing!" I observed; "and what will become of that sweet child?"

"He who feeds the sparrows will take care of her," replied Haggis, pointing solemnly above. "Surely yon motherless child will not be deserted by Him."

"I trust not, doctor—I trust not!" I answered. "And tell me, how does the black man we picked up get on? He was badly wounded, I fear."

"He has slipped his cable already for another world, as you sailors say," he answered. "He never spoke again after he was knocked over."

"That is bad, indeed," I observed. "Then we shall have no witnesses against those rascally pirates, and they may escape after all."

"Why, how can that be, mon?" asked the doctor. "There are enough on board here, sure, to swear they fired on the British flag, and did some damage, too."

"Oh, that is nothing," I answered. "They may take and murder every one of us, provided they are under their own flag; and nothing could be done to them in return."

"Hanging is far too good a fate for the fellows we've got on board," he observed. "They do nothing but curse and swear all day in their own language, till they are black in the face."

"Is the poor lady conscious of her approaching death?" I asked.

"No: she still remains in the same demented state, but far weaker in body, which makes me fear that she canna recover," he replied. "She has been removed into the captain's cabin, and I must go and see her. He insisted on my coming to lay down a bit, while he is acting nurse."

While the medico went to attend to his unfortunate charge, I ascended on deck.

The sea was smooth as glass, the light air which came off the distant shore, scarcely serving to ruffle for an instant its shining surface. The hot sun, rising above the land, had not served to dispel the haze, which floats almost constantly in the atmosphere, not rising in it, but remaining suspended, like the canopy of smoke spread over London on a calm day. Over the shore it was far denser, till, in the horizon, it assumed the appearance of a thick brickdust-coloured hue, out of which were seen emerging, like a series of azure clouds, the lofty hills above the far-famed, and not at all maligned, settlement of Sierra Leone.

As the day wore on, the breeze freshened, and our approach was more rapid. I was not at all prepared for the beautiful scene which gradually opened to our sight as we drew near. In the distance were the Sierras or mountains of the Lion, while from the water rose sloping hills, richly cultivated, and interspersed with large villages, handsome mansions, neat thatched cottages, surrounded with banana, orange, paw-paw, and other fruit trees, forming altogether a picture which one might suppose the abode of contentment, peace, health, and happiness,—alas! how different is the reality.

A pilot came alongside in a small boat pulled by four hands, and was taken on board. As he walked aft with the dignified air of a man who knows his own importance, he touched his hat to the captain, and informed us that his appellation was that of Jack Toggle, which, as it was given to him in his early youth, he could not get rid of, though he did not admire it himself. Since then, not only had he become converted to the truth, but had become a preacher of it, in a Chapel, in Free Town, which, on Sundays, was, he informed us, constantly attended by crowds of his African brethren. He was a stout, good-looking fellow, with a powerful voice, and self-possession, and I doubt not, is as much admired as many preachers of fairer hue in England.

At last we reached the anchorage of Free Town, and dropped our anchor once more to the bottom. The town is well laid out in broad streets, and from the houses being generally detached, covers a considerable extent of ground, in fact, they look like so many cottages ornée, elegantly built, tastefully painted externally, and surrounded by trees of various kinds. The broad mouth of the Sierra Leone river has the appearance of a smooth and extensive Lagoon, bounded on one side by the low, woody Bullom shore, and on the other by the verdant and gentle acclivity on which the town is situated, the background of which, gradually ascending, terminates in a semicircular range of moderate-sized hills, forming an amphitheatre decorated with lofty trees, and richly foliated shrubs, while every spot of the ascent, here and there studded with neat country seats, presented to our delighted eyes a picture of the most agreeable character, while the harbour bore on its unruffled bosom, ships of various sizes and rig, from every part of the world. While I was gazing on it, I felt a little soft hand placed in mine—

"Will you come and help take poor mamma on to the green shore, then ?" said the child, looking up with an inquiring glance into my face. "Massa Green says she is not able to go—she is ill, and I am sure the sweet green shore will make her well."

While the little girl was speaking, the captain came on deck and beckoned me towards him.

"Her last moments are come," he whispered; "she has returned to consciousness, and asks to see her child. Green is with her, and has promised to protect the girl, and he will keep his word—but we have no time to lose."

The kind skipper took the child's hand and led her below, whilst I followed. I am not fond of harrowing up the feelings of my readers by describing death-bed scenes, when no particular moral can be deduced therefrom. The mother recognised her daughter as soon as she was brought to her side, but the film of approaching dissolution was already dimming her sight. She had just strength to take the little girl by the hand, and place it in that of Green, who knew what it meant.

"Yes, yes, ma'am," he said, "I'll be a father to your child—do not doubt it. I've no babies of my own, and I don't expect ever to have any; I shall be too glad to take this one home to Mrs. Green, and she will be too happy to have her, and will be a good mother to her, depend upon it."

The dying woman understood him, and drew her child near her

to kiss her: in the act her head fell back, her features altered, the eyes became motionless—her spirit had fled. Thus died the unfortunate lady among strangers. Nothing of her history could we learn, except that she had pronounced the name of Markham, and called her daughter Eva. The child we found at once answered to the name, and said it was hers.

For some time she could not at all comprehend her loss, nor was it till the body of her mother was conveyed on shore to be buried, that a suspicion of the truth entered her mind. When she asked for her mamma, and was told that she had gone on shore, she cried bitterly at not being allowed to accompany her; and in order to pacify her, Green was obliged to explain to her that God would not let her see her any more in this world, but that in another and a better land she would be again united to her. It was interesting to hear the honest sailor in his homely way instructing the fair child in his own theological ideas, and to see the deep interest with which the little girl listened to him. Poor child! she was the only living thing—the only remnant of a proud ship, and her freight of human beings.

CHAPTER XI.

THE TRIAL.

It is time that I should return to those who had worked all the woe and destruction I have just described—the cold-blooded pirate and his fierce associates. I was on deck when they were brought up from below to be conveyed to a prison on shore. Fortunately the courts were sitting, and they were to be tried forthwith, so that we should not be delayed on this account any considerable time after we had completed our wood and water.

The first who appeared was Don Diego Lopez de Mendoza—but how changed from the gay and gallant cavalier who had received me in the cabin of the Esperanza—his beard was now of three days' growth, his linen soiled, his face unwashed, and his dress torn and bloodstained from the fierce struggle in which he had been engaged. He looked boldly around, though somewhat anxiously at the same time, for he was not quite certain that he was not forthwith to be hung up at our fore yard-arm—a fate he must have felt he not a little merited. When his eye fell on me, he instantly inquired, with a slight swagger in his tone, what was to be done with him. I answered that he would shortly be tried for piracy and murder on the high seas, and if found guilty, would in all probability suffer the penalty of the law. The three survivors of his lawless crew followed him with their arms in irons; a necessary precaution, for as they cast their scowling glances on either side, they evidently meditated revenging themselves on their captors. As they perceived, however, the guard on deck, the fortresses on shore, and the flags of the numerous British ships in the harbour, they felt the hopelessness of their case, and uttered imprecations, loud and deep, on our heads, but as they were in Spanish, our crew neither understood nor heeded them. When the Spanish captain reached the

gang-way, he turned round, and looking aft with the dignified air of an injured patriot, he exclaimed in his own language,—
"I call all here to witness that my ship was unlawfully captured, and that I have been treated as a common felon, and that my own government will not fail to seek for satisfaction from the British for the insult they have offered to them in my person."

Having thus delivered himself, he descended into the cutter, in which Seaton, with a file of marines, was waiting to carry him and his companions to prison.

"Remember, Mr. Seaton," said the captain, "if either of the men attempt to make their escape, shoot them: they deserve no mercy at our hands."

For the remainder of the day we were busily employed in watering the ship, so that I was unable to go on shore to see the lions of the place. Of the pure liquid, there is not only an abundant and constant supply, but it is of the very best quality—the only good thing the place produces; for, notwithstanding the beauty of the scenery, the climate is most deadly. While we lay there, deaths were occurring daily on board one or other of the numerous vessels which had put in to load with wood, an article of which much is exported. How can Africa be civilized with such a climate to contend against? How can the negro mind be improved and enlightened? Alas! I fear that with the example too generally set them by Europeans, such a consummation is yet far distant. They see white men robbing, murdering, cheating, lying, and all the time professing to believe in the doctrines of Christianity: yet we are surprised that the benighted Africans refuse to become Christians. No wonder that those who do so nominally, paint their saints *black*, and the Prince of Evil *white;* the latter, the patron of the men who can do such deeds.

The following morning, while I had the watch on deck, and was sweeping the horizon with my glass, I observed a small vessel in the offing, standing in for the land. As she drew near, I saw that she was a schooner of about eighty tons or so, that her canvass was very badly set, and that she was even worse steered, for she kept yawing about as if a drunken man were at the helm. I pointed her out to Captain Dainmore, who just then came on deck.

"She has probably lost most of her crew, and will have some difficulty in coming to an anchor," he observed. "Take the gig's crew with you, and lend her any assistance you may find she requires."

While he was speaking, up went the Spanish ensign by the signal halliards to the foremast head, while some other flag was hoisted at her peak.

"Why, what can they mean by that?" exclaimed an old quartermaster near me. "Them chaps hasn't much knowledge of seamanship, I'm thinking."

I was not long in shoving off, and pulling towards the schooner. I soon discovered that it was not for want of strength that her canvass was set in so slovenly a manner, for her decks appeared crowded with people, who, as I approached, hailed me with loud shouts. I had, however, no little difficulty in getting alongside, for as there was a strong breeze at the time, she was going rapidly through the water, and no one on board apparently had the slightest notion of heaving to, or of throwing me a rope. We fortunately contrived, notwithstanding the way she was yawing about, to hook on to her main chains, and I jumped on board.

I was certainly not prepared for the strange sight which met my eyes. There were more than a hundred blacks on deck, dressed out as if for a fancy ball or masquerade; a negro was at the helm, with a cocked hat and a plume of feathers in it on his head; he had on a blue checked shirt, and a long toledo buckled round his waist, while a pair of red morocco slippers adorned his feet, but of other garments he was innocently destitute, nor did he seem to be otherwise than highly proud of his costume. Some had on petticoats, and others hats; others wore inexpressibles, but, instead of making them cover their legs, they wore them as shawls over their shoulders; then, again, others had on waistcoats, without a rap else. Those were fortunate who could boast of tailed coats, and more fortunate still of surtouts, as containing a larger quantity of cloth, but the chief people alone had the prizes of various parts of the military uniform.

It had been long, I found, a matter of discussion, which was the most honourable—the cocked hat or the coat, and it was decided at last in favour of the cocked hat. He, therefore, who was selected as captain, wore the badge of honour—the plumed hat. He had been chosen for the office from possessing a greater amount of knowledge of seamanship than his companions, though, from the manner in which he steered, that was not, as may be supposed, very considerable. He had, however, done wonders; in fact, he seemed to be the only man on board who knew anything of the subject; and I discovered that the cause of the bad steering of the vessel was, that he was every instant compelled to leave the helm to show his people what to do, and he had even been engaged in attempting to range the cable and to bring up, when we went alongside. As I walked aft, he saluted me in English,—

"How do, sare, me captain?—glad see you—take helm?"

The blacks crowded round me, clapping their hands, and exhibiting every sign of satisfaction, while the captain gladly yielded up his post at the helm to one of my people. Having set the sails properly, and given a right course for the harbour, I endeavoured to glean from the black skipper the reason of the grotesque appearance of himself and his crew.

"Now listen, massa," he commenced; "no angry! What me done, me done right; if massa me, massa done same. Me once free man, king, like massa. Me go walk one day—many maus come—knock me down—de trees swim and turn round. Me wake in dark house—many niggers dere—me no more see me wives and piccaninnies. Den come white men—carry me on board ship—sail, sail—den come bang, bang! Englis ossifer come board—take Portigee ship. All come here, Sierra Leone. Den we all happy—dance, sing—stay some time—learn English palaver. Me go back to me country, near de Sherbro River. See me wives—see me piccaninnies—dance, sing, again. One day me want one new gown for me wife—me go in canoe wid rice to sell in Sherbro, and bring back gown. Me sell de rice, and get de gown—so bootiful—all red, and blue, and yellow—fit for Queen of England—when see boat of de white men. We pull very hard—pull, pull, pull away—no good. Ah! de white men take we—carry on board dis schooner—sink canoe—take de bootiful gown. Many niggers on board—many more come—schooner full. We sailed away for de Havanah—many womens on board—captain one great tiger—one halligator—one white devil! He beat we—flog, flog, flog every day till blood come—knock we down wid handspike—anything—swear—cruel—oh, very bad. So we say, 'Captain kill we—eh, not so—we kill captain.' Now, so happen, de womens shut up in after cabin, and de arms, de pistols, de swords, and de muskets, all in same cabin. Den de captain and de white men drink much, and go to sleep much, so when dark—very dark—dark as nigger's face, de women slip silent—silent—no noise—wid de arms to where we was. One bring pistol, one powder, one bring sword, one musket, till we got all de arms in de sip. Den de women come and pull off de irons, and den we all jump up togeder—we cry one loud cry—ah, dat cry wake captain—he jump up too, but too late—no get arms. We knock him brains out—we throw him overboard to de sharks—dey crush him bones. We kill all de crew—we throw overboard to feed de sharks—dey like him better den de nigger dat dey threw over, no dead, some days before. One lily-white boy we no kill—him good boy—bring water to poor nigger when captain beat much—wash him wounds—so we no hurt him. Den we say, we kill captain, we kill crew—where we go? who captain? who crew? Den all de niggers hold a palaver, and dey say—Blattoopam—dat is me, —him captain; so me captain. Den me say, 'Bout sip,' but dey crew no good—sip no come bout long time; last de boy help—de niggers pull—me steer—sip come about—we sail on, on, on. When me go sleep, boy steer—when boy sleep, me steer. Last me see dis port, so me sail in. Dere, sare, you have me history."

I found that Captain Blattoopam's account was corroborated in every respect by the boy's, whose life the Africans had mercifully spared in return for his humanity. They were certainly justified in acting as they did, and no one could pity the fate of the Spanish captain and his crew, brought about as it was by their own cruelty and folly, first, in ill-treating the slaves, and then allowing some of the women to go free, as it appeared they had done. The women who had been shut up in the cabin in which the arms were kept, conveyed them to the men, and instigated them to attempt the recovery of their freedom.

Soon after the black skipper had finished his account of the affair, I saw that there was something going forward in the forehold, and sending one of my people down, he reported that there were three white men confined there alive. I instantly ordered them on deck, when three of the most miserable looking wretches I ever saw appeared. Terror was in their aspect, and as they glanced around they seemed to expect instant death. Their only clothing were their shirts, torn and dabbled with blood. Their persons were dirty in the extreme, and their hair long and tangled.

"Oh, dem knaves! I forgot dem," exclaimed Captain Blattoopam, eyeing them with a glance of supreme contempt; "dey was passengers, so no kill dem."

Their lives had been spared at the solicitation of the boy, backed by the women, who considered, that as they had taken no part in ill-using them, they were not worthy of death. Poor wretches! it was melancholy to see white men quail before black savages as they did; nor were they assured that their lives were safe till they were clear out of the vessel.

We at last brought the little schooner safely up to an anchor, and delivered her over to the proper legal authorities, to be condemned as a prize, while the negroes were landed at the liberated African's yard, and soon after located at one of the villages in the neighbourhood, where, as they found numerous friends, they were heartily welcomed.

I must now return to the pirate, Don Diego Lopez de Mendoza, as he called himself. I saw nothing of him till I met him in court, where he stood arraigned for piracy and murder on the high seas, for attacking, under the flag of a power with which he was at peace, Her Britannic Majesty's brig Albatross, and for slaying and maiming some of her liege subjects on board the said brig. I am no lawyer, but as far as I recollect, these were the crimes for which he stood charged, as did also his three companions.

The officers and crew of the Albatross proved that we found a ship on fire; that we rescued a black man from the wreck; that the said black man stated that he had been a passenger on board the ship; that the ship had been boarded by a piratical schooner; and that the pirate had murdered some of the people, carried off the women, rifled the ship, and then set her on fire. We then proved that on the following day, the black, on seeing a schooner we had just boarded from thinking her a suspicious character, had positively asserted that she was the piratical schooner which had attacked the ship; that when ordered to heave-to, she not only refused to do so, and endeavoured to make her escape, but fired into her Britannic Majesty's brig, and for a time contrived to elude us; that, however, she afterwards ran on board us at night, with the evident intent of taking us by surprise, but that we had, instead, sent her to the bottom, and destroyed all her people, with the exception of the four prisoners at the bar. We also proved the death of the black, and of the unhappy lady who was rescued from the schooner. A smile of evident satisfaction lighted up the countenance of Captain Mendoza as this piece of information was translated to him, but his visage elongated again as little Eva was brought into court and placed in the witness-box. Child as she was, the judge consented to receive her evidence, if she were able to give any. At first, she was startled at finding herself in the presence of so many strange men, but as she gained sufficient assurance to look up, her eyes wandered round the court. When they reached the pirate they rested on him for a moment, and then, with a cry of terror, she flew into Green's arms, and tried to hide her face. When asked why she was alarmed, she answered,

"He took mamma and me from ship—he kill poor papa—he burn ship."

This closed the evidence against the prisoners; one would have supposed that it was conclusive, and sufficient to condemn them. Their defence was very ably conducted. It went to prove that Captain Mendoza was a very quiet, peaceable man, and that his companions were very orderly people ; that so far from setting a ship on fire, they would never wish to injure any one; but, when fired into by the Albatross, they believed that they were attacked by a pirate, and accordingly defended themselves to the utmost of their ability, and that when they ran into her at night, they did so from finding themselves in a sinking condition, as the only means of saving their lives. They then called upon the court to consider well before they harboured even a suspicion against innocent men.

The defence was worthy of Don Diego Lopez de Mendoza, who spoke at great length and displayed considerable oratorical ability. The judge summed up, and the jury, on returning into court, pronounced him not guilty. He, on this, bowed politely to the judge, and most profoundly to us, as if no matter of importance had occurred, and evidently expected to be allowed to take his hat and walk off with his companions, when some fresh actors appeared on the scene, who stated themselves to be the survivors of the crew of a brig attacked and plundered by him and his followers. This again entirely changed the form of his countenance, and he broke forth into curses loud and long, as the handcuffs, which had been removed, were again placed on his wrists, and he was conducted back to prison. The result of the second trial I did not hear till long afterwards, as we sailed the following morning to the southward, with little Eva as our passenger and guardian angel.

CHAPTER XII.

MARSDEN'S STORY.

WE were again at sea. I was walking the deck just before dinner with Frank Marsden, to whom I had become very much attached. We had a bond of union in the possession of similar tastes.

"You remember the promise I made some time ago, when Upton told us his story of Poor Tom Bunt?" he observed. "I have been endeavouring to fulfil it, and have put several tales together for the amusement of the mess. I was much struck with the account you gave me the other day, of the manner in which the slaves had regained their liberty, on board the schooner you visited in Sierra Leone, and I have founded a story on it, which I will read to-day after dinner, if you think it will gratify our messmates."

"I am sure it will," I replied; and just then the steward announced dinner.

The social meal was quickly concluded, when I took care to remind Marsden of his promise. Our messmates pricked up their ears at my announcement of his intention.

"Come, Frank, we shall be glad to hear what your story is about," said our good captain, who was dining with us. "If you will open the ball, I dare say others will follow; and the weather is so fine I don't think we are likely to have any interruption this afternoon."

"I wrote my story on purpose to read it to the mess, so I wont sham modest about it," replied Frank. "But I shall claim a favour from you in return, sir. It is that you will give us some of your adventures in the war time, when the service had better employment than hunting after slavers. I have heard you describe scenes, sir, which have made me long to have lived in those days."

"Those were glorious times I own, my boy, when England proudly lifted her head above all other nations, and stood forth as the champion of pure liberty, religion, and truth. Those were times when an Englishman was proud to acknowledge his country—and so he may justly now be, whatever her enemies may say about her," he added, after a moment's hesitation. "The era of England's greatness has not yet passed away I hope; and sure I am that when we engage in another war, we shall find British seamen doing their duty gallantly as before; British statesmen supporting them; a grateful nation applauding them, and a gracious Queen bestowing laurels on the victors. And that reminds me that we have not yet drank her Majesty's health. Gentlemen—the Queen."

Our fair sovereign's health was drunk with enthusiasm, as I trust it ever will be by her loyal navy. I am certain it was with no lip-service that every one at table added "God bless her."

"I will do my best to rummage up something from the stores of my memory for another day," continued Captain Dainmore. "So now, Frank, get under weigh as fast as you can, for all hands are ready for you."

Marsden accordingly went to his berth to get his manuscripts, and returning with them, prepared for his task. Besides the captain, we had all the officers of the gun-room present, for the senior mate, Seaton, had a watch, and was on deck; and we had two midshipmen; nor must I forget a very important personage, our little foundling, Eva. The lovely child was sitting on Massa Green's knee, while he was amusing her by cutting out figures from a cocoa-nut with his penknife. The moment, however, Marsden began his story, she opened wide her large blue eyes, and with lips apart, almost afraid to breathe, she listened attentively to every word he uttered. Frank smoothed his paper, cleared his voice, and began—

YARRA, THE SLAVE GIRL.

Beneath a plane-tree, whose wide-spreading leaves formed a grateful shade from the noontide heat of an African sun, was seated a young girl. She was a native of that mysterious, unknown land; yet although her skin was dark, her hair was long and glossy, and her form was such as a sculptor might delight to copy. Her features were delicate and regular, and her eyes large and lustrous, with a soft and languid expression, which betokened an

inocent and tender heart. A long scarf of fine grass-cloth, of
beautiful manufacture, which was thrown over one shoulder and
round her waist, served as an ample garment in that burning
time, and contributed a graceful drapery to her statue-like appearance. On her arms she wore heavy bracelets of pure gold,
though of rough workmanship, but her ancles were without any
rnament.

She was in a meditative mood, it seemed, for as she rested, half-
recumbent on the ground, she scarcely noticed the rich and beautiful scenery around her. No wonder, for to her the view was
familiar, as on no other had her eyes ever fallen. Behind her, in
the far distance, arose, above a grove of palm and cocoa-nut trees,
a line of lofty mountains of a blue tint, yet clearly defined against
the bright sky.

At her feet, the ground, covered with a forest of lofty trees, from
whose boughs hung in graceful festoons of many varied hues
numberless far-creeping parasites, sloped down towards a lake of
pure and sparkling water. There nature revelled in boundless
luxuriance. On every side were trees and plants, with leaves of
gigantic size and graceful form, with flowers of many tints to
please the eye, while birds of gaudy plumage flew from bough to
bough, filling the forest with their notes. Here and there were
to be seen a few cultivated spots, proving that the land was not a
desert, and at some distance appeared the palm-leaf roofs of some
human habitations. These cottages were of one story, the walls
composed of bamboo, and they were surrounded with a paling of
the same material.

It was a scene such as Africa alone can produce; and one might
suppose, that if uninterrupted peace and tranquil enjoyment could
anywhere be found in the world, it would have existed amid the
calm retirement which those shades afforded.

The young girl was the only being visible. For some time she
did not change her position; but when at length the shade of the
palm-tree reached a rock which rose above the ground, her eye
seemed more intently to watch that part of the lake below which
was seen through an opening in the forest. Her countenance on a
sudden lost that meditative look which it had before assumed, and
she rose from the ground as a small canoe, which looked like a
speck on the water, was seen to dart forth from beneath the trees
overhanging the banks of the opposite shore. The course of the
canoe was towards the spot where she had taken her post. Although
urged forward but by one person, it clove its way rapidly over the
calm waters of the lake.

The girl did not leave her position, yet one foot was advanced
and her head was bent forward, as if she would fain have done so,
and the bright smile which played round her countenance showed
that she looked with pleasure for the coming of some one she
expected. If it were the person in the canoe whose presence she
longed for, it must have been some strong instinct which made her
suppose that he was approaching, for the eye could scarcely distinguish that it was a human form in the little skiff, much less the
features of the person.

For nearly a quarter of an hour she watched with breathless suspense the course of the canoe, till it was again shut out to view by the umbrageous foliage of the many-tinted trees which fringed the margin of the water. The senses of those children of nature are more acute than those of more civilized regions, and it was by her ear that she seemed now to learn when the person she expected would appear before her, for there was no pathway visible by which he could approach from the water. At length she seemed to catch the sound of distant footsteps, and as she did so, she seated herself on the ground and busily occupied herself in the formation of a straw basket, the materials for which lay by her side. Was it female coquetry, or rather that timid modesty which seeks to conceal even the purest feelings akin to love. It is to be found in a maiden's bosom in every clime, whatever may be the hue of her skin. Her eyes were, however, raised constantly from her work, over which her fingers idly played; but he she sought came not; and, at length, the expression of her countenance again changed to one of doubt and fear.

She no longer even pretended to work, but her eyes wandered anxiously around in search of the expected one. Her impatience increased; she rose from her seat, and was stepping forward to advance down the hill, when a slight rustling of the leaves near her made her turn her head, and before she had time to fly, she found herself in the arms of a youth of her own swarthy race, yet one who might boast of as much manly beauty as she could of feminine perfections. His figure, though not above the ordinary height, was slight, well and strongly knit, and every line was full of grace, betokening strength and great power of activity. The slight garment he wore was of the same beautiful manufacture as that of the girl—of finely-plaited straw, but art, in truth, had done little towards his costume.

The girl uttered a cry, yet there was in it more of joy than fear, though she struggled to escape him. She did not, however, succeed; indeed, her efforts were not very violent.

"Ha, ha, my Yarra!" he exclaimed, laughing triumphantly; "you said I should not have a kiss, and I have won it in spite of you, dear one."

"I thought you had not left your canoe," she answered, disengaging herself, and sitting down on the ground at a little distance from him, by the side of her basket. "You did not behave fairly, Ado. Like the stealthy leopard you stole up, and took me unawares, or you would not have won so easily."

"My Yarra will forgive me, though. It was a great crime, but the temptation was not to be withstood," said the young African, imitating his mistress, by seating himself on the ground, at a respectful distance from her.

"Well, I will overlook the crime this time, as you have been long away, Ado," answered the girl, smiling. "But tell me, do you bring good news?"

"What would be good news, Yarra, eh?" asked Ado, laughing significantly.

"That your father and mother are well; that your brothers and sisters are well; that they have collected plenty of palm-oil and ivory; that——" answered the maiden.

"Ha, ha, ha! you know, sly one, that there is other news that I should call good news," said Ado, interrupting her. "That is the news I bring. I have brought gold-dust, and ivory, and palm-oil for your father, my Yarra, and now you shall be mine. Do you not call that good news?"

The girl looked at him.

"It might be worse," she answered, smiling.

Ado arose, and seated himself again, but it was a pace or so nearer. "I have been to the Fetish man, also," he continued. "He says that all will be well, and that we shall be happy when we are married; and that he will drive far, far away the evil spirits from our cottage. Is not that good news, my Yarra?"

"That the Fetish-man will drive away the evil spirits? Yes, certainly," answered the girl.

"Then I will take the gold-dust and the ivory and palm-oil to your father—shall I?" asked Ado.

"Yes. He would not thank me if I said no," replied the young girl, smiling; and Ado thereon found himself seated still nearer to her.

Love is the same all over the world, and young hearts feel its blessed influence, although old men seek to barter it for gold. The savage African chief is scarcely more ready to sell his child than is often the wealthy citizen of a civilized world.

The gifts were placed at the feet of Yarra's father, and the following day Ado was to carry his intended bride to his own home across the lake. Yarra, it may be seen, loved Ado dearly, and he was as fond and devoted a suitor as any in other happier lands. He loved her—he scarcely knew why. His was a generous and noble heart, full of gentle sympathies, unvitiated by intercourse with the world: and such must always love what they behold most beautiful, of a nature like their own.

The same power created the black man as the white, and implanted the same feelings within his bosom; the same qualities, to lead to virtue or to vice. Unhappily, in the benighted land of Africa, those which lead to vice are, too often, alone drawn forth, while all others are smothered, or lie dormant; but in some cases, surely the purer feelings must burst forth, and although the mind remains blank and uncultivated, the actions, guided by the sentiments of the heart, will be virtuous.

The lovers belonged to a peaceful tribe, who cultivated the ground for their food, and collected the rich oil from the palm-tree, to barter with other tribes nearer the coast, for articles which come in the big ships of the white men. They never went to war, unless first attacked, and refrained from stealing their fellow-men to sell into slavery, as they had heard others often did; indeed, they themselves had suffered from the practice.

The young couple were again seated under their favourite palm tree, and the selection of the spot proved that their eyes loved to gaze on the beautiful. Enjoying youth, freedom, and abundance, without a thought or care for the morrow, they were happy. By their side were gourds containing the refreshing milk of the cocoa-nut, and baskets with cake of maize, bananas, yams, cassava, and various kinds of tropical fruits, showing that they had come out there to enjoy their evening repast, away from the noise and bustle of the village.

"To-morrow, Yarra, you shall be my wife, my only wife, for I can love no other, and we will be as happy as the day is long," said Ado, looking into the young girl's face, and smiling.

"I shall be happy if I am where you are," answered Yarra; "but I have my fears that the Fetish will not be kind: the evil spirit likes not to see people happy."

"Hush, hush, do not call him evil," said the youth, almost shuddering; "even now he may be listening to what we say."

"Ah, may he?" cried the maiden, partly partaking of her lover's fears, and shrinking closer to him for protection. "We must pray to him not to hurt us."

"I frightened you, dear one," said Ado; "but think no more about it, he will not hurt us. We will talk of to-morrow, and of the music, and dancing, and feasting. What a free and joyous life we will lead!"

As he was speaking, a loud piercing shriek was heard. Yarra trembled.

"What is that?" she exclaimed.

Ado started to his feet and gazed towards the village, whence loud shouts and cries were heard to proceed, succeeded by reiterated terrific shrieks. Flames, too, were seen to burst from the cottages, and a number of women and children rushed forth towards where they were posted. Behind them came a concourse of men, among whom showers of arrows were falling, and they were followed and closely pressed by a far more numerous band, armed with clubs, hatchets, and bows. Yarra gazed with speechless horror at the scene; Ado looked also, and he made a step towards the combatants, as if he would have gone to aid his friends, but he soon saw by the overpowering number of the foe that his arm would be useless to drive them back. Another, too, required his protection.

"We must fly, Yarra!" he exclaimed; "we have the start of the enemy, and may still escape them."

As he spoke, he lifted the young girl in his arms, and before she could answer he commenced his descent down the steep sides of a deep ravine, which ran towards the lake, at a short distance from the spot where they had been standing. With unfaltering steps he sprang from rock to rock with his precious burden, steadying himself with one hand by the shrubs and luxuriant creepers which adorned the ground, while with the other arm he encircled the waist of his intended bride. For some time he continued safely advancing, till at length the steepness of the bank made him pause to select a secure spot to alight on.

"I will follow you safely on foot," whispered Yarra, seeing that the exertion was almost too much for her lover. "I can run faster than can you with me in your arms."

"I will not part from you," he replied, leaping down a precipice of many feet; nor had he been deceived in the nature of the ground. A bed of soft grass and leaves received him, and uninjured he continued his perilous way.

The bottom of the ravine was at length reached, but although the scene of conflict was hid from their view, the terrific noise of the combatants still reached their ears, growing every instant louder and louder, and warning them to seek a place of greater safety. Ado gazed despairingly up the opposite and still more precipitous side of the ravine into which he had descended. He felt that if he reached the summit he could scarcely hope to continue his course unperceived by the enemy. It occurred to him, however, that if he kept along the bottom of the ravine he might reach the lake, on the shore of which his canoe lay hidden among the bushes. He knew the path, for it was one up which he had come on the day when we first introduced the young couple to our readers. The danger in following the course which had at first presented itself was the probability of being seen by the invaders, and of being pursued by them. Yarra, however, agreed with him that they had no alternative left them, and hand-in-hand they therefore hurried on, threading their way among the thick-growing shrubs and lofty trees, which hid them from the sight of those above.

Before they could reach the lake, the shrieks and cries of their relations and friends, apparently close at hand, showed that the victorious enemy had driven them to the edge of the cliffs, where death or captivity must be their fate.

Peaceably disposed and unwarlike as they were, they had resisted to the last; but, as Ado had seen when they were first surprised, with so overwhelming a force opposed to them, they had not a chance of driving back the enemy. Yarra wept with grief for the destruction of her kindred, but still she encouraged Ado to persevere, even although here and there an arrow, shot beyond its mark, dropped through the boughs above their heads, and showed the near proximity of the foe. The lake was at last reached, but Ado had left the canoe at a spot along the shore still nearer the village, and consequently closer to the danger which they were endeavouring to avoid. Their only chance of escaping, however, was by reaching it unperceived. The thick trees, which still overhung the path, favoured them. Now they were obliged to descend almost into the water; then to climb some way up the bank; now to rush like lightning across some more open space, where it was impossible to find shelter.

The gentle and hitherto timid Yarra bravely imitated the example of her lover, nor hesitated a moment in their course.

The most dangerous spot was yet to be crossed—a space of some fifty yards wide, destitute of trees, and easily overlooked from the heights above. They paused for a moment ere they attempted to cross it, and then, hand-in-hand, they swiftly emerged from their shelter. A few yards more, and they might reach the canoe. They looked up to see if they were watched: no one was to be seen. Again they flew on, and were again about to enter beneath the shelter of the trees, when a loud shout made both the fugitives turn their heads, and they beheld, to their horror, a large band of the enemy on the summit of the cliffs, still contending with a remnant of their friends, who had there made a last and desperate stand. A few, urged to despair, rather than fall alive into the hands of their savage victors, were seen to throw themselves off the cliffs, to find a speedy death.

"We are perceived by the foe, but may still reach the canoe before they can stop us," exclaimed Ado, as he led forward Yarra, who had stopped, transfixed with horror. His words aroused her, and she again exerted herself to follow him. In another moment, the trees hid them from the enemy; but a few dropping arrows showed them that they had but just in time reached their friendly shelter.

Ado darted on to where he expected to find the canoe. It was still where he had left it, with the paddles safe in the bottom. A moment sufficed to launch it, and to place Yarra in the bows, when he, stepping in, seized a paddle, and, with a sturdy arm, urged the light bark from the shore. He had now one of two courses to pursue; either to attempt to creep close along in-shore, under the banks, in the hope of escaping the observation of the enemy, or at once boldly to push off across the lake. If there had been no other canoes, he would have preferred the latter course; but, being aware that there were many of great speed, and capable of containing several men, at a short distance off close to the village, he knew that as soon as they should leave the shelter of the bank, they would be perceived and followed.

He, in a low voice, intimated his purpose to Yarra, and she agreed with him. He accordingly guided the canoe so close to the bank, that the long reeds, which grew there, brushed its sides, as it rapidly passed like a snake among them, while the trees, bending gracefully towards the water, formed a leafy archway overhead.

They were now, it must be understood, returning exactly in the direction they had come. It was fortunate that they had pursued this plan, for scarcely had they proceeded many yards, when they heard the shouts of the people they had seen on the top of the cliff, and who were now evidently hunting for them on the shore of the lake, believing that they were still flying in the direction they were first seen pursuing. Ado guessed, however, that the large canoes would soon be discovered, and thus the means of pursuing them would be afforded to the enemy. These thoughts occurred as he continued his course in the manner we have described.

At length he reached the mouth of the same valley by which they had gained the lake, and here they must be again exposed to view, as there was a considerable space, owing to some peculiarity of the soil, altogether destitute of trees. Unhappily, down this very valley the enemy were even then pursuing some of their friends as they appeared in sight. Their flight was perceived, and they could even see some of the most active of the former diverge to one side, for the purpose clearly of cutting off their retreat. They were armed, too, with bows and arrows, and Ado foresaw that, should they not at once strike across the lake out of their reach, his life would be sacrificed, while Yarra would as certainly be made captive

There was no time for a moment's deliberation. The head of the canoe was now turned away from the shore, and in a few minutes the fugitives came in full sight of the village, and of the enemy posted on the summit of the cliffs. The real danger had now arrived, for as they opened a point of land near the village, Yarra, whose eyes were now turned in that direction, perceived a party of their foes pushing off three of the large canoes, evidently with the intention of pursuing them. She warned Ado of what was happening.

"Fear not, dear one," he answered, redoubling his efforts; "we have a long start; and if we are overtaken, I will die with you rather than be captured."

At such times few are inclined to speak without occasion. For another minute they were silent; when again Yarra exclaimed—

"They are following us, and have each a man in the prow, ready to shoot."

"Take then my shield to protect yourself," said Ado. "If you were injured, life to me would be valueless. If I am killed, then do as you think best."

"I will live to avenge you!" exclaimed Yarra, in an altered tone; "my heart would change to rock. But we may still escape them."

"We will strive to the last," said Ado, "and if we can reach my village, and they venture to follow us on shore, they may find a less easy victory than they expect."

These words were uttered at intervals, as he could gain breath from the exertion of urging on the boat. Thus they continued, while Yarra keenly watched the enemy pursuing them. Now the foe appeared to gain on them, now again to drop astern, as the rowers increased or lessened their exertions. One canoe at last took the lead, and the people in her seemed determined to overtake them. This beautiful lake, glittering like a precious jewel in a rough setting, is situated far in the interior of Africa. It is of several miles in length, though not more than three in breadth, and communicates by a narrow and short channel with that mighty river, the Zaira, whose waters, after a long course, fall into the wide Atlantic.

The sun, verging towards the west, shone down from an unclouded sky on the clear calm water, which, like a mirror, reflected every surrounding object. The paddle wielded by Ado seemed like some bright meteor, as he dashed it rapidly on either side into the lake, throwing, in its course, far above their heads, an arch of spray, beautifully tinted with the colours of the heaven-sent rainbow. The shower seemed to cool the air, and to add strength to his limbs. His muscles were, in truth, sorely taxed, and yet all his exertions, it appeared, would nought avail him or her he sought to save, for the foe was as eager in the pursuit as he was to escape. Alas! they knew full well that the young Yarra was a prize of high value. So thought Ado, for her charms were spoken of in all the villages around.

One, two, and three miles had been passed over, and yet he contrived to keep far out of the reach of the arrows of his pursuers. Another mile was won, and they had somewhat gained on him. Two more remained to be accomplished before he could reach his village. Had he not been the most accomplished oarsman of his tribe, he would long since have given in, but neither did his arm tire, nor did his strokes become less rapid. Yarra longed to aid him, but the canoe was too small to allow her to use a paddle, an art to which she was well accustomed.

The savage cries of their pursuers urged Ado onwards. He felt scarcely able to refrain from answering them; indeed, he every now and then uttered a shout of defiance to relieve his pent-up feelings. Another mile was passed In a short time more he would catch sight of the well-known walls of his native village.

He turned his head to take a glance at the enemy; the three canoes were in a line, one following the other, yet at some distance. He felt sure that he could reach the land before they could overtake him; his eye eagerly sought out the spot where he hoped to be in safety. On a sudden his voice was silent, a faintness of heart seized him He saw before him a thick smoke ascending and hanging in a dark cloud over the abode of his kindred. Forked flames, too, were bursting forth from the roofs where he hoped to find shelter. His village was on fire, and the hand of an enemy must have done the work. Perhaps even then his kindred were being slaughtered like those of his bride.

For some minutes he felt that he dared not tell Yarra, but still urged on his boat towards the spot. He might, he hoped, be mistaken; to reach it was their only chance of safety.

Yarra had, with the eye of love, been watching his countenance. She soon there read the tale of what he saw. She turned her head to look, and was too soon convinced of the dreadful reality. As they approached the spot, their ears were assailed with loud cries, and shouts of fighting men. Ado was not mistaken in his kindred —though taken by surprise, they had refused to yield, and were now assembled at a short distance from the village, striving bravely with the enemy Ado's canoe approached. He was perceived, and received with a shout of welcome. He leaped on shore, lifting Yarra on his left arm, while with his right hand he seized a heavy war-club. The satisfaction of his friends was of short duration, for the next instant the three canoes of the enemy were seen rounding a neighbouring point of land, and they found themselves attacked on both sides. As one party was discouraged, so was the fierceness of the other increased. The enemy attacked Ado's friends with renewed fury. Many were killed, but the young men and women were stunned with blows on the head, and made prisoners. Ado fought bravely, but hopelessly. The people who had followed him in the canoes singled him out, and attacked him on every side. For long he defended Yarra with his shield, regardless of his own safety. At length a blow on the arm made him drop his weapon, and several men rushing forward tore Yarra from his arms. In vain she endeavoured to escape; and as they bore her off she saw *im fallen and bleeding on the ground, while life seemed ebbing fast away from many a deep wound in his bosom. Her heart sickened at the sight. She no longer attempted to escape, but allowed herself unresistingly to be carried off among a crowd of other happess captives like herself.

The prisoners were mostly young men and women, and children. The older people were either killed or allowed to escape, as not worth capturing. They would be of no value in the slave-market.

When the young Yarra first found herself a prisoner, a sensation of dull despair deadened her senses, and she neither saw nor heard what was passing around; but in a short time consciousness returned, and she became keenly alive to all that was taking place, while the hope of making her escape entered her bosom. For Ado's sake she longed to be free—to learn if he lived—if he were dead, she too would die.

No time was lost by the victorious enemy in commencing their march, lest they themselves might be deprived of the spoils by other tribes, who would soon be in pursuit of them.

With their hands lashed behind them, and all attached to each other by cords, the unhappy prisoners were dragged on towards the river. Yarra listened to the conversation of her captors, and from what she gleaned, she learned that they had been instigated by some white men to make the attack, and that they were to return as fast as possible to a village near the coast, where they expected to meet some purchasers of their booty.

Poor Yarra had heard before of white men, and she believed them to be all that was bad and terrible. Her notions were not very distinct, but she fancied them the impersonification of the spirit of evil, who wanders about the world to injure human beings. They soon reached the river, on the banks of which were collected a fleet of canoes larger than Yarra had ever before seen, and into them were now crowded the inhabitants of several villages, which had been attacked for the purpose of taking captives. Among them Yarra recognised several of her own relatives and friends, but in vain her eye sought the form of Ado. Some of his village she spoke to, but they only increased her grief by reporting that he was dead.

The captives were without delay hurried into the canoes with blows and stripes, when their voyage down the river commenced. For two days they continued their course without interruption, but on the evening of the second they arrived in the neighbourhood of a territory, with the inhabitants of which the victorious party were at war. This compelled them to disembark so as to reach the port of their destination by a journey across the country of friendly tribes. Now began the physical sufferings of the unhappy slaves. As soon as they landed they were driven into a shed like cattle, and so crowded that they could not lie down, nor scarcely breathe, while the food which was distributed among them was bad and scanty. Near this large hut was another store, filled with a variety of valuable merchandise, such as elephants' tusks, palm-oil, and gold-dust, which had been collected from all parts of the interior. The following morning, as soon as it was daybreak, the slaves were dragged forth, and to each was assigned a heavy burden, with a threat that if any one dropped it, that person should be immediately killed. Even nursing mothers were not altogether exempt, but with their infants in their arms were compelled to carry a piece of ivory, a package of gold-dust, or some less weighty article. Thus for several days they travelled on, weary and foot-sore; at night herded together like cattle in a large shed, or gathered under the shelter of palm-trees, and watchfully guarded by their captors.

Yarra physically suffered less than most of her companions. She was young and active, and probably on account of her beauty her tyrants gave her a light burden to carry, lest, should she grow thin or ill, her price might be lowered in the market. At length the victors and their prisoners reached the territory of a chief, who went by the name of the King of Bembo. He was awaiting anxiously their arrival, in order to become the purchaser of the prisoners, for he was the most extensive slave-dealer on the coast. They were met on the confines of the territory by the king in person, with a number of his subjects, who had also come to trade on hearing of this expected arrival. The slaves were again lodged in a large shed similar to their previous habitations, but they were now washed and better fed, to appear to greater advantage in the eyes of their purchasers. For the first time they found themselves —their hearts bursting with the indignity—made the objects of traffic among men of their own race and colour. A new source of grief also awaited them. Relations and friends had hitherto been together and able to converse on the subject of their fate. They were now to be torn from each other—husbands, wives, and children were separated for ever.

King Bembo purchased some of the youngest and most valuable, his chiefs and subjects became the owners of others, till all were disposed of. Yarra, with several of her own people, became the property of the king, who, as soon as he had transacted his affairs, set out to return to his residence near the sea-coast. King Bembo was in a great hurry, for he expected to find several slavers on the coast, who would become the purchasers of the property he had just acquired. He therefore gave the unfortunate wretches no rest, but urged them on with the lash, day after day, for six days, till they reached their destination, in sight of the mighty ocean. Some fell down through weariness, and died, but that mattered little, provided he could get the others on in time, as, at the most, each had cost him but a few yards of cotton cloth, and he should receive several dollars for every survivor.

Yarra was particularly an object of attention to him. She shuddered as he told her that he thought of making her one of his wives, for he was a big, bloated, ugly old blackamoor; but he was very avaricious, and he considered that by selling her for a high price, he should be able to purchase, if he thought fit, five or six other wives, who would probably be of far more use to him than a young girl, who might pine and die if she were dissatisfied with her lot.

King Bembo's slave-store was on a slight elevation, in view of the sea, and not far from the mouth of a small river. In this place Yarra and her companions were at once placed, and from hence, as she gazed forth, she beheld, for the first time in her existence, the wide ocean spread out in boundless space before her astonished eyes, and what appeared to her a huge canoe floating on the surface of the river at her feet. Here they were better treated and more abundantly fed than before; indeed everything was done to enhance heir value, till a purchaser should come to carry them far away to other lands, of whose existence they had never before heard. They had not long to wait. King Bembo was seated in front of his hut, in a large rocking-chair, which was made a present to him by the master of a ship, which came from that land of freemen, the United States. He valued it much, for he had sold, at a cheap rate, a cargo of slaves to the same liberal-minded captain, and had received this, with a few other notions, as a compensation. King Bembo, as he rocked his fat body to and fro, was calculating how much he should get by his present speculation, when four or five white men appeared before him, coming up from the river. He well knew that they belonged to a small schooner, which lay full in sight before him, and that it was of great importance to them to get a cargo of slaves on board at once, and be off, as there was no British cruiser in the neighbourhood to interrupt them. Yarra, who, though narrowly watched, was allowed greater liberty than her companions, was seated outside the hut when they appeared. She beheld them with surprise, for she had never seen beings of that colour or appearance. Though swarthy and sunburnt, with large black whiskers, to her eyes they appeared of a fair complexion. They were dressed also in white, with large straw hats. As they drew near, and Yarra could read the lineaments of their countenances, her heart sunk within her, for she read there an expression of evil she had never before beheld. On them was stamped the impress of all the bad passions of civilized life. The one who appeared to be their chief saluted King Bembo as an old acquaintance, and they at once entered into an earnest conversation. At the end of it all the slaves were ordered out of the shed, and were arranged in lines according to their ages and sexes. The white men then commenced an eager scrutiny, pinching their legs and arms, and examining them in every way, to see that they were sound in limb and wind. One hundred only were selected, for it appeared that the schooner had already part of her cargo on board. They were forthwith assembled and marched down to the side of the river. Yarra had hitherto escaped notice; but as the white captain was going off, the king called him back, and pointed her out. He looked at her attentively, till her eyes could no longer meet his gaze. She then saw that he was again engaged in an eager dispute with the king. At the end of it she found herself standing trembling before them, and was then ordered to follow the white man to the boat. She looked round on every side, and thought of flying: but she saw how vain would be the attempt. With unwilling steps, therefore, and head bent down with shame and anguish towards the ground, she did as she was commanded.

What words can adequately describe the horrors of a slave-ship? The vessel on board which Yarra was conveyed was called the Andorinha, or the Swallow. She was under the Brazilian colours, and although little more than eighty tons burden, had on her slave-deck 150 persons. The space between the decks was only two feet four inches, so that the unhappy wretches could scarcely even sit upright, yet in this manner were they to be conveyed across the wide Atlantic. The men were chained two and two by the ankles, and were separated from the women and children by a wooden partition. A few of the younger women were, however, allowed to occupy a raised cabin on deck, but although not chained together, they were carefully locked in while the schooner remained in the river.

Her crew consisted of a captain, eight men, and a boy, and there were besides four other white men belonging to a captured slaver, and who had escaped in their boat; they were now returning to the Brazils. As soon as the provision and water for the voyage were got on board, the schooner's sails were loosened, and with a fine breeze she stood out to sea. If Yarra had before been astonished at sight of the ocean at a distance, she was much more so now that she felt herself on its heaving bosom. She had no fear; for although she knew not whither she was going, nor could she conceive what was to be her fate, she felt her spirits rise with the freshness of the sea air, and again she thought of the possibility of escaping. It was a vain hope, such as could possibly occur to none but a girl ignorant of the obstacles in her way, yet, notwithstanding, she entertained it.

The captain, Gaspar Brito, had, from the first, shewed her marked attention, if not kindness, and although she did not comprehend his object, she had conceived a great dislike to him. She, however, took advantage of her power, by going about the decks in every direction whenever the crew were so occupied as not to interfere with her. Poor Yarra, as she leaned over the taffrail, with straining eyes she watched the shore from which the schooner was rapidly gliding away. She was weary and sad. Her thoughts were of her native village, and of her kindred, whom she was doomed never more to see, and oftener still did they dwell on her well-loved Ado. She still persisted in believing that he lived, and that she should see him again, for she could not picture to her imagination that one so lately full of youth and health should be numbered among the dead. She started from her reverie by feeling a touch on her shoulder. She looked up and beheld the savage countenance of Captain Brito.

She did not comprehend his language, and happy for her that she could not, but his looks frightened her, and she endeavoured to fly from him. With a fierce oath he pursued her, and she would have fallen overboard in her terror, had not a young lad, one of the seamen, caught her by the arm and drawn her back again, when she took refuge among the other women in the cabin assigned to them on deck. With imprecations the captain came among them, and struck them indiscriminately with a heavy lash he always carried in his hand. Their cries and tears seemed to afford merriment to him and his savage crew, but not a word that was spoken could they understand. This was the commencement of their ill-treatment, and happier was even their lot than that of a larger number of the slaves.

As soon as they were out of sight of land, a few at a time were dragged up on deck to stretch their limbs, and to breathe the fresh air, but if they did not on the instant do what they were ordered, and often even without any cause, the lash descended on their shoulders, or they were kicked and beaten by the brutal crew till the blood ran from their lacerated limbs. Bitter was the feeling of revenge which sprung up in the bosom of the Africans. A few drops of water to cool their parched lips, and nauseous porridge of farinha was the only food they received. Day after day passed without any improvement, or hope of improvement, in their condition. Sometimes one or other of them sunk beneath their accumulated miseries, and the yet warm body was immediately hove overboard, to become the food of the sharks, by the Brazilians, with as much indifference as if it had been that of a sheep or pig. If any of the poor wretches gave vent to their feelings by cries and groans, the inhuman seamen would immediately rush among them with their thongs, and would strike right and left till they compelled them to be silent. Such was the general condition of the Andorinha. Yarra's heart burned within her as she witnessed the diabolical proceedings. A change was taking place in her feelings. She was no longer the timid, loving girl she had been a short time before, but she felt herself becoming the bold courageous woman, capable of performing deeds from which her nature would till then have shrunk.

While they were still within the cruising-ground of the British squadron, the Brazilians kept a vigilant look-out for strange sails, and also strongly guarded their prisoners, but no sooner were they fairly out at sea, and away from all danger of capture, than they gave themselves up to idleness, to gambling, and sleeping. They would perform none but the most necessary duties of the ship; their greatest amusement, when awake, being to thrash and kick the slaves who were brought up on deck to breathe the air. The only person who showed them any compassion was the lad who saved Yarra's life, José Lopez by name; and whenever he could do so unperceived by the crew, he would dip a jug in the water-tub, and bring it round to those who were suffering most from thirst. One day, just as he was about to perform this office of charity, he was seen by the captain, who that instant came out of his cabin. Without uttering a word, he flew at the poor lad with his ever active thong, and after increasing his passion by beating, he would have dashed out his brains with a handspike, had not Yarra thrown herself before him, and turned his rage upon her own head. The above description will give some idea of the condition of the slave schooner Andorinha, as she sailed swiftly over the waters of the Atlantic, at the distance of some three hundred miles from the coast of Africa.

Hitherto Yarra had not seen all her companions in captivity, for although allowed to wander about on deck, none of the women were permitted to go below. That morning a party of about thirty of the men were brought up, and made to walk on one side of the deck to stretch their limbs, but the seamen, whose business it was to keep them moving, at length growing tired of the occupation, they one by one threw themselves down to rest.

As Yarra was by chance passing near them, she heard herself called by name. She turned, and saw an old African lying on the deck, so ill and emaciated that he was apparently unable to move.

"Yarra," he said, "you do not recollect me, but I am of your tribe, and know you well. I have twice before been taken by dealers in human flesh, and have each time been rescued by the English, in whose warships I have served many years. Poor child! you never heard of the English; well, no matter; I have thus never reached the shores of America, or of the Islands, as a slave, and I don't intend to see them this time, except as a free man."

"What would you do?" asked Yarra, surprised at what she heard.

"Have you the courage to do as I direct?" said the old slave.

"I would dare anything to regain our freedom," replied the young girl, in a firm tone.

"It is well," answered the man, "we must abide our time. There are three other men who have served on board ship. They were taken with me in a canoe by these wretches who have us in their power. If we could contrive to get these shackles off our legs we might overpower them, and then we should easily find our way to an English port, where we should be safe. Now do not stay longer here, lest we should be suspected. You comprehend what is required, and we will leave you to find out the means of accomplishing it."

These words brought back hope to the young girl's heart, and she determined to find the means of freeing her companions.

The Brazilians had awarded a cabin to her and ten other women, in which was also kept the arm-chest. Aided by the female instincts of curiosity, they were not long in discovering its contents; and it at once occurred to Yarra, that if the Africans could be supplied with the arms, they might easily overpower the crew. At first she seemed afraid of communicating her projects to any of her companions, lest they might betray her, but still, if she could hope to succeed, it would be necessary to secure the assistance of most, if not all of them. First she spoke to one, to secure her co-operation, then to another, and so on, till all had promised to take part in the mutiny.

Two great difficulties had now to be overcome; to knock off the fetters from the ankles of the men, and to convey the arms to them. At first, they thought of gaining the assistance of José Lopez, but next, they considered that, though kind to them, he might still not prove faithless to his own countrymen, and they therefore were afraid of letting him into their secret. Fortunately, in the arm-chest they found a file, with the use of which one of the women was acquainted, and this she carefully conveyed to the old negro the next time he was allowed to come upon deck.

No sooner was their plan matured than the spirits of all the slaves revived. Of sanguine temperaments and light hearts, they saw not the difficulties in the way. A few words alone sufficed to convey their intentions to the prisoners below, who declared themselves prepared to obey the signal agreed on.

Two more days passed on in dreadful suspense. The whites were, seemingly, more vigilant than usual — perhaps they suspected something. The old African and his friends had, in the meantime, not allowed the file to be idle. While he worked, the rest rattled their chains, or howled, or sung, indeed made every other variety of noises to prevent the whites from hearing what was going forward. At last a day arrived, unusually hot, even for that scorching clime. The captain was afraid that if he kept all the slaves below he might lose most of them by fever, so he ordered up a gang of them on deck. Among them was old Doppo.

Overcome with the heat, the crew lay about the decks, or in their hammocks asleep. The only man who remained awake was the helmsman, and even he seemed to lose, at times, all consciousness of outward things as he listened to the idle flapping of the canvass against the masts, and as the hot sun struck down upon his head. The captain and his first mate were asleep in their cabins, and the second mate, who was officer of the watch, lay in the long-boat on deck, equally lost in oblivion.

On a sudden, the shackles fell from the ankles of several of the slaves on deck, and at the same moment a number more sprung up from below, armed with cutlasses, daggers, hatchets, and pistols. The helmsman, startled at the sight, was about to cry out, but before he could utter a sound of warning, a blow from a dagger laid him bleeding on the deck. Then arose the terrific shout of a hundred fierce spirits, eager to revenge their wrongs.

The white men, aroused from their slumber, sprang up; they well knew what those cries betokened. The enraged countenances of the Africans glared upon them as their eyes opened from their slumber. The mate leaped from the boat to find himself in the grasp of several stout Africans, who, before he could utter a prayer for mercy, hove him struggling into the sea. The most eager rush was made to where the captain slept, and before he was well-nigh awake, a dozen weapons had pierced his bosom. The work of slaughter was soon over. No mercy had been shown to the Africans, and in that hour of retribution they were little inclined to afford any. Yarra's eye had sought young José Lopez. In their blind fury several of the slaves had dragged him forth from his berth, not distinguishing him from the other whites, when Yarra sprung forward; she was just in time to hold back the arm of one who was about to plunge a dagger in his bosom.

"What!" she exclaimed, "would you destroy the only one who has shown us kindness and mercy? We will let him live to prove that we are not ungrateful."

Poor José, who had expected to suffer the fate of his companions, saw by her actions that his life would be spared, and, falling on his knees before her, took her hand, and kissed it in expression of his gratitude. Doppo, also, who was very glad to have José's assistance in working the vessel, at once assured him of his safety. The only other Europeans who had hitherto escaped, were the four passengers who lay trembling in the cabin, every moment expecting to be destroyed. For some time they were entirely overlooked.

As soon as the Africans found themselves complete masters of the schooner, they liberated from their shackles the rest of the men, and the women and children, who no sooner found themselves free than they gave way to the most extravagant signs of joy. They rushed into each other's arms, they danced, they sang, and shouted till their voices could shout no more. After some time they became more tranquil; surrounding Yarra, they proclaimed her as their chief, acknowledging that to her was due the honour of forming and enabling them to carry into execution the plan which had gained them their liberty.

She would modestly have declined the honour, but they insisted on obeying her, and she accordingly appointed Doppo to act as captain of the ship. Doppo was delighted at the honour; indeed, he was the only man fit for the office, and he immediately set to work to raise a crew to navigate the ship. For this purpose, he could only muster the four men who had been captured with him, and the lad José, till he recollected the passengers. On this the trembling wretches were dragged forth, expecting instant death, when they were told that their lives would be spared if they would undertake to perform the duty of seamen. This they eagerly promised to do; but Doppo, suspecting their intentions, appointed a guard to each of them, with loaded pistols, and with orders to shoot any one who should show a sign of treachery.

After a short consultation, it was determined to shape a course for Sierra Leone, as the only place where they had a chance of retaining their newly-gained liberty. Should they go to any other place along the coast but where the British flag was flying, they knew full well that they must again fall into the hands either of their own slave-dealing countrymen or the whites, who would sell them to another slaver. The difficulty was to find the way; for although Doppo was a fair seaman, he was perfectly ignorant of navigation, and, except one of the passengers, who had been the master of a vessel wrecked on the coast, no one on board was acquainted with the science. Doppo, however, very clearly gave him to understand, that if he did not take them to the port to which they wished to go, he should, without compunction, shoot him through the head — a hint the Brazilian was not likely to forget.

It must not be supposed that Yarra's spirits were elated at her success. She had gained her freedom, it is true; but what was liberty to her without Ado? Torn far away from her native country and her kindred, what chance had she of ever again being united to him? Yet her companions, more thoughtless, sang, and danced, and laughed, as if their lives henceforth were to be free from all care and trouble. Fortunately for them, the weather continued fine, and the wind fair; and for three days they advanced rapidly in their course. Doppo proved himself worthy of the honour bestowed on him, and established on board a very efficient discipline. He had stationed a look-out at the mast head, to give timely notice of any strange sail, for the greatest danger he apprehended was, falling in with any slavers, who would assuredly again capture them, and, though they might consider them too valuable to murder, would punish them for destroying the Brazilian crew.

"A sail in sight on the starboard beam!" sung out one of Doppo's men, from aloft.

"What does she look like?" inquired Doppo, exactly in the tone he had heard used on board ships of war.

"A large schooner, sare, twice as big as we," was the answer, in English, in which language he thought fit to carry on the duty of the ship.

"Which way is she standing?" he again asked.

"To the north-east, sare," was the answer.

"We must keep away, then, or she will be close aboard of us, he observed to himself. "Up with the helm, man," to José, who was at that post. "Square away the yards there. Now, Senhor Brazileiro, if that schooner come up with us, we will blow your brains out," he added, turning to the Brazilian captain, who was standing near, and devoutly wishing that the stranger might prove a slaver. Doppo walked the deck, with his spy-glass under his arm, exactly in the fashion with which he had seen officers performing their duty on board a man-of-war.

"When a hare runs, the dogs will follow." The large schooner had been apparently sailing on without noticing the Andorinha, but no sooner did she perceive the latter change her course, than she also kept away and crowded all sail in chase. The little vessel sailed well, but the stranger soon showed that she had a much faster pair of heels, for in less than an hour she had evidently come up much closer than when first seen.

The Africans at once perceived their danger, and all the horrors from which they had escaped again rose up to their imagination. No longer was the laugh and song heard; some even looked at the calm waters, and thought how far better it would be to seek rest beneath them than to submit to the tyranny of the white men. Doppo and the brave spirits talked of fighting for their freedom, though they felt that they could have little hope of success.

The Brazilians turned pale with fear, for they saw the threatening looks of their masters, and dreaded lest they should be sacrificed should the stranger prove a slaver. Poor Yarra's heart sunk at the thought that the chance of being again united with Ado was more remote than ever. As the stranger drew near, Doppo and his followers pronounced her, without a doubt, to be a slaver, and so also did José, though the rest of the Brazilians wished to persuade them that she was a simple British trader.

The only possibility of escaping from her was by the wind falling, when they might creep through the water faster than she could, but then she would probably send her boats after them. At all events, they determined to hold on to the last. Woman's wit was again to assist them. What force could not accomplish, it struck Yarra might be performed by stratagem. At her suggestion, all the women and children and most of the men were sent below, while a few only remained on deck, dressed in the seamen's clothes. The Brazilians were told to answer the hail of the stranger, and threatened with instant death if they did not speak as they were ordered. Every man then armed himself as best could, and awaited the result, with the Brazilian flag flying at their peak. The large schooner still rapidly drew near, but not a sheet nor tack did they start. She seemed, however, to suspect them, for, as she got them within range of her guns, she sent a shot flying over the water after them. This filled the hearts of most of them with terror, but at the same moment up went at their peak a flag Doppo knew well—the blood-red flag of England. He instantly ran aft and hauled down the Brazilian flag, and let fly his topsail sheets. No other gun was fired, and the stranger was soon alongside. There was now no doubt of her character—she was a slaver, but her cargo was no longer slaves. She had been captured by a British cruiser, and was now in possession of a prize-crew. The joy of the emancipated Africans knew no bounds, and loud were the congratulations with which the people on board the two vessels greeted each other, as they ran a short distance only apart towards Sierra Leone.

As Yarra looked over the side towards the other vessel, her heart bounded with joy, and in her eagerness she would have thrown herself into the sea, for on the deck of the stranger she beheld her well-loved Ado. The recognition was mutual, and by the intervention of Doppo, who explained to the officer the romantic history of the young people, they were allowed to be together. Many others also recognised acquaintances and friends; for it appeared that the large schooner had sailed from the same river, and had been mostly filled with people captured at the same time as Yarra and her friends.

We need not dwell on all Ado and Yarra said to each other. She told him all that had occurred, and he described to her how, on recovering on the battle-field, he found himself in the power of some of their victors, who had remained to pick up stragglers, and who would have put an end to his existence, had they not discovered that he was so slightly wounded as to be still of value, and that he was then sold by one dealer to another, till he was driven on board the schooner.

Both vessels arrived safely at Sierra Leone, where the Africans were immediately landed, and had plots of ground awarded to them, on which to erect cottages for their habitations. Here the Christian missionaries exerted themselves to enlighten the benighted minds of the settlers, and in many instances their efforts were blessed with success. Among their converts were Yarra and Ado, who were at length united with the holy rite of a Christian marriage, and have just cause to be grateful to the Great Being who, through much suffering, brought them to know the Divine Truths of His Gospel, and to learn that His world is ruled by the spirit of love and light, and not, as they before were taught to believe, by one of darkness and evil.

" Bravo, Marsden !" I exclaimed, " I must petition for the slave girl to add to my collection of tales. But how is it you ventured to introduce a black heroine? I vow, that while you were describing her, I felt almost in love with her myself, and could fully understand the anguish poor Ado must have suffered when he fancied he had lost her; yet, I dare say, if we went to see her, we should think her an ugly little nigger girl."

"I never thought about the colour of her skin while I was describing her," he answered; "or rather, I put myself in Ado's place, and fancied that true beauty could only be found of a dusky hue, and that a white face is a hideous defect. Pray let me ask in what does beauty consist? Does it not rather exist in expression than in form—in imagination than in reality? Does it not depend rather on the power of perception in the beholder than in the object itself? An uncultivated clown does not distinguish between the Venus de Medicis and Moll Flaggon; or rather, the latter is most to his taste. Ado would most certainly turn up his nose at the belle of a London season, dressed for her first Almack's, in her silks and lace attire, and would think her incomparably inferior to his own Yarra, in her robe of fine matting, thrown gracefully over her shoulder; so, indeed, I suspect, would a sculptor if he had to select one of the two for a model, particularly if the fairer damsel were addicted to tight lacing. Besides, let me tell you, I saw even at Sierra Leone some dark-skinned maidens, who were as symmetrically and gracefully formed as any of their white sisterhood, with features almost of the Caucasian cast. So I insist on it that Yarra was a very pretty girl, and in every respect worthy of being my heroine."

"A very good defence ye have made for the leddie, though I scarcely think mistress Ado required it," observed Haggis.

"By the by, Marsden, did you happen to see the young couple when you were on shore at Sierra Leone?" asked Sleepwell.

"Oh yes, purser, Marsden and I went together," put in Green. "We hunted out Mr. and Mrs. Ado, and they gave us all the particulars of their adventures; not in such choice language as you have just heard, but they told their tale very graphically, I can assure you."

"I thought so—I was sure Marsden could never have invented so many details," observed Sleepwell. "And now, who's going to spin the next yarn?" and he looked at the captain.

"I am not, I am afraid, in a story-telling mood," said the captain. "But it is your turn, master, to give us something amusing."

"I haven't had time to overhaul my log, to get anything ready," replied Green. "But I think by the cut of Upton's jib, he may enliven us with a yarn of some sort or other. What say you, Upton?"

"Why, master, that I cannot undertake to enliven you, though I may interest my hearers with some extracts from an old journal I was looking over this morning," returned the first lieutenant. "They led to a very sad train of thought, which I cannot shake off, but if you will listen to my tale, I will gladly tell it."

We all declared that we were in a sympathizing mood, and he accordingly gave us the following story, with permission to me to place it among my collection.

CHAPTER XIII.

A ROMANCE OF THE MEDITERRANEAN.—LIEUTENANT UPTON'S STORY.

HENRY LESLIE was one of my best and dearest friends. I had known him from my earliest days. He cut me out the first boat of which I was ever possessed: he taught me to pull an oar, to knot and splice, to reef and steer, and to manage the light skiff which floated on his father's lake. In truth, from his exciting tales and conversation I first imbibed that love of the ocean, and of all things appertaining to it, which has now become a very part of my existence. With him I first went to sea, where, continuing the instruction he had commenced on shore, he initiated me in all the mysteries of seamanship. There, though watching over me with the care and solicitude of a father, he kept me under the strictest discipline, for which I believe I loved him the better. He was then a mate, the senior in the mess, but was soon promoted. I almost regretted his good fortune, for I was afraid of being separated from him, but to my great joy he remained in the same ship, when he gave me the use of his cabin to study in and his books to read; a benefit I knew how to appreciate.

I cannot describe Leslie as he deserved. High-minded and generous, with a heart tender as a woman's, yet brave to an extreme, his appearance was highly in his favour; the blood of his race (for he was highly born) being marked by his noble bearing and his courteous and independent manners. By his equals in rank he was beloved, by the crews who served with him he was idolized.

Having good interest at the Admiralty, he always contrived to have me appointed to the ship to which he belonged; I thus served with him for several years in various climes. For some months we were in the North Seas, and then on the South American station; we were next sent to cruise on the coast of Africa, and in the West Indies, and, lastly, we served together in the Mediterranean, on board the Juno, 74. Although of a highly poetical and enthusiastic temperament, Leslie was generally considered by his shipmates to be rather unsusceptible of the fascinations of woman. In truth, he did not seek to win the affections of any, nor would he throw away his own on one who might not appreciate their value. At length, however, a change came over him. The last time we were in England together, while I repaired to the part of the country where my family were residing, he set off to enjoy the amusements of what is called the London season, which had just then commenced. He frequently wrote to me during our separation, describing the scenes and people among whom he found himself. Handsome, lively, and of good family and fortune, he was welcomed in those circles of the metropolis composed of men of the highest rank and talent, and of the most lovely and fascinating women in England, and consequently in the world.

Several weeks flew by, while he quaffed deep draughts from th glittering chalice of gaiety, the bitter and nauseous dregs of which prove how unwholesome is too often the bright-coloured potion. Yet he, it appeared, had not hitherto found it so. As far as I could judge by his letters, he had as yet escaped the attractions by which he was surrounded, and was looking forward with satisfaction to the time when his duty should again call him to sea, when he happened to be introduced to the family of the Earl of Ravelin. The earl had an only daughter, a young and very lovely girl, yet her beauty, as Leslie assured me, compared with her other perfections, appeared her least attractive quality. She was slightly formed, with a skin of snowy whiteness, and long fair hair, just tinged with an auburn hue; her eyes of deepest blue were shaded by dark eyelashes, which increased their soft and tender expression: and her height was sufficient to make her appear tall among others, without being conspicuous. Of the sweetest temper, graceful in mind as well as in form, with abundance of talent and wit, yet never obtruding it, and a voice of perfect melody, she was doted on by her father, and beloved by all who had the happiness of knowing her. Thus did Leslie describe the Lady Emily Manning; nor did I find, when I subsequently became acquainted with her, that he had at all overdrawn her portrait.

To see such a being was, in his opinion, to love her. To love her, as he felt she ought to be loved, was to deliver his whole soul into her keeping, to let his thoughts dwell alone with her, to weave every hope of future joy round her bright presence.

She, too, was of an enthusiastic temperament, nor did the devoted admiration of the young sailor fail of working that effect on her feelings, which the common-place attentions of those ordinary beings, the butterfly lovers and carpet knights of society, by whom she was generally surrounded, had no power of doing. She yielded her heart gradually but completely; she loved as woman only loves. Leslie discovered his happiness just as he received orders to join his ship. She did not disguise her fond affection, but referred him to her father, for his sanction to their union. The earl, as might be expected, exhibited no great satisfaction at the event.

"Before he could give an answer, he must examine the state of his daughter's feelings," he said. "Her happiness was his first consideration. Her preference might be evanescent; she might be happier with a more influential husband—he with a more wealthy bride."

The result of the earl's conference with Lady Emily was, a promise to Leslie, that on his attaining post rank her hand should be his, and that all his influence should be exerted to get him forward in the service. This was as much as the lover could reasonably expect, although more than two years must elapse before he could by any possibility obtain the desired rank and his anticipated happiness. When we are young, even a few years only before us appear far distant and indistinct. I, for one, considered this period a long time to wait, and was rather surprised at his philosophy in bearing this decision of the earl's with so much resignation. How many events, I thought, might not occur in the meantime to mar his bliss. Matters had thus been settled only the day before the Juno was ordered to sea, and he had but time to bid his mistress farewell, and to hurry down to join us at Spithead, before we sailed for the Mediterranean.

A considerable change had come over him since we parted. There was that pride in his eye, and boldness in his step, which every man must feel who knows that he possesses the pure affection of a lovely woman; but there was also at times a subdued melancholy in the expression of his countenance, which I never before observed, while his spirits had lost that buoyancy which formerly distinguished them. To all he was kind and gentle as ever; but even the men whispered among themselves, that Mr. Leslie had lost his heart while on shore.

As we touched at Lisbon and Cadiz, some time elapsed before we reached Malta; and ere we again sailed for the Ionian Islands, Leslie's commission, as commander, arrived from England, and at the same time his appointment to the command of a ten-gun brig, the Seahorse, then on the station. He was to supersede Captain B——, whose post commission had come out by the same packet; and as the brig was expected from the Levant every day, he remained at Malta to join her. Great was my grief at being thus compelled to continue on board my old ship; for had the Seahorse been there, I dare say he would have contrived to have taken me with him. I then thought this was the greatest misfortune which could have happened to me. How little do we mortals know what is for our benefit. Could we but remember that all things are ordered by Omnipotent Providence for the best, of how much dissatisfaction and ingratitude should we be guiltless; how much misery should we be saved. I make this observation from a deep conviction of its truth.

Although thus attached to Leslie, I should have quitted my own ship with much regret, for she was in every respect one of the happiest in the service, and had as nice a set of officers belonging to her as I have ever met. I will not describe any of them except our captain, Sir Roland Bertram. Of him I must speak, as he was my *beau ideal* of what a naval officer should be. His manners were polished, kind, and affable. He was a first-rate seaman, and brave as the bravest: humane in the extreme, he never punished if he considered that his duty to the service would allow him to avoid it, nor on the most trying occasions did he lose the calm equanimity of his temper. These qualifications, with a dignified and commanding person, secured him the respect and love of all who were brought within the sphere of his influence; nor is it too much to say, that in the service he was universally beloved. With such a captain, I passed three years of my life; and had not a circumstance occurred which, for a time, threw a gloom over my spirits, it would have been a period of happiness with as little alloy as falls usually to the lot even of young and buoyant hearts.

After quitting Malta, we visited Athens and several other interesting places in Greece; we then sailed for the Levant, running down the coast of Syria, and anchored at last off Alexandria. While the ship lay there, I, with several other officers, made a voyage some way up the mysterious and far-famed Nile, visiting on our way Grand Cairo, the pyramids, the catacombs, and many of the majestic ruins which border its banks. The pleasure which even now I experience at a retrospect of those days, shows me how much I must then have enjoyed the novel and varied scenes I visited, though I doubt, were I again to return there, whether the reality would equal the gorgeous splendour which time has flung over them on my memory. I must recollect, however, that I havo a tale—a sad one, alas! to narrate.

After an absence of some months, we again cast anchor in Valetta Harbour, where, to my great joy, I found that the Seahorse had arrived that very morning. As soon as I could, I asked and obtained leave to pay my friend a visit. On going on board the brig I learned that he was on shore, where I directly followed him, and found him at some lodgings he usually occupied, preparing to accompany a mutual acquaintance, Captain G——, to his housc to dinner. I was forthwith included in the invitation, and enjoyed a very pleasant party, to the agreeableness of which the daughters of our host much contributed. A ball was to take place the same evening at the Auberge de Provence, to which, of course, had not our inclinations led us, we were in duty bound to go. When we rose to join the ladies in the drawing-room, we found that the carriage had already conveyed them to the scene of festivity, and had returned for us.

In consequence of this arrangement, Leslie, who had taken my arm, and I, entered the ball-room together. We were advancing leisurely towards the farther end of it, when he suddenly started, the colour forsook his cheeks, and I felt his arm tremble in mine.

"Good heavens!" he exclaimed, in a hurried tone. "Can it be?"

I was not long in discovering the cause of his emotion. Before us sat a young lady; beautiful as the lily she seemed, but, alas! too, as delicate and fragile. Her eyes were large and lustrous—her skin was pure as the driven snow—but there was, I thought, that hectic glow on her cheek, which too often cruelly betrays the lurking presence of the most insidious of all diseases in many a fair bosom. Several officers of high rank stood round her, endeavouring in vain to win a smile from her lips; but no sooner did her eyes meet those of Leslie, than she exhibited equal agitation with himself. Withdrawing his arm from mine, he advanced rapidly towards her. She half rose to meet him; their hands were clasped, their eyes spoke language eloquent; and I had no longer a doubt that I beheld the Lady Emily Manning. But what cause had brought her to Malta I was at a loss to conjecture, as I felt sure that her appearance was totally unexpected by Leslie.

Her previous attendants one by one withdrew, and the lady and her future husband were left for a few minutes to the enjoyment of each other's society.

The fond lover did not, happily for himself, perceive the change which a few short months had wrought in the health of the object of his affections. He might well, indeed, have been deceived by the rosy blush which suffused her fair cheek, and neck of alabaster, as their eyes encountered. I was not so easily misled; for I had before seen the stealthy workings of consumption, and could not, I feared, mistake its fatal signs. It was therefore with a feeling of deep melancholy that I watched the happiness of my friend and his mistress till my sensations became too intense for sufferance, and I endeavoured to persuade myself that I must be deceived, and that the delicacy of her appearance, which had so much struck me, was rather natural to her than the result of illness. While I was still watching them, Leslie took Lady Emily's hand, and led her out to join a quadrille just then forming; and, as at the same time a friend insisted on introducing me to a lady with whom I was bound to dance, I was for a short period separated from them. When I next saw Lady Emily, she was dancing with another person to whom she had previously been engaged, and I found Leslie by my side.

"Congratulate me, my dear fellow, on this happy meeting!" he exclaimed, taking my arm. "You must have guessed doubtlessly with whom I was dancing. By the bye, I ought to have introduced you: pardon me for my neglect, and I will do so immediately. Is not our meeting extraordinary? Lady Emily and her father have been at Malta only a week. They formed their plans so suddenly that they had no time to let me know their intentions; for being offered a passage in the Minerva, which was on the point of sailing, they were even hurried in their preparations. They left England, she tells me, partly on account of Lord Ravelin's health, which has been indifferent lately; and also because the family physician advised her to spend a winter in the south of Europe, more as a precautionary measure, he assured her, than from the existence of any absolute necessity for her so doing. Some of her mother's family have been delicate; indeed, Lady Ravelin herself died of consumption, but no fears are entertained about her. I am rejoiced to say, that they are so pleased with Malta, that they intend to winter here, and then return home by way of Italy, when I trust that I shall be able to accompany them. Eh, my dear fellow! was any man so fortunate? Do not you almost envy my happiness?"

I could say nothing to throw a shadow over his enjoyment of the moment; but while I congratulated him on the arrival of his mistress, I felt how fleeting would be the happiness he prized. I was soon afterwards introduced by my friend to Lady Emily, and also to the Earl of Ravelin, with whose courteous and kind reception of me I was much gratified, as it showed the estimation in which he held his future son-in-law. He was a tall and very handsome man, though already advanced in life, and slightly infirm from recent illness, possessing also a most dignified and pleasing address, with a countenance which bespoke an amiable disposition. Lady Emily danced frequently throughout the evening, and appeared but slightly fatigued, when Leslie, with affectionate solicitude, handed her to her carriage. I could not help wishing that the family physician had been present to forbid her thus exerting herself.

Leslie directly afterwards quitted the ball-room, which had lost its only attraction, and as I walked home with him to his lodgings, he declared himself one of the happiest men in existence.

My duty compelling me to return on board, I did not see Leslie for two days. The next time I met him was on the deck of the Juno. I was doing duty one forenoon as mate of the watch, when the sentry gave notice that the captain was coming alongside. After calling out the guard to receive him, and manning the side-ropes, as I looked through a port to ascertain how soon he would be on board, I saw that he was accompanied by some ladies, and two or three naval officers and other gentlemen, among whom I recognised Leslie. Sir Roland Bertram was the first to come on deck to receive his guests, and to hand Lady Emily up the side, for she was, as I suspected when I saw Leslie, one of the party, as was also Lord Ravelin. After they had gone the rounds of the ship, tasted the grog and soup, and visited the ward-room and gun-room, they repaired to the captain's cabin, where, in the meantime, luncheon had been got ready for them.

"We shall require your assistance, Mr. Upton," said Sir Roland, smiling, as I was about to withdraw—(I was rather a favourite of his)—so I accordingly entered.

While the captain was showing Lord Ravelin and Lady Emily round the cabins, I heard him observe—

"That, Lord Ravelin, will be your private apartment, and this will be your daughter's, and we can easily arrange a small berth within call for her attendant, so that you will be as private as if on board your own yacht."

Taking the first opportunity to tell Leslie what I had heard, I asked him for an explanation; when he informed me that Sir Roland, who was an old friend of Lord Ravelin's, hearing that it was considered by the medical men advisable that Lady Emily should enjoy the sea air as much as possible, had offered to give them a cruise to the Ionian Islands, where we were about to proceed, and to return without delay.

"I am delighted to say," he added, "that I am to keep company with the Juno. I should have much liked to have fitted up the cabin of the Seahorse for the reception of Lady Emily and her father, but for her comfort the present plan is far preferable; in truth, a ten-gun brig is not exactly the sort of craft suited for a lady's abode."

He was right. The Seahorse, though a very pretty vessel for one of the old ten-gun brigs, and fast before the wind, was noted for being exceedingly crank. Thanks to the improving knowledge of our naval architects, we are not likely to have any more of them. The loss of many a gallant crew, encoffined in their hulls, pronounces their unworthiness.

It was a bright and glorious morning, when the blue-peter flying at the fore, a signal-gun was fired, our anchor hove up, and in stately trim our noble ship stood out of the harbour of Valetta, followed by the little Seahorse, who, with her slight spars spread with a crowd of canvass, was doing her best to keep way with us. She might have been likened to the young fawn following the majestic doe of the reindeer over its native wilds.

Lady Emily, who since her first visit to the ship had exhibited some slight symptoms of illness, seemed to revive with the pure sea breeze, and was able to walk the deck for some time together, either with Sir Roland or her father, without being fatigued. I observed her, as she did so, constantly turn her head towards the brig, with a look which would have given the fullest assurance to Leslie, had he required it, of her devoted affection. The sun went down, and again arose, and there was the Seahorse always at her post on our weather quarter, the wind continuing steady and moderate from the north-west. I suspect that we were in no hurry to make the voyage, for I observed that, whenever the breeze freshened, we always, by Sir Roland's orders, shortened sail, to enable the brig to keep us company, so that her lover's vessel greeted the eyes of our fair passenger every morning when she made her appearance on deck. How she loved to gaze upon the graceful fabric, to admire her buoyant form, the trim of her sails, the delicate tracery of her rigging, and then to expatiate on the delights of a seaman's life, the majestic beauty of the boundless ocean, his ever-moving home. She saw it bright and sunny; she knew not of the dark reverse.

There is less monotony in a voyage in the Mediterranean than perhaps in any other sea. There are so many places of interest to visit, so much beautiful coast scenery, such sudden changes of weather, and a climate in general so delightful, that it is deservedly the most favourite station. I am not superstitious, at least not more so than sailors in general are supposed to be; but, I knew not why, from the commencement of that voyage my spirits were low and heavy—there was a strange sense of coming evil, which I acknowledged to myself, yet trusted would prove fallacious. The sequel will show whether or not I was deceived. I might, I thought, feel the same ninety and nine times, and find the forebodings (shall I so call them?) false; but the hundredth, and this I fancied would be that one, they would prove fatal. There happened, in truth, several events which I could not help believing were ominous of ill. First, two sudden and violent deaths occurred. A seaman, one of the most active and best hands in the ship, who, in the most furious gale, when reefing topsails, was constantly at the weather earing, fell, during a calm, from the fore-topsail yard-arm into the sea, and although an admirable swimmer, sunk to rise no more. Another man, while we were practising at our guns, when about to fire, after looking along the sight of his piece, suddenly fell back with the lanyard in his hand; the gun went off, and as we rushed forward to raise him up we found that all assistance was vain—the vital spark had fled.

Following these events, one evening at the close of a sultry day, while Lady Emily was seated on deck, enjoying the fresh air which fanned her cheeks, a smoke was seen to ascend from the main-hatchway, and, at the same moment, several seamen rushed on deck with consternation depicted on their countenances. The officers hurried forward, and were met by the carpenter, who reported to the first lieutenant that the ship was on fire.

The drum beat to quarters, and the men, with perfect discipline, flew to their stations, while the first lieutenant, with the carpenter and his crew, descended to ascertain the extent of the evil. The suspense during their absence was awful, for the smoke, in dark columns, continued to rise, and extend all over the ship. What then must have been Leslie's feelings, when Sir Roland signalized him to keep closer, and to have his boats in the water ready to render assistance. He must soon have divined the fearful cause of the order, though, like us, ignorant of the extent of the danger.

For some time we could not tell whether the fire had originated near the magazine or spirit-room; but at length it was reported to be near the latter, and every man in the ship, knowing the particular office allotted to him, united like one perfect engine in quenching the rising flames. I need not describe the operations: the fire was at length got under, and the danger was past. Lady Emily, during those awful moments, remained calm and collected, clinging to the arm of her father, who leant over her with fond solicitude for her safety; and I saw a tear of gratitude escape from his eye, as Sir Roland informed him that we were no longer in peril.

A few hours afterwards, a gale came on, though it lasted scarcely a day. It was indeed providential that the accident had not occurred during its continuance.

"I don't like the look of that fire, sir," observed an old quartermaster to me, as he came aft; "if worse is not coming, I don't know the points of the compass—depend on it, sir."

We then for a spell had a return of fine weather, with frequent calms, when Sir Roland constantly invited Leslie to dine on board the Juno. He did so, I suspect, as much for the sake of his fair passenger, as to pay attention to Leslie. Those were happy moments for the lovers, for our kind captain took care to leave them as much as possible to the uninterrupted enjoyment of each other's society.

After touching at several of the Ionian islands, and at two or three ports in Greece, we anchored at Corfu, where we remained some days, and then once more shaped our course for Malta.

We were within three days' sail of our destination, when a little before mid-day it fell a dead calm, the Seahorse being less than a quarter of a mile astern of us. It was one of those days of loveliness, more frequently encountered in the Mediterranean than in most other latitudes, when the blue vaulted world, with its bright, sparkling sea, its green sunny shores, and pure elastic atmosphere, appears to be a habitation fitted rather for spirits of light and beauty than for beings prone, like man, to deeds of havoc and destruction. As I looked over the side at the fairy-like form of our tiny consort, I forgot that she was, like our more majestic ship, an engine to slay and alarm, and I could have fancied her some benign being, the guardian of the tranquil deep on which she floated. Lady Emily, escorted by the earl, just then came on deck to breathe the pure air, and as I gazed on her from a distance, I prayed that she might be spared to bless the earth with her grace and beauty, and to prove a wife worthy of my noble friend.

I fell into a reverie. I was aroused from it by the voice of Sir Roland ordering me to take a note on board the Seahorse. It proved, as I suspected, an invitation to Leslie. A boat was lowered, and, with another epistle from the ward-room mess, to invite some of their brother officers to dinner, in a few minutes I was on the deck of the brig. The midshipmen had also deputed me to invite some of their own rank, and, as may be supposed, no refusals were sent when I returned on board.

I was speedily followed by Leslie, who was too happy at finding an excuse, through Sir Roland's kindness, to spend some hours in the society of his mistress. With a joyous step, he sprang on board, brightness in his eye, a smile upon his lips, and his heart bounding with pride. As she sat on deck, he stood by her side, watching with the fondest affection every expression of her lovely countenance; nor do I believe that, even up to that time, had a suspicion of the frail tenure by which her life was held crossed his mind. Happy for him that it was so! They spoke of their present enjoyment, the days of happiness in store for them, the regions they would visit together, the shores of sunny Italy, the lands of romantic Greece, the cottage amid some lovely scenery, where they would settle tranquilly at last.

A gentle breeze had sprung up, which tempered the air playing under the awning, beneath which Lady Emily reclined. People talk much of the monotony of the sea, but, for my own part, I have never found cause to complain of it. Behold it sometimes, as then, shining with dazzling brightness — now dark and gloomy, like Lethe's stream—and anon lashed to fury by the raging tempest. As the eyes of the lovers gazed on it, so calm and beautiful did it look, that they forgot how treacherous and deceitful it could prove. They were watching a shoal of sportive dolphins, which were playing round the ship, and now and then one of those beautiful inhabitants of the Mediterranean, the nautilus, or Portuguese man-of-war, would rise from the deep, and spreading its tiny sail, skim along the surface of the mirror-like ocean.

"Oh that we could have a bark of our own, to sail together over these tranquil waters, and visit the lovely shores of this inland sea!" I heard Lady Emily say, as I passed near them.

"We may, some day, dearest," answered Leslie, pressing her hand, "when you shall be my Ocean Queen, and I will be the Monarch of our little world."

I may appear to be somewhat minute in my description, but every event of that awful day was too indelibly stamped on my mind ever to be erased by time. At length, as the evening drew towards a close, though the wind continued light, and the sea calm, the aspect of the sky gave tokens of a change in the weather. To a landsman's eye all seemed as before, but, dead to leeward, there appeared suddenly a small white cloud, just rising out of the sea; it looked like snow-capped mountain in the distance. All the officers of the ship, as well as our guests, were collected on deck. I saw Sir Roland glance his eye round the horizon, as did one or two of the officers, and then exchange significant looks with each other.

"Leslie," said Sir Roland, beckoning to him, "you had better get on board your ship, and make all snug. We shall have a breeze soon. Bear a hand, my good fellow," he added, as Leslie passed him, "you have not a moment to lose."

The lovers exchanged a tender pressure of the hand, and Leslie tore himself from her side. The boats of the Seahorse were piped away, and in a minute were pulling rapidly towards the brig. The fair girl watched her lover as long as she could distinguish his features, when, faint from the exertion she had made to appear well before him, she sunk down on her couch.

"Lady Emily, I must entreat you to go below, for we shall have a strong breeze presently, to which you ought not to be exposed," said Sir Roland, approaching her.

"Oh no, no!" she answered; "let me enjoy a little longer the pure air of heaven. I am not afraid of the storm, I assure you."

And she rose and walked to the side of the ship whence her eye could watch the Seahorse, nor could all the persuasions of Sir Roland and the Earl induce her to alter her determination.

In the meantime the hands had been turned up and every preparation made for getting the ship snug, should the threatening tempest approach us. The little cloud had now become a dense mass of white mist, rising, as it were, against the wind, and rapidly extending over the whole horizon, while overhead not a cloud floated on the pure blue sky. The circumstances I am describing, it must be remembered, either occurred simultaneously or quickly succeeded each other.

"What do you think of the look of those clouds to leeward, Mr. Bernard?" said Sir Roland, addressing our first lieutenant, an old officer who had seen much service.

"I have seen such before, sir, in these seas, when our ship was struck by a white squall, which left us a complete wreck, with twelve of our people killed by the vivid lightning which accompanied it."

"God grant we may escape the like," said Sir Roland; "but we will be prepared for the worst. Shorten sail, Mr. Bernard."

"Ay, ay, sir," answered the zealous first, as he hurried forward to obey our chief's commands. "There are few moments to spare if we would save the sticks," he added; and then in a sharp, ringing voice issued the necessary command to take in the lofty sails. The men, who were expecting the orders, sprung up the rigging, and rapidly and quietly they were obeyed. Again he cast his eyes around on the dense white masses of clouds now advancing every instant with increasing speed from the north-east, the rays of the setting sun tinging their edges with a ruddy hue. Onward they came, not directly towards us, but forming a wide circle, as each moment they grew thicker and thicker. As yet not a sound of the approaching gale had been heard, but suddenly a rushing noise, like the rolling of a thousand chariot wheels, struck our ears.

"Man the fore and main clue-garnets, spanker-brails,—jib down haul—clear the fore-topmast staysail," sung out the first lieutenant, with rapid voice; "shorten sail—lower the topsails." These orders followed in rapid succession.

Darker and darker grew the clouds, as wheeling round they appeared to windward, and then, like a mighty squadron of cavalry charging with loud shouts a square of infantry, they rushed impetuously down towards us with a fierce and tremendous roar, the furious wind ploughing up and rending in its rapid course the face of the ocean into wild leaping and foaming waves. Volleys of terrific thunder resounded through the sky, while lightning, blue and vivid, darted from the darkening mass, and, playing around us, threatened us with destruction.

Like some furious demon intent on ill, the squall struck our noble ship. Proud as we called her, she yielded helplessly to its powers. In an instant, though every halliard and sheet was let go, she was on her beam-ends, the water rushing in even at her main-deck ports. At that instant a loud shriek was heard—the lightning had struck two of our people, and their blackened corpses rolled to leeward. The same flash shivered the main-topmast, when the squall taking it, carried it with its spars and rigging over the side; the fore-topmast staysail was blown like a gossamer web from the bolt ropes, and carried away far to leeward; and thus, instead of running before the gale we lay helplessly exposed to its fury.

I have attempted, in a few words, to describe the scene, but I feel how far anything I can say must inevitably fall short of the terrific reality. The stoutest seamen stood aghast, and every officer waited with breathless anxiety for what might next occur. So occupied was everybody with the condition of the Juno, that no one thought of looking how it fared with the Seahorse. At that awful moment my duty took me to the after part of the quarter-deck. The shock had sent Lord Ravelin, unable to save himself, to the lee side of the ship, but Lady Emily, unsupported, held with convulsive energy to the weather bulwarks, her eye straining in the direction of her lover's vessel. It was then a cry, faint, but full of agonized terror, struck my ear. I rushed forward, Lady Emily had sunk upon the deck. I looked around. The Seahorse was nowhere visible, but I fancied that as I gazed towards the spot where she had been, that I saw the mast of a ship sinking beneath the foaming waves. At the same moment a mist-like form, of human shape, with flowing drapery, appeared, borne down to leeward on the blast, where, joined by another shape, they seemed to ascend amid the clouds towards the heavens, and a stream of melody of joyous sound, I thought, came back upon my ear. I bent down to raise Lady Emily; but she moved not, she breathed not. I took her hand, it fell listlessly by her side, and the sad conviction forced itself on me that she was dead. I shouted for aid, but the tempest drowned my voice, and the increasing darkness prevented me from being seen.

The ship still lay on her beam-ends, the sea rushing into her ports to leeward, while the foam, in masses like a snow-drift, dashed over her on the weather side. The atmosphere grew darker and darker; the clouds, which seemed to press us down with their weight, discharging deluges of rain and hail, sent forth peal upon peal of thunder, and flash after flash of lurid and forked lightning; the wind howled and roared with deafening violence, laughing to scorn the voices of the officers, as they attempted to issue their orders; while night setting in, added to the horrors of the scene. Headsail was again hoisted, but the ship refused to wear. The last resource on such an occasion now alone remained for us; the masts one after another, must be cut away. It was a desperate remedy, but it was the only chance of saving the ship.

Sir Roland, watching every occurrence with a seaman's eye, had not stirred from his post. His deep voice was now heard through his speaking trumpet.

"Stand by to cut away the masts!" he cried.

Some of the best men came aft, their axes gleaming in their hands. The lee mizen shrouds were cut away, the weather followed, and a few strokes sent the mizen-mast, with all its top hamper, dashing amid the billows. Still the ship lay helplessly on her side.

"Cut away the main-mast!" cried the captain.

The seamen sprang to their stations. The mast fell with a crash into the ocean. It was a moment of most intense anxiety. The ship felt the relief afforded her, and rising on her keel slowly turned her head from the blast. Away she flew before it, rivalling the scud in speed, and throwing the foaming waters high over her bows. As I before observed, words cannot convey an adequate idea of the terrific realities of the scene, or the rapidity with which the events I have mentioned followed each other. But a few minutes had passed since the gallant Leslie and his officers had stood on our deck, in high health and spirits. Now, alas! where were they? His graceful bark and all on board lay engulfed beneath the raging billows, and our noble ship, almost a wreck, was hurrying on—perhaps to destruction.

Such are the chances of a sailor's life.

I had during this period been endeavouring to protect the form of Lady Emily from the fury of the tempest, calling loudly for assistance, Sir Roland was the first to hear me.

"Great Heaven!" he exclaimed, "I fancied she had been conveyed below: and Lord Ravelin, where is he?"

"He was but just now standing near his daughter," I answered. "I fear that he has been hurt."

As soon as some of the crew came aft with lanthorns, Lord Ravelin was found on the deck, stunned by the blow of a falling spar, and he was in this state conveyed to his cabin; as was Lady Emily to hers. The surgeon was instantly summoned, and anxiously we awaited his opinion. He soon again appeared, the expression of his countenance betraying the truth. My fears were too sadly realized. Lady Emily—the young, the loved, the beautiful—was no more. The shock of what her eye alone beheld had been more than her strength could bear. In that moment of terror, her spirit, too gentle for this rough world, had quitted its fair but fragile tenement, and those who loved in life were not by death divided.

To this day I have been unable to divest myself of the idea that I beheld her spirit, conjoined to that of my friend, ascending to regions far purer and more blessed than this. My imagination might have misled me, and yet to my senses the vision appeared clear and defined. If such things can be, then surely I was not deceived.

The white squall subsided almost as rapidly as it had commenced;

the wind shifted back to its original quarter, the sea went down, and the moon and stars shone forth upon the dancing waves.

Beautiful and calm looked the laughing ocean, and nothing was there to tell of the scene of strife which had just occurred. Contriving to rig jury-masts, we stood back to the spot where we had last seen the Seahorse, but, alas! not a trace of her was to be found, nor has there been to this day.

Sad and melancholy was our short voyage to Malta. I had lost my best friend: the aged Earl had been bereaved of his only child. He lingered on for some time, but before the year had closed he followed his daughter to the grave. They sleep where rest their noble ancestors, whilst the boundless ocean is the gallant Leslie's tomb.

By the time Upton had concluded, the evening had drawn on, and we were obliged to separate to our different avocations. The unnautical reader must not suppose from these pages that naval officers have nothing to do but to amuse themselves by telling stories; but there are numerous occasions when the eye is too fatigued to dwell on a book, and when permission to sleep is denied, when a well-spun yarn or friendly conversation affords the greatest relaxation which can be enjoyed by us poor sailors. Jack spins his fo'castle yarn with high gusto to his credulous messmates for'ard, while his officer narrates his adventures with equal pleasure in the gun-room or on the quarter-deck.

Forsooth, we had indeed something else to do besides spinning yarns. Frequently during the time I was on the coast have I been ten days together away from the ship in a small boat looking out for slavers. During all that time we were unable to land, to stretch our legs, or cook our provisions, for we were on an enemy's coast, and should have been cooked ourselves if we had attempted it; and if we fell in with a slaver, we had no choice but victory or death; for, if overpowered, we had not a chance of escape.

Day after day, and night after night have I been alone on the dark waters, and perhaps not a friendly cruiser within one or two hundred miles of me; my food hard biscuit and salt junk—my couch the starboard side of the stern sheets of the boat, with a blanket rolled round me as my only covering, exposed to scorching suns and damp fogs, to rain, wind, and lightning; and when I mention this, I trust my countrymen will feel, whatever may be said to the contrary, that officers, while thus employed, are at least honestly earning their salt.

CHAPTER XIV.

SLAVER HUNTING.

WE spent some time cruising off the coast, now running along shore, now standing out to sea, in the hopes of falling in with slavers; we chased several, but for some time they all managed to escape from us. As long as we kept at sea, the ship continued very healthy, and we began to laugh at the prognostications of Haggis, until, from the information he had received, our captain considered it his duty to send the boats up some of the rivers in search of vessels taking in their cargoes. I shall not forget the first expedition of the kind, when I was sent in command up the River Bonny. At early dawn we shoved off, I in the pinnace, and Green in the second gig, in high spirits at the prospect of something to do, and pulled across the foaming mouth of the river. Mangrove bushes line the banks on either side of the dark and silent stream. As we pulled on, after landing for a short time to breakfast, I took to moralizing as I sat in the stern sheets with a cigar in my mouth, the greatest luxury in that climate.

Green was a delightful companion, for although no scholar, he was very well informed; he had seen a great deal of the world; he knew everybody, and everybody, it appeared, knew him; indeed it was a common saying on board, that wherever Green went he was sure to find an acquaintance. We pulled up the stream all that day, and slept in the boats, exposed to the damp, heavy fogs, which, even in the best of seasons, are so destructive to Europeans. The following morning we again pulled on, but without hearing even of a slaver. Well, I was laughing with Green, and asking him if he had any friends in those parts to give us information.

"Perhaps I may have," he answered, "but I'm not quite certain. Jimbo Pimbo, my own correspondent, is defunct, I believe."

Scarcely had he spoken when we saw a number of negroes, in spite of the alligators, bathing in the river. We pulled towards them, when, to the delight of us all, one of them popped his head out of the water, exclaiming, "Ah, Massa Green! How him do? Glad see Massa Green. Know him, Pillalloo?"

Upon which, Massa Pillalloo, catching hold of the gunnel of the boat, hauled himself on board, and seated himself, dripping as he was, in the stern sheets. It appeared that he had been taken as a slave, and recaptured, and remained some time on board a ship to which Green belonged. He assured us that there were no slavers in the river, but promised to gain us every information he could for a future visit.

Some time after this we were off Loanda, when we received information that a large schooner had been seen hovering off the mouth of the Coanza river, and that a number of slaves had been collected at the slave dealers' depôts in the neighbourhood.

On hearing this not unwelcome news, we lost not a moment in heaving up the anchor and getting under weigh, though we were obliged to use not a little circumspection to circumvent the persons connected with the diabolical traffic on shore, who were certain to send off information of our movements to their agents.

The wind was off the shore at the time, and in a minute after Captain Dainmore received the information, we were under a spread of canvas standing out to sea. In the offing we met the sea breeze, and altering our course, we hauled up for Coanza, carrying every stitch of sail we could set. Every one was on the look-out as we neared the place; for prizes are not to be picked up every day, even though one may risk one's life to find them. Now let it be understood, that although every officer is glad to take a prize, and has no objection to the cash which may chance thereby to reach his pocket, I believe that a high sense of duty, and a wish to put a stop to the nefarious traffic, are the motives which animate Her Majesty's officers on that deadly coast; and I fling back with disdain the foul aspersions which have been cast on the members of my noble profession by men who, because they themselves are influenced by mercenary motives, believe that the art of buying cheap is the greatest talent to be desired, and fancy that no other men are ruled by more noble, more worthy sentiments. Notwithstanding the heat of the sun, some one was constantly at the masthead, looking out for a sail in-shore, till night closed in, and a thick mist rose over the world.

We had, by our calculations, run our course, and were about off the mouth of the Coanza soon after daybreak, but so dense was the fog that nothing could be seen of the land, while we ourselves were equally invisible. We, however, kept the lead going, and stood on. Some hours passed, and the mist still continued hanging over us like a heavy pall, till at last the rays of the sun burst through it, and the blue sky was seen above our heads, while all around us the mass of vapour looked (as Seaton called it) like a lofty wall built up to keep us from the world beyond.

"I shall just run aloft and see if I can get a peep over the battlement," he observed, laughing; "who knows but what an enemy is not far off on the outside."

He had not been many minutes aloft when he exclaimed, "A vessel close on board of us, on the starboard bow!"

The cry was repeated by the look-out at the masthead, and Seaton came sliding down on deck. "A large schooner," he exclaimed to Captain Dainmore, who had just come out of his cabin. "She's at anchor, apparently, but I could only just see her mast head above the fog."

"The Andorinha, there's no doubt about it!" he exclaimed; "the fellow is taking his slaves on board, and does not dream who is near. Port the helm—keep her up a little—how are we going now?"

"Right for her, sir," answered the look-out aloft.

"See all ready to have the boats out, Mr. Upton. We'll not let him escape if we can help it."

A cheerful "Ay, ay, sir," was the answer, and the boats' crews set busily to work to get them into the water at a moment's notice.

On we stood, expecting every moment to be up to the stranger, when suddenly the mist lifted, and we found ourselves close on board a large vessel, with two rafts alongside, crowded with black human beings, whom a white crew were busily employed in transferring, like bales of merchandise, to her decks.

The low mangrove-covered shore was about a mile off, with a little bay, and a sandy beach abreast of us, while a third raft of triangular shape, with a large sail set, and covered like the other, with negroes, was coming off to the schooner, and was now about midway between her and the shore. Alongside the vessel were several boats which had assisted in bringing off the rafts.

A simultaneous cry of rage and joy arose from among the motley crowd of blacks and whites as our approach was perceived; the Spaniards and Portuguese at finding that the prey was to be rescued out of their hands, the slaves from knowing that we were come as their deliverers.

Though, however, we were tolerably sure of capturing the schooner, we were not quite so certain of securing her crew, for no sooner did they see us, than cutting the rafts adrift, and their own cable at the same time, they leaped into three different boats; and pulled off in as many directions verging towards the shore—the crew of the third raft also at the same time altered her course so as to distract, as much as possible, our attention.

Upton, Green, Seaton, and I, were each in our separate boats; the first boarded the schooner, where the only whites he found below were the *stevadores*, or stowers of the cargo, a mongrel tribe of Portuguese, and he had some difficulty in saving them from the vengeance of the blacks, whom in their vocation they had cruelly treated. Green threw some of his men on board the rafts, and then dashed after one of the slaver's boats, while Seaton and I pulled away in chase of the third raft, and the boats which had her in tow. It was an exciting scene; our men cheered, the blacks shrieked, and we all strained every muscle to rescue them. When we first saw the rafts, they had exactly the appearance of the blackened timbers of a ship destroyed by fire, for as the negroes are all made to squat down, nothing but the black heads appear, dotting the surface it seemed of the water. Just as we separated in chase, another raft was seen, hurried by the tide out of the Coanza river, and I accordingly hailed Seaton to pull after it, in hopes of getting on board before the whites could gain command of it, to haul it again on shore.

These rafts were of considerable size, and built, in a triangular form, of the trunks of palm-trees, cut away below the branches, and which are almost as buoyant as cork. They are lashed together with ropes, and rows of water-casks are made fast to their outer edges, as bulwarks to keep off the sharks, for heavily freighted as they are, the centre is sunk completely under the water, so that the miserable blacks have to sit up to their waist in the sea. Each raft conveys from one to two hundred persons. On the top of the casks, a platform is built, on which is placed the farinha, the flour, and other food, on which the slaves are fed, so that each raft contains the supply of water and provisions of its passengers for the whole voyage.

They are built some way up the Coanza, and are guided down the stream and across the bar by means of ropes, made fast to each angle, and, by hauling on one or the other, the raft is made to sheer off clear of any point or obstruction in the way.

No sooner did the white people in the fourth raft see that they were pursued, than, jumping into their boats, they towed it with such good will towards the shore, that, aided by an eddy, they reached it before Seaton could get up to them, and then set to work to loose the slaves and to drag them on shore, so as to be out of our each, while some of the Spaniards opened a sharp fire on him from behind the bushes, in the hope of crippling him before he could get up to them.

As the raft, of which I was in pursuit, was farther from the shore, her chance of escape was less, though, to do the Spaniards and Portuguese on board her justice, they did their best to get away and to carry off their captives. When they saw that their efforts were of no avail, they jumped into their boats and pulled off towards the shore. Without stopping to board the raft, which I left to take care of itself, I followed them, sending the contents of three muskets after them to bring them to, but that did not stop them. Their boat's keel grated on the beach before we could get hold of them, and, without stopping to look behind them, they jumped out and ran off into the bushes.

My people would have followed, but I was obliged to call them back (not a little against my will, for I should have liked to punish the rascals), to take charge of the raft, which was drifting near the shore. It was fortunate I did so, for, as we shoved off through the surf, a large body of blacks, and whites, and whitey-browns, came down, in the hope of this taking place, when they would probably have got hold of the greater part of the cargo. Had they dared, they would have fired at us, but they were probably afraid, if they went too far, we should land and chastise them.

We got back to the raft just in time to tow her off shore, to the great joy of her passengers, who had watched our proceedings with intense interest, for several of them had been before taken and liberated by our cruisers, and therefore knew that we came as their friends. The poor wretches had other enemies to contend with, in a shoal of sharks which surrounded the raft, and were actually rubbing their snouts against the water casks, in the hope of picking off the negroes on the other side of them.

It was, indeed, frightful to see the monsters make a rush at the rafts, with force sufficient, one would have thought, to knock them to pieces, and to know that, if such should happen, probably every one of the poor wretches would be devoured; and, as it was, one of my people, in stepping from the boat to the raft, was nearly seized hold of by one of the ravenous creatures. Jack Dobson never leaped higher in his life than he did on that occasion.

After considerable exertion, I and Seaton, who had come to my assistance, got the raft alongside the schooner, where we met Green and Upton, on their return from their unsuccessful chase of the slaver's boats. We, however, remained masters of the schooner Andorinha, and captors of seven hundred slaves, including those already below and on board the three rafts. About one hundred were supposed to have been retained in captivity on board the fourth raft, which escaped.

Those in the hold were overjoyed at being released. The *stevadores* had chained their ankles to bolts in the decks, making them sit down on their heels and hams, without affording them an inch of spare room in which to turn their bodies, with sufficient food and water only to support existence; and were it not for the sake of landing them in tolerable condition, they would probably never be allowed to breathe the pure air of heaven, from the commencemen to the end of the voyage.

I do not pretend to possess more of the milk of human kindness than my fellow-men, but I do say that this diabolical traffic must be put down by some means or other, and that it is worthy of the exertions of all the intelligent and philanthropic men of the world —I will not say alone of England—to discover the means by which that purpose may be effected.

Our blockade of the African coast is absolutely necessary if we would succeed; but it is equally absurd and useless if we at the same time encourage the employers of slaves, and eagerly seek for their produce. The only method by which slavery can be abolished is, to form a crusade against all employers of slaves; to hold no communion with them, either commercially or politically; to refuse to receive their produce on any terms; to make slaving piracy; to condemn all vessels of which there is the slightest suspicion; and to hang all men, white, brown, or black, of whatever nation, caught in the act.

Till strenuous measures are taken, many hundred fine fellows may be sent annually to die on that pestiferous coast, without producing the slightest effect. We are ready to do our duty—we are ready to go, to toil, to sicken, and to die; but you gentlemen of England—you legislators who sit at home at ease—let us feel that we are to die for some good purpose; let us know that our efforts are backed up by efficient regulations at home. But I fear that all I can say will have little effect; we are to have cheap sugar at every cost; cheap sugar is the order of the day! For cheap sugar we are to barter away our souls!

"Oh, no," I hear some one answer, "it is the principle of the thing; we alone advocate the true principles of political economy."

To this I answer, I, too, am a political economist; I, too, advocate the principles of political economy when they do not militate against other principles. But there exists another economy which is called moral economy. That moral economy takes precedence of political economy. By the laws of the first you are to worship your Maker, and to do to all men as you would be done by, to act honestly and justly; by the laws of the second, it appears you are to buy sugar cheap.

These are a sailor's notions on the subject, whose only boast is that he is an honest man, and loves and respects honesty, and abhors knavery, quackery, and all the works of the devil. He may be wrong; if he is, some of the rulers and governors of the land, and a mighty chief of cotton men, are right. But I am telling a tale, and not writing an essay on politics.

We got all the negroes on board, with water and provisions, which the raft fortunately supplied, and made the poor wretches as comfortable as circumstances would permit. On returning on board the Albatross, I found that the captain had settled that I should to take the prize to Sierra Leone; and accordingly, having a few clothes and necessaries put up, I returned on board her to assume the command. The breeze was at first against us, but it shifted round in the evening, and enabled us to lay our course for our port of destination. We had a run of some days before us, so I set to work to consider how I could best keep the slaves in health, with a due regard to our own safety, for of course it would have been unwise to trust to them entirely, lest any bad spirits among them should persuade the rest to attempt the capture of the vessel, with the hopes of getting on shore free from all restraint, and of enjoying the plunder of the vessel, which, to negro imaginations, was very considerable.

Of food and water there was an abundance, and I had the negroes on deck a hundred and fifty or so at a time; and having got a number of apologies for musical instruments manufactured, I found some of them were willing enough to play, while the rest danced away to their hearts' content. As soon as they were tired, I made as many of them as there was room for sit round close to the bulwarks, and had another party up to dance. I had also some Kroomen on board, sent from the Albatross, on whom I could place full reliance, so I made them go round to tell them stories to amuse them. The result of my care was, that all were orderly, healthy, and contented, and that we reached Sierra Leone in safety without any deaths. I was right glad, however, to be off my charge, for, besides the responsibility, there were numerous inconveniences which it is very easy to imagine, but which few will thank me for describing.

I here saw the last of my friend Don Diego Lopez de Mendoza, as did the world in general, for he made his exit on the ignominious gibbet, for which he had so long been qualified, in company with his less noble followers. He appeared on the scaffold with the greatest nonchalance, smoking a cigar, and surrounded by several priests of the Romish Church in their proper vestments, who exhorted him to repentance, and chanted forth the last prayers to accompany a departing sinner on his way. Taking the cigar from his mouth, he informed the spectators that he was an innocent man, and that the British Nation were barbarians to hang him, when a more civilized people would have sent him out of the world with a bullet—the more decorous way for a cavalier like himself to die. As no one believed him to be innocent, he departed this life without a pitying sigh. He had been condemned, I found, for another atrocious case of piracy, when he left his prize with holes in her bottom, expecting her to sink, which, fortunately for the survivors of her crew, she did not do, but they having stopped her leaks, managed to bring her into Sierra Leone in time to prevent his escape.

CHAPTER XV.

PEPE, THE PIRATE.

I SPENT several days in that place of bad celebrity, Sierra Leone, and, though I did not suffer in health, I was heartily sick of it; very glad, therefore, was I when I beheld the Albatross standing into the harbour. I was on board almost as soon as she had dropped her anchor, and was welcomed cordially by all hands.

We only remained sufficient time to complete our wood and water, and again sailed to cruise off the mouth of the Niger. We had a somewhat calm, but altogether a pleasant time down to our cruising ground, and got on famously with my "Voices from the Ocean." We were seated round our mess-table when Green was called on for a story.

"That scoundrel, Don Diego Lopez de Mendoza, who paid the penalty of his crimes t'other day on the scaffold, reminds me of another fellow I have met of the same water, but whose fate has hitherto been more fortunate. I knew the rascal well, his name was Pepe; and as his history is a romance in itself, I will tell it for Fairfield's especial benefit; so now, my boy, out with your note-book and catch the jewels which fall from my mouth. I would rather you than I had the trouble. Listen, then, to the history of

PEPE, THE PIRATE.

HOW PEPE WENT TO SEA, AND BECAME CAPTAIN OF A SLAVER.

Thanks to railroads and the new police, gentlemen of the road, highway-robbers, have pretty well disappeared from the thoroughfares and the wild heaths and woods of Merrie England. In Ireland to be sure, a mail-coach is now and then stopped, and lives, if not purses, are more frequently taken than is pleasant to contemplate or altogether creditable to some party or parties unknown—lords or beggars—the hereditary rulers of the hereditary rebels; but wander where one will, with the exception of one or two countries, a genuine brigand or a professed robber has become almost a traditionary character, and the adventurous traveller has scarcely the chance of pulling the triggers of his pistols, except to exhibit his skill as a marksman on some harmless bird, or to silence a roving cat. Spain is one of the happy exceptions, and even from thence many a disappointed tourist has to return home without one thrilling adventure worthy of record in his note-book, unless he has sufficient imagination to invent one for the amusement of his friends. On the wide ocean, once the scene of so many daring exploits, the same deplorable dearth of openly professed robbers is to be found. Now and then, to be sure, a good respectable cutthroat is heard of, who carries a black flag at each mast-head, makes all the men he captures walk the plank, like the grand Turk marries all the women, and lives a jolly, roistering life till he blows himself up into the air, or goes to the bottom with his colours nailed to the mast like a brave man. For my part, when such a gentleman is found, I think he ought to be cherished the more for the rarity of his character—hung, of course, if he is caught, but respected as long as he manages to range at liberty. For a reason not very dissimilar, I hold in the greatest esteem a certain Senhor Don José Montes Pepe, a hidalgo of the highest honour and integrity, who flourished not many years ago, and extended his reputation to all parts of the world.

Whether Don Pepe owed his existence to honest and respectable parents, may be strongly doubted; of his birth and education, therefore, the less said perhaps the better — his enemies even asserted that he had no right to the Don before his name—but thus much he could affirm, that less honest gentlemen than himself had assumed it before him. Pepe first saw the light of this sublunary world not far from that spot famed in history, the now decayed town of Palos, whence the great discoverer of the western hemisphere set out on that important expedition which served to extend the eyes of mankind wider than they had ever opened before. I do not know that in consequence of this locality Pepe troubled his head much about Columbus, or ever read his voyages, but at a very early age he exhibited a strong predilection for a sea-life. Finding that his friends, who, for certain reasons, intended him for the church, did not coincide in his views, he bolted, carrying away, to supply his immediate wants, as much of their money as he could lay his hands on, and, into the bargain, some silver and gilt utensils used in the sacred mysteries, and which were under the charge of a certain holy friar in a neighbouring convent. Scandal says that to one of the pious fathers he bore a strong resemblance; but of that nothing certain can be learned. Knowing that were he caught consequences far from pleasant would ensue, besides the loss of his wealth, Pepe made the best of his way on board a ship on the point of sailing for South America. As he could pay for his passage, no questions were asked, and he was treated like a gentleman, having the air and manners of one to perfection, being a very good-looking fellow into the bargain, with a tall, manly figure, and an intelligent countenance. In fact, he had always been a great favourite among the ladies, who being, as is acknowledged since the days of our fair mother, Donna Eve, at the bottom of all mischief, had persuaded him that it would be a great pity so nice a young man should have his crown shaved, and sleep for the rest of his days in a cold cell within the walls of a convent. So, as I have said, he went to sea. Knowing, however, that he might have some difficulty in replenishing his pockets, he was not idle during his voyage, but by being always wide awake, he soon made himself acquainted with all the details of seamanship, so that by the time the ship reached Monte Video he was no contemptible sailor. He liked the style of life so much, that he determined to go to sea again at once; but the seductions of the sex in the New World, as it had done in the old, again proved his bane, showing also that the change of climate has not altered their natures. He went to their tertullias, he sang and danced, he made love, and would have married, had not the ladies already been provided with husbands; he laughed and he smoked, he drank and he gamed, regardless of the future, till one night on his return home, happening to look into his chest, he found it empty, or rather full only of old clothes; he searched his pockets—not a dollar could he find in them. He then sat down like a philosopher, and after meditating a little on affairs in general, and his own in particular, he came to the conclusion that he was not worth a maravedi. Other young gentlemen might have been disconcerted at this discovery, but Pepe instead went to bed, and determined to think the matter over on the morrow. He had no relations or rich monks to rob, or there would have been no difficulty about the affair, he thought. He had also not a few debts, for his credit was extensive, and he patronized all the best tradesmen in the place. It struck him, however, as he was dressing in the morning, after a refreshing night's rest, that he required change of air for his health, so he ordered a new kit as soon as he went out, paid—not his bills—but a round of visits in the evening to his fair friends, and at night went on board a fast schooner, the captain of which was an acquaintance of his.

During his second cruise, he contrived to improve still further his nautical education, though, as he spent his money as fast as he got it, he was not the richer for all his toil. Thus, for three or four years, he remained constantly at sea, undergoing all its vicissitudes and increasing in knowledge, till at last he shipped on board a schooner, bound for the coast of Africa, to take in a cargo of slaves, which were then to be sold in one of the West India markets. The speculation was successful, for *Blacks were up* when they arrived, and only a third had died; thus Pepe again found himself supplied with funds to carry on the war. So pleasantly passed his life on shore, that he was in no hurry again to go to sea; and when the slaver sailed, he was nowhere to be discovered.

Pepe must at this time have been a bad calculator, for his money was soon gone, and his credit did not last much longer. His resources were, however, in one respect inexhaustible—he always contrived to keep up appearances, the true way to greatness. He had, by his good looks or his soft tongue, won the affections of the wife of a wealthy planter. The husband, to get rid of Senhor Pepe, offered him a berth on board a richly-freighted merchantman, bound for Cadiz, in Old Spain. Pepe accepted the offer, and sailed; but he had his reasons for wishing not to go home; he preferred seeing more of the world first; so he persuaded the crew to take a cruise with him down the South American coast, where he sold his cargo to the Portuguese, and ended by selling the ship. He then gave their share of the profits to his men, bought a fast schooner, fitted her out with guns, and as he was in no way particular as to morality of character, he had no difficulty in shipping a crew.

Behold Don Pepe at length launched as captain of his own ship. He had found slaving so profitable before, that he determined to try a speculation on his own account; and as he had plenty of dollars to purchase half-a-dozen cargoes, he forthwith sailed for the African coast. Surely he must have been born under a fortunate star, for again success blessed his labours, and he cleared an enormous profit; but when are mortals content? Pepe immediately sailed on another voyage: a new passion had entered his soul, and the sex had gone to leeward—he was beginning to grow avaricious.

In the mean time, England had discovered that she and the rest of the world had for many centuries been actively engaged in a very nefarious traffic: and that, if she did not put a stop to the slave trade, a number of most unpleasant occurrences would assuredly come to pass. She had also persuaded some of her allies and friends, by dint of strong arguments, to join her in her philanthropic project, promising to take all the trouble upon her own shoulders, which her said disinterested friends not only fully intended that she should do, but also slily purposed to increase the load as much as they could, calculating that with the kind aid of the climate her officers would have no sinecure appointment of it, and would soon induce her to abandon the enterprise. Neither Spaniards, Portuguese, nor Frenchmen, however, have any idea of the curious composition of John Bull, or they would not for a moment have dreamed of such a thing. John has determined to get rid of the slave trade, and depend upon it he will some day succeed, though he may first have to expend a good number of lives in the undertaking.

But to return to Pepe's adventures. One fine morning, as the El Carmen, the name of his new schooner, was off the mouth of the Nunn river, out of which she had come during the night, with about two hundred slaves on board, he observed a strange sail five or six miles away to the northward. The haze was too thick to make her out clearly, but Pepe had a strong suspicion that her appearance boded him no good; in fact, he could not divest his mind of the idea that she was a British cruiser. The breeze which had come off the land at night had completely fallen, the sea was smooth and shining, and the long, low line of mangroves on the pestilential shore looked dark and dreary. Pepe walked the deck of his vessel with a glass under his arm, which he every now and then turned towards the strange sail; for though she, like El Carmen, was then becalmed, she might first get the breeze and bring it down with her. If she were also a man-of-war, she would have boats, he recollected, and might very probably think fit to overhaul him with them. Now, although his vessel carried six long guns, and he and his crew were perfectly ready to fight if required, as he did not care one jot for the honour and glory to be gained thereby, he saw no manner of use in risking his own life, or the lives of his people, if it could possibly be avoided. He therefore got out his sweeps, and with his boats towing ahead, pulled away to the southward.

The El Carmen was a fast craft, and soon made good head-way, but her proceedings were observed by the stranger to the nor'ward. Captain Pepe had mounted into the main rigging, and kept his eye intently fixed on her. For some time he was unable to make out anything to alarm him; but at last, as his telescope ranged over the intermediate space of water, he discerned three little black spots floating on its surface, no bigger apparently than so many black beetles swimming in a horse-pond.

Having satisfied himself, however, that they were ship's boats, and probably full of armed men, who would prove ugly customers if they once managed to get on board his vessel, he descended on deck and ordered the boarding nettings to be triced up, the guns to be loaded with grape and canister, and to be run out, and the arm-chest to be thrown open, and pikes placed ready to repel the enemy. The schooner was soon in fighting order, and the crew, having done everything necessary, like brave men, prepared for the worst.

Although the enemy's light boats pulled three times as fast as they did, still they continued at their oars to prolong the time before they could be attacked, in the hopes that a breeze might spring up and carry them clear. Pepe did his utmost to encourage them in their labours, even to putting his hand to the hawser which worked the sweeps. In this he was ably seconded by his mate, a creole, Diogo Nunez by name, a sharp, active little fellow, the life and soul of the ship's company. He appeared a realization of perpetual motion; he was here, there, and everywhere at the same moment, shouting, jumping, and laughing; now giving one fellow a pull by the ears, now another a kick on the breech, in the most amiable way possible, just to expedite their motions; he was the idol of the men, and as brave and tough as he was full of fun and wickedness, for, to speak the truth, he was a sad scamp into the bargain.

"Well, Diogo, how far off are the boats from us now, should you say?" asked Captain Pepe of his mate.

"A good league and a half, Senhor Captain," answered the mate, coming down from the main rigging. "As we are slipping at the rate of three knots an hour through the water, it will take half an hour before they can be up with us. In that time, by the blessing of the saints, a breeze may spring up, and then, good by to their lordships. I should like to give some of them to the sharks before we part company."

"Ay, if the whole crew of yonder craft, and every one of their hated nation, went to the inferno, it wouldn't matter," muttered the captain between his closed teeth. "What business have they to interfere in our lawful traffic?"

"None, I should think, the vile heretics! Courage, my men!" shouted the mate. "Pull away with a will; I see a breeze playing on the water ahead of us."

This last remark was not true, but it served Diogo's purpose, and that was all he cared about. The crew redoubled their efforts, and for some time longer kept out of range of the boats' guns. The boats came on steadily abreast of each other, and none but British seamen would have pulled as did their bold crews under a burning sun, but the prospect of a skirmish nerved their arms. Pepe was watching them through his glass. "Carramba, we shall have some tough work with those fellows," he observed to his mate. "Get in the sweeps. We must let the men rest a little, to be prepared for them; but stay, look to the westward,—what's that?"

"The saints be praised, a breeze on the water," cried Diogo, clapping his hands.

"We'll keep the sweeps going then. Pull away, my lads, the holy Virgin favour us!"

As he spoke he pointed seaward, where a line of darker colour could be seen gradually expanding and advancing towards them. The sails of the schooner, however, still hung sluggishly against the masts, but the yards were at once braced sharp up to meet the breeze. It did not come as soon as expected, and the consequence was that the boats got rather closer than was pleasant, as was proved by a shot from a gun in the bow of the largest, which came flying over their heads through the fore-top-sail.

"Shall we give them one in return?" asked Diogo. "It may silence their tongues."

"No, no, we'll reserve our compliments till they get nearer," answered the captain. "Perhaps, after all, we may not have to pay them, and there's no use throwing powder and shot away."

Pepe was in an economical mood, like Joe Hume. Every instant the boats were drawing nearer—in another minute the largest fired again, and the shot passed through the main-sail. Pepe cast his eyes anxiously towards the point whence he expected to see the breeze come. It seemed to be in a coy mood, just touching the face of the water and flying off again, ashamed of what it had been about—a third shot struck the topsail and knocked one of the crew overboard.

"Curses on the heretics! we must fire now," exclaimed Diogo. Pepe nodded his head. "Train a gun aft to give it them."

Just then the sails were seen slowly to bulge outward, the schooner sensibly increased her speed through the water, the sweeps were plied with redoubled vigour, so were the oars, if that were possible, of the British crew. Each moment the breeze strengthened, and every sail drew well. She was, however, obliged to keep close hauled to retain her distance from the land. The sweeps were, therefore, still continued at work, for, notwithstanding all the efforts of the Spaniards, the boats gained on them.

"Shall I fire now?" asked Diogo, who had been looking anxiously along the sight of a gun run out at one of the after ports.

"No; hold," answered Pepe. "It will do no good as yet, for you will hardly hit them at this distance, and it will only make them in a still greater hurry to come up with us."

"As you like, Senhor Captain," replied Diogo, shrugging his shoulders. "Then I must suggest that we just throw them a little bait to stop them for a minute or so. It will be the loss of a few dollars; but that will be better than risking the whole cargo."

"You are right, Diogo," said Captain Pepe. "I should not wish to kill them, but our safety demands it. Here, Antonio, get up three or four of the most sickly of the slaves, and bring them aft immediately."

The captain's orders were quickly obeyed, and four emaciated wretches stood trembling before him. The weakest was first selected and brought aft. The poor wretch evidently thought that his life was to be instantly sacrificed, but so stupified was he, that he did not make even a struggle for existence, looking on with a stare of amazement at the proceedings of his masters. They, following Diogo's directions, made fast several large pieces of cork under his arms and round his neck, sufficient to buoy him up, and then, careless of his imploring looks for mercy, lowered him by a rope into the sea: one end was let slip, and the poor wretch was left floating by himself in the broad sea, with numbers, doubtless, of the ravenous monsters of the deep swimming at no great distance round him. Had he been allowed to retain his knife, he might, perhaps, have been able to defend himself from them, but buoyed up as he was, he had not the means of encountering them. As he dropped astern of the schooner, he cast a reproachful look with his large full eyes, at the Spaniards, which seemed to say, " Was it for this, cruel men, that you tore me from my sweet and shady groves, to become the sport of your malice? May the fate to which you have abandoned me soon be yours !" Something, in fact, to this effect he spoke; but his words did not reach the slaver's ears. They were busy in making ready another unfortunate wretch to throw overboard, while they watched eagerly to see whether the boats would stop to pick up the first.

The breeze was every instant freshening, but the sea still remained so smooth, that the boats continued to make good way; Captain Pepe kept his glance roaming from them to his canvass, and many a look did he cast over the side to see how fast the El Carmen was slipping through the water, that he might give the order to get in the sweeps as soon as possible, to rest the people for further exertions should they become necessary, while now and then his eye fell upon the black head floating between him and the enemy.

"It is to be hoped no sharks will scent the bait, or our object will be lost," observed Diogo, with admirable *sang froid;* " it would be a pity to expend any of the cargo uselessly."

None of the monsters, however, appeared, and the Spaniards had quickly the satisfaction of seeing their manœuvre succeed, for no sooner did the Englishmen observe the negro in the water, than one of the smaller boats pulled towards him, and was of course delayed some time in getting him on board, his additional weight also serving to decrease their speed. As soon as their humane conduct was perceived, another black was lowered, like the first, into the water, but he, seeing that his companion was safe, did not appear very much alarmed at what was going to happen to him. No sooner, however, did the pursuers perceive that this trick was to be repeated, than the barge recommenced firing as fast as the gun could be loaded, in the hopes of counteracting its effects, by knocking away some of the schooner's spars.

" The fools are in a merciful humour," exclaimed the little villain Diogo, rubbing his hands with glee, " so much the better, we must expend a few more negroes; but that matters little, for they are no great loss; they cost little, and would probably have died before they reached the end of the voyage."

Four negroes had thus been thrown overboard, and successively picked up by the humane English. A fifth was now prepared. He was a stout, strong youth, full of animal life, it seemed, but he perhaps had some disease, which made him of less value to his captors. He struggled with all his might when he found what was to be done with him, for he had not seen his fellows picked up, and fully believed that he was to be sacrificed, perhaps to propitiate the water-demons of the whites. At last they succeeded in making the floats fast to him, and in forcing him to the stern of the vessel. Scant ceremony was used with him, and as a punishment for his resistance he was hove overboard. For an instant, carried down by the force of his fall, he sank beneath the water, but soon rising again, he struck out towards the approaching boats. His efforts were of no avail. At that instant a dark body was seen to glide away from the side of the vessel, more ill-omened from its silent movement. A loud shriek was heard, the hapless wretch threw up his arms, as if grasping at the air, and was dragged down by his ruthless destroyer into the fathomless deep; a crimson tint marking the spot where he had disappeared. Even the rough slavers shuddered at the catastrophe they had contributed to bring about.

"We must have no more of this," said Captain Pepe, who was a humane man in his way, and averse at all times to shedding of blood.

"No," observed Diogo, shrugging his shoulders, "there will be no use in it, if the sharks are to pull them down instead of letting the boats pick them up. Ship the hatches again, or if the spars are hit, some of the splinters may be falling below and injuring our cargo. Here comes another shot."

The iron missile came hurtling along, and striking the helmsman, laid him a corpse on the deck, then, killing another man, after knocking the binnacle to pieces, struck the mainmast, whence it glanced off through one of the lee ports into the sea. Diogo flew to the helm, while the second mate, a black, savage-looking fellow, pointed one of the stern guns at the boats.

"Yes, you may fire, and take care to hit one of the villains," cried Don Pepe, his anger being aroused at the loss of his people.

The mate fired, but as the smoke blew aside, the boats were seen approaching as before.

"I must now try my hand," said the captain.

He fired, and it was evident from the confusion in one of the boats that somebody had been hit, if the boat herself had escaped. On they still came, but it was very clear that they gained nothing on the schooner. Notwithstanding this they persevered in the hope of the breeze again falling, or of some other circumstances favouring them. Pepe looked aloft with a satisfied air, every brace was taut, every sail drew well, and as he glanced to windward he observed the bright sparkling foam leaping upward from the fast increasing breeze.

"We shall do now, and may laugh at the rascals," he exclaimed: "in with the sweeps, we no longer want them. Bravo! the saints are in good humour with us. Ten candles to the shrine of our lady of the rock."

"And ten thousand curses on the villains who have killed three of our best men," added Diogo, frowning at the boats, in which expression he was cordially joined by the second mate.

Don Pepe, mindful of his gentility, jumped up on the taffrail, and making a polite bow with his hat, wished the enemy good-by. A few more shots were sent after him, but they soon fell altogether short of the schooner, and El Carmen bounded gaily on her way. The wind had come round a little more to the northward, so that she was now able to stand off shore; at the same time Don Pepe well knew that the British cruiser was not likely to give up the chase as long as she could keep him in sight, and the same breeze which was now filling his sails was also sending her along through the water. Every means, therefore, were used to increase the speed of the schooner, and as she was a very fast craft there appeared a good chance of her getting away from her pursuer—but alas! in this world, nothing is certain. Just as Senhor Diogo was in the midst of a jovial song, into which his spirits broke forth as the enemy's boats sank beneath the horizon, the look-out at the masthead hailed the deck, to announce a sail on the weather-bow.

"Diablo!" exclaimed Diogo, stopping short in his song. "What does she look like?"

"A square-rigged craft, I should say, but her royals are only just rising out of the water," was the answer.

"What's that?" asked Don Pepe, coming out of his cabin—a round house placed on the after part of the deck—into which he had gone to indulge in a siesta after the chase. "Another sail, do you say? whereabouts is she?"

The point was indicated by the man aloft. Don Pepe, after muttering a few carrambas and similar Spanish ejaculations, slung a spy-glass over his shoulder, and went aloft to scrutinize the strange sail himself. He came down again without saying a word, and then sent Diogo up to form his opinion.

"Well, what do you make of her?" he asked, as soon as the mate rejoined him on deck.

"A large brig, senhor; and, by the squareness of her yards and the cut of her canvass, I should say one of those accursed English cruisers which are playing the devil with our trade."

"Not a doubt about it, Diogo; and we shall have some difficulty in eluding her," observed Pepe, as he paced the deck with hurried steps.

"He has us fairly jammed in with the shore, and with the other vessel to windward of us; if we go about on the other tack, we shall have to encounter her, to say nothing of fighting the boats, which would be sure to cut us off, though we might easily manage them. What is to be done now, Diogo?"

"Stand on as we go," answered the mate. "The vessel from which we have escaped is an enemy, that's certain. This one may, after all, possibly prove a friend."

"She does not look like one," said Pepe.

"She is too big, I fear, to beat off with our guns," observed Diogo.

"What must we do then?" asked the captain.

"Trust to the saints," replied Diogo, crossing himself. "They have hitherto proved our friends."

The schooner, with a spanking breeze, was now slipping through the water at the rate of nine knots an hour at the least, running all the time parallel with the coast.

That the stranger did not intend to allow them to pass without attempting to overhaul them, the slavers were soon convinced by the course she was steering. Their only hope, therefore, of escaping her unwelcome supervision was, by their greater speed, or from some lucky shift of the wind. Should a breeze blow off the shore, which was not very likely to happen, they would then be placed to windward, and the stranger would have considerable difficulty in working up to them. They even longed for one of those black squalls, which sometimes come off the coast of Africa with terrific violence, rendering the air dark as midnight, but the sky over the land remained bright and clear as before.

They were steering nearly due south, and as the stranger's courses appeared above the horizon, she was seen to be keeping about south-east, which would, before long, bring her close up to them. It was pleasant sailing, the sea sparkled, the fish leaped up from their ocean homes, the woods on the low shore looked verdant, the sun shone brightly forth from an unclouded sky, the breeze blew fresh and pure over the watery space towards the west, but from the smiling land on one side arose pestiferous exhalations, and from the other came on the avengers of wrong and tyranny. A cleverer man than Captain Pepe might have been puzzled how to escape from the two.

"Is she a friend or a foe, think you?" he asked of his mate, who was scrutinizing her through his telescope.

"One of those cursed Englishmen, as I'm a Christian!" answered Diogo. "We shall know soon. Ah, he's signalizing us. There, up goes his ensign. I thought so; the tyrant flag of England."

"Then, by St. Jago! we must fight for it," exclaimed the captain.

Thereupon he made his crew a very neat speech, the purport of which was, that they would be made mincemeat of, and lose the profit of their voyage into the bargain, if they could not contrive to beat the Englishman or get away from him; that honour and glory were very fine things, but that discretion was a better; though, for his part, rather than lose his ship and cargo, he would blow the slaves, himself, and them, up into the air together.

On this, instead of giving three cheers, they all piously crossed themselves, examined the primings of their pistols, felt the edge of their swords, and saw that all the guns were well loaded. Every stitch of canvass El Carmen could carry was packed on her, and away she flew as fast as the breeze could impel her. It was evident, however, that those who guided the movements of the English ship of war had determined that she should not escape them, and, as they had the weather gage, the game was in their own hands. Nearer and nearer they drew to each other, till at last they came almost within range of each other's guns. The hearts of the Spaniards beat quick as, with firm-set mouths and stern eyes, they gazed at their opponent.

CHAPTER XVI.

PEPE'S ENGAGEMENT WITH THE BRIG.—HE SHOWS THAT HE IS A MAN OF SPIRIT.

THE British ship was the first to fire, but her shot fell short. Several other guns were discharged, in rapid succession, without doing any damage; at last one struck the schooner, and, piercing her side, fell among the unhappy beings confined below. The fearful yells and shrieks which succeeded almost unnerved the hard hearts of the slaver's crew, and, when another ball sent one of their number to his last account, they could no longer restrain their rage, but let fly their whole broadside at their opponent. It however did her little damage, and she was about to return the compliment, by raking them as she shot ahead of them, when they were just in time, by keeping off the wind, to avoid so dangerous a salute.

The wind by this time had shifted more to the southward, so the British ship still kept the weather-gage, and both vessels were now hotly engaged, running almost free directly upon the coast. The wind was increasing rapidly, and the sea was getting up. Several times was the slaver hulled by the shot of the brig, and each time arose the same fearful yells as before. At last one of her shot struck the fore-topmast of the brig, just above the cap, and the instant after, both it and the bowsprit being carried away, the vessel, deprived of her head-sail, flew up into the wind.

A shriek of delight escaped the Spaniards as they beheld the condition of their enemy; but they were quickly silenced, by finding that their own condition was little better; for their own mainmast, already wounded severely, pressed by the spread of canvass they carried, notwithstanding the increasing gale, was seen to totter, some of the weather shrouds had been shot away, and a heavy send of the sea carried it fairly away close to the deck, when falling overboard, it towed alongside by the lee rigging.

Thus, in a short time, were the two vessels reduced to almost complete wrecks, while a lee-shore, towards which they were driving, appeared within four or five miles of them, threatening them with destruction. There was enough, indeed, to make a stout heart quake. A heavy sea came rolling in across the broad Atlantic, the dark green waves topped with white crests of foam, while a heavy surf dashed on the low sandy shore; each huge billow, as it broke with a loud roar, threatening to carry back in its reflux anything which might get within its influence.

The brig of war, notwithstanding her shattered condition, seemed determined not to be balked of her prey; for while some of her crew were cutting away the wreck of her foremast, getting up a jurymast, and securing the mainmast, the rest were working the guns as they could be brought to bear, many of the shot from which struck the schooner—the wild tumult of the waves, and the roar of the wind in the rigging, being now added to the shrieks of the miserable blacks, who were thus unresistingly slaughtered. While thus desperately fighting, the two vessels drove together towards the shore.

It must be confessed, that Don Pepe did not like the state of affairs, and, mild-tempered and amiable as he generally was, as he stood issuing the necessary orders, he turned many a fierce look towards the vessel which was driving him on to destruction, and vowed that, if he escaped with his life, he would be revenged on her and all which sailed under the same flag. Even after the mainmast had been cut adrift, it was found impossible to bring the schooner again on a wind, and their only hope now of not going on shore consisted in riding out the gale at anchor. A very poor one it was, for, of course, the brig would anchor also, and do her best to sink them.

Just as they were preparing for this desperate alternative, Diogo reported that he perceived the mouth of a small river, directly ahead of them, and pronounced it to be one with which he was well acquainted.

"There is not much water on the bar," he observed, "but if we keep in mid-channel we may drive over it, and once inside we are safe."

The two best hands were, therefore, sent to the helm, while Diogo went forward to con the vessel towards the narrow entrance. Every man on deck held his breath as they approached the wild, broken water, for they well knew the awful risk they were incurring, but few thought of the human beings crowded below, who had not a chance of escape should they strike. The shot from the enemy still pursued them, but did no further damage; and almost to their disappointment they saw the brig haul up to the wind, and then finding that she could not beat off, let go two anchors.

"She drifts, she drifts!" exclaimed Pepe, with exultation. "She will be driven on shore, and then we shall have our revenge."

But Senhor Pepe was mistaken, for by the time the cables were veered out the brig brought up and rode buoyantly to the gale. The slavers had enough to do to take care of themselves. The prospect ahead, as has been observed, was not tempting. In the distance was a dark forest, low mangrove-bushes lined either side of the stream, the shore exhibited a dreary expanse of sand, and they had good reason to know that amid those raging billows many a hungry shark was likely to be sporting, ready to make a feast of them should they be compelled to swim for it.

"Starboard the helm," sung out Diogo, from forward; "so, steady. We stand well for the deepest water."

"Every man hold on," cried Pepe, grasping the stump of the mainmast; but the warning was scarcely required, for all the crew had secured themselves in the best way they could.

The schooner approached the bar. She was amid the wild foaming waters. A mountain wave came rolling in with a loud roar, her stern lifted high in the air, and she seemed about to slide down into the deep gulf before her, but the wave advanced, and she rose again with her bow now aloft; before she was again on an even keel, another came on foaming and raging; it struck her, and flying over her resisting frame, deluged her decks. A cry of terror and despair arose from the crew, and two of their number were carried far away from all help; but the vessel still careered onward, floating amid the boiling waters. Another minute of dreadful suspense passed, and she had escaped the dangers of the outer bar; but a second one was before her, which she must pass before she could be in safety. A few fathoms of comparatively tranquil water intervened. She drove on towards it; the sea twice broke over her, a terrific squall struck her, and before she could let go her anchors she was cast upon the muddy shore, and the remaining mast went by the board, killing several of the crew by its fall. The remainder were too well pleased at finding themselves in comparative safety to think much about them, but they had yet no easy task to get themselves and their human cargo on shore. One boat alone remained, and lowering her on the lee-side, they opened the hatches to get up some of the blacks to carry on shore. Even Pepe shuddered as he looked below, for so many shot had hulled the schooner, that her crowded slave-deck was a complete shambles, the dying and the dead mingled amid the living. The survivors raised a loud cry as the first were taken up, fully believing that they were about to be murdered in detail; while even the Spaniards could scarcely bear the dreadful effluvia which arose from the revolting mass of humanity.

Some little way inland was a large hut, built expressly for the reception of slaves ready for embarkation, and here, after some time, the unfortunate survivors of the blacks, landed from the schooner, were collected together. Too stupified to consider or care what was next to happen to them, they sat down on the ground, where most of them forgot their griefs in sleep, while the Spaniards kept watch outside.

By the time all these arrangements had been made, night had come on; but the rest which visited the slaves was denied to their masters, for no sooner did they light a fire to cook their suppers, than several persons were seen approaching from among the trees. The chief of the new comers announced himself as King Bobo, sovereign of the surrounding territory. He was habited in a cocked hat with a feather, and half of a petticoat thrown over his shoulder as a royal mantle; while his attendants, if not so strikingly, were more simply dressed in every variety of garment, few, however, boasting more than one article each. After a long harangue, which was highly applauded by his attendants, King Bobo demanded by what right Captain Pepe had landed on his territory, and taken possession of his storehouse? Don Pepe, whose temper had been somewhat ruffled by the attack of the English, answered briefly by pointing to his gun, and intimated that if his sable majesty did not quickly take his departure, he would hasten his movements. On this, King Bobo looked very indignant, but observing something dangerous in Pepe's countenance, soon brought his palaver to a conclusion, and, followed by his subjects, hurried off into the woods. Diogo, who knew the blacks well, warned his captain that it would be necessary for them to be on their guard, but the night passed away without their receiving any further visits. The Spaniards had cause to be uneasy, for they were aware of the treacherous character of the blacks of that neighbourhood, and, as they had been obliged to divide their forces, they felt that they should have some difficulty to defend themselves should they be attacked. Part of the crew, we ought to have remarked, had been left to watch the schooner, to protect her from being plundered, while the rest guarded her living cargo.

The storm had subsided as rapidly as it had commenced, and when the morning broke, not a cloud obscured the blue sky; the wind had gone down, the sea had grown calm, and the surf no longer broke upon the strand with the loud continuous roar it had hitherto done. Suddenly the party who were guarding the hut were startled by the report of a musket fired in the direction of the schooner. Others followed in quick succession. They leaped on

H

their feet, and grasped their arms, when Pepe, ordering four of his men to follow him, set off towards the spot.

We must now return to the British brig, which we left at anchor off the coast. She rode out the gale in beautiful style, and at daybreak was ready to make sail for the nearest port, where she could hope to find a new mast. Not a breath of air, however, was blowing, so it was impossible to weigh the anchors. As the officer of the watch walked the deck, thinking what had been the fate of the people on board the schooner they had driven on shore the previous day, he observed the mist gradually clearing away over the land. At last he stopped in his walk, and turning his spy-glass towards the coast, he surveyed it narrowly. As he did so, it struck him that there was an indentation, very like the mouth of a river, almost abreast of them, and, looking still more attentively, he made out the hull of a vessel, which he could have no doubt was the schooner. Having satisfied himself of this, he sent down to inform the captain.

"Not a doubt about it!" exclaimed Captain Hownslaw, rubbing his hands. "We'll have the rascal before the day is many hours old, and punish him for the mischief he has done us. Call the boats away, Mr. Snubbem; or stay—let the boats' crews have their breakfasts first."

The men were not long in laying in their provisions; and, under the command of the first lieutenant, an eager party, in three boats, was soon pulling towards the shore.

As they neared the land, they found a heavy surf breaking over the bar at the mouth of the river, and for some time even their brave leader hesitated about advancing; but the sight of the enemy's vessel increased their eagerness—and what daring deeds will not British seamen undertake when their spirits are aroused. After pulling some way along the wall of white breakers, a narrow clear line of water was perceived, and dashing through it amid the wild tumult of the waves, they were quickly again in safety. The second bar was likewise crossed without a casualty, and giving three cheers, they pulled towards the schooner.

Thus far not a sign of an enemy had appeared, but as the sea on the outside was still breaking over her, they pulled round her head and stern to board her on the inside. The bowman of the leading boat had just hooked on, when they were saluted by a hot fire from an enemy hid among the trees, but no one was wounded; and on leaping on board they found the deck of the schooner deserted. When it was also ascertained that not a black or a Spaniard remained below, and that there was nothing to be done, the commander of the expedition quickly ordered the crews into their boats again. In half a minute the English were scrambling up the mud banks to drive their concealed enemies from their ambush, with loud shouts vowing vengeance against them for their cowardice in not daring to show their faces.

In the mean time, Captain Pepe and his party were hastening to the assistance of their comrades. As he was hurrying on, he caught a glimpse of the sea through an opening in the woods, and there, floating calmly at anchor, he beheld the brig which had chased his schooner on shore.

"It is those cursed Englishmen again," he exclaimed; "on, my friends, and let them feel the temper of Spanish steel."

The execrations of his followers against the British, satisfied Don Pepe that they were in a right humour for the work in hand, and before many minutes had passed they reached the scene of action. They found their friends posted behind a bank naturally formed by the force of the waters of the river, while the attacking party were endeavouring to cross the space of soft mud which intervened between them. Pepe, at a glance, took in the position of affairs, and saw that if his people behaved with coolness the day might yet be his. Ordering each of them to pick off his man, he gave the word to fire, but after the exertion of running, or from their too great eagerness, their aim was unsteady, and two only of the English fell. This also served to inflame the rage of the rest, and, encouraged by their gallant leader, before the Spaniards had again time to load, they extricated themselves from the mud, and, with cutlass in hand, rushed up the bank.

"Fire, fire!" cried Pepe, as the Spaniards were hurriedly loading.

An irregular volley was discharged, which did no further damage than sending a ball through the lieutenant's cocked-hat, and the slaver's crew were compelled to throw aside their muskets and defend themselves with their swords. They now showed themselves to be true men, and fought as bravely as lions. The two parties were well matched, in point of numbers and courage, and the combat was long and furious. It seemed doubtful how it would end, for several on both sides had fallen, when one of the Spaniards, who had been left to guard the slaves, was seen running towards them, shouting loudly to his friends.

"Carramba!" shouted Don Pepe, "they are of more consequence than fighting these bull-dog Englishmen;" and uttering a few words to his men, which the British did not understand, the Spaniards simultaneously leaped down the bank, and, dispersing in all directions, fled through the woods.

The English, as soon as they had recovered from their astonishment at this proceeding, of course followed, but near the bottom of the bank they found themselves in front of a deep bog, through which it was impossible to wade, and while they were looking about for a passage to pass round it, the Spaniards had already got out of sight. Though burning with anger at the loss of so many of his men, the English commander saw that he should only expose his party to still greater loss by following the enemy, for, as the latter were evidently well acquainted with the country, they had the advantage of him in that respect, and had also, in all probability, formed some plan to lead him into an ambush.

Most unwillingly, therefore, he ordered his men to return to the boats, which they did with some difficulty, carrying their wounded comrades in their arms. The two who had fallen in the mud were past all aid, and when the party returned, they found them already almost covered up in the black compound. As soon as the boats were reached, the lieutenant determined to endeavour to get the schooner afloat, but on examining her condition it was found impracticable to move her, so firmly imbedded was she in the mud. One course only remained, and Pepe's fine schooner was consigned to the flames. This work accomplished, the British recrossed the bar in safety, and returned to their ship, when, soon afterwards, a breeze springing up, they made sail for Sierra Leone to repair damages.

We must now return to Don Pepe. The information brought to him while he was engaged with the English was, that the few Spaniards who had been left to guard the slaves had been attacked and overpowered by King Bobo, who was then busily engaged in carrying them off.

Now it must not be supposed that his sable majesty was influenced by any philanthropic motive in liberating his fellow-countrymen; but having undertaken to furnish a certain supply of blacks to a slave dealer located some miles to the south, he was honestly anxious to fulfil his engagement. This information induced Pepe wisely to retire from a combat in which only honour and glory were to be gained, to protect property which he valued so much more.

As soon as he and his followers had assembled, they hurried towards the hut where they had left the slaves, and as they approached it their ears were saluted by the sound of drums, mingled with the shouts and cries of great numbers of human voices.

Advancing a little farther on, they perceived a concourse of people assembled, with arms of various descriptions in their hands, and in front of them stood King Bobo, exciting their courage by an harangue which they, every now and then, interrupted to give expression to their sentiments, by the sounds the Spaniards had heard. Pepe, on this, halted his party to prepare to engage the blacks if necessary, and having examined their arms, they again advanced boldly towards them. This at first somewhat staggered King Bobo and his subjects; but being a brave fellow, he did not shrink from the spot where he stood. This example encouraged the rest, and even Pepe judged it would be more prudent to hold a palaver before proceeding to hostilities. His sable majesty was the first to speak, by demanding why the Spaniards had landed on his territory, and had, without asking leave, taken possession of his hut. The only answer Pepe could make to this was, that he had landed very much against his will, and that as he found the hut unoccupied, he had made use of it to shelter his slaves.

"And I," replied the king, "as you could not take care of the slaves, have taken care of them for you. They are now free men, and have gone off to their homes. You, shall, however, have the use of the hut, and I will supply you with provisions till you can return whence you came. Your ship is ours, so you must not go near her again. Now you may take possession of your house."

At this the Spaniards felt not a little foolish, for they had been completely outwitted by the blacks, but there was no use expostulating, for every one of the slaves had been carried off, and there was, therefore, nothing left to fight about. King Bobo now drew off his people with the intention of plundering the schooner, but no sooner had they gone than the Spaniards perceived a thick smoke rising in the direction where she was. This was followed by the report of several guns, succeeded by a terrific explosion, which shook even the ground on which they stood.

"The El Carmen has blown up," exclaimed Diogo. "That was her death wail, and those accursed Englishmen have done it. I hope King Bobo and his blacks had time to get on board first and bear her company to heaven."

This charitable wish had not been accomplished, for in a few minutes his majesty and his army came running back in great consternation at the catastrophe which had occurred. Had the Spaniards seized their opportunity they might have revenged themselves on the blacks, but they had enjoyed fighting enough for one day, and besides, as Pepe moralized, there was nothing to gain by it. Poor Don Pepe had certainly been the greatest loser by the events of the last two days. He had lost a number of his crew, he had been robbed of his slaves, he had now lost his ship, and found himself surrounded by enemies, without any immediate prospect of escape, while he was dependent, too, upon them for wherewith to support existence. Braver men might have succumbed beneath so many difficulties, for although twenty of them remained alive, their ammunition was nearly exhausted, and they could scarcely hope to succeed in fighting their way to the nearest river, when they might expect to find some vessel to take them off. Diogo was the only man who knew anything of the country, and he reported that about fifteen leagues to the southward there was another river, resorted to by slavers, and also by merchantmen, who went there to load with palm oil and ivory.

After some consultation it was determined forthwith to proceed thither, and, for the purpose of being allowed to travel in safety, to propitiate King Bobo and the neighbouring potentates by as large promises as they could be induced to receive. The next morning, matters being amicably arranged with the king, they started on their journey; and whether twenty stout fellows with muskets on their shoulders, or the promises they made, had most effect on the minds of the blacks, it is difficult to say, but certain it is that at last the whole party reached the neighbourhood of the Danda river in safety. Here the greater number remained concealed, while Pepe and Diogo went down to the banks of the stream to reconnoitre. The first object which met their eyes was a fine schooner lying at anchor in the centre of the river.

"What can she be?" asked Captain Pepe.

"An American slaver or an English merchantman," answered Diogo.

"Suppose we venture on board and learn," observed Pepe.

"Agreed," said Diogo; "but how are we to get on board?"

After looking along the shore for some time, they observed a canoe at a little distance off with two blacks in her, fishing.

On this, Pepe held up a dollar and intimated that he wished to be taken on board the schooner. The blacks soon understood him, and in a short time the two Spaniards stood on the deck of the Fair Rosamond, one of the finest traders out of Liverpool. They found that one half of the crew had died of fever, many were ill below with the same complaint, and that she had barely hands to navigate her home. On this, Pepe framed his own story. They were Spanish seamen, who had escaped from a vessel wrecked on the coast, their shipmates, with the exception of one, were all dead, and they were anxious to get off in any craft which would take them. The English master, an unsuspicious, honest seaman, at once gladly offered to ship them, and they promised to join him on condition that they might return to bring off their sick shipmate.

"Of course, of course," answered Captain John Brown; "I think all the better of you for it. You shall return when you like, and please God we'll get out of this cursed hole by to-morrow morning at daybreak, if the weather holds fine."

"All goes well," whispered Don Pepe to his lieutenant, as they pulled on shore in the canoe. "By to-morrow morning we shall have again a craft of our own, and then we will have our vengeance on the English."

The captain did not look amiable as he uttered these words, but Diogo rubbed his hands and grinned with satisfaction at the thought of what they were to do.

Towards the evening, the two new hands returned on board the Fair Rosamond with their sick companion. The latter was carefully placed in a hammock below, while Pepe and Diogo set about the duties allotted to them with praiseworthy alacrity.

"I wish we had a few more hands like these fellows," observed Captain Brown to his mate. "It isn't often one finds Spaniards as smart as they are."

"They are smart enough, sir," answered the mate; "but the big one seems a mighty fine gentleman for a foremast-man, and I don't altogether like the looks of the little chap."

"Well I don't see anything suspicious about them," observed the captain.

"I don't say there is, sir," said the mate; "only I don't quite like them. I wouldn't wish to wrong any man, but do you know, sir, that when their sick shipmate came on board with them, it struck me that he looked no more ill than you or I do. When I passed his hammock just now he was pretending to be asleep, and snoring as loud as a sou'wester, which, if he were down with the fever, he wouldn't do, depend on it."

"Well, I hope there's nothing wrong," replied Captain Brown; "but keep a good watch on them, and as there are only three of them, they can't do us much harm, I should think."

"Ay, ay, sir," answered the mate, "depend on me for that."

This conversation took place in the evening, just as the first watch was set in which the two volunteers were placed. The watch below, wearied with the exertion of bending sails and getting the ship ready for sea with so few hands, were fast asleep in their hammocks. The captain had turned in, and the first mate kept the deck. The night was somewhat dark, for though the sky was clear, and the stars shone brightly forth overhead, there was no moon, and a thin mist rising from the river screened all objects at a little distance off. Pepe and Diogo were leaning over the bulwarks forward, and conversing in a low tone which served, it seemed, to afford them infinite satisfaction. The mate walked uneasily up and down the deck, keeping his eyes wandering on either side, while his ears were also broad awake to detect the approach of an enemy. Suddenly he was startled by a slight splashing noise which sounded like the dip of numerous oars in the water. He listened attentively and endeavoured to pierce the obscurity, for his suspicions were aroused, and he had during that day been oppressed with a presentiment of coming ill, though from what quarter it might arrive he knew not. The noise continued, till at length he was certain that he heard the regular fall of oars.

"There's mischief abroad," he muttered; "I'll rouse up the captain, and arm the people. These black rascals are traitorous, and I don't like the Spaniards."

At the same moment, he dived below to awaken Captain Brown, to whom, in a few words, he explained his fears, and again sprang upon deck. As his glance fell upon the water, he perceived three large canoes close aboard of the schooner, and, directly confronting him, stood the tallest of the Spanish strangers.

"What do these boats want here?" he asked.

A blow from a handspike, which laid him senseless on the deck, was the answer; and, before any of the English crew had time to defend themselves, the canoes ran alongside, and twenty Spaniards climbed up the sides of the schooner. The cry of some of the crew who were cut down, aroused the pretended invalid below, and, leaping upon deck, he joined his comrades. When, therefore, poor Captain Brown made his appearance, he found his vessel in possession of a set of villains, and himself a prisoner. At first, the Englishmen, prompted by their nature, attempted to resist, but they were soon overpowered: and now Don Pepe had an opportunity of exhibiting the magnanimity and generosity of his temper. Politely bowing to the unfortunate master, whom some of his followers had bound to the main-mast. he apologized to him for the necessity he had been under of depriving him of his command, and explained to him that if he and his people would quietly go on shore, their lives would be spared, but if not, he should be under the necessity of giving them as food to the alligators and sharks.

"But we shall all die of the fever on shore," urged Captain Brown.

"Patience, my friend; it would have been our fate had we remained," replied Captain Pepe, and his argument was irresistible.

Two or three of the Englishmen had been murdered by the blood-thirsty Spaniards before Pepe had time to put an end to the slaughter. The master and his mate, who soon recovered, were treated with every attention which circumstances would allow, and as the morning dawned he ordered them with the rest of the crew, who were bound hand and foot, to be put into the canoes which remained alongside, and to be taken on shore. This done, a favourable breeze having sprung up, the sails were loosened, the anchor was hove up, and Diogo, acting as pilot, the Fair Rosamond, under the command of her new masters, stood over the bar. Don Pepe's heart bounded with satisfaction, as he once more found himself the owner of a fine well-armed vessel, with abundance of provisions on board. That she was not very honestly come by was a matter of perfect indifference to him.

"Viva a liberdad!" he exclaimed; "our necks, through the tyranny of mankind, are in jeopardy of a halter. There's no use concealing the fact from ourselves, and so I propose that we take good care to merit it. Every man's hand will be against us, but if we are true to each other, they may try to catch us in vain, and while we lead a roving, jovial life, the wealth of the world may be ours to pick and choose from as we list."

"Viva, viva, our brave Captain Don Pepe!" was the unanimous answer to this harangue.

A code of laws and regulations he drew up were signed without hesitation by all hands. A black flag was hoisted, and a salvo fired in honour of it; and thus Don Pepe became an open and avowed Pirate.

CHAPTER XVII.

HOW PEPE BECAME A BENEDICT.

A FINE ship was proudly sailing over the waters of the Caribbean Sea, with a favourable breeze, towards the Mona passage between the islands of St. Domingo and Porto Rico. Her last port was Cartagina, and she was about four days out. Although the John and Mary carried eight guns on her upper deck, half of them were non-combatants, for the simple reason that they were made of wood, commonly called "quakers," while her crew consisted of some twenty hands or so, including officers and boys. In fact, she aspired to no higher rank than that of an honest trader belonging to the port of Liverpool, whither she was now about to return, touching at one or two places on her way, after a successful voyage to the Spanish Main, having hitherto escaped all the dangers of tempests and robbers.

She might have measured about four hundred tons or more, and as she now carried studden sails on either side, alow and aloft, with her guns run out, she cut a very formidable appearance; so thought honest John Brown, her master. She had several passengers on board, both Spanish and English, and among the former was a young and pretty widow, with her still more youthful and lovely sister, a rich merchant, and a soldier, while most of the latter were mercantile men of different grades. Captain Brown was proud of his passengers, proud of his ship, and proud of the rich freight she bore.

It was a lovely day, the sea was smooth and sparkling, and the sun shone brightly forth from a blue unclouded sky. An awning, however, spread over the deck, sheltered the passengers collected there from his too scorching rays. How completely, on such occasions, people enjoy the *dolce far niente* of life. The crew were busily employed in the various sedentary occupations of seamen, while the gentlemen were lolling about reading or talking, and the ladies were writing, or singing to the music of a guitar. Captain Brown was earnestly recounting to an interesting audience some of the adventures of his life.

"It's now about two years ago when what I am going to tell you happened," he continued. "I then commanded a fine schooner trading to the coast of Africa, with the same man I now have as mate, honest Bill Simpson there. Well, we had been for some weeks in the Danda river shipping our cargo, and had lost nearly half our people by fever, when just as we were ready for sea, we were boarded by a set of rascally pirates, who turned us on shore, and ran off with our vessel. To be sure they might have murdered us outright, and so they would but for their captain, who was such a polite villain, that he made us a low bow instead, and wished us a pleasant trip on shore. I cannot tell you how I felt as I saw my vessel going over the bar, and I am very certain that I should have died had not another trader come in a few days afterwards and taken us on board. Well, from that day to this I have never heard anything more of the Fair Rosamond, though I have good reason to suppose that the pirate who got hold of her was no other than the famous Captain Pepe, whom everybody in the West Indies is talking about."

"What a dreadful man Captain Pepe must be," observed Donna Marina, who understood a little English.

"Dreadful! a regular devil incarnate, marm," answered Captain Brown.

"What is he like, Senhor Captain?" inquired Donna Isabelita, the widow's pretty sister.

"Like, marm! why he isn't a bad-looking fellow, as far as I can remember; about the same height and figure as the major there, I should say," answered the captain.

"Dear me," observed the young lady, "he does not look like a pirate."

"Perhaps not, marm," replied Captain Brown. "Beauty is only skin deep, remember."

"I should so like to see this far-famed Captain Pepe," said the widow.

"That's more than I should, marm, except at the end of a thick rope," answered the captain.

"Why, what should make us afraid of Captain Pepe, or a hundred pirates like him?" observed Mister Theophilus Fiz, a little Jamaica Creole, who, with a straw-hat on his head and in a suit of nankeen, was pacing the deck with his hands in his trousers pockets. "Haven't we got powder and shot and eight guns, with plenty of men to fight them? I should just like to see Captain Pepe trying to play off his tricks on us."

He elevated his voice as he passed in his walk near the Spanish major, who now looked up from a book of music he had been intently studying, and smiled. He now rose from his seat, and approached the ladies.

"Oh, major," said Donna Marina, laughing, "do you know that Captain Brown says that the famous pirate, Pepe, is very like you."

"A high compliment, truly, the captain pays me, if he refers to my personal appearance," replied the major, bowing. "For I have heard some ladies, who once were Pepe's guests, aver, that he is a remarkably handsome man, although his morality, it appears, does not stand very high in the estimation of the world."

"As to his good looks I can't say," struck in Mr. Theophilus Fiz, "but that he's a precious scoundrel I've no doubt, and I should just like to fall in with him and his craft to show him how I would treat him, the piccarooning rascal!"

"Senhor Fiz is a bold man," said the major, bowing.

"A sail broad on the starboard-bow," cried the look-out from the mast-head.

"Which way is she standing?" inquired the master.

"Across our bows," was the reply.

"We shall see more of her by and by, then," observed Captain Brown, as he continued his quarter-deck walk.

In the monotony of a prosperous voyage every incident is of interest, and the prospect of meeting a strange sail upon the world of waters is sufficient to arouse the most lethargic from their slumbers. The passengers, therefore, few of whom probably were in general much given either to physical or mental exertion, were eagerly looking out from the deck for the appearance of the stranger's sails above the line of the horizon. At last, one by one her top-gallant-sails, topsails, and courses rose as if from out of the water, shining like pure snow in the rays of the bright sun, and Captain Brown was soon able to pronounce her a large, square topsail schooner, but whither bound, or under what flag she sailed, it was impossible to say. There was something, however, in the cut of her sails which seemed to attract Captain Brown's attention, as he continually kept his telescope turned towards her, while his countenance wore a doubtful, if not an alarmed expression.

"That seems a valuable glass you have, Senhor Captain," observed the major, walking up to him; "will you permit me to test its powers?"

"Certainly, sir, certainly," answered the honest skipper; "you will find it not a bad glass, I flatter myself;—bought it myself—cost five guineas—one of Dolland's best—day and night—see a man's nose five miles off."

While the master was thus running on in praise of his glass, the major, who evidently was not attending to a word he said, had his eye for a few seconds intently fixed upon the stranger, and as he returned the instrument into the hands of its owner, a strange gleam might have been observed to pass over his countenance.

"Well, major, what do you think of her?" asked the master.

"I am too little of a seaman to form an opinion," was the answer. "I merely wished to try the power of your glass," and returning it with a bow to the master, he walked aft.

For some time longer the two vessels drew nearer each other without the stranger making any alteration in her course, and as she became more distinct, so the anxious expression of the skipper's countenance increased in intensity. First he rubbed the object-glass of his telescope, then he adjusted the instrument, then he rubbed his own eyes, but still he was not satisfied.

"Well, captain," asked Mr. Theophilus Fiz, "what is that vessel we see out there?"

"Why, sir," answered Captain Brown, "that's more than I can say. I don't like her looks, that I own; she's too rakish a craft to be honest, I fear. Like your high-flying beauties on shore, I've learnt to mistrust such-like ladies. Some of them are all fair and above board, and are as near real angels as I could wish any woman to be, both outside and inside. Perhaps, too, that schooner there may be a government vessel, or a fair trader, but she don't look like one, that's all."

"What does Mr. Simpson say about her?" asked Mr. Theophilus Fiz, with a slight degree of trepidation in the tone of his voice. The mate was at that instant approaching.

"Here, Simpson," said the master, "take the glass, and say what do you make out of that vessel?"

The mate looked long and steadily.

"Why, sir," he answered, "that she's as wicked, rakish-looking a craft as I ever saw afloat, and I shouldn't be surprised if she's one of the piccarooning villains that swarm about these seas, ready to pounce upon any vessel unable to defend herself."

"But do you mean to say that any pirates would venture to attack us when they see that we have eight guns on our decks?" asked Mr. Fiz.

"Perhaps no, and perhaps yes," was the unsatisfactory answer. "But wooden dogs can't bite, you know."

"What is that you are saying about pirates?" asked the rich merchant, who had just then come on deck. "I hope we've no chance of falling in with them. Mother of Heaven protect us from such an event!"

"What have we to fear with so brave a man as Don Fiz to fight for us?" said the major, smiling. "Besides, my dear sir, no pirate—if pirate yonder craft should prove—would dream of interfering with a ship like ours, armed with eight guns; nor can they be aware that we have so large a treasure on board, as I understand there is."

Don Fernandes started.

"Who says that we have treasure on board?" he asked, with alarmed countenance.

"Oh! it is the most advantageous way of remitting money to England just now; so I take it for granted that Don Fernandes would carry some of his gold with him, and every one knows that he is the possessor of unbounded wealth."

On this the major, who spoke, made the rich man a profound bow, though an acute observer might have seen a smile lurking about the corners of his lips and gleaming in his eyes.

"We'll show our colours, at all events, to prove that we are not ashamed of them, and try if the stranger will answer them," said the master; and, in a minute, the broad red flag of England was blowing from the peak.

Scarcely had it fluttered an instant in the breeze, before a similar ensign was shown by the stranger.

"All right!" exclaimed Mr. Fiz, rubbing his hands with satisfaction; "a friend, at all events. If she had been a pirate, we would soon have sent her to the bottom of the sea, however."

"If!" exclaimed the master. "A friend, indeed! You don't pretend to say what a man is made of by the colour of his coat? And how do you know that the fellow does not lie with his buntin' on purpose to deceive us? What do you say, Simpson?"

"Not a doubt about it, sir; and now I think of it, as well as I can judge at this distance, she's very like a Spanish schooner which was lying not far from us in Cartaginia little more than a week ago."

The master now took his mate aside, and consulted with him earnestly for some time. The result of their conversation did not transpire; but it very soon got noised about the ship that the schooner in sight was a pirate. That the captain thought she was so was soon evident, by his giving orders to prepare for action. The crew set about their duties with alacrity, as true British seamen always will when danger is at hand. Ammunition was handed up, the guns were loaded and run out—at least the four real ones were loaded, while the others looked equally formidable at a little distance; at the same time, the studden-sails, royals, and topgallant sails were allowed to stand, and every stitch of canvass the ship could carry was packed on her to increase her distance from the suspicious stranger. This done, the crew went to their quarters.

While these operations were going forward, the passengers exhibited the troubled state of their feelings in a variety of ways. Donna Isabelita wept and clung to her sister, who sat still with their eyes fixed on the strange sail; the rich merchant turned pale, and, with an expression of doubt and alarm on his countenance, dived into the cabin, where he remained some time among certain cases and packages; while Mr. Theophilus Fiz strutted about the deck, under the persuasion that he was the most important person on board, and, consequently, vapoured more furiously than ever, in a vain endeavour to hide his fears. The only person to whom the approach of the hostile bark appeared a matter of perfect indifference was the major, though he every now-and-then cast a glance towards her to ascertain her position, but immediately again returned to his music-book and guitar.

"Why, Senhor Major, you seem to take things very coolly," observed Mr. Fiz, as he passed him in his walk. "We shall want you to fight presently. I suppose you'll not object to do that?"

"Bah! not at all. I will take the wooden guns under my charge," was the major's answer, with a slight sneer in the tone of his voice.

"Let me tell you, it wont be a joking matter," said Mr. Fiz. "If we don't fight, we shall be captured by the pirates to a certainty, and have all our throats cut."

"Not if we consent to join the pirates. It is what I intend to do, if we are overpowered. Bah! those fellows lead a jovial life, depend on it. Ah, Senhor Fiz, you will make a dashing pirate!"

"I a pirate!" exclaimed Mr. Fiz, in a tone of horror. "What would my friends and acquaintances say, should they hear of it? No, Senhor Major, I have lived an honest man, and I hope to die one."

"Ah! you are no philosopher, I see, Senhor Fiz," observed the major, with a shrug of his shoulders, and a twirl of his moustache. "You will have to try your courage soon, depend on it."

While this conversation was going forward, notwithstanding all the efforts made to increase the speed of the ship, the schooner, with the British ensign flying, was gradually approaching her from the eastward. The ship's best point of sailing was nearly before the wind, or, rather, with it on the quarter; and to keep it there her course had been altered a couple of points, Captain Brown hoping thus to get well ahead of the schooner, and, perhaps, to knock some of her spars away before she could come to close quarters. She was now within the distance of a couple of miles, and neither in her hull nor rigging did she appear like an English vessel.

"We will soon see what she really is," observed Captain Brown. "Haul down our flag and hoist the Spanish ensign, Simpson, and, depend on it, the fellow will soon show other colours."

The captain was right, for no sooner were the colours changed than up went the flag of Spain from the peak of the schooner also.

"I thought so!" exclaimed the captain, as he again hoisted the British flag. "It shall never be said, however, that John Brown fought under any flag but his own. Whatever happens, don't give in till the last, for, depend upon it, we have little mercy to expect from the crew of yonder craft."

The seamen, with a cheerful shout, promised to do their best. The stranger did not again change her colours, and just then a shot from one of her guns came flying across their bows. A second followed, but went wide of its mark, and, as the missile left the gun, a black flag was seen flying from the peak of the stranger. There was now, therefore, no doubt of her character. The mate was as brave a fellow as ever stepped; but discretion, he thought, on an occasion like the present, was the best part of valour.

"Hadn't we better haul our wind, and, if we must fight, keep the weather gage; though, for my part, the less we have to say to yonder piccarooning craft the better?" he observed to Captain Brown.

"It's no use, Simpson," answered the master; "we've no chance of getting away without fighting, though we'll do our best for the sake of our owners and passengers; and I only hope if those piratical rascals come within range of the John and Mary's guns, they'll have cause to remember her as long as they remain unhanged."

The schooner came dashing on, looking so light and delicately formed that it seemed impossible she could have power to injure the stately ship. She still continued firing, but as her shot flew high no one on deck was injured, though the sails of the ship were more than once pierced, and now-and-then a brace or a topmast shroud was shot away, but were quickly again repaired. As she approached nearer, her shot told with more effect; while as far as

Captain Brown could judge, as yet not one from the John and Mary had hit her.

At last the master lost all patience, and, pointing one of his four guns himself, he fired. His eye followed the course of the ball, but he had apparently no better success than the rest, for not a rope was shot away—not a splinter was seen to start from the deck or sides of the schooner.

"Well, I can't tell what's in the guns that none of them do their duty," he exclaimed, turning away with vexation. "Simpson, do you try your hand as a marksman, and see if you can't clip that fellow's wings a bit."

"Ay, ay, sir," answered the mate, casting his eye along one of the guns; "I'll try and knock a feather out of him at all events."

He was as good as his word, for the ball struck the bulwarks of the schooner, and evidently committed some mischief. Her revenge, however, was complete, for, in return, the shot from her whole broadside came rattling among the masts and rigging of the ship. Down came her fore-topmast on the deck, and the slings of her main-topsail were shot away, while numberless other damages occurred.

Before the crew could clear away the wreck of the spars to work their guns, the schooner had fired two more broadsides with still more disastrous results. Shot after shot followed, till so complete a wreck did the ship become, that she could only be kept directly before the wind. Poor Brown was in despair, but still he encouraged his crew to fight on bravely. The passengers trembled with alarm, except the major, who looked calmly on as if the work going forward were an every day occurrence; and now-and-then he descended below to comfort the ladies, who had been conveyed there to be out of danger. Just as he got on deck he saw the schooner passing under the stern of the ship, while a man standing on her taffrail hailed in English to ask if she surrendered.

"Not while I've a gun to fight," returned Captain Brown.

"We shall see," answered the voice, as the schooner, putting up her helm, ranged up on the larboard side.

In a few seconds the bower-anchor of the schooner was hooked in the mainchain plates of the ship, and a savage band of pirates were climbing up her lofty side. One gun had been got over to that side, and was pointed down to the deck of the schooner. The major had been most assiduous in dragging it over and loading it. Captain Brown waited till the bulwarks of the vessels ground together. "Fire!" he exclaimed.

The priming blazed up from the touch-hole, but the gun did not go off. The mate primed it afresh, but it again flashed in the pan.

"Curses on the lubber who loaded that gun!" he exclaimed; and his brave fellows, without time to reload the gun, had to defend themselves from the impetuous attacks of the pirates.

Though the English fought bravely, they were soon overpowered by numbers, entangled as they were also by the spars and rigging which had fallen from aloft.

The major was the only person who took it coolly, for instead of attempting to defend the ship he retreated aft, and was detected by Simpson in heaving a rope on board the schooner to assist the pirates on board. Before the mate had time to punish him for his perfidy, the deck was won by the Spaniards, and the survivors of the English driven below.

The leader of the pirates was a tall, good-looking man. He had been the first on board, and had crossed blades with Captain Brown, whom he quickly disarmed and threw on the deck. There lay the poor master looking up at his captor, and expecting every instant to receive his death-blow, surrounded by the dead and dying of his crew, while the savage shouts of the victorious pirates sounded in his ears.

His captor, whose sword was uplifted ready to run him through the heart, seemed to be examining his countenance attentively. In another moment the poor master would have ceased to live, but at that instant some of the buccaneers dragged forward the rich merchant, Don Fernandes, and other prisoners, and the major appeared on deck escorting the two fair donnas.

"Here's a fat fellow, who seems lined with gold," cried the pirates, producing numerous gold pieces from various parts of the merchant's dress.

"Oh, Senhor Brown, Senhor Brown, save me, save me!" exclaimed Don Fernandes, wringing his hands. "Why did you not run away faster? They have robbed me of the little saving of my life, and I am a beggar."

"Ha, ha, ha!" laughed the major, but said nothing.

"Senhor Brown!" exclaimed the leader of the buccaneers, "I thought so. You are a brave man, Senhor Brown, and have fought your ship well; rise, your life is safe. It is no disgrace to be conquered by me, for learn that I am Pepe, the Pirate."

"Pepe, the Pirate!" cried all the passengers in concert.

"The handsome man who is so polite to the ladies," said Donna Marina, glancing her bright eyes at him.

"The dreadful scoundrel who cuts all the men's throats!" ejaculated Mr. Fiz, ready to sink through the deck with fright.

"The man who knows to a fraction the value of every cargo afloat," muttered Don Fernandes. "I am a ruined man!"

"He does not look as if he would do us any harm," murmured Donna Isabelita, clinging closer to the major's arm.

"Not while I am with you, my charmer," answered her gallant protector.

"Are you not the man, then, who ran away with the Fair Rosamond?" asked Captain Brown, as he rose to his feet.

"The very same, at your service, my friend. Necessity compelled me to deprive you of her," said the pirate.

"And now you have deprived me of another vessel!" cried the poor master. "I am an unfortunate wretch!"

"The fortune of war," answered Don Pepe.

Among the survivors was Simpson, the mate, though his head was tied up with a handkerchief, beneath which the blood was trickling down.

During this conversation the major, who, although held by each arm by the pirates, retained his admirable self-possession, was approaching the chief.

"What!" he exclaimed, "my old friend, Don Jose Montes Pepe!" and, rushing forward, he threw himself into his arms.

"Ah! do I see the gallant Major Mendez, who so nobly saved my life at the risk of his own?" cried Don Pepe.

"The same; and for his sake he now entreats you to spare the lives of the prisoners in your power."

"Say no more about it, your wish is granted," returned the pirate; "set their minds at rest on that score, provided no attempt is made to hide the treasure on board. Make them look sharp about it," he added, in a whisper, "for we sighted a strange sail this morning, and she may be, perhaps, an English man-of-war."

The honest mate had been excessively puzzled at this scene, till he remembered having seen the major heave a rope on board the schooner during the action.

"Oh, you scoundrel!" he muttered. "If you didn't come on board on purpose to betray us into the hands of the robbers, I'm a Dutchman."

"But," exclaimed the major, tearing himself away from his friend's embrace, "in my joy at seeing you I for a moment forgot to introduce the fair donnas under my protection. They both have considerable property in the Havanah," he whispered; "one is a widow, the other a spinster. The widow has her deceased lord's property besides. You take the widow, I will be content with her sister."

Having given his friend this information, he introduced him with all form to the senhoras, who returned his courtesy most graciously, and made up their minds that pirates were much abused and maligned individuals.

When Don Fernandes observed the high favour in which the major stood with the pirate, a gleam of hope crossed his mind, for that gentleman had been especially attentive to him from the commencement of the voyage.

"Oh, Senhor Major, in mercy's name intercede for me with these gentlemen, for they look as if they were about to hang me at once," he cried.

"Sorry for it, senhor, but I have no interest," answered the major; "your gold will avail more than my interference. The ladies are my only charge."

"Gold! gold! I have no gold!" exclaimed the terrified merchant.

"Ho! ho! ho!" was the only answer the major deigned to make. The work of pillage now began, while the master and his crew were lashed back to back round the masts, where they might see their property carried off by the freebooters. Directed by the active major, they were not long in discovering the money-chests of the merchant, which were forthwith transferred to the schooner, no one heeding the protestations and entreaties of Don Fernandes. While these operations were going forward, Don Pepe was paying the most devoted attention to the pretty widow, which she received with evident pleasure; and every now-and-then, as the major passed Donna Isabelita in the performance of his duties, he took the opportunity of pouring some soft words into her ear, which seemed far from disagreeable. A great change had taken place in the manners of that worthy; for instead of the indolent, phlegmatic soldier he had hitherto appeared, he now seemed an active, energetic seaman, whom the pirates implicitly obeyed—an alteration which did not fail to attract the notice of both Captain Brown and his mate. With grief almost amounting to madness, Don Fernandes had seen chest after chest of his gold go over the side, and now the pirates commenced loading the schooner with the lighter and more valuable part of the cargo. The luggage of the passengers of course was not spared, and even the persons of them were searched, to the great dismay of poor Mr. Fiz, who fully expected that it was preparatory to his being thrown overboard. At last, some trunks and boxes containing female gear were handed on deck.

"Oh, those are our trunks!" cried Donna Marina, as she saw them. "Where are they going?"

"On board my schooner," answered Don Pepe, with a profound bow. "They will be safer there than in this ship."

"Madre de Dios!—how dreadful!" exclaimed the widow. "But what are we to do, then?"

"Follow your trunks, lovely senhora," replied the pirate, with a tender pressure of the hand. "The Juanetta will afford you tolerable accommodation, and the attentions of a devoted slave must make up for all other deficiencies."

A smile was the only answer the fair widow made.

The major, as we will still call the pirate's lieutenant, now reported the schooner fully laden, and hinted that he heard strong indications among the crew of a wish to hang up some of the captives; and as he was speaking, some of them dragged aft poor Simpson, who had made a stout resistance to the last, while others seized poor Theophilus Fiz to execute as their first victim.

"The bloody-minded villains!" exclaimed Don Pepe, with an angry brow, as he rose from the side of Donna Marina. "They are never content except they are allowed to commit murder; but they shall not be indulged. What are you about to do with those men, villains?" he exclaimed, in a loud tone, which sounded in every part of the ship. "The first man who attempts to injure them shall die. How often, as to-day, have I not brought a prize into your hands?—how often have I not led you to victory? Without me you well know you could do nothing, and therefore I will be obeyed. Hear me then; let those men go free, and get every one of you on board the schooner."

The pirates, with sullen looks, but without answering a word, obeyed. When the crew of the boat alone remained, he, with his own hands, released Captain Brown.

"You are a brave man," he said, "and deserve to live. For your sake I spare the lives of all on board, on condition that every one promises never to appear as witnesses against me or any of my followers. Go and learn the determination of the rest."

"I am very certain all will agree," eagerly cried Mr. Fiz, who had overheard the speech; "don't we, Captain Brown? Thank you, Senhor Pirate. There's no use even asking the rest. I, for my part, will vow I never cast my eyes on you before."

I

While Captain Brown went round to notify the pirate's offer to his passengers and crew, Don Pepe took the hand of Donna Marina.

"Fair'lady," he said, "I am bound for the Havanah, and can offer you a quick passage; your property is already on board."

"I must not be separated from my baggage," she answered, looking towards the schooner.

"And you, sweet Isabelita, will you proceed in the ship?" said the gallant major, imitating his chief.

"I must not be separated from my sister," was the young lady's discreet answer.

As may be supposed, there were no dissentient voices to Don Pepe's proposal, and in another minute he and the major, with their fair charges and a black maid, were on the deck of the schooner, which stood away to the westward; the crew of the John and Mary were busily employed in repairing damages, while the ship continued on her course.

By daybreak next morning a sail was discovered, four or five miles off, on the starboard bow, standing towards them. When poor Fiz, who had just come on deck, heard of it, he was terribly alarmed.

"Oh dear! oh dear! this is the last time I am ever caught at sea," he exclaimed. "If it is another pirate, we shall this time be all murdered outright, and the ship sent to the bottom."

"I almost wish she may be," said poor Brown. "After all my losses I can never lift up my head at home."

"Oh, don't be down-hearted now," answered the little Creole: "I believe, if it were not for you, not one of us would have been alive at this moment, so depend on it, if we ever get home safe, we will make your losses up to you."

As the stranger drew near, she proved to be a sloop of war, with the flag of England flying from her peak, while the condition of the John and Mary explained what had occurred. When the sloop got within hail she was ordered to heave to, while a boat from the man-of-war boarded her.

"By your appearance we thought that you had been engaged with an enemy," said the lieutenant who came on board, "and I'll be bound it's no other than the very fellow we've been sent to look after, the notorious Pepe."

"All I can tell you is, that we were knocked about as you see; that we were robbed of every thing the pirates could carry off; but that, after we surrendered, no one was ill-treated," answered Captain Brown.

The officer having ascertained from some of the crew, who were not so conscientious as the master, the course the schooner had steered when she left them, after assisting them in getting somewhat to rights, returned on board his ship. The sloop of war then made sail in chase, while the John and Mary was allowed to continue on her course—Captain Brown considering himself very fortunate in not being detained to give evidence against the pirates if they should be captured.

CHAPTER XVIII.

A PLAN TO CATCH PEPE NAPPING, BUT HE IS FOUND WIDE AWAKE.

His Britannic majesty's sloop Sea-gull had now been out six weeks from Jamaica, cruising in search of Captain Pepe. She had fallen in with several vessels plundered by him, and had boarded numbers of others from whom she received information of his movements, but for some reason or other she had never been able to get hold of the bold freebooter. At last her captain began to suspect that he had been purposely misled, which was in reality the case. In fact, Pepe had agents, not only in every port, but on board every cruiser and merchantman in the seas, so that it was as difficult to elude his vigilance as to discover his movements. He has often been known to board a vessel, and, when pressed for time, to demand only certain chests and packages, which always proved to be the most valuable. He never shed blood if it could possibly be avoided, nor was he ever known to ill-treat the prisoners who fell into his hands, provided they made no resistance.

The commander of the Sea-gull was now in hopes of falling in with the pirate before he could get into port to dispose of his cargo. The sloop, therefore, stood away for St. Domingo, the coast of which island she ran down, speaking every vessel she met, but gaining no satisfactory intelligence of the pirate schooner. Sometimes, indeed, a craft answering her description was heard of, but if it were her, she always managed to elude her pursuer, or else the chase turned out to be some Yankee trader, or other peaceably disposed vessel. At last Captain Hesketts, the commander of the Sea-gull, was almost in despair of finding the cunning pirate, and vowed if he ever came up with him, he would blow him and his band of miscreants out of the water together, while the crew whispered among themselves, that the vessel they were so vainly looking after must be the Flying Dutchman, or one of those phantom barks well known to cruise over the ocean to lure mariners to destruction. Captain Hesketts was not a man to give up his object any more than the famed Vanderdecken himself. One evening, just at sundown, he sighted a large schooner standing for the coast of Cuba, to the south of which he then was. He fired a gun to bring her to, but to no effect, and not ten minutes afterwards, another vessel was seen going towards the same coast, a little more to the eastward. It was impossible to say which of the two it was the most advisable to chase, so he followed the one first seen.

All night the Sea-gull kept the chase in sight, beating up to the nor'ward, and at daybreak next morning she was seen close in to the Cuba coast. Just, however, as the sun arose, a thick mist came over the shore, beneath which, as it advanced, wafted slowly along by the land-breeze, appeared, shining brightly in the rays of the rising sun, the topsails of two vessels, three miles or so apart from each other. That one was the chase there was no doubt, while the other was probably the sail seen on the previous evening. A few minutes afterwards, however, it fell a dead calm, and the mist gradually settled down over the sea, obscuring the shore and the two vessels from the sight of the English. It was indeed provoking; but as probably both vessels were becalmed as well as the Sea-gull, her commander determined to send away the launch in search of the one last seen, while he followed the one he had chased during the night. The launch was accordingly lowered into the water, and, with a crew of fourteen hands, under the command of Mr. Brookes, the second lieutenant, sent away in the direction of the stranger. After pulling to the north east for about an hour, the mist cleared away slightly, and exposed, close aboard of them, the sail of which they were in search.

"Give way, my men, give way," shouted Lieutenant Brookes, "and the pirate will be ours in five minutes."

In less than that time they were alongside a low, rakish-looking schooner, but instead of any opposition being made as they sprang on board, they were received by a demure, puritanical-looking personage, who, in the nasal twang of a true Yankee, informed the officer that he was the master of the schooner Pilgrim, from New York, and asked the reason of their visit.

Lieutenant Brookes apologized for his mistake.

"You are a civil fellow, and deserve a civil answer," said the master of the Pilgrim. "Now, I guess it's Pepe, the piccarooning Spaniard, you're looking after. Well, then, about the end of the middle watch, last night, as we lay close in shore, we saw two boats come out of a creek right abreast of us. As they pulled close to us we gave them a shot over their heads, but they didn't like our looks, I calculate, so they went away back again in the very direction from which they came. Now, I guess they are some of the very chaps you are looking after; and if you want them, there you'll find them, as snug as rats in a hole."

Thanking the American master for his information, the English lieutenant returned to his boat, and pulled away towards the shore, in high hopes of capturing the renowned freebooter.

"Now, I calculate, some one will put his nose in a trap," muttered the Yankee skipper, as he squirted a stream of tobacco-juice in the direction the English had taken. "Well, that's no business of mine," and he continued his quarter-deck walk, whistling for a breeze.

The launch had got within a quarter of a mile of the shore, before any opening could be perceived, when, as the officer thought he must be mistaken as to the spot, he observed a narrow line of blue water running up between the trees which lined the very margin of the sea. "Give way, my boys, give way," he shouted; and in a few minutes the boat was threading a narrow passage, with rocks and trees on either side, leading into a broad lagoon. When, however, Lieutenant Brookes looked round the lake-like expanse, and saw not the sign of a vessel, he began to suspect that the American had deceived him; yet, before giving up the search, he resolved to examine the place to discover if there were any other inlets in which a vessel might be concealed. For this purpose they skirted round the shores of the lagoon, and had not pulled long, before they reached a thickly-wooded headland, on doubling which, they discovered the entrance of another lagoon. Not a sound, however, was heard, not a boat floated on the smooth surface of the lake, when, on a sudden, the solemn silence was broken by the sharp bark of a dog.

"There are persons concealed not far from here, depend on it," cried the lieutenant. "Give way, my lads, and if Pepe is among them, we'll carry him off a prisoner."

The persevering seamen, although fatigued by their incessant exertion, pulled up the channel for some little distance, till they reached a little bay or nook, where, at the farther end, almost concealed by the lofty trees, they saw a large schooner with a row of guns bristling from her ports, and boarding nettings triced up on either side. Without considering the disparity of force, they at once made a dash at the stranger. Not a soul appeared on deck, nor was the silence which reigned over the scene broken by any sound, till, as they were approaching near, a loud derisive laugh sounded in their ears, and a black flag was run up at each mast-head. The effect was startling, and sufficient to appal the stoutest hearts, but the seamen encouraged by their officer, quickly recovered their courage, and as they gave way again, uttering a loud cheer in answer, in an instant they were alongside of the schooner. As they climbed up the side of the vessel they endeavoured to cut with their tomahawks and cutlasses the boarding nettings, which formed a strong protection to the people within them. The brave lieutenant was the first to make a way through, but no sooner did he leap down on deck than a lasso was thrown by an unseen hand over his neck, and he found himself dragged rapidly over to the other side of the vessel, without the slightest power of resistance. At the same moment, from the hatchways, and from behind the bulwarks, from every spot where they could have been concealed, up sprang some sixty stout seamen or more, and with loud shouts and cries fell upon the English who had followed their leader. One after one, as they leaped down on deck, they were treated as he had been, till the whole party were fairly caught and pinioned. The more they struggled the tighter the ropes were drawn, and the louder they swore the more uproarious became the derisive laughter and abuse of their opponents. It was a very disagreeable position, and considering the sort of characters into whose hands they had fallen, not without a considerable amount of danger. Few men like to feel ropes round their necks—the Spaniards might at any moment be tempted to run them up to the yard-arms; and that such would be their fate their commander was convinced, from the fierce looks and expressions which passed among their captors. The one who appeared to be the captain of the pirate band, had hitherto not spoken, though foremost in seizing the British lieutenant. He was a tall, fine-looking man; his costume was rich and elegant, betraying the nautical dandy, with not a slight dash of the privateer. As he advanced towards the captive officer, he made him a bow of mock politeness.

"So, Senhor Tenente," he began, "you wished to pay us a visit it seems. It is thus we receive those who are unwelcome. Now dare say you expect to be shot, or hung, but you are mistaken, we are not butchers,—we must, however, give you a lesson you will not easily forget—not to put your head into a lion's mouth. You shall then be welcome to your boat, to find your way back to your ship as best you can."

"We are your prisoners, and you may murder us if you like; but depend upon it, if you do, you will some day hang for it," answered the lieutenant, who understood a little Spanish, and was enraged at the pirate's coolness; "and let me ask you who you are who dares to oppose the British flag?"

"I—I am Pepe, and care no more for the British flag than I do for my pocket handkerchief."

"Pepe! I thought so," answered the lieutenant; "and depend on it, if you are caught you will grace a yard-arm."

"Probably!" was the only answer, as the pirate turned away, and without further notice the Spaniards began belabouring their prisoners in the most unmerciful manner, though the officer escaped the same punishment, while the men swore that they would some day have their vengeance on the scoundrels. They were then led below, and compelled to perform all the most menial offices, with knives held at their backs to urge them on, and every now and then a pirate would prick his weapon into the flesh of his captive, to expedite his movements.

The lieutenant had remained on deck for some time ruminating on his fate, when he was roused by a pirate with a kick, and ordered to go below to wait at the captain's table. Brookes had no power of resisting, so he was compelled to obey What was his astonishment, however, on entering the cabin to find it ornamented in the most costly style, while at the table sat two young and beautiful women. At the head of the board was Pepe, and at the foot his quondam friend and lieutenant.

"We have sent for you to prove how well an Englishman can serve his masters," said the pirate, in a scornful tone. "Now take care that I am not deceived."

"In Heaven's name, do not resist," whispered one of the ladies, near whom the officer was standing. "It will make him furious, and the consequences may be fatal to you."

"I am in your power, and it would be madness in me to refuse," answered the officer. "Besides," he added, with a low bow, "when I serve ladies so fair as these it can alone afford me pleasure."

"Bravo!" exclaimed the pirate, clapping his hands. "An Englishman turned courtier. You deserve to be free at once. I only wished to prove you. You are a brave fellow, and shall sit down and join our feast. Here, Domingos, cast loose this gentleman's arms. Now allow me to introduce you to Donna Marina Montes, my lady wife, and to Donna Isabelita Mendes Pinto, the wife of my particular friend and lieutenant, Don Rodrigo Mendes. a lineal descendant of the celebrated traveller, Ferdinand Mendes Pinto, of whom you no doubt have heard."

On this name being mentioned up sprang our friend the major, for no less a person was thereby indicated, and, with a profound bow to the astonished lieutenant, handed him a seat. The ladies bent their heads gracefully and smiled sweetly, and in a minute afterwards the English lieutenant and the Spanish pirate were hob-nobbing at each other in the most amicable way possible. Pepe's mood seemed entirely changed. He laughed, talked, and joked; the ladies joined with spirit in the conversation, of which the major, or rather Don Rodrigo Mendes Pinto, monopolized the greater part. After the repast was concluded, Donna Marina and her sister, accompanied by the husband of the latter, took their guitars, and sang, till Lieutenant Brookes almost forgot where he was, and how he had lately been engaged.

"You little expected to find such a reception as we prepared for you on deck," said Pepe, addressing his guest, and laughing; "still less to see the manner we live on board. For much are we indobted to the ladies you see before you. That they were here you knew from my friend Captain Brown, of the John and Mary— Ha, ha, ha! He complained to you of our treatment of him, and gave you every information to discover us. I know all about it. Nothing escapes me—Ha, ha, ha!"

"It is the case," answered the lieutenant. "Your information seems boundless."

"Yes, you are right. There is not a vessel which sails on these seas of which I have not the most exact account, and scarcely a man-of-war either on board of which I have not a spy. Now, while you were looking for me in one direction, I took good care to be in another, and was well employed in visiting the Havanah, where my friend and I had the happiness of being united to our respective brides. Carramba! they are women of spirit, and instead of remaining quietly at home preferred coming with us to sea. What think you of that, Senhor Tenente! We are happy men, are we not?"

"Certainly, senhor, as long as you avoid the rope," answered the officer.

Pepe's brow grew black as night, and Donna Marina cast an imploring look towards the rash speaker.

"I may do something to deserve it yet," answered Pepe. "And those words may yet cost you dear. Here, Domingos, conduct this British officer on deck again, and let all his men be collected from below."

The order was instantly obeyed, and with scarcely time to bow to the ladies, who had evidently interested themselves in his fate, the lieutenant found himself again bound and standing on the deck of the vessel, surrounded by his men. Their boat was still alongside, but without sail, oar, mast, or spar of any kind. Without further ceremony their limbs were loosed, and they were ordered to find their way into the boat. She was then taken in tow by two of the pirate's boats, which at once pulled out towards the sea.

"What's going to happen now?" exclaimed one of the Englishmen. "The rascals are not going to take us out here to shoot us, I hope."

"More likely to cast us adrift, and let us float about till we are starved," said another.

"Silence, men," cried their commander; "you are still afloat in your own boat, and must not despair. Our ship will certainly be off here before long to look out for us, and I have every hope we shall be picked up."

The men said no more, but sat looking anxiously towards the pirates, expecting every instant to see them lift the muskets by their sides to their shoulders, and give them a quieting volley. On, however, they pulled across the lagoon through the outer passage, and at length cleared the land, directly out to sea. On, on they pulled, till even the pirates, hardy as they were and accustomed to the climate, began to weary. At last they cast off, and, with shouts of mocking laughter, returned to the shore. Leaving the English crew to their fate—death by hunger and thirst, with the most dreadful torments, was what they must expect if not succoured. For some time even the stoutest gave way to despondency, till they were aroused by the voice of their commander. A word from him cheered their spirits. He reminded them that they still had the means of sending the boat through the water, for that the pirates had neglected to take the bottom boards and thwarts out of the boat, or to deprive them of their clothes, while some still had their knives hanging round their necks. Under his directions they tore up the bottom boards and manufactured a spar—not a very stout one, but sufficient for the sail they could set upon it. With their shirts sewed together they formed a sail, while the linings of their jackets served to form ropes and yarns to strengthen their masts. The remainder of the bottom boards and some of the thwarts served for a rudder and oars. These preparations took them till dark, till when they were afraid to move lest the pirates should observe them. They then made sail in the direction their ship had gone—for the wind was fortunately fair—and paddling at the same time, by daybreak the next morning they had run many leagues along shore. They were afraid to pull very close to land, lest they might be observed by any other piratical bands; but they kept a bright look-out all the time for their own ship, in the hope that she might have put back to look for them. In vain, however, they toiled on, under a tropical sun, without a drop of water to quench their burning thirst; not a sail appeared dotting the smooth surface of the shining ocean.

One by one the men sank back, exhausted from their labour, but their officer urged them on by words of encouragement, taking his turn at the paddles with the rest. Even he, however, felt his strength decreasing, when, towards evening, as he was casting his aching eyes round the horizon, the white canvass of a ship, shining in the rays of the setting sun, met his sight, a little on the larboard bow. Their course was altered a point or so to meet her, but still the chances were very much against their being seen during the night, and even then she might not prove ready to succour them.

It was an anxious time; for the sun went down, and darkness rapidly covered the face of the deep, and, as yet, the ship was far distant. Soon the veil of night completely hid her. When last seen, however, she was, so far as they could judge, standing towards them, close hauled on the larboard tack, but a shift of wind might make her go about, and then to a certainty miss them.

The wind was so light, that neither she nor they could make much way through the water, and thus their anxiety was of necessity prolonged. At last the moon, to their great joy, rose above the waters, her pale beams falling on the white canvass of a ship, not half a mile ahead of them. They shouted, as if they could be heard at that distance. She steadily advanced towards them; again they shouted, and an answering cheer came down to their ears. They could not be mistaken, she was the Sea-gull, and in a few minutes they were on her deck, and receiving the congratulations of their shipmates on their narrow escape.

No sooner had Captain Hesketts received an account of the adventures of his lieutenant, than he determined at once to go in with his boats and attack the pirate. Fortunately for his purpose, the breeze freshened, and, long before daybreak, the Sea-gull was off the mouth of the lagoon where Pepe lay concealed. The corvette stood in as close as she could venture, when all her boats being speedily manned, they at once pulled in for the lagoon, led by Lieutenant Brookes, who, in spite of his fatigue, insisted on piloting the expedition.

In the most profound silence they advanced through the outer passage across the lagoon, and into the inner creek. In another instant they expected to be engaged with the formidable pirate, but, on rounding the point, the schooner was nowhere to be seen. They pulled to the head of the creek; not a sound broke the stillness of night, not a sign of any vessel appeared.

"He has shifted his berth to no great distance, probably, and we may still find him," observed Lieutenant Brookes.

The boats accordingly pulled round the lagoon into every creek and bay, and the sun was already high in the heavens before they had explored half of it.

They brought up for a short time to refresh the men, and then continued their labours, but in vain; not a sign was there of Pepe or his vessel.

Our hero, for so ought Pepe to be called, was not so quite green as the English supposed, to be caught in the way they expected; for no sooner had the boat full of prisoners got out of sight, than he ordered the cables to be cast off from the shore, and slowly warped the schooner towards the mouth of the lagoon. As soon as it was dark, he ran out and stood away to the eastward, while the English, as he calculated they would, were looking out for their ship from an opposite direction.

He thus easily got off unperceived, but, as he had appointed a rendezvous in a lagoon a day's sail more to the eastward, in order to dispose of the remainder of his cargo, before he returned to Havanah, he made the best of his way thither. The vessels he expected arrived at the same time, and, having given him gold in exchange for his various commodities, again took their departure. Pepe ought to have done the same, but Donna Marina was unwell, or unwilling, to go to sea that day, and Donna Isabelita wished to spend a longer time in the romantic spot where the vessel lay concealed.

It was a lovely evening, the heat of the day was cooled by a gentle sea-breeze, the tall and graceful trees, behind which the sun had just sunk, cast their shadows on the smooth waters of the narrow inlet out of which every instant leaped numerous fish, rippling its surface as they again fell into their tranquil home. The two ladies were seated on the deck of the schooner, their sweet voices accompanied by their guitars, while their husbands lay at their feet admiring their beauty and listening to their melody.

The pirates, after the work of the day was over, lay about the decks either asleep, or playing at cards, or narrating their adventures—the great resource of seamen of every age and clime. Discipline had become very slack of late on board; the ladies, it is to be feared, had something to do with it. A man had been stationed at the foretop-mast-head, to keep a look-out towards the sea; he had left his post, and had only just returned; with a sharp cry he aroused those on deck to sudden activity—

"Five boats pulling up the creek with the ensign of England flying at their sterns."

"To arms! to arms!" resounded along the decks. The pirates rushed to their stations, and their guns were loaded and run out.

"Lower a boat and carry the ladies on shore," whispered Pepe to his lieutenant. "We must not expose them to the work we have on hand."

The order was instantly obeyed, in spite of Donna Marina's entreaties to be allowed to remain on board.

"Who was stationed at the mast-head?" exclaimed the captain. "Come here. You did not give due notice of the approach of those boats. If we are captured, it will be owing to your negligence. Receive your reward." As he spoke, he levelled a pistol, and the man fell dead. "Let that be a warning to you, my men," he exclaimed, in a fierce voice. "We must have no further trifling, for depend on it, we have no mercy to expect at the hands of our enemies."

As he spoke, the boats were close aboard of them. "Fire!" he exclaimed, and the whole broadside of the schooner was discharged at the advancing boats. The iron shower did not stop them for an instant, but the crews, with loud shouts, sprang more vigorously to their oars. Many, however, were killed or wounded, and more than one shot passed between wind and water. In an instant they were alongside,—one boarding on the bows, another astern, and the seamen were scrambling up the sides of the pirate schooner. Nothing could withstand their fury, and the pirates knew what they had to expect, for among them they recognised their late captives. The struggle was fierce, for the Spaniards fought with desperation, but they were at length compelled to give way; many were cut down, some were driven below, but the greater number leaped overboard. The English seamen wished to follow them in their boats, but so well had the broadside done its work, that they were found half-full of water.

The pirate's late captives were the most savage; and as they were swimming for their lives, several were shot dead by the muskets of the marines. What had become of Pepe no one could tell. He might have escaped on shore, or been killed in the water. An empty vessel and a dozen Spanish prisoners was all that remained to the victors. When the leaks in the boats were stopped, and they were baled out, a few men being left on board to guard the prize, the remainder pulled on shore in search of the pirates who had escaped. They wandered about in every direction, but not a sign of them could they discover, and at length they were compelled to return on board the prize. She was got safe out, and the pirates were tried and hanged.

Some years afterwards, Lieutenant Brookes, then a commander, was ordered in his ship to look into the magnificent harbour of Havanah. While he lay there he was invited by a British merchant residing there, to make a short excursion into the interior. The first night they stopped at the house of the merchant, the next at a magnificent quinta, belonging to one of the most wealthy and respectable men in the island.

"He is rather an extensive dealer in slaves," observed the merchant, "but that is thought nothing of here. He has a charming wife, a lovely sister-in-law, and is one of the most courteous and hospitable men I know."

"By all means, let us pay him a visit then," said Captain Brookes.

The two visitors were ushered into a magnificent saloon with highly polished floors, and mirrors, for that was all they could perceive, as the thick blinds were closed to exclude the heat of the day. The owner of the mansion, a dignified, fine-looking man, of middle age, received them with the greatest politeness.

"Allow me to introduce you to my wife, Donna Marina Montes, and to my fair sister-in-law, Donna Isabelita Mendes Pinto."

The ladies answered courteously, and were evidently smiling. It was a pity they could not be seen. Captain Brookes fancied he recognised the voice of his host. At length the servants brought in a dozen or more wax-lights. Captain Brookes examined the countenance of his host more attentively.

"Pepe, the Pirate!" burst from his lips.

"The same," was the answer, "and happy again to have Senhor Brookes as his guest—ha, ha, ha!"

Captain Brookes vowed that he never spent a pleasanter evening in his life than he did in the mansion of the wealthy and respected planter, Don José Montes, the *ci-devant* Pepe, the Pirate.

CHAPTER XIX.

FURTHER PARTICULARS ABOUT DON JOSE MONTES PEPE, BY LIEUTENANT FAIRFIELD.

"I FANCIED that I recollected the name of Pepe when you mentioned it," I observed, when Green had concluded his narrative. "And now I remember all about our amigo. I also fell in with him when I was in the West Indies, and heard of him constantly. I am sorry to say, that Donna Marina has had as little success in reforming him as wives in general have in improving their rakish husbands. She has, however, perhaps made him more cautious, and, as he has run his head into one noose, he takes care to keep it out of another. If he is no longer a pirate, he is as great a dealer in slaves as any in the Havanah, and, it is well known, that his vessels commit a little quiet piracy whenever they have an opportunity, without fear of detection. He is said to be prodigiously rich, and to own more slaves than any one in the island."

"In fact, you would say he is a notable instance of the success of villany, and a shining example to all men to turn rogues," observed Haggis.

"Exactly, doctor. If there were not another and a better world, where we hope to moor ship at last, many a man might be content to bring up in the unsheltered bay, where Don Pepe has chosen to anchor," observed our good captain. "But, remember, he has bad holding ground; the wind may shift and drive him out to sea, without compass or provisions, or dash him to pieces on the rocks. When a villain is painted, that reflection should occur to every one. But you were going to give us an account of your adventures in the West Indies, Mr. Fairfield."

"I was, sir, and I will gladly do so," I replied. "I was at that time junior lieutenant of the Victor, brig-of-war. We had been cruising for some time in different parts of the Carribean Sea, when we at length returned to Jamaica. We had not long lain in Kingston harbour, when it was up anchor again, and we were ordered to make the best of our way to the Havanah. On leaving the island, we stood over to the Cuba coast, when, the wind coming off the land, we were able to lay our course to the westward. The evening was drawing on as we passed point Escondida, and by the time we were off the mouth of the bay of Guantanamo, it was almost dark. Guantanamo is a fine, deep bay, the shores are beautifully wooded, and highly picturesque, and there are besides numerous snug little harbours in it, where a vessel may be secure, either from the storms of heaven or from mortal foes.

"We'll just look into the bay, and see if, by chance, any slaving gentlemen are brought up there," said Captain Benham, our commander. "We shall be out again before dark. It never does to leave any spot unsearched; if you do, what you are looking for is sure to be there."

So we made a board over to the west shore, and then stood right up the bay. None of us, however, expected to find any vessel in there. We stood on for about a mile or so, when, as we opened one of the harbours I spoke of on the west shore, we observed a brig lying at anchor, with her sails loosened, just ready apparently to get under weigh. She had hitherto been concealed from us by a high point, thickly covered with trees.

"About ship," exclaimed the captain. "We must get alongside that fellow and overhaul him, for if he's virtuous I'm very much mistaken."

About we went, so as to keep outside of her, that she might not slip away, but, after making two or three short boards, it fell a flat calm, and there we lay utterly unable to move.

"Out boats," cried our skipper: "it will never do to wait here all night without paying that fellow a visit. Wilson," to our first lieutenant, "you will lead in the gig; Fairfield, do you take the pinnace. We will try to get up to you if there should come a breath of wind to help us along. Stay, however; first fire a shot, to see if the fellow understands good breeding, and will send a boat on board us."

The gun was fired, and the noise went reverberating among the rocks and trees which fringed the bay, but it drew no response from the stranger. We were all the time anxiously watching her with our glasses. We could make out that she was a large vessel, and pierced, apparently, for some six or eight guns on each side. We observed, also, a number of boats passing continuously between the brig and the shore.

"They have found out what we are, and are landing their slaves, I am afraid," said our captain. "Bear a hand and get the boats ready, my lads; we must put a stop to that."

The boats were soon in the water, for every man worked with a will. Wilson leaped into his boat and shoved off, and I followed in the pinnace. Our crews gave way in style, and the ship's company cheered as we left the side. We went through the water at a tremendous rate, and soon reached the mouth of the smaller harbour, in which the brig lay. When thus far, we opened another point, and, as we did so, the masts and spars of a large schooner came into view. There was just sufficient light for us to see the Spanish ensign run up at her peak. Before we had pulled many strokes farther, a shot from the schooner came flying over our heads.

"What can this mean?" I thought. "She does not take us for a pirate, I suppose. Perhaps she is one herself."

"That ere football was plaguy near," said Tom Harding, the coxswain of the pinnace. "The sooner we gives them chaps as sent it the taste of our cutlasses the better for us, my bo's."

He had scarcely spoken, when a whole shower of shot came hurtling through the air, and dashing up the water on every side around us. One came so near, that it actually sent the spray over us, and went skipping on a long way astern of us. Wilson waved his hand for me to follow, and on we dashed with greater energy than before. There is nothing like the sound of firing in their ears to make British seamen hurry on to the place whence it comes.

As we advanced, however, the schooner could not fire at us without running a chance of hitting the brig. The latter vessel had not all the time fired a single shot. This seemed very strange, and I could not account for it. The brig lay with her head towards the shore. Not a soul could we see on her decks. Wilson pulled up on the port side—I boarded on the starboard. We expected to be saluted with a shower of shot and grape, but to our surprise not the slightest opposition was made. We sprang upon deck at the same moment, and as we did so we distinguished some of the brig's crew tumbling in a tremendous hurry down below, evidently expecting that we should cut them to pieces. I suspect that if our people had got at them, they would at all events have broken their heads, for they were very justly in a great rage at having been fired at by her consort, for such we supposed the schooner to be. The brig was a very large vessel, nearly three hundred tons, I dare say, and was, moreover, strongly armed with a long swivel-gun amidships, and six long nines. This puzzled us still more to know why she did not attempt to defend herself, for if her guns had been well worked, she might have sunk both our boats. Here we were, masters of the ship. We accordingly looked down the hatchways, and summoned the crew to appear before us, not, however, without some suspicion that they might fire at us from below, or play us some cowardly trick. At last, after bawling at them for some time, a fellow made his appearance with a lantern in his hand, followed by several others in the usual dress of Spanish seamen. Among them I observed one on whose coat some gold lace was glittering.

"Hillo, who are you, sir?" I exclaimed, catching hold of the gentleman. "Come forward and show yourself."

"Sono aspirante de Marinha," he answered, in a terrible fright, lest I should cut him down.

He meant to say that he was a Spanish midshipman, but what business he and his crew had on board that vessel we could not tell, till he contrived to explain to us that she was a prize captured by the schooner, which schooner was a Spanish man-of-war.

"Tell that to the marines," said Wilson. "She is some rascally pirate, or she would not have fired at us. We'll, however, overhaul the vessel, and see if we can make out more about her."

We accordingly made the Spaniards understand that we wanted all the lanterns they could muster, and when they were brought, while Wilson kept the deck, I went below to examine the ship throughout. The crew looked very vindictively at us as we passed, but I also thought that I could distinguish a derisive smile lurking in the corners of the mouths of most of them. I had soon convincing proofs that she was a slaver, outward bound. Her hold contained a large assortment of printed cottons of gay colours, to barter for slaves; a large copper cauldron to boil the farinha, the food on which they are fed, and, besides that, abundance of planking to form the slave deck. I reported what I had seen to Wilson on my return on deck.

"She is a slaver, there is no doubt of it," he observed. "And I suppose the story of the Spanish midshipman is true. However, take the jolly boat, and go on board the schooner to learn further particulars. I will remain in charge of this vessel till you return." "Ay, ay," I replied; and calling my boat's crew, I was soon on my way towards the schooner. As I got near, I discovered that she had a spring on her cable, and that she was gradually bringing her broadside to bear directly on the brig. It was with no very pleasant sensation also, that, as I looked up when we were almost aboard of her, I perceived that her guns were depressed so as to bear directly down upon us; except, however, that one felt rather flattered that such vast preparations should be made for the reception of an English jolly boat. No opposition was offered to our clambering up the sides as we best could, but the gangway was not manned, nor was any other respect paid, such as we had a right to expect on visiting the ship-of-war of a friendly power. Well, when I got on deck, I beheld a sight for which I certainly was not prepared. The whole deck, fore and aft, was lighted up with lanterns, the crew of, I should say, at least, two hundred men, were at their quarters, and there were sixty marines drawn up in martial array, with shouldered muskets, and swords by their sides, looking fierce enough to swallow us whole if we had shown fight. You may just fancy me, with my handful of seamen, stepping over the gangway. Directly facing me stood the mighty commander of this band of heroes, with a crowd of officers, covered with gold lace and cocked hats, grouped behind him. He was a short man, and very fat, and he seemed to have selected the largest cocked hat ever manufactured to cover his head, in order to add to his dignity; but what he highly prided himself on still more, was a pair of huge moustaches, which curled up in the true Don Whiskerandos style. He looked very like a vain turkey-cock, when a farm-yard is visited by a stranger. I heard some loud grumblings as I first caught sight of this fearful personage, which afterwards resolved themselves into sundry ferocious oaths, at least, so I suspected from the expression of his countenance, and the words *maldicho, carramba*, &c., which came out among them; but this mattered very little, as neither I nor any of my people could understand a word he said. Taking our silence for contempt, I suppose, he grew furious, twirling his moustache with fearful energy, and stamping on the deck, as if he were anxious to summon some one from beneath to his assistance; at last, he wound up by clapping his hand on the hilt of his sword—a movement which was followed by all his officers. I stood firm. Not so my men, who grasped their cutlasses, and I heard one of them whisper to another—

"We shall have a scrimmage may be, arter all, with them here strange Dons. We shall have enough to do to heave them all overboard."

And, by Jove! I believe if I had led them on, they would just as willingly and merrily have leaped down among the Dons, and laid about them with right good will, as have stood quiet where they were. At last, I thought it was time to say something, so in a sort of lingua franca, I asked the captain why he had fired at us; but the only answer I got was a further volley of oaths, winding up with "*non intendo ustedes.*"

"I ask you," I repeated in English, "why did you fire at us when you must have seen our flags, and known that we were friends?"

The captain on this shook his head, and, turning round, called to some one in another part of the ship. Immediately a man came aft and saluted us in very good English, with "Your servant, sir."

I was afraid, from his accent, that the fellow was an Englishman, though he might perhaps have been an American. The captain again uttered a very long sentence, looking fiercely at me all the time.

"He asks, sir," said the interpreter, "how you and your people ventured to go on board the brig yonder, when he fired you off?"

"Tell him," I replied, "because I was obeying orders. I belong to a British man-of-war, and my captain desired me, with another officer, my superior, to overhaul the brig. We have done so, and we have full evidence that she is a slaver."

Again the Spanish captain spluttered forth a long sentence, which the interpreter explained—

"He knows that she is a slaver, sir," he said, "and he has therefore captured her under the same treaty that you capture slavers; and, as she is his prize, he was consequently very angry that you should venture on board without his leave."

"He may say what he likes," I replied. "But now ask him how he dared to fire on the British flag, when he must have known that if he were doing all that was just and above board, we should be on friendly terms?"

Again the moustache was twirled, and the stamping recommenced, while the man delivered my message.

"Oh, by St. Patrick, them chaps won't grow aisy till they've had some blood drawn!" said an Irish lad who pulled the bow oar. "If Mr. Fairfield would but say the word, and let us try our cutlashes on their heads, it would do them a wonder of good."

"Silence!" I exclaimed, really afraid lest some overt act of my people might give the cowardly Spaniards an excuse to set on us.

The interpreter now again spoke. "He says, sir, that it was too dark to see your ensign—that there have been some piratical craft cruising about in these waters lately, and that he thought your boats belonged to one of them, which had come in to re-capture the brig."

"You may tell him that I believe he lies incontinently," I felt very much inclined to say, but I did not, and merely answered, "Very well—I am not the person to judge of the truth of his statement, but I am desired to request that he will immediately come on board the brig, to explain matters to my superior officer, who has charge of her, for, if he does not, we shall most certainly carry her off as a prize."

On this there was a great deal of talking, and then the captain's gig was hauled up alongside, and he tumbled into her in a great hurry, and away she pulled as hard as his men could bend to their oars towards the brig. I immediately followed, but the jolly-boat did not pull as fast as the Spanish gig, though my people gave way with a will to see the fun.

When I reached the quarter-deck of the brig, a wonderful transmogrification of characters had taken place. There was Wilson drawn up to his full height of six feet four, I should say, with his sword in his hand, and surrounded by his crew—a fine set of fellows they were—with their shirt-sleeves tucked up to their elbows, and their cutlasses in their fists, looking very much as if they meant mischief. I scarcely at first recognised the little Spanish captain among the crowd. His cocked hat was in his hand, and he seemed busily employed in sweeping the deck with it, while his large head went bobbing away, and his left foot kept scraping away at the same time, like a hen making a hole in the dust to bask in.

"And how dared you fire into my boats?" thundered Wilson, in a voice which made the Spaniards tremble. "Let me tell you that I have a great inclination, if you cannot offer a proper explanation, to bring the guns of the brig to bear on your schooner, and to blow you out of the water. When a breeze springs up, our ship out yonder will stand in here and make you pay dearly for your audacity."

"Oh, Senhor, it was a mistake, entirely a mistake, I can assure you, on the honour of a Spanish hidalgo," returned the little captain, in a trembling voice—so Wilson, who understood Spanish, afterwards told me. "We could not distinguish your flags, and took you for an enemy. The fact is, we only this morning made prize of this brig just outside this place, and we brought up here to wait for a breeze off the land to continue our voyage to St. Jago da Cuba, where we were bound, to deliver her over to the court of adjudicature. We were on the point of getting under weigh when you made your appearance. What I tell you, Senhor, is the entire truth, I again repeat, on the sacred word of honour of a true Spanish gentleman," he added, with further bows and gesticulations.

The account seemed plausible enough to Wilson, and as there was no doubt of the schooner belonging to the Spanish Government, he could not doubt the word of the commander. I cannot say that I was quite so credulous; I could not help fancying that there was a trick somewhere or other.

"Very well, Senhor Captain, a good voyage to you," said Wilson. "I think there is no fear but that the brig will be condemned."

"Oh, no fear, no fear," returned the Spaniard; "I look upon her as our property already."

With mutual protestations of affection and esteem, which, on the part of the Spaniards, might have been interpreted into the directly opposite feelings, we returned to our boat, and pulled back to the Victor. Our captain was satisfied with what we had done; but, as a matter of precaution, determined to watch our friend and his prize safely into St. Jago da Cuba. We accordingly kept a bright look-out on their movements during the night, lest they might slip away to sea unobserved. The calm continued till daybreak, when a light breeze from the northward sprang up and filled our sails. Directly afterwards we saw the brig standing out of the harbour, followed by the schooner. We hove to for them, greatly, we afterwards had reason to know, to the disgust of the Spanish captain. All appeared going on right, and as soon as they got round the points, they hauled up for St. Jago. St. Jago da Cuba, as the Spaniards call it, is, as you know, about thirty miles from the bay of Guantanamo. As the day drew on, the breeze freshened up a little, and all the vessels went gaily dashing on towards the port. Our captain, while it was still calm, sent to ask the Spaniard to come and dine with him, but the latter was too sulky, I suppose, to accept the invitation, for he did not make his appearance. By three o'clock in the afternoon we got into St. Jago, and saw the brig and schooner safely at anchor close to each other. Our captain, however, was too old a cruiser to be yet content, so we also brought up, till we had ascertained, beyond a doubt, that the brig was delivered up to the proper authorities. The next morning, when I came on deck, I looked out towards the spot where she was at anchor, half expecting to find that she had given us the slip during the night; but there she was sure enough; and on going on shore during the day, we found that all was right, and that she was now in the power of the law. As legal proceedings in Spain are proverbially slow, our captain did not think it worth his while to remain to see the result of the trial, of which, indeed, there could be no doubt, so we once more continued our voyage to the Havanah. I ought to have described the brig. She was a beautiful vessel, perfectly new; indeed, she had not been to sea before, and, from her look, I should say, was very fast. In a word, she was, in every respect, fitted to act as a slaver or a pirate. She was called the Panchita. After a quick passage we reached that magnificent place, the Havanah. We spent ten days there before we sailed for Jamaica. I was one day walking through the streets of the town with an English merchant, settled there, when a gay cavalcade dashed by, headed by a fine-looking, dignified gentleman, with a cigar in his mouth, and his cloak thrown jauntily on one side.

"Do you know who that is?" asked my friend Hardy.

"No," I answered. "One of the most respectable inhabitants of the place, I suppose."

"One of the greatest rascals," he replied. "That fellow is not only the greatest slave dealer in the island, but he owns several vessels, whose crews are strongly suspected of being guilty of piracy, whenever they have an opportunity, without fear of detection. Not three weeks ago, a vessel of his sailed from hence, strongly armed, and with a crew capable of any atrocity. She was a fine brig, the Panchita."

"The Panchita!" I exclaimed; "why, that was the very brig we boarded in the bay of Guantanamo. Her career is soon ended then, for she was captured by a Spanish schooner of war, the Regulo, Don Huasco de Montebellino, commander, and is long ere this condemned as a slaver."

"Don't be too sure of that," he observed. "Ha, ha, ha!—pardon my laughter, but I am sadly afraid you have been gulled. Why, that same Don Huasco is the bosom friend of Don Montes Pepe, the cavalier who passed just now; and as the Panchita is his property, I don't think the little chap would venture to capture her. It would be as much as his life is worth, if he ever came back here—no, no, I smell a rat," and he laughed again.

We had not gone on far when we observed the same cavalcade returning, and what was my surprise to see our captain and two or three of my brother officers riding alongside of Don Pepe. When they got abreast of us, that gentleman reined up his steed, and addressed my companion, looking also pointedly at me.

"He invites us to come to an entertainment he gives to-day, at a country house he has a little way out of town," said my friend. "It wont do to refuse from our scrupulous delicacy, seeing that your skipper has already accepted—so I'll say that you will be delighted to come."

Before I could even frame an excuse, had I wished it, for I certainly doubted how far I was justified in going to the house of such a rascal—knowing him to be such—I found that the engagement was made. My friends, in their ignorance, were not certainly to blame. On this, Pepe expressed his high satisfaction, and ordering two of his attendants to dismount, my friend and I were supplied with their steeds, and away we all ambled cheek by jowl towards our reputable amigo's mansion. The house was spacious, with verandahs all round, and commanded a fine view of the harbour, the shipping, and the distant ocean. After we had washed our faces, and brushed the dust from our garments, we were introduced to the lady of the house, Donna Marina, who, as Green describes her, was really a very handsome woman; and her sister, also, Donna Isabelita Pinto, was still very pretty and engaging in her manners. The entertainment was superb—with viands and fruits of all descriptions, and a number of sable attendants in scanty garments, some of whom might have been dispensed with to advantage. I particularly observed the vast profusion of plate; but what was curious, it was of every variety of pattern, and evidently cast in many different countries and times. Some even looked most suspiciously more fitted for a church than a sideboard—but I might have been mistaken. After dinner, an extemporary poet got up, and recited and sang till he sent some of us to sleep, and after smoking several cigars, we all got into net hammocks, and snoozed away for a couple of hours. We had then coffee, and a number of ladies coming in with a band of music, we had a regular ball, which lasted till past midnight. When we were about to take our leave, Don Pepe would not hear of our going.

"Oh, mis amigos," he exclaimed, embracing our skipper most affectionately, "I cannot allow such a thing—you have come here for a week at least; this is only the prelude of our festivities; Donna Marina would never forgive you if you deserted us at this juncture: so go you shall not."

The end of it was, we enjoyed a very comfortable night's rest in the luxurious beds he had prepared for us.

"Depend on it, the rogue—I beg pardon—our respected host, has some reason for detaining you," whispered my friend, as we went to our chamber. "I should advise you to look to it, or you may be gulled—(I beg your pardon)—as you were in the case of the Panchita."

I had no opportunity of speaking to Captain Benham till next day, and when I told him what I had heard of my friend's caution, he would not at first credit it.

"Nonsense!" he exclaimed; "all scandal, depend on it. Such a respectable, fine fellow as our kind host cannot be the character you insinuate. I never met a more gentlemanly courteous man—a regular Spanish grandee of the first class. Why, he was telling me only last night about his father and grandfather, and how it was they first came over to settle here. Oh no, it's impossible."

"Was he telling you the truth, sir, do you think?" I asked.

"By jingo, I never thought that he might possibly have been romancing all the time. Well, I will look to it," was the answer.

"But I think it right, sir, to tell you that Mr. Hardy (my friend) suspects that something is going on which he is anxious to conceal from us. Probably one of his vessels is ready for sea, and he wishes to get her off while we are here, and the Victor is quietly at her anchors."

The captain gave a long "Whew!" "I'll tell you what it is, Fairfield, I suspect you are right, but we must not excite the gentleman's suspicions—you must go back to the town and get on board as quickly as you can; then take my gig and pull round the harbour in every direction, just as if for your amusement, and observe if there be any suspicious-looking vessel getting ready for sea. At the same time, get Mr. Hardy to institute inquiries on shore, and if you find that you are right, tell Wilson to have everything ready for sea, and send and let me know. We will meantime remain on here, and then, when every preparation is made, we will post off and get on board as the anchor is run up to the bows. I beg Don Pepe's pardon if our suspicions are wrong, and if correct, he has only fallen into the trap he has laid. I don't much like it, however."

When I mentioned to Don Pepe the necessity there was of my returning to my duty on board my ship, he expressed deep regret, and insisted on furnishing me with a horse and a guide.

"The road is difficult to find, and as you are in a hurry, I will send you by a short cut," I understood him to say, but my knowledge of the Spanish language was at that time very limited. A fine horse was brought to the door for my use, and my attendant was also mounted, and off we set. I certainly did not observe accurately the direction we took: indeed, relying on my guide, I was thinking of other things. I remember that we soon quitted the road, and on we went for a considerable distance over mere horse tracks, without seeing scarcely any human habitations, the country every instant growing wilder and wilder. At last I became convinced that we had taken the wrong direction, and had gone directly towards the interior of the island. I instantly turned my horse's head, and told my guide that I must make the best of my way into the town. He pretended to understand me, but either did not do so, or again purposely misled me; for after several hours' riding, I found myself again directly in front of Don Pepe's mansion. The hospitable owner was there to receive me, and with the blandest of smiles, asked me how I had enjoyed my ride, or some thing to that effect. I was very indignant, and could scarcely find words to explain that I had wished to return to Havanah, and not to take a pleasure ride. While I was still spluttering away and making hideous grimaces, in my vain endeavours to speak Castilian, who should arrive but Captain Benham and my friend Hardy.

"What, Mr. Fairfield, come back already?" exclaimed my captain, as soon as he saw me; "you bring important news, I hope."

"I can only say, sir, that my suspicions are confirmed," I replied, and explained in a few words what had happened.

"Ho, ho! that does look something like it," he observed. "Well, make the best of your way on board, late as it is, and do as I directed you,—there is more reason for it than ever."

"Ay, ay, sir, I'll not lose a moment, depend on it," I replied: and then turning to Hardy, I begged him to explain to Don Montes Pepe, that my duty required me to be on board without delay, and to beg that he would send some one who would lead me by the most direct cut into the town.

"The latter part of the request I shall not give," said my friend: "I intend to go with you myself. I cannot reconcile it to my conscience to trust you to the tender mercies of such piccarooning villains as are some of our host's followers. Why, man, if he does not wish you to arrive at Havanah to night, they would murder you without the slightest scruple."

I cannot say that I was sorry for Hardy's determination, though I at first begged him not to give up his amusement on my account. We were soon in our saddles, and accompanied by two of his servants, who had come out to escort him, and two whom Pepe insisted on sending with us, we set off for Havanah. A ride of two hours took us there, without any adventure worth recounting. I got on board the brig just as it fell dark, and, if Pepe's object were to make me lose a day, he had certainly succeeded. Wilson was not at all surprised at all I told him.

We at once set to work to get the ship ready for sea. The next morning I took the gig, as the captain had directed me, and pulled into every nook of that vast harbour, narrowly examining every craft I saw, but, though I observed several rakish-looking schooners and brigs, I could not fix upon any one of them as particularly of doubtful character. I had almost given up the search in despair, and was about returning on board, thinking that our suspicions had been ill founded, and that Don Pepe was, after all, a maligned and highly honourable gentleman, when I observed, over a point of land to the eastward, what looked very like the glitter of a topgallant sail, as it is first loosened, though it might have been a white bird just taking wing. Determined, however, to satisfy myself, I told the people to look out for a long pull, and put the boat's head towards the point I speak of.

I have never found seamen grumble when they know that there is a good object for exertion, and my lads bent to their oars as if there were not such a thing as a tropical sun overhead, so that we soon neared the spot. Before we got there, I took off my coat, and the gold lace from my cap, and made the men bind their handkerchiefs round their heads, so as not to excite the suspicions of those on board the vessel, if vessel there were; however, I knew that whatever she might be like, I could not even go on board her, much less take possession of her. In another quarter of an hour, we rounded the point, and there lay, in a snug little cove, as wicked a looking craft as I ever set eyes on.

She was a schooner, with taunt, raking masts, and square yards, and a long, low hull, just the cut of a vessel for a slaver. She was full of people; some were aloft bending sails, others were at the same time setting up the rigging, and others were hoisting in her stores and water. So busily employed was every soul on board, that I do not believe they ever observed us. I longed to pull in and reconnoitre more minutely, but I had seen enough to convince me that she had some particular reason for being in so desperate a hurry. I therefore pulled back to the brig as fast as I could, and told Wilson what I had observed. He agreed with me, that we ought to let the captain know of the circumstance, and, accordingly, packing up a carpet bag, as a pretence for sending to him, we despatched it, with a note, under charge of his coxswain. As we expected, before night, he and the rest of our shipmates returned on board, they having taken an affectionate farewell of Don Pepe, greatly, probably, to his disgust.

Everything was ready for sea, but we had no pilot on board, for the master knew the harbour too well to require one; nor was any other sign given of our intention of sailing, for we felt certain that our late host would be carefully watching our proceedings. However, we waited till it was perfectly dark, and then got up the anchor, and loosened the sails as silently as we could, when, a light air coming from the south-west, we were able to stand clear of everything out of the harbour.

When off the little bay I spoke of, we hove to, and Captain Benham ordered me to take the gig and pull in, with muffled oars, to see if our friend were still there. I had no little difficulty in finding the spot in the dark, but at last, after half an hour's search, I hit on it and pulled in. In vain I looked about for the schooner. I tried right round the bay, and passed the very quay near which she had been moored. As I did so, I fancied that I heard a derisive peal of laughter, but I might have been mistaken; at all events, the schooner was gone. Not a little disconcerted, I returned on board, more fully convinced than ever of Pepe's roguery. The puzzle was, which direction we were to take, for, by the delay which had occurred, she had already some hours' start of us. Our only satisfaction was, that in the morning, when Pepe found that we had sailed, he would be left in uncertainty whether we had made a prize of his schooner or not. At last, it was determined to beat round the west end of the island, for the navigation of the north side is dangerous and difficult. To make a long story short, and to arrive at a very lame conclusion, whichever course our friend took, we never saw her again, and the chances are, she is still employed in adding to the wealth of Don Pepe.

I have, however, none yet done with the Panchita. On our way back to Jamaica, we put into St. Jago, and, on making inquiries for the brig, we found that the captor had brought her to trial as being a pirate instead of a slaver, and that by this piece of legal irregularity, the poor man had lost his prize. We were speaking on the subject to an English merchant, who was dining on board with us, and we also recounted our adventures with Don Pepe. When he had heard them, he burst into a loud fit of laughter.

"And so, my good fellows, you suppose that Don Huasco de Montebelino, the captain of the Spanish man-of-war schooner, has suffered by his innocent mistake!" he observed. "Don't you think he made it on purpose? I can tell you I know he did, and they sailed together directly she was released, as amicably as possible. Don't you know the dodge? It is beautifully simple; Don Pepe gives the Spanish officer a handsome gratuity, provided his vessels get free beyond the 70° of longitude, outside of which the British men-of-war seldom cruise. So his Catholic Majesty's ship sticks close to the slaver, and if a British pennant heaves in sight, he directly takes possession, and you cannot touch her. He is certain then, if compelled to bring her to trial, to make a flaw through which she may easily escape. The Spanish government know all about it, and wink at everything which is done to assist in the slave trade. Now I know it for a fact, that the royal schooner accompanied the slave brig through the windward passage, and did not quit her till she was beyond all fear of pursuit."

We thanked our guest for his information, which was very valuable.

"Oh, I forgot to tell you," he added, "that very brig will be just as ready to commit piracy as to carry slaves. I know that the man who is in her as master, in the last vessel he commanded, never got across to the African coast, and yet returned with a cargo of slaves."

"How did he manage that?" we inquired.

"By a very simple method; he met the slavers on their homeward voyage, and running alongside one of them took all her slaves out of her; when in his more gracious mood, paying for them in cotton goods to enable her to purchase more, or not unfrequently making her go back with an empty hold, her people glad even to escape with their lives. Pepe, it is said, orders his captains never to kill if they can possibly help it; so he is looked upon as a humane and generous man."

I might keep you all day with descriptions of Pepe and his doings, for when I left the West Indies he was still as flourishing as ever.

My messmates thanked me for my account of Pepe.

"Don't you think it very likely that Don Diego Lopez de Mendoza was one of his captains?" said Upton; "it has more than once occurred to me that such was the case."

"By Jove! I should not be at all surprised if he were, and that his vessel, which we sent to the bottom, was my old friend," I exclaimed; "I never thought of it before."

"It may be she was, but ye maun gang far before ye will discover the truth, considering that poor child is the only being alive we got out of her," observed Haggis, sententiously; and that settled the question.

"Cannot somebody else give us a story?" said Green. "I am tired somewhat of Don Pepe, and so, I dare say, is Fairfield, and he wants something for his grand *ouvrage*."

"A sail on the lee-bow!" sang out Seaton through the sky-light.

"How does she bear?" asked the captain.

"About four miles south-south-west, sir," was the answer.

"How was it you did not report this before?" asked the captain; "she must have been in sight some time, surely."

"No, sir, we have only just made her out," answered Seaton; "there is a good deal of haze in the air, and it is thicker down about where she is even than here. We have just risen her courses above the horizon."

"Which way do you make her out to be standing?" asked the skipper, as we went on deck.

"About north-west, sir," answered Seaton.

"We'll keep away there a couple of points to cut her off," said the captain. "If she's a friend she'll not alter her course, and if a slaver, we must do our best to get up with her before dark."

The coast of Africa was now broad on our larboard beam: a long, dark line rising above the water, and the wind, which had been blowing the greater part of the day from seaward, now came off the land hot and sultry, and smelling of the burning sands. We were consequently to windward of the stranger, and as there was rather more wind where we were than she had, we had the advantage over her.

She was a large brig, but when we came to examine her with our glasses, all hopes of her proving a slaver vanished, for her high sides, her low masts, and short yards, all betokened her to be an English merchantman of the old build. A great improvement has, indeed, of late years taken place, especially among vessels from Liverpool and out of the Clyde.

As we were both going through the water pretty rapidly, we soon approached each other. We showed our colours, and the brig hoisted the red ensign, when Captain Dainmore ordered the signal to be made for them to heave-to, and told me to board her and learn what information I could about slavers. The merchantmen generally manage to pick up, either from the blacks or from each other, some little knowledge as to what is going on, and besides the slavers, knowing they can do them no harm, approach them fearlessly. The brig obeyed the signal, and I was soon on board.

The master, who was a very respectable-looking old gentleman, received me on deck very politely, and apologized for not coming on board us.

"But you see, sir," he observed, in a sad tone, pointing to his crew, "we are sadly short-handed. If we had remained up the Gaboon much longer, I should not have had people enough to carry the ship home. Now look at those poor fellows with their sallow cheeks and thin limbs. A few months ago they were as strong, rosy, and hearty, as any ploughboys. It makes my heart bleed when I look at them; and if any bad weather come on, I don't know how we shall manage. I've lost just one half of my people. God help me!"

I told him that I trusted Providence would send him fine weather, and then inquired if he had seen any suspicious-looking sails as he came along the coast.

"I did, sir, and very suspicious they were; I was not, indeed, quite comfortable till I lost sight of them. There were two schooners; I don't know which way one went, but the other I made out clearly standing for the mouth of the Bass river."

"When was this?" I asked.

"Just two days ago, sir," he answered. "In my weak state I was afraid lest they might take it into their heads to board me, and walk away with some of my cargo. Such gentry play those tricks now and then. I am laden chiefly with palm oil and ivory, a cargo they have a great fancy for, as it is impossible to identify it."

"What is your name, captain, may I ask?"

"Brown, sir; at your service," he answered.

"What, John Brown!" I exclaimed, involuntarily thinking of Green's story.

"Yes, sir," he answered, somewhat surprised at the tone in which I had pronounced his name, "John Brown."

"Did you ever command the John and Mary, in the West India trade?" I asked.

"I did, sir," and he sighed deeply.

"Did you ever fall in with Pepe the Pirate?" I added.

He started, and a frown came on his placid countenance.

"I should think I did, sir;—the audacious scoundrel! Twice, sir—twice. That villain has been the ruin of me; and here am I, in my old age, obliged to toil on, without a hope of leaving my family properly provided for. How do you know anything about the rascal, may I ask, sir?"

I told him that I had myself met him, and that Green had given me further particulars.

"Green! oh yes, I know him well; a kind, good fellow he is. I told him all the story myself, all about Pepe from the time I first had the misfortune to set eyes on him. I should like to see Mr. Green again; but I must make the best of my way home, and I do not like to give my poor boys the fatigue of getting a boat into the water. Give my kind regards to him, and tell him John Brown will never forget him."

I tried to persuade the old man to accompany me on board, but he would not come; and I told him that we had put an effectual stop to the depredations of one, we believed, of Pepe's cruisers, as a consolation to him.

"I could have wished the villain a better end," he observed; "but I must not keep you, sir; and mind, don't forget the schooner we saw going up the Bass," he hallooed after me as I stepped into my boat. "Nor Green. Heaven bless all of you, and preserve you from this horrid coast."

I waved adieu, and shoved off. The brig's fore-yard came slowly round, her sails filled, and she stood once again on her course. When I got on board we did the same, keeping rather nearer in shore than we had before done. All were much interested in my account of Captain John Brown; and Green regretted that he had not himself gone on board the brig to visit the poor old man, whom he had known, he said, for some years, and who, though a capital seaman, and of most excellent character, seemed always to have been persecuted by fate. From him, indeed, he had got most of the particulars which he had given us of Pepe the Pirate.

CHAPTER XX.

A TRIP UP THE QUORRA.

"CALL the boats' crews away, Mister Fairfield." This order, given in the clear tones of our commander's voice, roused me from a reverie into which one morning I had fallen, when, being officer of the watch, I paced the deck of the Albatross, lying at anchor off the mouth of the Nun River, one of the embouchures of the far-famed Quorra or Niger. The hot sun rolled his course majestically through the deep-blue sky, on which not a cloud floated to dim the lustre of his burning splendour, not a breath of air disturbed the glass-like surface of the ocean, whose slow heaving swells, making the vessel roll from side to side, alone gave signs of its sleeping power, while anxiously we waited for the sea-breeze to set in to drive back the suffocating odour which, even to the distance we were from the land, came off from the scorched earth. Over the low swampy shore there hung also a wide extending mist, blue and gauze-like, yet sufficiently thick to render indistinct any objects within its influence. Now and then, also, to remind us of the clime in which we were, a flying-fish would rise from its liquid home, and taking a short spirt through the more subtle air, his scales, like jewels, glittering in the sunbeams, would fall again with a gentle splash into the calm sea. Or, as I looked over the side, I could see the long snout and dark back of more than one huge shark swimming round the ship, ready to pick up any offal thrown overboard, or perhaps a stray midshipman, or other small boy, who might chance to fall into the water; and as the cook emptied his bucket from the galley, I observed several of the monsters making a rush altogether at its contents, showing, as they turned up their white stomachs, their huge maws and triple rows of teeth. I had been thinking just before how much I should like to plunge into the blue crystal sea, to cool my heated skin, well dried as it was by the torrid sun of Africa; but this sight banished any such wish. I could not help fancying how lustily they would have tugged at my arms and legs had they found me among them. I shuddered at the very idea, and prayed Heaven such might never be my lot.

My next thought was of a pleasant stroll among the tempting groves I saw through my glass, looking so cool and shady; but I soon recollected the stories I had heard of the deadliness of the black fever, and the treachery of the black men, and I as quickly abandoned all wish to go there for the *pleasure* of the thing.

We had anchored off the river the previous night, in consequence of information we received from the English vessel we had fallen in with some days before.

As yet the African fever had not paid us his unwelcome visit, and we began to flatter ourselves that we were to be altogether exempt from the plague which spares so few. From the length of time we had been on the coast, we had reason to be thankful, though we still had much to go through. We had at Sierra Leone shipped some Kroomen, with which class of men every vessel on the coast is supplied to do the hard work, such as watering the ship and cutting fire-wood; as that sort of labour would soon destroy Europeans unaccustomed to the climate. These blacks are indeed a most useful set of fellows, either as axemen, boatmen, or sailors. In appearance they are far superior to any other race of negroes I have met with; they are generally tall and well proportioned, their limbs are muscular, and their gait erect and firm. It is said, and from what I have seen I believe it, that their spirit is of so unyielding a nature that they are never taken as slaves, as they would either destroy themselves or those who attempted to master them. To see the native majesty of their step, they look as if they were born ever to be free. There is a nobility itself in their whole bearing. In truth they are, as we used to call them, *highly-polished black gentlemen.*

It may be as well to prelude the account of our expedition up the Quorra with a description of the geography of the place. The coast here trends east and west, forming the northern shore of the Bight of Biafra. The Nun river is the westernmost embouchure of the Quorra. About twenty-two miles east of the Nun is the Brass River; both of them having sand-bars across their channels: the last, as I have good reason to know, boasting of three, over which the sea at times breaks with terrific violence.

After separating from their parent stream, the mysterious and mighty Quorra, they each run a course of about sixteen miles to the sea, thus forming a low swampy island, covered with mangroves—a nice place, as may be supposed, for the generation of fevers and such like pleasantnesses. There are three bars, it must be remembered, on the Brass River, about three miles apart.

I had been in a reverie, as I was saying, thinking of I need not say whom, when the words, " call the boats' crews away," aroused me to the stern realities of the cruel world. I was all alive in a moment, and repeating the order; the boatswain's shrill whistle sounded along the decks, summoning the watch below. The next instant the people were seen tumbling up on deck; the tackles were hooked on to the yard, the boom boats were hoisted out, the gripes cast loose, and a gig and canoe, which hung on our quarters, were lowered in the water; spars, sails, oars, arms, ammunition, and provisions, were handed in, cutlasses were buckled on, and we were ready to start. Upton, in the pinnace, commanded the expedition; I was in the cutter; Seaton had the gig, and to our fleet was attached the canoe, manned by Kroomen, which was to act the part of a light squadron in reconnoitring. Our orders were to proceed up the river Nun into the Quorra, to look into every creek and bight in our way, and should we not be fortunate enough to fall in with a slaver, to return to the ship on the following day, so as not to be exposed more than one night to the noxious air of the river.

At about 10 a.m., we shoved off from the ship's side, with a hearty cheer to speed us on our way from the shipmates we left behind. We were all in high spirits at having something more to do than the daily routine of duty afforded us; nor were our hopes small of making a prize during the trip. Even the heat, which added many a shade to our already well-browned physiognomies, served to boil up our ardour without making it evaporate; so that we were up to anything which might come in our way.

As we neared the entrance of the river, a line of white breakers appeared directly across our course, towards the roughest part of which the canoe, which was leading, with a black pilot on board, paddled on, and, much to our surprise, went right over it without shipping a drop of water, while we, who, after waiting some time, selected the bluest water, were half-drowned by the sea breaking over us. The flood, however, soon made, and we had a fair tide to carry us along. After a long pull we entered the Quorra, which is here rather more than a mile wide, though higher up it is considerably broader; the country on each side appearing to consist of extensive swamps, covered with mangrove, cabbage, and palm-trees.

Out of the moist ground arise those noxious exhalations, which, near, look like the smoke of damp fire-wood, and which caused that blue haze we had seen at a distance in the morning. Oh, how hot it was! We could have cooked a beef-steak in the stern sheets as quickly as by a kitchen fire; so you may suppose that we ourselves were frying pretty rapidly: we should have been nice morsels for any cannibals who were choice in their food.

On we pulled, notwithstanding, shoving our noses into every nook and creek we could find, but, except our own little fleet, not a bark was there to be seen floating on the dark, leaden waters. Scarcely a thing with life appeared, except now and then, when near the shore, an alligator would poke his long snout above the water, as if to ask the white man what he wanted, that he ventured into his dominions; but receiving no answer, would as quickly again disappear beneath the slimy tide, thinking us not worthy of further notice. Although we distinguished not the voice of man nor of beast, it could not be said that silence reigned over those regions; for there was the rush of waters, the crackling of the leaves, the hum of innumerable insects, which flitted in every direction—even the hot air itself seemed to utter sounds, but all so composed and harmonized, that they appeared but one deep solemn *burr-ush*, which we called the *noise of heat*. I do not think any words can describe it; it must be felt to be understood.

After pulling steadily onward for about four or five hours, enjoying during the latter part of the time a sea-breeze, which, somewhat cooling the air, gave us an appetite for dinner, we brought-to near a clear space of ground, where we lighted our fires, for which there was an abundance of wood in every direction—dry enough in all conscience—and set to work to cook our food.

Eating may not be a very romantic occupation, and that is the reason authors make knights and ladies fair, in their stories, get on very well without it; but, to my mind, it is always in reality the most amusing part of an expedition. While we were boiling our pork and yams, and frying some fish we had caught in the morning, with a few oysters which we had picked off the mangrove trees at low water, on our way up, some black fellows came down to see what we were about. My readers may smile at my talking of picking the oysters off the trees, but I did not say they grew there. Oysters, it must be known, must cling to something; so finding the boughs of the mangroves hanging in the water, they get hold of them, and probably catch much more food than they would at the bottom of the sea, though of course they can't be expected to know that they ought to let go again when the tide falls.

These black gentlemen were, I doubt not, from their costume, characters of great importance—if not kings in *propriâ personâ*. One wore a broad-brimmed Spanish hat, a regular sombrero, with an ostrich feather stuck in it, a marine's red coat, a pair of Wellington boots, and a sort of petticoat, or rather kilt, coming down to the knee, of green baize. Another was habited in a pair of red slippers, a soldier's cap, and an old naval cloak, which he carried with the air that an ancient Roman on the stage wears his toga, or Pollione, for instance, in Norma, his robe. A third was dressed in a woman's pink silk bonnet, hind part before, which set off his black physiognomy to great advantage; a pair of tight net drawers, and one top boot—how procured I cannot tell—but not a rap of anything else, though he seemed as proud of his finery as his companions were of their more complete costume. Of the rest, some had similar incongruous habiliments, and others rejoiced in a state of primitive nature.

As this extraordinary group drew near, we received them with shouts of merriment, which they seemed to take rather as a compliment than otherwise, their chief observing, as he strutted about with the self-satisfied air of a peacock, "Me bery fine, massa, d—n your eyes."

They were a disgusting set, covered over with loathsome sores, arising from the pestilential air they breathe, and the unwholesome food, such as alligators and cat-fish, on which they exist. They either would not, or could not, speak much English, nor could we elicit any information from them as to whether there were any slavers in the river; so we were not sorry, after enduring their society for nearly an hour, to get rid of them, by hinting that their room would be more agreeable than their company, and giving them a bottle of rum, which was what they came for.

We then returned to the boats, where, for an hour or so more, we remained to rest the people, who were much overcome with the heat and fatigue, sheltered from the sun by some lofty cotton-trees, whose boughs overhung the water. To make ourselves as comfortable as circumstances would allow, we brought the after-parts of the boats together, where we officers lighted our weeds, and leaning back in the stern sheets, talked of past events, and adventures in store for us, with that half-dreaming tone which lassitude produces. It was very pleasant, though, watching the blue smoke of our cigars, mingling in curling wreaths with the glittering air, as it escaped beyond the shadow of the trees, the calm water gliding by, observing the strange shrubs and plants which surrounded us, and listening to the suppressed jokes of the seamen, as they lay on their oars, not forgetting the chattering of a million parroquetes, which all on a sudden commenced such a noise as I never heard before; it burst forth like a mill suddenly set going, or like certain deliberative assemblies where there are all talkers and no listeners. The birds seemed to have a prodigious deal to say, and to be in a great hurry to say it. It was most laughable to listen to them. While we were thus passing the time, or rather killing it, we heard a low, floundering, flapping noise in the water, and looking out, in order to discover whence it proceeded, we saw, not thirty yards from us, the long snout of a huge alligator protruding above the stream. Slowly he lifted his vast form from the water, and began to climb up the bank, attracted doubtlessly by the smell of the fragments of food we had left on the shore. A low *hush* from the Kroomen warned us to be silent, and presently we saw two of them spring from the canoe, with long spears in their hands, when with noiseless steps they approached the awkwardly-moving monster. When he had waddled a considerable way up the bank, they advanced rapidly towards him, and being no longer afraid of his retreating, one of them leaped before his jaws, to attract his attention, while the other, springing behind him, ran his long spear right through his tail, and pinned him to the ground as an entomologist does a cockchafer or beetle. Now began the tug of war. Round and round spun the astonished alligator, with the spear as the pivot of his gyrations, Nap, the Krooman, holding on like fury, making the most horrible grimaces, and screaming in his agitation lest the beast should break away from him. In the meantime the other black was attacking the vast reptile in front, now poking his long spear into one eye, now into the other, as he could take aim, now thrusting it down his throat, then wounding him in the neck. Sometimes I thought the alligator would have broken loose, when the Krooman would have run no inconsiderable chance of slipping down his jaws; but the spear was tough, and Nap held fast, till at last a home-thrust pierced the brain of the beast, and he sank down in the agony of death. A loud shout from all parties acknowledged the gallantry of the victors, who immediately set about cutting some delicate *morçeaux* from the carcass for their own especial eating, none of the whites feeling an inclination to join them in their repast. One does not like to feed on a beast, which, for what one knows to the contrary, may have the day before been dining off a little black child.

Soon after the combat we again got under weigh, and continued our explorations up the river, but with the same want of success as at first. Now and then, as we proceeded, we caught sight of a canoe, which was sure to give us a long chase before we could come up with it, and then the black crew were certain to know nothing of any slavers, perhaps to be scarcely aware that such a traffic existed. It was wearying work, but we persevered till darkness rendered any further search useless. We accordingly brought up for the night on the west bank of the river, near the driest spot of ground we could find, and after taking our supper, we made ourselves as comfortable as we could in the boats, in the same way that we had done in the afternoon, all of us having been cautioned on no account to sleep on shore.

In the meantime, Upton despatched the Kroomen, who were still fresh, to reconnoitre farther up the river, where there was some probability of the slaver we were in search of lying concealed. For an hour or two we remained wrapped up in our cloaks, endeavouring to keep out the air, which felt something like a blanket wetted by hot water; some of the party at times smoking, but none of us indulging in conversation. There was a thin crescent moon in the heavens, which threw a pale uncertain light over the scene, and as I lay half awake and half dozing, I fancied I could see dark forms gliding over the face of the waters—the spirits, I thought, of those brave hearts which had sunk beneath the noxious influence of that baneful clime. On such occasions, and at such moments, the imagination often runs away with the sense, and it is now almost painful to recal the absurd fancies of my brain, which I then thought realities.

Suddenly we were all aroused into action by the piercing, yet not loud whisper of the chief Krooman's voice. It sounded like a ringing yet deep hiss. His words were "Ship live there!" His light canoe, which we had not seen till he spoke, now ranged up alongside Upton's boat, when he explained that he had seen a vessel some distance up in a bight on the west bank, the same to which we were then made fast. Within thirty seconds we were pulling with silent voices and rapid strokes towards the point he indicated, a thickly-wooded promontory intervening, which even in daylight would have shut out our view. An hour's pull brought us into the neighbourhood of the stranger; but nothing could be seen, except now and then a long dark canoe darting like a black snake in and out from among the bushes, which made us feel pretty sure that the crew of the stranger, if a slaver, had already information of our approach, and would be prepared for us.

"He here—he here," said the Krooman, as we came up with the canoe, which had been previously piloting the way, and in another moment we rounded a point, when through the obscurity we could distinguish a low, black vessel, her masts almost concealed by the thick foliage of the trees which surrounded her. With steady nervous strokes we pulled on towards her, all three boats abreast, with the canoe in the rear, though the Kroomen were as ready for a skirmish as the most fire-eating of the whites.

Not a word was spoken, the regular splash of the oars, as they clove the water, alone broke the silence which reigned over the tranquil stream. I breathed rather faster as we advanced, and, I believe, even those most accustomed to the sort of work we were upon, felt a certain awe creep over them as we neared the stranger. The thought of the last parting embrace of one dearly loved, of future bliss destroyed, of hopes become vain, would occasionally occur, yet it was not so much the dread of death, as the uncertainty of whence danger might come, which at that moment tried my feelings.

Some plot was evidently prepared, and we concluded that they had probably a masked battery on shore, which would open on us as we got higher up the creek. Nothing moving, however, was to be seen on shore, nor could we observe any one showing their heads above the bulwarks on board. We made out clearly at last that the vessel was a schooner, moored so that her broadside bore directly down the creek, that her ports were open, her boarding-nettings triced up, and that she seemed prepared to make a determined resistance. We were not, therefore, doomed to expend much more of our patience.

"At her, my boys!" cried Upton, and, giving three hearty cheers, which woke the dull silence of night, we dashed on together, expecting every moment to find a shower of shot flying about our heads; but not a gun was fired—a long, low growl, and then a fierce bark, was the only answer.

"Carramba! maldicho perro — silencio," muttered a voice on board the vessel.

"Ho, ho!" I thought, " she is not deserted, at all events."

The water flew from the bows of the boats—a few strokes more, and we were within pistol-shot of her, when, as if to make amends for their previous apathy, there opened such a shower of iron and lead on our heads, that I thought not one of us could have escaped without having some of the missiles lodged in our bodies. Rather inspirited than otherwise by this warm reception, we gave another hearty cheer, and our boat-hooks were in a moment made fast to their chains.

We were not long, you may be sure, in scrambling up her sides, but, to our surprise, instead of a fierce tussle, as we expected, not another shot was fired, not a cutlass raised to defend her. Forcing our way through the boarding nettings, we jumped down on her decks, thoughtless of any treachery. In truth, it was more than probable that the Spaniards had laid a train of gunpowder to the magazine, and, having lighted it, had escaped to the shore, in the pious hope that we might all be blown into the air.

On such occasions, one seldom stops to consider. It however happened, that as the first of our party leaped upon her decks, the last of the schooner's crew was seen tumbling down her hold, with the exception of three or four who were lying between the guns forward, in the last stage of a fever, which had, we afterwards found, carried off their two mates, and nearly half their complement of men. Their captain being also down with the fever, they were left entirely without officers, owing to which circumstance it was that we had so cheap a victory.

I shall not forget in a hurry—ugh!—the dreadful stench which exhaled from the hold as we looked down to see what had become of the gentlemen who had honoured us with a salute. Below were about eighty negroes, shipped that very day, now manacled and chained to the decks, among whom the crew were endeavouring to shelter themselves to avoid the vengeance they might well expect from our people at this wanton attempt to destroy us. They had doubtlessly expected to send us all to the bottom by one broadside, when they fancied we should give them no more trouble.

We soon had them all upon deck again; when, to prevent them from doing any further mischief, we put their hands into the bracelets they had prepared for the remainder of their living cargo. We then stowed them away again among their black captives, to the no small astonishment of the latter, who scarcely supposed that the same ornaments they wore would fit so admirably the hands of their late masters.

While this operation was going forward, I took a lantern, and found my way into a round-house on the after-part of the deck, where I discovered the captain of the schooner in his berth, unable to move from sickness. He could speak a few words of English, which he employed to inform me that his people had fired without his orders, for that knowing we were such incarnate devils at fighting, it was hopeless attempting to resist us.

He vowed by the Virgin Mary, by all the saints in the calendar, and by his own patron saint in particular, that as soon as he heard the guns going off, he had ordered his men to desist, and to save their lives as they best could, while he was ready to die with grief lest any of us should be hurt.

I had tolerably strong misgivings that this account was very far from the truth; for I suspect, that had the broadside sunk us, he would have put a very different face on the matter.

As soon as we had secured the crew of the slaver, we set to work to get her under weigh. This took some time, for the sails were unbent and stowed away below, and the running rigging was unrove. All hands, however, worked with a will. We first were obliged to cut away the branches of the trees entangled in her rigging, and then we had to cast off her warps and to tow her out into the stream before we could bend the sails. When all things were put to rights, a watch was set, and the remainder of the people lay down to rest.

The next morning we towed her farther out, where she could feel the little breeze that was then stirring; nor shall I forget quickly the pleasant feeling I experienced, when, as daylight appeared, we got the canvass on the vessel, and she glided down towards the mouth of the river—OUR PRIZE.

She proved to be a fine one-topsail schooner, called the Cherubino; and by her build and the easy way she slipped through the water, we judged her to be very fast. After breakfast, the prisoners were allowed to come on deck; and it was curious to observe their downcast looks compared to the self-satisfied manner of our men at their success. At the top of high-water, the wind increased considerably, setting nearly right up the Nun; so we stood over to the eastern shore of the Quorra, intending to try the Brass entrance. We had been beating down for some hours, when the look-out hailed that a sail was coming in by the Brass river.

"Hurra!" cried Benson, a merry fellow, whose jovial spirits, neither the suns of Africa nor the snows of Iceland could overcome—"Hurra, boys! another prize or we are Dutchmen."

"Give me my glass," exclaimed Upton. eager to ascertain the

L

fact, and his telescope being handed to him, he mounted with it to the fore-yard-arm. After a long scrutinizing look, he descended again on deck, rubbing his hands with glee. "She is not a bit like a quiet trader, at all events," he observed, " but as ill-looking a craft as ever I saw, and if she prove honest, I will agree with Benson, that we are Dutchmen."

The tide and a strong wind being both in favour of the stranger, she approached us rapidly, and we were not long in making her out to be a large square-topsail schooner, with the Spanish colours flying at the peak, and some private signal at the fore. Seeing this, we again hoisted the Spanish ensign, and hauling our boats under our lee-counter, dodged quietly on, while she came up the stream.

It was a time of considerable excitement and suspense. That she was a slaver, there was little doubt. Being naturally suspicious, she might think something was wrong, and by hauling her wind, being by far the largest, and very likely the fastest, vessel, she might contrive to escape us; we could not tell, also, what secret signals the slavers might possess, by which to communicate with each other; and of course, if they began to speak to us, and we could not answer, they would see that all was not right. However, Upton, like a good sailor, had plenty of resources at hand. He ordered all the people to lie down, except the man at the helm, and a few others, who mounted Spanish hats and caps, as did he, with Seaton and myself, and a most bandit set of fellows we forthwith appeared. All went on very well till the schooner was within a mile of us, when up went a small flag to her fore-topmast-head in place of the one before there, followed by several others. A quantity of flags had been found in one of the lockers, and Upton immediately ordered a like number to be hoisted, taking care that they should not blow out clearly enough to be distinguished by the people of the other vessel, who would set it down to the stupidity of our signal-man. This was done not to lose time, for while the signals were being bent on, Upton ordered one of the Spaniards to be brought on deck, selecting a jovial, contented-looking fellow, who seemed one of the most likely of the crew to enjoy life.

A fat little man, with large sparkling eyes and thick lips, now drawn somewhat down, not knowing what was going to happen, stood trembling before him. Upton having put on the fiercest look he could muster, welcomed him on deck with a loaded pistol in his hand, and being at all times the very pink of politeness, addressed him with the little Spanish he could speak, in terms similar to these:—

"Senor Espanol, I shall regret to be compelled to treat you as I intend to do, if you do not answer me faithfully; but necessity, you are aware, has no law. You see this pistol; I shall shoot you through the head with it, if by any chance that schooner escape us."

The Spaniard, who had hitherto seen nothing but the pistol, and from Upton's gestures and words expected fully to be summarily dismissed from the world, breathed more freely. Looking round, he now for the first time observed the approaching vessel. "Carramba!" he muttered to himself, "these devils of Englishmen are in luck to-day—paciencia!"

Taking a look at the flags, he desired to be led to the captain's cabin, where from a drawer he produced a much-soiled manuscript book of signals, and after examining it carefully, Upton every now and then stimulating his wits with the muzzle of the pistol, he interpreted the signal, by saying that the schooner, which he let us know was the Santa Maria—an odd name for one of her calling —was asking where the slaves had been collected for her. "Tell them opposite the creek where we took you," said Upton, and the Spaniard obeyed by bending on the proper flags to the signal-halyards.

The effect was as we could wish, for she immediately stood over to the eastern shore, thus every instant getting more to leeward. She then signalized that the coast was clear, and that we might run out without danger. She had thus evidently not seen the Albatross. So far all was well, and reminding the Spaniard what his fate would be if she escaped, we recommended him to keep a bright look-out on her movements. He smiled with not a little scorn on his countenance, thinking probably from the Santa Maria's greater size, weight of metal, and number of men, that we might find we had caught a Tartar.

On she came with all her canvass set, and by carefully shifting our boats towing alongside, to our great joy, we weathered her before she suspected anything was wrong. She now brailed up her fore-sail, topgallant-sail, and maintop-sail, preparatory to bringing-to, at the same time making a signal for the captain of the Cherubino to come on board and receive his letters.

"Ha, ha! At all events I will obey that order presently," exclaimed Upton, laughing. "Keep the vessel away after him."

Our only fear now was, lest the crew, showing the white feather, might run the Santa Maria on shore and blow her up before we could board her.

As may be supposed, as soon as the Santa Maria saw us come bowling along after them, instead of heaving-to, their suspicions were aroused, particularly when up went the freedom-bearing flag of England at our peak, and we fired a gun as a signal for her to heave-to. This, as may be supposed, had no effect, and a second, which we had got forward, lodged a shot in the head of her main-mast. It wounded the jaws of the gaff, though the sail did not come down. Her captain, however, as he soon convinced us, was not a fellow to yield tamely; for sending people aloft, he secured the spar again, let fall his sails, and hauled his wind, evidently intending to fight his way past us, and beat out of the river again by one of the other channels, or to sink us if he could. One of these things he thought he could do, as he had not seen our boats towing astern. Knowing his own vessel to be very fast, he hoped to weather us on the first tack, and to disable us from following him by knocking away some of our spars. For this latter object he worked his guns most manfully, aiming always at our rigging, the shot passing through and through our sails, though for some time no spars were wounded.

L 2

CHAPTER XXI.

A TRIP UP THE QUORRA.

We were, you must understand, to windward on the western shore, the wind being about west-south-west. Every instant the breeze increased, which was all in favour of the Santa Maria, as being a larger and stiffer vessel, she could carry her canvass better, and go through the water faster than we, with our heavy boats astern, could do; she was, indeed, rapidly fore-reaching on us.

Had not her captain been a brave fellow, he would have run her on shore and deserted her; but this he had no thoughts of doing while a hope of escape remained. We also, of course, might at once have attacked her with our boats, but we should have done so at a much greater risk of life, for with the strong breeze there was blowing, the enemy might have sunk some of them while we were attempting to get on board her. We should have been obliged, also, to leave one boat's-crew, at least, on board the Cherubino, to work her and keep the prisoners in order. Taking these things into consideration, Upton determined to board the Santa Maria with the first captured schooner, having the boats as a last resource.

If we were anxious before, we were now doubly so. All depended on how the wind held. A different slant might carry her out clear by the Brass, but if she attempted the Nun we should cut her off, or she would fall into the hands of the Albatross. The probabilities, therefore, of her escaping without coming to close quarters were but slight, but still the chance which remained was sufficient to give us abundance of excitement.

Upton seemed to be in every part of the ship at once; now taking a sight along one of the foremost guns and firing it himself, generally with some effect; now hurrying aft, to see that the sails were well trimmed; next looking over the side, to observe how fast we went through the water; and then watching the movements of the enemy. We could see our shot as they passed over the slaver or through her sails, strike the palm or tall cotton-trees on the opposite bank of the river, sending the white splinters in every direction, sometimes lopping off a branch or shivering the dry trunks like lightning; his shot producing the same effect on the opposite side, to the great surprise of the parroquetes and the no small astonishment and terror of a few negroes who had come down to see what all the noise could be about. The last-mentioned jetty inhabitants of the groves, having a little human wisdom in their woolly heads, beat their retreat in double quick time; the latter only chattered the faster and louder. I don't mean to say that I could exactly hear them—only I have no doubt of the fact, so I beg that the truth of my story may not be disputed.

It was amusing all the time to watch the countenance of our Spanish signal-man. He could not help wishing for the success of his countrymen in the Santa Maria; though not being aware that

Englishmen do not generally murder their prisoners in cold blood, he could not tell if her ladyship escaped, whether we might not, as we threatened, blow out his brains—the chance of such a consummation being far from a pleasant subject of contemplation to a man. Upton's eye at last fell upon him, when he ordered him to be taken below to be out of the way of the shot. The wind now veered a point more to the southward, and the Santa Maria could not weather a promontory which ran out from the eastern bank of the river.

"They are, after all, going to run her on shore!" I exclaimed. In another moment she would have been on the slimy bank.

"No, by Jove! she is about again!" cried Upton, as the enemy shot a-head, and the wind, again shifting, placed her well to windward of us.

"We will be even with them. Man the boats. Fairfield, do you remain in the Cherubino with four of the Kroomen, and two out of each of the other boats. Run on board the enemy if a change of wind enable you to do so; at all events, keep blazing away at her till you see us fairly on her decks. Now put the schooner about."

The men being selected who were to remain with me, the rest, while she was in stays, jumped into the boats and shoved off. During the time the boats were pulling in a direction to cut her off, as she was then standing, I continued firing away at her hull, so as to distract her people's attention as much as possible from them. She soon, however, almost ceased firing at us, turning most of her guns at the advancing boats, though fortunately not being well served, scarcely one of their shot touched them. I was more fortunate with my artillery; thanks to one of the Kroomen, who rejoiced, I remember, in the name of Fuzbos.

"Me hit shooner, Massa," he observed, making a sign that he should like amazingly to have a slap at the enemy.

I gave him leave to fire, and he was as good as his word. The shot hit the already-wounded mainmast, cutting away the main and peak halliards, bringing the mainsail down on deck, and sending the main-top-mast and topsail over the side. We had just time to fire another shot, which killed several of her people, when the boats were alongside. The really hot work now began. No sooner were the boat-hooks on to the chains than our people were saluted with showers of langrage from three or four guns, pointed low to receive them, bullets from pistols and muskets, and thrusts from pikes; but besides these little disagreeables, the Spaniards hove into the boats bottles full of gunpowder, which, breaking as they touched the planks, they followed them up with shovels full of hot coals, the explosions, partial as they providentially were, burning some of our people in the most dreadful way. Fortunately, there was a good deal of water in the boats, so that the powder which fell into their bottoms was damped; and Seaton, in the cutter, bethought him of pulling out the plug, when he saw what the enemy were about, and swamping her before he sprang up the side of the schooner.

Upton, discharging his pistol at the head of the Spanish captain, and turning aside the thrust of a pike, was the first on the deck;

and then commenced such a hewing, and slashing, and cutting, and thrusting of cutlasses and pikes, as I never saw before. The Spaniards, to do them justice, defended themselves bravely; but this work could not last long.

The boats had boarded on the weather side and quarter. I now came up on the lee bow, and, with five Englishmen and two Kroomen, leaped on their decks. This reinforcement gave fresh confidence to our people, and proportionably disheartened the Spaniards, who began tumbling down their hold at a great rate, others singing out for quarter most lustily. To the honour of our seamen, they seldom bear malice: no sooner did the enemy sue for mercy than they ceased to strike.

Upton and I, like two generals, met at the head of our men, on the after-part of the Santa Maria's deck, and were congratulating each other on our victory—in very brief terms, it may be supposed —when our attention was called by a loud cry from the seaman left at the helm of the Cherubino.

"By Jove!" exclaimed Upton, "the prisoners are getting loose."

And so it was. As I, with my men, had sprung on board the Santa Maria, some of her crew had contrived to swing themselves on to the bowsprit of the smaller schooner, to get out of harm's way; when, no one observing them, they slipped below. Their first impulse was, of course, to knock the manacles off the hands of their friends and of some of the blacks; then, seizing some cutlasses and axes, to endeavour to free the Cherubino from the Santa Maria. They either forgot that we had our boats to pursue them, or, perhaps, they thought them disabled.

They were, when we perceived them, cutting away most lustily; numbers of negroes, as well as whites, were hurrying up from below; and the three hands who had been left on board were driven aft, and were contending for their lives. Here were the tables turned with a vengeance: but Upton and I, leading on our men, soon drove the Spaniards back into the hold of the Cherub, and were within a minute complete masters of both vessels. We had, however, not a little difficulty in again fixing on the manacles to our numerous prisoners.

CHAPTER XXII.

THE BAR OF THE QUORRA.

WE now anchored the two schooners to repair damages and fit them for sea. We had lost one man killed, three badly wounded—among whom was poor Seaton—and four slightly, who were still able to do duty. Four of the Spaniards were killed, and ten or twelve badly wounded in the two vessels.

Not knowing what to do with so many prisoners, who far outnumbered our people, Upton determined to set some of them on shore, among whom was the captain of the Cherubino, who had taken no part in the fray, and our friend the signal-man. According to custom, they were permitted to carry with them their wearing apparel, their books, and instruments. In consequence, each claimed a large trunk; and I remember hearing the seamen who handed them into the boats exclaim that they were very heavy. We afterwards discovered that they were full of dollars for the purchase of slaves. The men also landed with a good deal of money concealed about their persons. We were better up to their tricks another time.

It seems an anomaly that no punishment should be inflicted on wretches carrying on an Heaven-accursed and illegal traffic, who are to fire into our ships and kill our people, while a smuggler, who snaps a pistol at a revenue officer, would probably be hung or transported for life. I believe that till slavers are treated as pirates, their business will never be completely destroyed. At present, high pay, with little or no risk, tempts the best Spanish and Portuguese seamen to join ships fitting out for slaving voyages. They frequently receive three or four times as much, or more, than they would in an honest calling; while the owners and captains make many hundred per cent.

The remainder of the people we distributed between the two vessels, the greater number being on board the Santa Maria.

It was now coming on to blow very fresh, with sudden squalls and heavy rain; and by the time the people had taken some food, and both vessels were got ready for sea, the day was drawing to a close. Notwithstanding this, Upton was anxious to avoid spending another night exposed to the pestilential air of the river. It had gone two bells in the first dog-watch before we got under weigh, and as we had some distance to beat down before we could reach the bars on the Brass river, and by six o'clock it is dark in those latitudes, we could not hope to clear them by daylight. However, Upton was not to be deterred from his intention. He led in the Santa Maria, towing the pinnace and cutter, I following in the Cherub, with the gig's crew and some Kroomen as my ship's company, he having the rest of the people with the wounded on board the big schooner.

The signal was given, the anchors hove in and stowed, and away we went at a great rate through the water, heeling over to the furious gusts which every now and then came in from the sea, giving notice of what we were to expect. The Santa Maria was under her mainsail, closely reefed, and jib, but I preferred carrying my square topsail also, closely reefed, of course, to enable me to keep my vessel better in hand, and fortunate it was in the sequel that I did so. By the time that we had got well into the Brass Channel, the sun sank behind the groves of mangroves in a wide extended flame of angry red, darkness following with rapid strides upon the departed day.

As long as I could see the Santa Maria I kept in her wake, but as she much outsailed the Cherub, by dusk she ran us altogether out of sight, and I was left to find my way as I best could; the black pilot being in the other vessel, it was very far from pleasant work, I assure you. For a long time we continued tacking across the stream, making, however, but little way, while the dark mangrove-bushes, forming a long low line, marked the shore on either side, and a-head appeared a wall of white breakers through which our course lay.

Night had now set in, and darkness covered the face of the deep. Overhead were threatening clouds, which every now and then sent forth deluges of rain, which were blown in our teeth by the furious blast; below was the silent mysterious stream, with its voracious and terrific inhabitants, whose prey, should we strike the hidden rocks, we might any instant become. At no period of my existence had time appeared so long. I thought we should never get into clear water. I had, in truth, seldom before commanded a vessel placed in so critical a position as the Cherubino, and I was consequently doubly anxious. I was every moment on the topsail-yard looking out for dangers to be avoided. At last the roar of the innermost bar sounded on my ears, and before long I could see the white frothy waves close on our weather-bow, but as for a space of unbroken water, none was to be found.

"The Santa Maria has passed safe over, and so must we," I thought. "So here goes. Keep her well full," I sang out to the man at the helm. "Take her right through it."

Away flew the Cherubino, heeling over so that the water washed into our lee scuppers. The line of white-crested waves was close under our bows.

"Hold fast, every man!" I cried.

The hatches had been battened down. The little vessel seemed to know her danger, but to be determined to surmount it. Gallantly she breasted the foaming waves. The first sea struck her, sending the water (for it was more than a spray) fore and aft, over our decks, wetting every soul through and through to the skin. One of the men, from the sister isle, I remember, vowed that it had washed an alligator right down his throat—claws, tail, and all; and when some of his messmates ventured to doubt his assertion, he declared "that it was a porpoise, or a whale at *laste.*" The next roller which came in made every timber in her frame quiver again, to the horror of the poor wretches below, who must, from their cries, have been expecting instant destruction — the final summing-up of all their woes. She rose bravely over it, a slant of wind well off shore filled her sails for a moment, and we were again in smooth water. This was, however, only the first of the three bars we must attempt to cross. Again we glided rapidly onward, heeling over to the breeze, to the no small terror of the Spanish crew, who had, it appeared, but little confidence in our knowledge of the dangers to be encountered. It was tack and tack for nearly another hour; when, as we were approaching the second bar, and I was on the fore-yard, looking out through the darkness in a hopeless endeavour to pick the best channel, I saw suddenly blaze up, towards the entrance of the river, the bright glare of a blue-light: another and another followed in rapid succession.

"Good Heavens!" I mentally exclaimed; "the Santa Maria must be on shore, and is making signals of distress. Perhaps the lights are burned to teach us to avoid the same danger."

No time was to be lost in fruitless conjecture. We were close upon the second line of broken water.

"Neck or nothing. Lord help the unfortunate beings below!" I ejaculated. "Keep her a good full," I cried, as I descended on deck.

As the saying is, every man holding on with nails and eyelids, lest a sea should come on board, we dashed through the barrier. Scarcely were we again in smooth water, than up went a rocket before us, another blue-light was burned, and a prolonged hail was borne down to our ears on the blast—I had before heard such a cry; it was that of strong men stricken with terror. The light appeared low; so that there was little doubt it must be burning in a boat. Perhaps the Santa Maria herself had gone down, and the survivors had escaped in the boats. If so, what had my small vessel to expect! Again the same cry was repeated, louder than before.

"A boat broad on the weather-bow," cried the look-out forward. There was now no doubt on the subject.

"One of the boats adrift," I cried. "Down with the helm. Heave the top-sail aback. Stand by, to let go the anchor," were the hurried orders I gave. "It is our only chance of picking them up," I thought. "We can then veer over to the boat as she drifts by. The risk is great, but the chance must be tried." I had not much time for calculation, you may be sure. "Let go the anchor," I sang out lustily; but the men forward saw the danger, and pretended not to hear the order.

Not a moment was to be lost in words of remonstrance. Drawing a pistol from my belt, I rushed forward, threatening to shoot the first man who showed a sign of disobedience. The men no longer forgot their duty. With an axe I had seized, I cut away the lashings and stoppers. Away ran the cable through the hawse-holes at a furious speed, as the vessel, her head to wind, drove before it. I thought it would have parted, as it came up at the end of sixty fathoms with a tremendous jerk, our stern being already among the breakers on the bar. A heavy sea came rolling in.

"Hold fast for your lives, in earnest," I sang out.

It broke directly under our bows, rushing on board, and sweeping everything before it. I thought at the moment the schooner would never have risen again. As it was, she was half full of water. The shrieks of the unhappy slaves below were terrific. I had released some of the Spaniards to assist in working the vessel, at some slight risk of their proving treacherous, but as there was little chance of their escaping if they were so, and none of their gaining anything, I trusted them. Another sea came on board with less violence; the boat was directly behind it, a little on our larboard bow.

"Starboard the helm," I cried. "So, steady."

The vessel edged quickly over. The boat came hurrying onward. In another moment if we missed her, she would be among the breakers, and nothing could save the people in her.

"Steady, so."

A dozen ropes were over our side for them to catch hold of, and I must do the Spaniards the justice to say, that they appeared as anxious to save their late enemies as we were. A huge sea bore her on. "Hurrah! we have her!" Four men were standing up in her, and as she surged alongside, they seized the friendly ropes and sprang on deck. The boat hurried by, and in another instant was dashed to pieces among the breakers.

"They are all gone!" exclaimed one of the men, as they leaped on deck. "We broke adrift as she got among the breakers of the last bar, and down she went like a shot."

"Good heavens! all those fine fellows lost!" I exclaimed. "Poor Upton! Do thus end all your aspirations for fame?" I thought, and then turned my attention to our present exigencies.

I now learned that, when crossing the last bar, the two boats had broken adrift, and that the men, fancying they should be safer in the larger one, had got into her; but that, however, they had found their strength insufficient to manage her, which they might have done the smaller boat.

"Hands up anchor," I cried, "we may yet find some one clinging to the wreck." The hands were all at the windlass, but our combined strength could not move the anchor. "Work with a will, my men—work with a will," I cried; but nothing would do. We hove the bow of the little vessel almost under water, the sea dashing over us all the time; but the anchor remained firm. At last, I saw that there was no chance of getting it up, so we slipped, and again made sail for the mouth of the river. We had yet another bar to cross before we could get into the open sea. It was with feelings of extreme anxiety that we approached the last line of breakers, rolling in with far greater fury than the two others, and among which we had too much cause to believe our brave shipmates and their unhappy prisoners were already engulfed.

We found the wind blowing stronger than ever, as we approached the sea, and chopping about within three or four points, with sudden squalls. It was probably in one of these squalls that the Santa Maria was lost. We hoped to be more fortunate, and if we could once get in the open sea, there was little to fear.

As we were standing towards the eastern bank, the look-out man sang out, "A rock on the weather-bow."

The cry was startling, for we could not tell how many more there might be ahead. As we flew by, a gleam of lightning suddenly darted from the sky, and, to my great relief, instead of a rock, exhibited the Albatross' pinnace which the four men had deserted. Putting the vessel about, in another minute I had the boat triumphantly in tow. To make a long story short, after an infinite succession of tacks, we at last reached the outer bar. An unbroken line of foaming rollers appeared before us. There was no use attempting to pick our way; so, keeping our sails well full, we steered directly for the centre. Bravely our bark breasted the raging billows, as the poets say; one after the other they came rolling in, seeming about to overwhelm her; but like a gallant hunter, she successively rose to them.

At last one more gigantic than the rest came thundering onwards

"Hold on, my men—hold on," I cried, scudding up the main rigging, followed by the rest of the crew, except two men who were lashed to the helm. The little craft plunged right into it, the clear water washed over the decks, and she seemed as if never about to rise again;—but neither was her day come, nor was ours. After each plunge, she lifted up her nose as buoyant as before, when in came another big tumbling sea. For a moment she staggered, as her decks were again deluged; and then joyfully rising once more, she sprang over it, as, like a sea-fowl when rising from a dive, she shook her head to free herself from the water. With a shout of joy we found ourselves clear of the treacherous stream and running rapidly through the clear sea.

Now that we were ourselves free from peril, the fate of our companions was brought more forcibly before our minds. In vain we looked along the line of white breakers which fringed the dark shore —nothing like the hull of a vessel could be seen.

"Poor Upton! We should have been congratulating each other on our success, and now who can say that you and your men are in the land of the living?" Such were the tones of my meditation as I walked the deck of my prize, while we were making a sufficient offing to bring up till the morning, when I purposed to run in again and look out for any vestiges of the wreck, or to carry off any of the people who might have reached the shore alive. To endeavour to procure some hope to my mind, I called aft the men we had saved from the boat; but they still persisted in declaring that the Santa Maria had gone down at the moment they broke adrift from her. I consequently dismissed them, and continued my solitary walk and gloomy reflections.

I was just going to put the vessel about for the last time before dropping our anchor—we had but one left us—when suddenly a bright light burst forth to seaward. To us it was a star of hope. Keeping the vessel up for it, before long the look-out sang out, "A ship on the weather-bow." My night-glass had constantly been turned in the same direction. "The Santa Maria, by all that's prosperous!" I exclaimed, joyfully.

After standing on some little way farther, I put the schooner about, and soon proved that my conjecture was right, for there was the Santa Maria herself, riding safely at anchor before us.

Passing close under her stern, I hailed—"We have got the men from the boats safe on board."

"Have you, my dear fellow? Thank God for it!" exclaimed Upton through his speaking-trumpet. "Drop your anchor under my lee, and I will come on board of you."

Scarcely had he spoken, when a loud heart-cheering "Hip, hip, hip, hurra!" arose simultaneously from the crew of the Santa Maria, to which my people answered with right good will—"Hip, hip, hip, hurra!" It awoke the silence of the night with a vengeance. There's nothing sailors like so much as a good hearty cheer on fitting occasions. It made my heart bound when I heard it. All's well that ends well.

Upton soon came on board and thanked me for saving his people, whose loss had caused him much grief, as he could not help feeling that their death would be laid at his door, owing to his persisting in taking the vessels out of the river, notwithstanding the dangers to be encountered.

CHAPTER XXIII.

THE FLYING DUTCHMAN.

WHEN we had got a good offing, as the wind was light, and there was every prospect of a fine night, we anchored both vessels till the return of the Albatross. We considered that there was no use knocking about to look for her, as our people were already so worn out, that those who had the watch on deck could scarcely keep their eyes open. Upton said that he could not stay with me long, for he did not like to leave so many Spaniards as there were still on board with his own crew, thus weakened by the people he had in the boat. He told me, however, that he had warned Benson, the midshipman who had accompanied him, and who was officer of the watch, to keep a sharp look-out on the Dons, lest they should attempt to retake their vessel. I had less fear on my own account, for we had fewer prisoners in comparison, but I determined still to be watchful.

It was very natural that the Spanish prisoners should hate us, and should be burning to revenge themselves, if they could do so with impunity. Our chief regret was for poor Seaton, who, as I have said, was the only officer wounded. Unfortunately, the assistant-surgeon had not come off with us, but Upton, who understood something of anatomy, expressed his opinion that our young shipmate was not materially hurt, and that, provided fever did not attack him, he would do very well. With the exception of one man, the rest were not, he conceived, in danger. The two schooners lay so close together that we could almost carry on a conversation with the people on board the Santa Maria, and Upton, every now and then, as we walked the deck, hailed her, to assure himself that all was right. I perceived a feverish excitement in his manner, which I was also conscious I possessed myself, and he observed to me, that though fatigued, he had not the least inclination to sleep.

"This climate plays sad havoc with a man's constitution, Walter," he said; "nothing but a good heart and sound body can enable one to brave it out. Fortunately, I believe I possess both. But as one does not know what may happen any moment, a shot from one of those rascally slavers may lay one low, or such a catastrophe as we have just escaped may finish one's career: if my hour should be near at hand, I make you my executor."

"I'll do whatever you wish; but nonsense, man—don't talk in that style," I was answering, when he interrupted me with vehemence.

"It is no nonsense, Fairfield, I tell you. What else can one expect among noxious exhalations, and burning suns, slaver's bullets and cannon-balls, assassins' knives, sharks and alligators, lions, baboons, and buffaloes—nonsense, forsooth—the only wonder is that one manages to counteract their nefarious machinations to possess themselves of one's body and personal effects—the soul, the essence, the ethereal part, such base-born brutes cannot touch, thanks to the main-topsail halliards which keep it out of their reach."

I thought he was quizzing me with this string of words, and laughed heartily at the odd combination, yet I felt a strong inclination to answer him in the same strain.

"You may laugh, Fairfield, laugh your fill," he continued, in the same strain; "but it is sad, sober earnest I am talking—I am, indeed—I would it were otherwise. I would that the spirit of joy and lightness could put to flight the demons of wretchedness and obscurity which hover over us. It is a fearful combat, and sadly unequal—a mighty host of evil beings arrayed against a mere handful of celestial messengers."

He was silent for a moment, and we took a turn on the deck.

"Fairfield," he exclaimed, on a sudden, with fearful energy, grasping my arm in so strong a vice that I thought he would have broken it, "what in the name of mercy is the matter?"

"On my word, Upton, I cannot tell, except you are much overworked and rather excited; and if you will lie down and take half-an-hour's sleep, I think it would be better for you," I replied.

"Sleep! there is no sleep for those in authority, at such times as these. Benson, ahoy!" he shouted. "Keep a bright look-out there."

"Ay, ay, sir," answered the midshipman from the deck of the Santa Maria.

"Is there any stir among the Spaniards aboard?" Upton inquired.

"No, sir, all as quiet as mice," was the answer.

"See to them, sir, and pistol any one who dares to show his ugly nose on deck," exclaimed poor Upton. "We must take care they don't recapture the ship—they would try it if they dared. I'll be on board of you presently, when I've settled some important business with Mr. Fairfield."

"Ay, ay, sir," answered Benson, rather puzzled to make out what his officer was talking about.

Suddenly an uncontrollable fit of laughter seized me, and I was astonished at my own voice, so strange and wild appeared the sounds. "What you were saying is perfectly true, my dear fellow; but let us be merry while we can," I exclaimed, intending to be very wise. "We have done a deed this day Alexander or Cæsar might have been proud of, and I doubt if either of them would have managed to carry the Santa Maria and Cherubino clear over those bars as we did. Ha, ha, ha!" and I laughed at my own conceit. "Do you believe in spirits, Upton; beings of the nether world?"

"Yes—no—yes, yes," he answered, hurriedly. "Benson, ahoy! who is that man standing between the masts of the schooner there?"

I saw the midshipman move to either side of the deck to look.

"There is no one standing up there, sir," he replied.

"You speak falsely, sir!" thundered Upton, who even in his madness (for with that dreadful malady he was, I feared, afflicted) retained his polite mode of expression. "I mean that dark fellow who is grasping hold of the two mast-heads and flinging somersets between them. He is big enough, I should think."

I could hear poor Benson laugh, as also the watch who were on the look out, but he was sorely puzzled to know how to answer the first lieutenant's joke."

"If he were there, sir, he must have gone overboard, for I don't see him," he answered, judiciously.

"Don't speak of it just now, Upton," I whispered. "But, by Jove! what is there?" and I pointed to windward, towards which direction he turned his gaze. "If that be not the Albatross coming down upon us under all sail, my eyes strangely deceive me."

"Of course it's she," said Upton, calmly. "Don't repeat the nonsense I have been uttering. I should know her at any distance; she seems in a desperate hurry too; royals set, and studding-sails out on both sides. You remark the new cloth in her fore-top-gallant sail, which is shining bright in the moonbeams?"

"I do, I do," I said, for I saw it clearly, and several other points he remarked on. "What can our good captain mean by carrying such a press of sail at night, and so near the coast?"

"He has had misgivings about us—supernatural warnings," said Upton, solemnly. "But thank Heaven he comes, for we shall now have medical assistance for the sick and wounded; they, poor fellows, much require it; and I have been longing to get them safe on board."

As we were speaking, we were looking intently at the brig. I never saw her to such advantage—in the soft pale moonlight, her sails glistened whiter than usual, her masts seemed tauter, and her yards squarer than in reality, but we considered this was owing to a slight ocular deception. She seemed, as she glided majestically over the waters, like some beautiful spirit, sent on a beneficent mission to sea-worn mariners. We were rather surprised at the rapid progress she made towards us, for the wind had dropped to almost a calm, or at least there was scarcely more wind than would have sent her along at the rate of two knots an hour. Down she came directly upon us. Upton grasped my arm.

"Fairfield," he said, "I suppose she'll heave-to under our stern, and I must go on board and report what we have done. Not a bad day's work; but I have an inexpressible dislike to the idea of presenting myself before our captain and shipmates. The doctor will put me on the sick list the moment he sees me, though I'm as well as ever I was in my life, and as fit for work. Fairfield, you must go and state that I am engaged in my duties on board. See, here she comes!"

I think I stated that the two prizes were lying abreast of each other with their heads to the northward, and that my vessel, the Cherubino, was the innermost one.

"How superb the Albatross looks!" continued Upton, his outstretched arm pointing towards her. "By Jove! she's coming down directly for us. Does it strike you, Fairfield, that perhaps she may not have seen us? We must let her know where we are, at all events. Benson, ahoy! fire one of your larboard guns to let the Albatross know our whereabouts."

"Ay, ay, sir," sang out Benson.

"Now, Fairfield, I suppose you've got a gun loaded on board—bear a hand, man, and fire it."

I directly ordered a quarter-master, who was doing duty as my first officer, to see that a gun was loaded as a signal, and to fire it without delay.

Before, however, there was time to do so the Albatross was down upon us. She saw us, it appeared, or, if not, she, fortunately for us, selected a course which avoided us both. On she came directly between the two vessels. As we watched her approaching, we could see the water hiss and bubble up under her bows, and could hear the rippling sound it made. I longed to hail her—I felt that I ought to do so, but my tongue was tied to my mouth. A man was stationed on the forecastle on the look-out. I could distinguish his features clearly in the moonlight.

"There's Tom Hudson on the larboard bow, Upton," I said; "don't you see him? In what an odd way he looks at us!"

"Ay, yes—I observed it," answered my brother officer. "There's a fixed leaden gaze in his eyes. The fact is, the man is only half awake. For my part, I am not quite certain even now that he sees us."

The brig glided by us. There were two more of her people looking at us over the gangway, and as her quarter came abreast of us we could see three or four officers walking on the poop. One was Captain Dainmore—another was Green.

"Ah, and there's Haggis too! I wish that he would give us a little of his skill," suddenly exclaimed Upton. "But I say, Fairfield, who in the name of wonder is that fourth fellow? If I did not know that I was myself on board here talking to you—ha, ha, ha!—I should think that it was myself."

I looked attentively as he spoke, and sure enough there was a tall figure of the very height and air of Upton walking alongside the captain. Who he was I could not tell, for there was no other officer on board at all like Upton. What was also very strange was, that not one of them seemed to take the slightest notice of us.

"By Heaven, I must speak her!" suddenly exclaimed Upton, almost gasping for breath.

"Brig ahoy!" he shouted, in a tone which sounded like a wild scream.

"Ay, ay, sir," was the answer, and I knew that it was Benson's voice.

"Albatross, ahoy!" again shouted Upton.

"I don't see her, sir," answered Benson. "All ready there with the gun."

The Albatross glided past us in all her beautiful proportions, and was soon under our stern. I thought she would instantly shorten sail and heave-to.

"Don't see her!" exclaimed Upton. "Why, man, where are your eyes?"

Just then "bang"—the gun from the Santa Maria exploded. The sound struck on our ears with extraordinary loudness. Almost at the same moment, a piece on board my vessel was fired. We both started. Our nerves were sadly shaken by the day's work. Our eyes were still fixed on the Albatross, when we saw her topgallant masts and yards rise in the air, followed by her top-sails—

her studding-sails went away on either side—her courses melted from view—her hull split in two, and seemed to sink into the ocean, and she was gone. We rubbed our eyes and gazed on the spot—the moonbeams played on the water, but no vessel was to be seen. For some minutes after this extraordinary occurrence, we stood still without uttering a word, and gazing on the spot where our ship had been.

"What can have become of her?" at length Upton exclaimed, as if he had been seriously meditating on the matter. "I trust in mercy no accident has happened to her; but do you know, Walter, I agree with Shakspeare, that there are more things in heaven and earth than are dreamed of in our philosophy. Speak, man, speak—what has become of the Albatross and of all the brave spirits in her? Have she and they melted into thin air?—where are they?—tell me?"

I had myself before been excited, but the noise of the gun had recalled me to my proper senses, and my brother officer's extravagance served to calm me. "I trust well, and at no very great distance from us," I replied. "The report of our gun will probably bring them down upon us. I'll tell you what it is, Upton,—we have been cheated by some optical delusion, and though I can in no way account for it, I do not believe that we have seen the Albatross at all."

I suspected afterwards that the appearance was more in our own feverish minds, rather than the orb of vision.

"Not seen her, man!" he exclaimed. "Are we to mistrust our own senses, because materialists venture to doubt the existence of a spiritual world? If we have not seen our ship, we have seen the Flying Dutchman, who, by the by, has no business to be up here—or else some demon-commanded bark, sent to warn us of impending danger. Ask Benson if he has seen her,—my throat is dry, and I cannot hail."

"Benson, ahoy!" I shouted; "do you see anything of the Albatross?"

"Yes, sir," he answered, to my very great surprise; "I see her coming down before the wind on my larboard bow. Don't you see her, sir?"

"No," I replied, fairly puzzled again, "I have not made her out."

"You must be as blind as a badger, then," shouted the midshipman with a strange laugh. "Why, she's not three cables length off from us, and big enough, in all conscience."

"That's not a proper way of speaking to your superior officer," I exclaimed. "You don't see her, you know."

"My superior officer be ——. I do," was the answer. "Yes, there."—He turned round and hailed, as if he were speaking to the Albatross, but he got no answer. He hailed again.

"By ——, if you don't choose to be civil I'll wake you up a bit with a cannon-ball," he exclaimed. "I'll let you know who's captain of the Santa Maria *pro tem*. Tomkins, fire the larboard aftermost gun. It's loaded, I know. Elevate it, man, and blaze away and be d——d to you."

"Hillo," I thought, "a pretty state we are getting into; we shall be stark staring mad before the morning."

At that moment bang went the gun—it was a mere chance that it had not been fired into us. Benson directly after spoke us.

"I've sent the Albatross to kingdom come, I believe, sir, for she's nowhere to be seen, either north, south, east, or west," he shouted.

"I can't make it out at all."

"I should think not," I replied. "But never mind, Mr. Benson. Who succeeds you as officer of the watch? Go and call him, and tell him he is to take charge of the deck, while you enjoy half an hour's sleep."

"Ay, ay, sir," answered the midshipman, who was aware that he had been somewhat irregular in his language, and directly afterwards an old quarter-master announced that he had taken his post.

I had some work in persuading Upton to lie down, for he most required rest, but at length I succeeded, indeed, I did not like to let him go on board the Santa Maria in the state he was. For two hours I paced the deck, anxiously wishing for the morning. At last Upton awoke, and, to my great satisfaction, appeared himself again. He then returned to his own schooner, and I lay down to recover my fatigue. The firing had done some good, for it served to keep the Spaniards quiet, and to let the Albatross know our whereabouts. As morning broke she appeared, beating up from the northward, and by eight o'clock she was up to us, for as the destination of the prizes we knew would be to the northward, there was an object in our running down to her. I need scarcely say that she had not been near us during the night, and that whatever we did see, it was not the Albatross. The story got about the ship, and gave rise to all sorts of Flying Dutchman yarns, and foreboding prognostications respecting the fate of the schooners. Neither Upton, Benson, nor I suffered from fever, as I feared we might, and to our great satisfaction, Haggis pronounced a favourable opinion on Seaton's case.

The Spanish crews, notwithstanding their resistance to lawful authority, were allowed to escape not only with impunity, but with their bag and baggage, among which we afterwards discovered they had stowed away not a small number of dollars. We afterwards heard that in several instances the identical fellows who had got off so cheaply, after slaying and wounding Her Majesty's liege subjects, were again fallen in with at their old work. Now, if we had *treated them as pirates*, and *run them up at once to their own yard-arm*,* not only would they have been prevented from following their own accursed trade, but the example would have deterred others from pursuing a course which might lead to such disagreeable results. Now, the very high pay a slaver's crew receive, enables her to get the best men to be found in the Brazils or elsewhere. If they ran a risk of their lives, none but the most daring would venture to engage in the vile traffic. However, while the Brazilian authorities encourage it by every means in their power, our task is almost hopeless.

To strengthen my assertion that the infliction of death is the only

* Nothing *short* of that mode of proceeding will stop the Slave-trade:—and more, it would be the *most humane* manner of proceeding—after giving due notice of your unswerving intention of so proceeding. Depend upon it that it would not have to be done *twice*, when it was seen that you were in earnest. But let there be no compromise.

means of putting a stop to slaving, the observation of a Greek pirate has just occurred to me. I belonged some years ago to the ——, brig-of-war, in the Mediterranean, when we captured a Greek mistico, with a crew of the most determined desperadoes on board I ever met. Her captain was a remarkably fine young fellow, a complete Adonis in appearance, but with an eye which betrayed the devil lurking within. To our minds the proof of her piratical exploits was perfectly clear, but when sent to Malta for adjudication, the captain and crew were acquitted, and allowed to proceed on their way. Not many months had elapsed when we again fell in with our handsome friend, an hour or so after he had plundered an English merchantman, whose crew were perfectly ready to swear to his identity. When brought on deck, he stood in an attitude of proud indifference, and when asked by our commander how it was he ventured to commit a crime of such atrocity, after having been before treated so leniently,

"Oh!" he responded, with a scornful laugh and shrug of his shoulder, "had you wished to put an end to my pirating, you ought to have hung me at first. Then I should have comprehended the meaning of your threats."

We were engaged the whole day in getting the two schooners in fit trim for their voyage to Sierra Leone, where it was necessary to take them for adjudication. As the Cherubino had actually slaves on board, and the Santa Maria was fitted with slave decks, and had her water casks stowed in her hold, there was no doubt of their being condemned. Captain Dainmore had determined to give us a day's rest before we sailed, which I, indeed, absolutely required. I was to have charge of the Cherubino, which, as having slaves on board, was the most valuable prize, and Hawkins, one of our mates, was to take command of the Santa Maria.

CHAPTER XXIV.

WHAT HAS BECOME OF THE SANTA MARIA?

BEFORE dark I went on board my new command, while Hawkins took charge of the Santa Maria. I had twelve British seamen, and six Kroomen, and he had ten of the first and four Africans. Both vessels, according to their requirements, had been provisioned and victualled for upwards of thirty days. I cannot say that I anticipated any pleasure in the voyage. There is something very far from delectable in the odours and noises on board a slave ship, even although there are, as was the case on board the Cherubino, comparatively, only a few negroes. Then I had no companionship but my own thoughts and a few books during the space of at least three weeks or a month, the average passage from the mouth of the Niger to Sierra Leone. If a man is in the least liable to be haunted by blue devils, it is the position of all others in which they are sure to attack him with tenfold fury.

"It is a very fine thing to command a ship," I thought, as I stepped on the deck of my charge. "But I shall sadly miss the cheerful voices of my companions in the Albatross, their long yarns and pleasant conversation."

I had, however, little time for meditation for the first day or so, my duties on board being so multifarious that they required all my attention. As soon as I got on board I had to divide my crew into watches, and to appoint each to their separate offices, while I had to act the part, not only of captain, but of master, purser, surgeon, and nurse, and I may also say of chaplain. My second in command was the young midshipman, Jenkins, who, although a smart lad, had no experience, and could afford me but little assistance.

Soon after day-break the next morning, a light breeze from the north-east springing up, the Santa Maria and I got under weigh, and shaped a course for Sierra Leone. For five or six days the weather continued very favourable, and we made good progress, though we had to shorten sail at times to squalls, which soon again blew over. At last it fell a flat calm, and both vessels being close together, Hawkins came on board me, under pretence of asking my advice on several matters, but I suspect, in reality, for the sake of society.

The most important question he asked was, whether, should a vessel which looked like a slaver appear in sight, he might chase her and endeavour to capture her.

"The chances are you would catch a Tartar, Hawkins; and if you did not get your head broken, you would find yourself sold as a slave among the blackymoors. With negroes on board, I should not be justified in going out of my way to help you, and therefore, while you remain with me I cannot give you permission to do as you wish."

I did not at the time think of this conversation, but it occurred to me afterwards. When at length a breeze did spring up, it came from the westward, and we had the prospect of a long beat before we could get round Cape Palmas.

Before the wind we found both vessels sail very equally, though the Cherubino was the smallest, but when we came to haul our wind my vessel beat the Santa Maria hollow, for she being light, with scarcely, indeed, sufficient ballast in her for safety, made a great deal of lee way. On seeing this I cautioned Hawkins to be careful, and to shorten sail in time, especially at night, when it was more difficult to see the squalls before they came.

We exchanged signals with two of our own cruisers, and we fell in at different times with a Spanish and Portuguese man-of-war; they each sent a boat on board, and seemed very much disappointed when they found what we were; indeed, from their looks I suspected they not a little longed to retake us. Indeed, I believe the ships of both those nations on the coast of Africa are employed very much more in protecting the slave trade, than in attempting to put it down.

We had been out two weeks, and Hawkins had kept pretty close to me, when one evening just before nightfall, I had run him very nearly out of sight. It was of too much importance for me to make the best of my way to allow me to heave-to for him, and I therefore continued my course under easy sail, hoping that during the night he would come up with me. I watched for him with some anxiety when I came on deck to take the morning watch, but not a sail was in sight on either board, the dark sea heaved and fell within the narrow confines of the black canopy which hung over us, unbroken by a single line or speck which hope might picture to be my missing consort. When the sun should have appeared, a dense mist, such as is rarely to be found except on the African coast or the streets of London in November, so completely enveloped us in its thick shroud, that not a fathom could we see beyond the end of the bowsprit.

Although the wind was light, it had come fair, and there was sufficient to send us along at the rate of three or four knots an hour. At last, as the day wore on, the stronger sea breeze set in, and blew off the fog in heavy wreaths over the land. As the horizon cleared, I fully expected to see the Santa Maria, but nothing of her was to be perceived from deck, and Jenkins, who went up to the mast-head, reported that not a sail was in sight. This was very vexatious, but it could not be remedied. To put back to look out for her was out of the question, and if I hove-to, she might very likely pass me either in shore of me or in the offing, so I continued my course.

We had sharp work of it during the afternoon, in shortening and making sail, as the squalls came heavily down on us off the land, and once, had we not let fly everything, the schooner would have been thrown on her beam-ends, or would have completely turned the turtle.

The next day, at the end of the forenoon watch, a sail hove in sight, which at first we were in hopes might be our missing consort, but she soon proved to be the man-of-war schooner, Pickle. A midshipman from her boarded me, when I told him of my anxiety about the Santa Maria, and on his hurrying back, the Pickle immediately made sail to look for her. Soon afterwards another schooner was seen in the same direction.

"I hope she may be the Santa Maria at all events," I heard Jenkins exclaim.

"Not likely, sir," observed old Bill Leadline, who had come with us, and was acting as boatswain on board. "I never expects to see she again. When I heard of the strange sights Mr. Upton, Mr. Fairfield, and Mr. Benson seed off the mouth of the Niggar river, I knowed harm would come of it. Depend on't something has happened to her; and I an't altogether comfortable like about ourselves."

"What are you talking about there?" I asked. "Come aft here, Leadline, and let me hear. You think some misfortune is going to happen to us?"

"Yes, sir," he answered bluntly, as if he had made up his mind to the worst; "I do."

"Well, then, keep your thoughts to yourself, and don't frighten the people with your nonsense. Now, I believe, that we shall get safe into Sierra Leone."

"Beg pardon, sir, may I be bold to ask, sir, what was the reason of them supernatural sights as it was said was seen aboard the two crafts t'other night?"

I laughed as he spoke, though I felt ashamed of myself, and could not find fault with him for the freedom he was taking. "All fancy and moonshine," I replied. "Depend on it, nothing I or any one else saw would have any effect on our fate; and let me assure you, that nothing was seen at the time you speak of; so now go and call the watch, it is just eight bells."

With regard to ourselves, Leadline was at all events wrong, for without any adventure worth narrating, or without the loss of a single slave, we arrived safely at Sierra Leone My first inquiries were for the Santa Maria. Nothing had been heard of her; I hoped, therefore, to see her on the following day, but several passed and she did not arrive.

The Cherubino was condemned as a lawful prize by the court of mixed commission, and her slaves were landed and lodged in the liberated African yard, till a spot was fixed on for their future abode.

I went out to visit my late charges a few days after they had been there, and they all appeared delighted to see me. They were employed in building their huts with wattles and red clay, and in thatching them with long rye grass.

I entered a neighbouring village, under the escort of some of my friends, and found many of the cottages not only comfortable, but furnished with many articles of African luxury; indeed, from all I saw, I should say that the liberated slave has decidedly improved his physical condition in leaving his native home, and, I hope, by the exertions of the Christian Missionaries, his moral state also.

While I was thus anxiously waiting the arrival of Hawkins, the mail from England came in. There were several letters for me. The handwriting of one I knew at a glance. I eagerly tore it open. It was from Edith—my own Edith.

Now I am not fond of introducing my own griefs, nor even my joys, before the world, for it can scarcely be expected to sympathise with the one or the other; but the contents of her letter are so intimately connected with my story, that I am compelled to allude to them.

My feelings were of intense grief—bitter disappointment. The hope of my life had fled; henceforth all was to be a blank. She was not to be mine!

I have as yet spoken little of her. She was the daughter of Colonel Mowbray, an officer commanding a regiment in India. She had consented to be mine without asking his leave; but trusting to his love, had written to him, feeling confident of obtaining it. Poor girl! she knew not the heart of a man of the world.

Her father's answer came; but how different from what she expected, and I had been led to hope. It strictly forbade our marriage, and ordered her, on pain of his severe displeasure, to hold no correspondence with me after she had written to communicate the fact. She would have a fortune, and must therefore wed with one of equal wealth, at least.

This was to be her last letter. She would not deny herself the satisfaction of expressing her affection; she said everything her tender nature could suggest to soothe my feelings—to draw the sting from the cruel wound she was compelled to inflict: but she must bow to the stern decree.

The bright visions which had animated my existence had departed. The malignant fever might now claim its victim. Such were my first feelings. I was no longer myself. I ate, drank, and talked mechanically; but as I never mentioned the cause of my wretchedness, the change which all perceived was put down to the effect of the climate. I felt that could I have gone home all might be well; but parted from each other, she might be influenced by false reports—might be persuaded not only to obey her father's commands, but to forget me—to marry another. That thought was madness.

Oh! if I could be with her—could speak to her—could tell her all I felt and all I thought—she would never consent to give me up while her heart remained faithful.

We were both young—we could wait; and Hope whispered to me that I might gain rank and fame, and perhaps wealth, and be worthy of her even in her father's sight.

But she was forbidden even to receive my letters. I however had still the liberty of writing, and could not yield her up in silence. Yield!—my heart rebelled against the word. I would not yield her up till she was torn from me.

I employed my time in writing numberless letters. Many I destroyed, and some I sent; but as their contents cannot prove interesting to the public, I will not transcribe them.

I was thus employed when a black boy poked his woolly head into the room, to tell me that an officer, who was ill at the hospital, and had just been landed from a merchant brig, desired to see me.

"Who is he?" I asked.

"Me not know, Massa—him berry bad—many mans land wid him berry bad too."

I hurried off to the hospital; my mind misgave me as I approached that mansion into which so many enter, but so few depart, except to their long last abode. I was shown into the officers' ward, where, on a bed, a phantom of his former self, lay poor Hawkins worn out with fatigue and sickness.

"Why, Hawkins, my poor fellow," I exclaimed, "though I have been very anxious about you, I am sorry to see you in this plight. What has happened to you?"

"That's what I want to tell you, sir," he answered, in a weak voice. "I am not so bad as I look though; I am more starved and worn out than ill. You must know that when we lost sight of you in the fog, I was very much vexed, thinking that you might suppose I was after some mad scheme to hunt up slavers on my own account, so I determined to carry on all sail to overtake you. I had been on deck for several hours, constantly shortening and making sail, for it was very squally, you know, and we still saw nothing of the Cherubino, when at last I was obliged to turn in and take a snooze. Davis had charge of the watch—he was, I am afraid, somewhat addicted to liquor, but he appeared to me perfectly sober when I went below, and I charged him to shorten sail the moment a squall appeared, and to call me directly anything occurred. I had been asleep about two hours when I found myself jerked into the middle of the cabin, and heard loud cries from the people, and the noise of the sea rushing up the deck. How I found my way through the skylight I scarcely know, for I recollect nothing distinctly, till I discovered that I was holding on to the outside of the weather bulwarks, with all the crew, and that the Santa Maria had turned the turtle. The sea was fortunately smooth, and as the vessel was empty, there appeared a hope that she might float some time, but our position was very far from enviable. We had no boats, and even if we had, and should succeed in reaching the shore, either the negroes or the slaver's friends were very likely to put an end to us. I, however, felt that it would never do to yield without a struggle, and saw that our best chance of safety was to build a raft from the spars and upper part of the bulwarks, which we might chip off. Providentially, Finson, one of the carpenter's mates, had been chopping wood when the schooner went over, and had kept his axe firm in his hand, while he clambered on to the side of the vessel. By this circumstance, I believe, through Heaven's mercy, our lives were saved, for without the axe we could never have cut away the planks to form the raft. I first mustered all hands, and found that the only one missing was Davis, who had charge of the deck at the time of the accident. He had not been seen, and was supposed to have slipped overboard and sunk at once. I then explained my plan, and the men cheerfully set to work. My great fear was lest the vessel should turn completely over so as to prevent us from getting either the planks from the side, or at some water casks which had been lashed to the bulwarks for immediate use. Accordingly, we first commenced ripping away the planks from the bulwarks, and piling them up ready for use, and by this means we got at the water casks.

"Fortunately, they were securely bunged, and cutting the lashings, we got them alongside, and made them fast to the planks already loosened. You see I was afraid of securing anything to the vessel herself, lest she should go down and carry any of our treasure with her. Having got a good supply of planking to form a raft, my next care was to cut away the topmasts, and topsail, and top-gallant-yards of the schooner, out of which to make the framework, but I saw the risk that on their removal, she, losing their support, might go completely over. Of course, the yards being under the masts, they supported them, and there was, therefore, no risk in detaching them, so we cut away every rope which held them, knowing that if the schooner went down, they would float clear.

"To perform this work without throwing additional weight on the heads of the masts, I had some canoes built of the planks, on which the men floated out to perform the work. They were certainly not very water tight, for they consisted simply of three or four planks placed one above another, to form the bottom, and two others for the sides, lashed together with ropes: and, it struck me, that if we could have had enough of them, we might, by this means, have reached the shore.

"We at the same time secured the jib-boom, which we got without much difficulty, and the fore-top-gallant sail, which might serve as a sail for our raft. We now began to form the raft, by making a frame-work of the stoutest spars, while the others were placed across them, with the planks on the top of all. In the centre we put our two precious casks of water between two spars, which served as keel for our raft. As I expected, as soon as the support of the masts was removed, the schooner turned keel uppermost, and all chance of getting anything more out of her was at an end. The only provisions we had secured was a small cask of biscuit, which floated out of the cabin skylight. It was hardly enough to keep body and soul together for two days, with the strictest economy, and was almost completely wetted through, so that I felt that there was every probability of dying of hunger, though I did not tell the people so, but tried to keep up their spirits as I best could.

"By sinking the heel of the top-gallant mast we formed a mast on which we hoisted the top-gallant sail, and with a light wind from the southward, as there was nothing more to be got from the wreck, we cast off, and left the Santa Maria to her fate. She was already settling down, and I don't suppose floated an hour after we lost sight of her. Away we stood to the northward, going at the rate of two knots an hour. My greatest hope of safety lay in our falling in with some vessel, but numbers might pass without seeing us.

"The men were cheerful, and even made light of our misfortune, obeying with alacrity every order issued. Fortunately, we had the whole day before us. The sun came out, and I had the biscuits dried, and then issued a mouthful to each man, with a mug of water. My great care was never to let thirst get the better of them. Starvation is very bad, but, I believe, thirst more speedily drives people out of their minds.

"You may be certain all this time we were looking out for sails, but hour after hour passed away, and none appeared. At last the night came on, and while one half of the people kept watch, the other lay down to sleep, though there was scarce room enough for them to stretch their limbs. I will not attempt to describe the dreadful thoughts which passed through my head that night, and certainly I could not have believed that I should have been able to endure many such hours again.

"The morning came, and there we were, still as far from help as ever, with a smooth shining sea on every side around us. Not a speck like a sail was there in the clear line of the horizon to cheer our hearts with even a prospect of relief. I had served out the bread at stated intervals, but that could contribute to keep us alive a very little time longer. I trembled for the future. Even the men began to be down-hearted, and sat moodily without exchanging a word with each other.

"Suddenly we were startled by the cry of 'A shark, a shark!' for I had sunk into a sort of doze, worn out with fatigue, mental and bodily. I looked up to see Simmons, who had been sitting with his legs in the water, draw them suddenly up, while the tail of a shark, as the monster turned round alarmed at the cry, almost knocked him off the raft.

"'Wait a bit, messmates,' he exclaimed, 'we'll see if we can't nail that ere chap. Jones, do you stand by with your hatchet, and if he plays that ere trick again, just give him a nick over the small of the back,'—(I never before heard of a fish having a small of the back)—'and do the rest of you be ready to haul him in. He'll make precious fine salt junk, I'll warrant.'

"'Take care what you are about, my men, that you don't capsize the raft, or lose your legs,' I exclaimed.

"'No fear of that, sir,' answered Simmons. 'Now be ready, lads.'

"Without more ado, I saw him shove his naked leg overboard, and move it backwards and forwards as an attractive bait to the sharks, while he kept his eye intently fixed on the water to draw it back at the proper moment. He had not long to wait; a ravenous brute saw the tempting morsel, and made a grab at it. At the instant he drew in his foot, almost as the shark's long snout touched it. The action startled the fish, he whisked his tail in the air, over the edge of the raft; as he prepared to descend, it was caught hold of by the men, and down on it came the carpenter's axe with a tremendous blow.

"'Haul away, my lads, haul away!' sang out Simmons; and almost as soon as the shark could have swallowed one of us, to his infinite surprise and disgust, he found the knives of our hungry fellows cutting rashers out of his back. I don't mean to say he felt, because the blow on his spine had deprived him of all sensation, but his fierce eyes showed what he would have been at had he caught any one of us outside the raft.

"When the people had satisfied their hunger off the raw flesh of the shark, they cut off slices to hang up to dry, and then hove the remainder overboard. Scarcely had they done so, when, on looking astern, we saw the water alive with the monsters, attracted, doubtlessly, by the blood and flesh of their comrade. Our men only laughed.

"'No fear of wanting beef now, my lads,' sang out Simmons. They forgot what would be our fate if the raft were capsized. Day after day passed by, and our water was nearly exhausted, though of food, such as it was, we had sufficient.

"On the sixth day, a heavy shower of rain came down, and by spreading out our sail we were able to catch nearly enough to refill our casks. This and the shark's flesh saved our lives. I wont tire your patience—indeed, I am not very well able to speak—by telling you all that happened. Three days more we waited, and not a sail had we seen. We were so low down in the water that our horizon was very circumscribed, and even when our sail was seen, it probably was believed to belong to a canoe. It was just as day dawned, I had stood up to stretch my limbs after a broken sleep, when, on looking windward, I saw a brig standing on the same course as we were, but somewhat on our starboard hand. She might see us, or she might take no notice of us, and pass us at a distance. We shouted as if our voices could be heard by the people on board. I never endured such an half-hour of suspense as that from the time we first saw her till she made us out. As soon as she did so, she stood for us, and we were all speedily hoisted on board; but so weak and wretched, that we could not walk across the deck. The brig proved to be the Jane, Captain Williams, bound for this place, on her way to Liverpool. We had fortunately a quick passage here; and I hope our poor fellows will soon get round again. They want good food and dry beds more than anything else, for raw shark's flesh is not the thing to live on exactly every day in the week. I am more grieved about the loss of the schooner, and the suffering of my poor fellows, than I can well express."

I comforted Hawkins as well as I could, and left him in better spirits than I found him. I next visited the men, who were already recovering, with even one day's rest. I had now an object to take away my thoughts from myself, and I soon felt its beneficial effects in the returning elasticity of my spirits, and the bright light in which I viewed affairs in general. I advise all my friends who have mental or physical griefs, to exert themselves to relieve those of others, and they will soon find their own diminished, if not forgotten altogether. In my letters to England, I had made every inquiry in my power to discover the relations of poor little Eva, but without any success; and we, the officers of the Albatross, had determined not to deliver her into the hands of any one who had not a legal right to take charge of her.

Several days more passed before the Albatross came into harbour, and by that time Hawkins and the late crew of the Santa Maria had so far recovered as to be able to return to their duty. On returning on board, I was glad to find Seaton, and the rest of those who had been wounded in the Quorra affair, on their legs again, as well as ever. My messmates remarked the change which had taken place in me, and thought that I was going to be attacked with fever. Haggis even recommended me to invalid on the first opportunity, for he thought that I could not withstand the complaint; but as I knew my only chance of promotion and success was by remaining on the coast, I determined to brave the worst. I therefore again resumed my duties on board, and sailed once more for the south.

However, I longed for excitement—for something to do more novel than chasing slavers—and was not long in finding it. We were off a place called Badagry, where there is a missionary station, the teachers of which have so well performed their duty that they have converted a large number of Africans. This caused the jealousy and hatred of a neighbouring king, who threatened to destroy the settlement, root and branch, if all hands did not instantly consent to abjure their faith, and turn out the missionaries. Just at this juncture the Albatross appeared off the coast, and the missionaries sent a boat on board with a letter requesting assistance. As our captain was in a hurry to proceed farther south, I volunteered to do duty on shore with a boat's crew, and he was pleased to approve of my proposal. I accordingly picked some good men, and pulled on shore, where I was cordially received by the missionaries, who told me that the blacks were totally unable to manage the big guns, and that they had very few muskets in the place; I therefore immediately set to work to examine the means of defence.

There were six guns on very rickety carriages, and they had no sights, and though there was powder, they were destitute of ball. The first thing I did was to repair the carriages, and to draw lines with chalk along the top of the guns to serve as sights, and then to cut up some bars of iron, which were not a bad substitute for grape shot; and the next was to point two of my guns up the river, and the others in the different directions by which the station, which was on the top of a gentle rise, could be approached.

These dispositions were made before night; and having set a guard, I went to bed. I was startled out of my sleep by what sounded to me the war-cries of the enemy, and, jumping up, I hurried to the door to lead on my men. When in the open air, I found that the sounds were very different to what I had supposed, and that they proceeded from the black converts of the missionaries singing the midnight hymn of praise—a practice they had been taught to pursue in time of danger or affliction.

The next morning the army of the enemy appeared. When summoning their king to hold a palaver, I told his sable majesty that I would annihilate him and all his people if he did not take himself off. Fortunately, a large basket was floating down the river, and I assured him that I would treat him as I treated it. Accordingly, I took my chance and fired: the shot knocked the basket to atoms, to the great delight of my own people, and the evident dismay of the besieging forces. This fortunate occurrence having happened, I allowed time for its effect to work · the king, after consulting with those who had accompanied him, asked leave to return to his army, to hear what they thought of the matter.

I answered that he was perfectly welcome to go where he liked, but to remember that if he ever approached the station with hostile intent, the big guns would treat him exactly in the same way that they had treated the basket. The hint was taken; and I believe to this day the missionary station has been undisturbed.

I mention the story to show the advantages of an armed neutrality; and I wish Messrs. Cobden, Bright, and Co. would take a lesson from it, and learn that as long as England shows what she can do, no one will venture to attack her. By knocking the basket to pieces, I gained a bloodless victory, and made friends with the foe. I did more—for many of them were afterwards induced to visit the station, and become Christians.

I spent some time with those good people, whose exertions in the great cause of teaching the heathen the way of truth deserved all praise; but I was not sorry when the Albatross appeared off and took me on board.

CHAPTER XXV.

MARSDEN'S SECOND TALE.

WE were once more standing off the coast, on a voyage to St. Helena—that never-to-be-forgotten little rock, where the fallen Napoleon breathed his last—and as we had every prospect of fine weather, our yarn-spinning propensities were again summoned into action. Marsden was called on for a story, and producing a MS., he read the following legend:—

THE FATHER'S CURSE.

Not a cloud floated in the intense blue sky, not a breath of air stirred the shining surface of the slumbering ocean. The hot sun, in his meridian splendour, shed his burning rays full upon the unsheltered head of a human being, who, deserted and alone, rested by a few frail planks upon the watery plain. No land was near to cheer his heart with hopes of release; far as his eye could reach was one wide expanse of silvery brightness, canopied by the azure arc of heaven. It seemed to the hapless mariner that this was the entire world, and he its sole inhabitant, the raft on which he lay the only spot whereon to place his foot. Dreadful thoughts crossed his brain.

Could this be true? Had another deluge swept all his fellow-men from the face of the globe?—or, had he been transported to some other world, such as he had heard tell, where those bright stars, at which so oft he had gazed in his midnight watch, twinkling far distant in the sky—a mere mass of water without land or inhabitants? Day after day, and night succeeding night, had he floated alone, moving onwards over the face of the deep, yet reaching no land and meeting no bark to give him relief.

The raft was composed of some shattered spars, lashed to the mast-head and main-top of a large brig, with a few planks nailed above them, to which was secured a sea-chest and a small cask with a hen-coop placed so as to form a bulwark to the seas. A spar fixed in the centre, and stayed up on either side, served as a mast, with a boat's sail, which now hung uselessly down, hoisted on it, an oar passing through the top, doing the work of a rudder.

The form which lay on this frail construction was one of manly beauty, though care, anguish, and hardship had made deep inroads on it, as his furrowed brow, his hollow cheek, and dim sunken eye full well attested. The hue of his countenance, which once might have been fair and bright, was now sallow from gnawing hunger, and tanned by exposure to the clime of the scorching tropics; his hair, once black as the raven's wing, now tinged with grey, hung in long dishevelled tresses over his shoulders, while his beard exhibited proofs that many days had passed since it had last been trimmed.

His tall figure, once full of grace and strength, was now gaunt and attenuated, like some noble tree, branchless and stripped of foliage, when blasted by the fiery bolts of heaven. Even thus reduced and prostrate as he was, there was something majestic and daring in his mien, defying, even to the last, the terrors of death; yet, his habiliments were those of a common seaman, though such he could scarcely be; a check shirt, a pair of loose trowsers, and a red sash, in which was stuck a dagger, or rather a long knife, such as carried by Spanish sailors, completed his costume.

For a long time he lay completely prostrate on the raft—apparently, the fell tyrant was assuming his all-potent sway; his miseries in this life were soon to end, his crimes to meet their just reward in another. Slowly he raised himself up on one arm, for his strength was too much exhausted, it seemed, to allow him to stand; his dim eyes wandered around the horizon, but the same view of sea and sky met their aching sight as had greeted them for so many days. He spoke, but his words were so faint he could scarcely hear them himself, yet it was some relief to break the dreadful silence which reigned over the ocean.

"Can it then be true?" he whispered, in a tone of anguish. "Am I doomed to wander ever thus over the wide desert sea, cut off from all communion with my race? or else to bring upon the heads of those who succour me the same fate which unrelentingly pursues me? That old man's burning curse scorches my heart—his words ring still loudly in my ear. Ah! but I myself am grown a dotard like him to believe that they could have influence over me. 'Tis chance alone which one day places wealth and power in our hands, the next one robs us of it, and chance may yet bring help, and place me once more on the deck of as brave a bark as the one which sank beneath my feet. A coward would long ago have died with half the anguish either of mind or body which I have suffered; but, while a spark of life remains, I will not yield. Even now, perhaps, a breeze may be bearing down some ship to succour me."

As he spoke he gradually raised himself from his recumbent position, though with pain and difficulty, and grasping the mast for his support, looked anxiously around. His hopes were again disappointed, and, overcome by the exertion, he sank once more down upon the raft. How long he thus remained he could not tell, when his eye rested on a speck of white, which seemed like the wing of a sea-fowl poised on a distant wave, or a fleecy cloud floating on the blue sky; yet as he gazed, his practised eye made out the royals of a ship just rising above the horizon. With starting eye-balls he watched to discover whether she was coming towards him, or perhaps only passing along in the distance to tantalize him the more, yet on she came, her top-gallant-sails appeared, then her top-sails, and by the time half her courses had risen above the water, he perceived that she must be a large ship, he thought probably a richly-freighted merchantman from the far-off lands of India. The sun shone brightly on her broad spread of canvass, which, as she glided calmly onwards, seemed to expand and tower upwards to the skies, glistening like a moving pillar of snow, or one of those vast icebergs which float over the dreary seas of the north. Ere her hull had yet appeared, a strain of music, soft as a seraph's song, came wafted over the wave upon his astonished ear; louder and louder it grew as the ship swiftly approached, yet not a breath of air rippled the surface of the sea, though her sails seemed full, and swelling with a strong breeze.

At last the lofty hull appeared, with a battery of guns frowning from her sides. Gay pennants floated from each mast-head, and a broad ensign flew out from her main-peak. As the seaman gazed he beheld the decks crowded with people. Bright and happy faces were there, not only of a brave and gallant crew, but among them were female forms, young and lovely as the angels in heaven, while the music, which had before been soft and melancholy, burst forth into joyous and martial strains, between the pauses of which merry and careless laughter struck upon his ear, and he could see that the persons on deck were footing it in the light dance, the seamen forward, those of higher rank in the after-part of the ship. In vain he raised his voice to cry for help, no one heeded him; a fair young couple were gazing over the side of the ship upon the blue waters, but their eyes fell not on him. They were joined by others who rested awhile from their amusement, but none regarded the deserted mariner. The noble ship sailed proudly on; the mimic waves she raised as she clove her way through the water, lifted his raft and rocked it to and fro. As the ship passed close abeam of him, he again tried to hail, but his voice died away unheard, overpowered by the sound of the music. Onward she went; he could look through her stern-ports into her cabins, which seemed garnished with every luxury and ornament. So close was she to him, that he could perceive the smile on the cheek of beauty, the glance of love and admiration in the eyes of the men as they pressed the hands of their fair companions; but of the hundreds who paced her decks not one appeared to heed him.

His heart sank within him; in vain he attempted to raise himself; in vain he shouted; a burst of wild mocking laughter echoed back his voice as the ship slowly receded from him; the forms which peopled her decks grew less and less distinct, the music each instant grew fainter; a bright gauze-like haze seemed to envelope her as gradually her hull sank beneath the horizon, her courses next disappeared, her top-sails, topgallant-sails, and royals followed, and he was again left alone upon the broad sea. He closed his eyes in agony of spirit. Was it a mocking phantom of the brain, or was she one of those spectre-barks of which he had heard, but whose appearance he had sceptically disbelieved, sent to tantalize him as a punishment for his crime—or, still more dreadful thought—had he himself, by some magic charm, become invisible to the eyes of his fellow-men? Such must be the case; he could not doubt the dreadful truth. That the ship he had seen was no phantom he felt assured. Her hull and dark guns, her taunt masts, the delicate tracery of her rigging, the features of her crew and passengers, were too clearly seen, to leave him in further uncertainty as to the fact. As thus he thought, he uttered a deep groan, and, for the first time, wished for death.

He closed his eyes, expecting never again to open them in life, while thick crowding fancies, mingled with recollections of the past, came over his brain; his crimes, dark and terrible, rushed back upon his mind; accusing angels prejudging and condemning him; every scene in his past life came before him—a dreadful drama;—too full of horrors to be told; yet one act there was, more palpable than the rest; so clear it seemed, that he, with others, again appeared to perform their parts. He spoke, and phantom shapes responded in words distinct upon his ear—

THE SEAMAN'S DREAM.

He stood beneath the verandah of a large mansion; in the far distance towered the magnificent ranges of the lofty Andes, the trees and the shrubs of the tropics were around, exulting in luxuriant vegetation—the lofty cotton-tree and ruddy shaddock, the cocoa-nut, the refreshing plantain, and citron and lime-trees, with innumerable other shrubs and plants, while to the west the ground sloped away towards the wide-spreading sea, on whose slumbering surface, just rippled over by the gentle night breeze, a crescent moon shed a long line of silvery light, casting a soft and mellow hue over the whole scene, the subdued splash of the waters upon the beach alone breaking the silence of the night. It was a time fitted for lovers' interviews—the communion of genial spirits. At a short distance from the shore lay a fine schooner. She was riding at single anchor, tending off shore with the land breeze, her sails were closely furled, not a light shone through her ports, and her crew appeared to be asleep below, for not a human being was seen on her decks or on any part of her rigging.

In one of the miniature bays formed by the rocks running out from the shore was a small skiff, with two men in her, who sat silently on the thwarts, resting on their oars, their eyes directed towards the spot where he stood. They were dressed as Spanish seamen, with red caps and sashes of the same hue, in which were stuck the never-absent long knife and a brace of pistols. He took two or three turns, with his arms folded on his breast, looking up at the verandah, in expectation of seeing some one appear there. Again he stopped, impatient at the delay.

"I am here, beloved one," he exclaimed, in a suppressed tone.

Scarcely had he spoken, when a window leading into the verandah opened, and a young girl stepped forth and leant over the balustrade. She was very beautiful, her eyes were full and dark, her ringlets of raven hue.

"Who calls?" she said, in a low, silvery tone. "Alfonso!" Her words were Spanish.

He stepped from beneath the shade of the verandah.

"It is I, my beloved," he answered; "fasten this, dearest, to the rail, and I will anon be with you."

As he spoke he threw up his scarf, and she doing as he bid her, he swung himself up by it, and in a moment she was in his arms. They stood thus long together, gazing over the moon-lit sea towards the schooner which lay at anchor, and while he pointed at the beautiful craft he urged her with impassioned words to make it her home.

"But my father, my poor father, I cannot quit him in his old age to mourn alone," she exclaimed, clasping her hands in doubt and fear,—" I, his only child. 'Twill break his heart were he to find that I had fled from him."

"He may find sufficient cause of grief and anger if you remain," he answered.

"Oh, Mother of Heaven, it is too true!" she uttered, shuddering. She was silent for some moments before she again spoke. "Oh, Alfonso," she exclaimed, in a beseeching tone, "you promised in the sight of Heaven to marry me."

"I did, beloved one, and mean to fulfil my word."

He, the betrayer, knew that he spoke falsely.

"Then why delay the ceremony?" pleaded the young girl, "you know how devotedly, how fondly, I love you."

"Yes, yes, dearest, and I value your love more than all the gold hoarded in your father's coffers. But think you that he, proud and wealthy as he is, would give his only child to an unknown and nameless stranger, whose only possession is yonder gallant bark, and his sole retainers a few brave hearts who compose her crew. The idea is hopeless; yet fly with me to some other land, where our hands may be united by the bands of the church as our hearts are already by the stronger ties of love, and together we will return to petition for your parent's forgiveness and blessing, and surely he will not then deny it you."

As he spoke, he pressed her passionately to his heart. His eloquence prevailed. Her happy home, her parent, her days of childish innocence, all were forgotten. In another moment he, the dark traitor as he knew himself to be, had sprung over the balustrade, holding with one arm her form, while with the other he grasped the wood-work, and lowered himself with her to the ground. As she lay almost unconscious in his arms, he bore her to the boat, and placing her by his side, seized the tiller, while the men, with rapid strokes, pulled towards the schooner. Before the boat had gained a greater distance from the shore than a pistol-ball could reach, lights were seen gleaming from the windows of the house, and the sound of human voices came down upon the breeze. They awoke the unhappy girl from her trance. Shrinking from his side, she gazed towards the beach. His eyes followed the direction of hers, and there he beheld, standing on the yellow sands with outstretched arms, the figure of a tall man. His silvery hair, on which the moonbeams shone, streaming in the wind. Through the gloom of night she yet recognised her parent.

"Oh take me back to my father; I cannot—cannot leave him thus!" she exclaimed, in tones of anguish.

"Give way, my men, give way!" he shouted, and the boat flew through the water.

The old man lifted up his hand in a menacing attitude, but no voice reached the ears of the ravisher, as he held his victim closer in his arms, lest she should elude his wiles by throwing herself into the sea.

In a few minutes the boat reached the schooner, which, lately seemingly so deserted and quiet, was now a scene of life and animation. As he, their chief, trod the deck, every part of the vessel swarmed with men, the anchor was hove up, the sails loosened, and as the land-breeze filled them, she stood out to sea. In one fleeting moment how many events rushed through his memory.

From the time when he thus bore away his victim, five years flew by, each year heaping crime upon crime. In many a hardy fight did he engage, again was enacted the chase, the combat, and the capture—again the shouts of the victors, the shrieks of the vanquished, sounded in his ears—again he saw told out the heaps of gold he had attained—again he saw it quickly squandered. Various were the climes he visited, from the icy poles to the torrid zones, but he found not peace nor happiness; yet had it been possible, the lovely being by his side might have afforded it, but though her love for her betrayer was such as can exist alone in woman's tender bosom, he felt that there was an upbraiding look in her eyes, which condemned him for treachery.

Her cheek, too, grew paler and paler, her bright eyes lost their lustre, her lips the smile which used to welcome him as he returned to their island home from some daring and perilous expedition. Even he, at length, perceived the change, and the dread of losing the only being whom he had ever loved, or had learned to love him, softened his stern heart. One child had been born—a girl—a delicate flower, lovely as her mother. For the sake of her helpless infant, the hapless Isidora wished to live. She won Alfonso's promise to grant her the only request she would make, and she then besought him to restore her, ere she died, to her father, that she might leave their child to his care. His word was passed to fulfil her wish. A gallant vessel, laden with wealth, and manned by a sturdy crew, stanch to their captain, bore Isidora and her lovely daughter to her father's home. The anchor was again dropped off the well-known coast, and a boat conveyed a covered litter to the shore. Alfonso had ascertained that the old man yet lived, and his daughter was now borne into his presence by four of the pirate crew. Alfonso, wrapped closely in his sea-cloak, stood at a distance to watch what would happen.

The father drew aside the curtain of the litter with trembling hands. "What stranger seeks my roof?" he asked.

"One who was once no stranger," exclaimed Isidora, raising herself feebly on her couch. "She is one who comes to die beneath the roof which gave her birth. Father, forgive your hapless Isidora while she yet may hear those blessed words, and protect the only remembrance of her which she can leave, this innocent child."

The old man gazed at her for an instant, when his paternal love triumphing over all other feelings, he clasped her in his arms.

"Isidora, my child, I blame you not," he cried; "I know the deceit and treachery which were practised to tear you from me, and may Heaven forgive you as I do. Your child shall be mine, and may blessings descend upon her head."

The old man mentioned not Alfonso's name, and if he regarded him as he stood at a distance, he considered him as some stranger who demanded not his attention.

A chamber, in which in her infancy she had slept, was prepared, and thither Isidora was conveyed with her child.

For many days Alfonso watched outside the house, unable to gain admittance without betraying himself. His crew already murmured at the delay, but he could not leave her thus without saying one word of farewell, without even a petition for forgiveness for the wrong he had done her. At length, waiting till the night had closed in, he sprang into the balcony, from which five years before he carried her off, and gently opening the window, he stood in her chamber. Their child slept by her side. Her nurse had that moment quitted her, and they were alone. He pronounced her name. Starting from her sleep, she uttered a faint cry, before consciousness fully returned.

"Isidora," he said, "I come to bid you farewell—eternal, alas! it must be—to crave your pardon for the foul wrong I have done you, for the blight I have cast upon your young life."

"Speak not of that, Alfonso; the time that has passed cannot be recalled, but the future may still be in your hands. Quit, then, the dreadful life you have led. Seek pardon from Heaven, nor leave me till death has closed my eyes."

"Impossible, Isidora!" exclaimed the pirate, vehemently; "I am wedded to it, and have no power to dissolve the bonds."

"If you love me still, speak not thus; or if you love me not, then pronounce the fatal words, and let me die at once."

While they were yet speaking, footsteps were heard approaching the chamber—but even should they be foes who came, Alfonso disdained to fly. Folding his arms across his breast, he there stood to brave the worst. The door flew open, and at the entrance of the room appeared Don Bertolo, with a drawn sword in his hand, followed by a number of armed retainers.

"Wretch!" exclaimed the old man. "Behold your accursed work in that lovely flower, blighted in her early youth. Your life shall answer for your crimes."

Alfonso stood unmoved, as Don Bertolo rushed towards him.

"Oh, spare him! spare him!" exclaimed Donna Isidora, raising up her feeble form from her couch, while her little daughter, startled by the strange sounds, crept to her side. "Spare him! he is the father of my child; my husband, and to me ever true!"

At these words Don Bertolo restrained his hand.

"Know, then, dark traitor, that if I slay you not, it is that your blood runs in my kindred veins, but to the punishment of Heaven I leave you. May your heart, as you have made mine, be desolate; may you wander over the wide ocean, year after year, your feet never resting on the dry land, your eyes never rejoicing in the sight of the green fields; may your presence bring disaster and misery, till all your fellow-men learn to dread and shun you, and then, forsaken by your partners in crime, may you die without a pitying hand to close your eyes!"

In vain did Isidora attempt to interrupt her father while he was uttering this fearful curse, but clasping her daughter to her bosom, she exclaimed,—

"Oh, retract that dread sentence, my father; and you, my child, pray Heaven, without ceasing, that the curse may be remitted from your father's head."

The child heard and understood her mother's words, and deeply were they engraven on her memory. They were the last the unhappy Isidora ever uttered. As her daughter pressed her lips upon her brow, she started back with dismay, for the cold damp of death was already collecting there. At the cry of grief the child uttered, Don Bertolo rushed to the bed-side of his daughter. He, too, soon there discovered the fatal truth, but instead of giving way to sorrow, fury filled his bosom.

"And you have done this, accursed villain!" he cried, turning a look of hatred at the pirate, while he pointed at the corpse of his child. "While she lived, for her sake you were safe from my vengeance, but now she is gone, your spirit shall answer at the tribunal of Heaven for her death. On, my friends! and punish the murderer of my daughter."

As he spoke, he rushed towards Alfonso with his drawn weapon, followed by the armed men who had entered the room with him; but the pirate was not thus to be taken at advantage. Keeping his eye fixed on his assailant, he retreated towards the window. With one bound he cleared the balustrade, and, swinging himself safely to the ground, took his way towards the shore. As he hurried onwards, he turned his head ever and anon towards his pursuers, who, headed by Don Bertolo, were rushing after him. Once or twice he thought of stopping and selling his life dearly, but the recollection of Isidora and his child softened his heart for the moment, and for their sake he resolved to avoid further bloodshed. When, however, he reached the beach, no boat was there; but half-way between him and his vessel he saw one pulling towards the shore. He waved his sword, which shone brightly in the moonbeams, and shouted loudly to his men to redouble their efforts. They saw the signal, and knew that their chief must be in danger. His enemies were already close to him. They halted and fired, but not a shot touched him. Then on again they rushed with loud cries to overwhelm him. Undaunted, he stood at bay, his sword whirling round his head, keeping even the most daring at a distance, till his boat touched the strand, and his followers leaped forward to his assistance. Surrounding him, they drove his assailants back, and then, before they could again rally, bore him unscathed to their boat. As they quickly launched her into deep water, the aged Don Bertolo reached the strand, and again the father's fearful curse, uttered in the chamber of Isidora, rang in the pirate's ears,—

"Go, wretch; wander over the wide ocean, year after year, your feet never resting on the dry land, your eyes never rejoicing in the sight of green fields! May your accursed presence ever bring disaster and misery, till your fellow-men learn to dread and shun you, and then, forsaken by your partners in crime, may you die without one pitying hand to close your eyes."

As the pirate crew heard these words, they beheld the tall figure of Don Bertolo, with outstretched arms, standing on the shore, the moonbeams playing on his white locks, as, uncovered, they streamed in the wind. They, too, remembered them, and superstitious terrors took possession of their minds.

That old man's prophet-like figure, and his dreadful curse, were ever present like an accusing angel to Alfonso's mind; though no sooner did he again find himself upon the deck of his own bark, with a daring crew ready to obey his behests, than his accustomed hardihood returned, and in a firm voice he ordered the anchor to be weighed, and sail to be made on the schooner. Away flew the terror-inspiring vessel on her dark mission of plunder and destruction.

Years again passed away, and the hardened pirate laughed to scorn the old man's curse; but the hand of Heaven, if slow, is sure to strike the sinner, when the measure of his sins is full.

Alfonso now commanded a large ship, and many hundred men obeyed his orders. She was richly laden with costly merchandize from various distant climes, the spoil of numerous ships which now lay beneath the ocean waves—the sepulchres of their murdered crews.

For many days had the pirate crew sailed on, exulting in a prosperous voyage, when a fierce hurricane arose. The ship drove before it under bare poles, for not a thread of canvass could be exposed to its fury. Onward she flew till a dark line of rocky coast appeared under her lee. The anchors were let go, but the cables snapped off like threads of cotton, and the bravest saw that death, with all its horrors, must be their lot. The proud ship struck—the masts went by the board—the wild sea rushed over her, each wave sweeping hundreds from their hold into the watery gulf yawning beside them—till at length the pirate chief himself, of all his band, alone remained alive. A wave, which shattered the ship into a thousand fragments, carried him towards a rock rising above the water. He instinctively clung to the tangled sea-weed which hung round it, and climbed to its summit, whither the spray alone could reach him. He gazed around; a wild and dreary scene met his view: but his heart was hardened, and his spirits did not quail; on the contrary, he took a fierce delight in surmounting the difficulties which surrounded him; and forming a raft with the broken spars and pieces of the wreck which were washed on the rock, he hoped to reach the still distant shore. The storm had expended its fury when he committed himself to his raft; but no sooner had he quitted the rock than the wind came off the coast, and before he could again secure himself, he was blown out to sea. He beheld the shore gradually sink beneath the horizon; and when he gazed around, and saw nothing but the wide desert sea, and the arch of heaven overhead, he remembered the old man's curse.

The pirate started from his sleep, for those dreadful words seemed again to ring loudly in his ears. He lifted his head, and looked out upon the ocean; but some time passed before his mind could comprehend the present. As his eye wandered towards the horizon, it rested on another sail, which approached him rapidly, but though still the same ill-omened calm continued, her sails appeared full, like those of the former ship which had passed him. As she came on, a dark mist seemed to surround her, through which an ensign, black as night, was seen flying from her peak, her hull and masts were of the same colour, while ever and anon a low and mournful wail struck upon his ear. Onward sailed the mysterious bark directly towards the spot where the raft floated, and as she passed, the heart even of the bold pirate shrunk with dread, for as he gazed, he beheld her decks crowded with hideous beings, some shrieking and moaning, others, as they leaned over the side of the ship, mocking at him, beckoning him on board, and then breaking into wild shouts of derisive laughter, mowing and gibbering, changing ever and anon their shapes. Every part of the ship and rigging was full of them; skeleton forms also were there fixed against the bulwarks, or the masts, from whence appeared to proceed the sounds of agony he heard. But there was one shape more dreadful than all the rest; he who steered the demon ship. Dark as night was his visage, of vast proportions his form—fire darted from his eyes, withering all things within its range. The hull and tall masts of the ship seemed mirrored in the smooth sea, the which, as she clave in her course with a rushing sound, became tinged with a lurid glare. The form beckoned to him with a menacing attitude, and as the ship, in a ruddy mist, gradually disappeared, the voices of her spectre-crew filled the air, repeating the awful curse of Isidora's father.

He sank back, horror stricken, and wished for death to relieve him of his load of misery. Thus he lay, for how long he knew not: he was alone conscious of a change in the atmosphere; a fresh breeze blew over his face; he felt the raft, hitherto so motionless, lifting and falling on the rising waves, as it drove onward before the wind. The cool breath of heaven somewhat revived him; but he feared to open his eyes, lest they should rest on horrors similar to those he had witnessed. Suddenly he was aroused by a voice hailing him in his own language; but so often had he been deceived, that, believing some other phantom was sent to tantalize him, he dared not open his eyes, dreading a repetition of the same horrors. Again the hail was repeated, and he felt the raft grating against the side of a vessel. At length, opening his eyes, he saw a human being lowered from a ship's side, and in the act of springing on the raft.

"Is he yet alive?" asked a voice from the deck.

"He yet lives, senhor, but appears almost starved to death."

"Hoist him up then carefully upon deck," said the first speaker, in a tone of authority.

The pirate made a sign that he comprehended what was going forward, but his voice failed him. He could still scarcely persuade himself that he was not dreaming, when he saw the raft, which had so long been his home, cast adrift, and soon afterwards found himself the occupant of a handsome cabin, surrounded by the commiserating and anxious faces of his fellow-men. A cordial poured down his throat revived him; and words of Christian kindness, such as he had scarcely before heard, sounded in his ear. By degrees his faculties resumed their powers, and he quickly forged a specious tale, to satisfy the inquiries of his preservers. He discovered that the ship which had rescued him was a large merchantman, one of the rich galleons of Old Spain, which bore the produce of the mines of the American provinces to the mother country.

A few days saw the wave-tossed stranger perfectly recovered, and all on board readily acknowledged his bold and commanding bearing, which stamped him as a chief among his fellows, though few felt their love kindle towards him. There was something forbidding in his aspect; and he seemed to shun social intercourse with any, evidently preferring to walk the deck in solitude, and to commune with his own thoughts.

"Have I at length escaped from the effect of the old man's curse; and shall I again see the green land of my birth?" he muttered to himself. "Yes, I may laugh the dotard's threats to scorn : fate alone has hitherto been against me."

"A sail on the weather-bow!" shouted the man from the mast-head.

"What does she look like?" demanded the captain.

"A large top-sail schooner," was the answer.

"Which way is she standing?" asked the captain.

"Across our course, to all appearance," replied the man at the mast-head.

Alfonso, on this, ascended the rigging to ascertain the truth; nor was he long before he convinced himself that the man was right in his conjectures. He also discovered that the stranger was no other than a consort of his own, from which he had been some time separated before his shipwreck.

"What do you, senhor, make her out to be?" asked the captain, as he reached the deck.

"A craft which I should, at all events, advise you to avoid," answered Alfonso; "she looks wicked enough for any mischief; and there are, to my certain knowledge, vessels in these seas which are daring enough, and strong enough, to attack the proudest merchantman."

"The holy saints protect us from such! But what reason, senhor, have you for thinking ill of this vessel?" asked the captain.

"Perhaps from mere suspicion of her character; perhaps, because I have seen her before," answered the pirate. "Now, take my advice—avoid her by every possible means, at the same time that you prepare your people for fighting, should she venture to attack us."

At these words, the captain turned pale ; for although he had a numerous crew, and heavy guns, he was well aware of the advantage a light schooner had to out-manœuvre him. As the ship kept steadily on her course, all hands were on deck watching the stranger, who continued in the same position she was when first seen on the weather-bow, gradually drawing nearer and nearer. Sometimes her sails were filled, and she stood away on the same course ; then again she was seen to haul her wind and back her top-sail; and, as the night closed in, she was about two miles distant. Whatever she was, she caused great alarm on board the Spanish ship, and neither crew nor passengers showed any inclination to go below for repose. The guns were loaded and run out, and the people were at their quarters.

Thus passed the first watch of the night, when they began to hope that they might be allowed to continue on their voyage without molestation; and at last the watch below were ordered to their berths, while the guns were run in and secured. The stranger thought differently, and continued pacing the deck, his eagle eye scanning the horizon in every direction, as far as the thickening gloom would allow; but, as the night advanced, the moon sunk beneath the waves, and a mist arose through which no human sight could pierce. A change had come over the pirate's mood—perhaps he wished to redeem the past; or, rather, with all his crimes, he felt gratitude towards those who had preserved him.

The morning watch had just been called, and the ship was sailing steadily on her silent course, when the dark hull of a vessel was dimly discerned on the weather-quarter, and, before those that saw her could cry out, a shower of balls and shot was discharged among them, tearing up the deck, and wounding and killing many of the people. The drum beat to quarters, but, before they could cast loose their guns, a loud grating noise was heard, as the stranger vessel ground against theirs, and numbers of dark forms were seen climbing up their side. In vain they attempted to defend themselves. The pirates were bold and fierce; neither age nor sex were spared. The crew were cut down without mercy, and the late peaceful deck was now a scene of the wildest tumult and bloodshed, horrors of every sort, the shrieks and oaths of the combatants, the flashing of fire-arms, the clashing of swords, mingled in wild confusion. Alfonso kept the pirates at bay, but at length a pistol-shot from a distance brought him to the deck, and at that moment the pirates, with loud shouts, proclaimed themselves the victors.

"Alas!" he exclaimed, ere losing all consciousness of the present, "I am in truth, then, doomed to bring destruction on all who protect or confide in me."

When he recovered, he found himself in the cabin of a schooner. Forms and faces he well knew were around him; they were those of men steeped in every crime—men whom he himself had led to many a desperate and lawless adventure.

"He revives," said a voice. It was that of a man who had always been a stanch supporter of his. "Long live Captain Alfonso! he alone is worthy to command us."

While the seamen echoed the cry, the pirate had time to collect his thoughts; his plan was quickly formed. Though suffering from intense pain he rose from the couch, and supported himself on his feet.

"Thanks, my friends," were the first words he spoke, "you find me among you once more in a strange way. Some may be suspicious of me; I will go on deck and stand a fair trial."

The pure air of heaven restored his strength, as with a bold and haughty brow he stood near the companion-hatch, while the band of desperadoes clustered round the main-mast. Several corpses lay wrapped in flags upon the deck—among them was the body of the late chief of the pirate schooner. To this circumstance Alfonso owed the proposition of being elected captain. There were, however, numerous dissentient voices among the crew.

"How comes it that he was fighting on the side of our enemies?" shouted some of them.

"Perhaps he betrayed the last ship he commanded," suggested others.

"I never betrayed a comrade," answered the pirate, "nor to those who confided in me have I proved false. I had vowed to protect those people on whose side you found me fighting, and while I had strength to wield a sword it was devoted to them. Where are they now?"

"At the bottom of the sea, where you must follow them," shouted twenty voices.

"If they no longer exist, my duty is at an end," said the pirate, calmly; "as to your threats, you well know I fear them not. If you wish me to become your chief, I will be true to you; if not, we shall part before long. I serve no master but the laws I assist to frame. I give you five minutes to decide. Must I leave you to your own devices, or shall I lead you, as heretofore, to victory and wealth?"

The effect of this bold speech was electric, and the very men who had the instant before been the loudest in condemning him to death, now cried out, "Long live Captain Alfonso."

A daring front, unflinching courage, and prompt answers will invariably succeed with uneducated and lawless men, for to such is the only authority they bow.

For six weeks had the pirate Alfonso been reinstated in his command over this band of miscreants, but during that time not a sign of land had greeted his aching sight.

No sooner were they approaching some island to which the crew wished to repair to refresh themselves and refit the ship, than a vessel would heave in sight, tempting them with the hope of her proving a prize worthy of capture. Frequently the manifold chances of the sea enabled her to escape, but many an unhappy bark fell into their merciless hands, and the deep ocean became her tomb, and that of those who manned her. "The dead tell no tales, and the deep reveals no secrets," was the pirate's adage, but sometimes with fearful certainty they learnt its falsehood. Who can say what is death? Cannot the power of Heaven sound the fathomless deep?

It was a lovely night, the full moon and glittering stars were shining brightly from the dark sky; the sea, on which their light played, was as calm as childhood's slumbers; the gentle breeze which rippled its surface, like the smile on the infant's lips.

The pirate chief walked the silent deck; the wakeful helmsman kept his eye aloft, or else upon the compass, the look-outs forward scanned the distant horizon, but no one watched their captain's movements. Dark thoughts were in his bosom, the evil deeds of his life came crowding on his memory—deeds which he felt had steeped his soul so deep in sin that pardon would be hopeless. Even then was he pondering on fresh exploits, atrocious as the former, when his glance fell upon the resplendent ocean. Entranced he stood, his breath restrained; for there beneath the moonbeams he beheld a form of majestic beauty, in garments of white drapery and a face most angelic, which yet, as he gazed, assumed the features of his lost Isidora. Those features wore an expression of mournfulness, and a beseeching look still full of love and tenderness, while by her gestures she seemed to beckon him to follow her, pointing to some unseen object in the distance. The lips of the beautiful apparition appeared to move, but no sound reached his ears. Like one entranced he stood gazing at it, till he longed again to clasp that form, once so loved, in his arms.

"I come, I come, Isidora!" he exclaimed, and rushed to the side of the vessel as if to throw himself into the ocean to reach her, but as he spoke, the sound of a human voice dissolved the spell, the fair illusion mournfully shook her head, and began rapidly to pass from his sight. Each instant fainter and fainter it grew, till nought remained but a gauze-like mist of the same lovely form expanded into vast proportions, through which the moonbeams were seen playing on the water, and the stars shining from out of the clear sky. That, too, finally mingled with the surrounding atmosphere, and Alfonso no longer beheld it.

"A sail on the weather-bow," shouted the look-out forward, and just in the wake of the moonbeams, in the direction to which the phantom had pointed, the white canvass of a ship appeared.

"Brace up the head-yards; get a pull of the lee-braces!" exclaimed the captain, rousing himself by great exertion. "We must overhaul yonder craft."

"Watch on deck, rouse up, rouse up!" cried the petty officers, repeating his commands.

In an instant the deck of the schooner was alive with men, promptly obeying the order. The chase, by this change of course, was thus brought right ahead. No one again lay down, for when a prospect of making a fresh prize offered itself, the crew, greedy for wealth which they could not enjoy, were far too interested in the affair to think of sleep. After the lapse of an hour it was clearly seen that they were quickly nearing their intended prize, but the light was not sufficient to enable them to distinguish her character; she might be a ship of war, and they might be running into the lion's mouth. The chase did not perceive her danger, for she neither altered her course nor made more sail. At length they made out that she was a large ship, but with the uncertain light of dawn which just now broke upon the world, they could not tell whether she carried guns or not.

Hope urged them on; no matter, the booty gained without fighting for was seldom of much value. As the sun rose from his ocean-bed, his rays streamed full upon the sails of the chase, enlarging her proportions, and making her appear still nearer to them than she really was. At the prospect of the combat, the fierce energies of the pirate chief were aroused; he even forgot the vision of the night, and all his worst passions assumed their sway.

"Try the range of our pivot-gun on the chase," he exclaimed.

The eager crew cheered at the order, but the shot fell far short of its mark. Every man in the ship was on deck, with a cutlass buckled to his side and pistols in his belt, ready to rush a savage horde on board the devoted prize. A second shot was fired with like effect as the first, on which the ship, till now apparently unconscious of the approach of an enemy, suddenly spread a whole cloud of canvass, the effect of which was soon apparent by her increasing her distance from her pursuer. As the sun rose in the sky, the breeze increased; and majestically the noble ship ploughed her course over the deep. The proud flag of Spain was hoisted at her peak, but she gave no other sign that she was aware of the vicinity of a stranger.

The pirates' breasts were filled with rage at the thoughts of losing what they judged would prove a rich prize, and every effort was made on board the schooner to overtake her. Every stitch of canvass they could pack on her was set, but instead of their gaining on the ship she continued to distance them. At last, however, the breeze, which in southern latitudes is ever uncertain, began to fail her, though they still took advantage of what remained of it. The vast sheets of canvass lately puffed out with the strong breeze were seen to flap against the masts, and soon she became almost becalmed.

On this the pirates gave a shout of joy, for they now felt certain of their prize; undaunted, however, she quickly took in her studding-sails and other light canvass, brailed up her courses, and gave every sign that she was ready for the contest. A shift of wind had placed her in the position she had occupied when first seen, well on the weather-bow of the schooner, which gave her an advantage she did not fail to make use of. The pirates cheered as they approached her, while they stood at their guns, waiting anxiously for the order to fire. It was awful to contemplate the meeting of those two strange barks on the world of waters, in dead silence, intent only on each other's destruction. The ship seemed well aware of the character of her opponent, and just as the schooner got within musket shot of her, a fresh breeze enabled her to keep away, her ports were of a sudden thrown open, and a heavy broadside poured into the pirates' vessel. On this their shouts were changed into shrieks and execrations, for many of their best men were laid low; still they advanced, for their spars were uninjured, and they hoped to rake the ship as she had done them, but as she delivered her fire she again hauled her wind, her commander, whoever he might be, evidently being on the watch to prevent their so doing. For some minutes not another shot was fired, but at length the pirate chief allowed the bow chasers to be trained forward and discharged, in the hopes of knocking away some of the ship's spars; she, in return, firing her stern guns. In this way they closed, but when they had got within about a hundred yards of each other, the pirate put up his helm and brought his broadside to bear upon the enemy; who, at the same time, kept away and returned it with interest.

In this manner the two vessels ran off before the wind, discharging broadside for broadside as fast as they could load, the heavy metal of the ship being somewhat balanced by the greater rapidity with which the stronger crew of the pirate fired. With loud yells and execrations, the pirates, stripped to their waists, worked their guns beneath the full blaze of a tropical sun, which was alone suf-

ficient to fever their blood to fury. Numbers fell, but their death only served to increase the courage and rage of the rest, and spars came tumbling from aloft; the hull was pierced in many places, and already the water was rushing into her in awful quantities. Amid the wreck and havoc, the dying and the dead, Alfonso stood unharmed; but no longer was his voice heard encouraging his fellows to fresh exertions, for as he watched the hostile ship he beheld floating amid the wreaths of smoke the form he had seen during the night watch, with her head now drooping in an attitude of deep grief, yet still beckoning to him and pointing to the deck of the ship. Suddenly he was aroused by that terror-inspiring cry—
"The schooner is sinking! the schooner is sinking!"
"Run the ship then on board, and take her instead," he exclaimed, forgetful at the moment of all else.

On this the helm was put down, while a sturdy band stood ready with their grappling-irons to heave into the rigging of the enemy. One broadside was manned, and the remainder of the crew were prepared, with cutlass in hand, to follow their chief on board the enemy. The side of the schooner grated against that of the ship, but she suddenly rolling over, the grappling-irons missed their hold, and fell into the water; at the same moment the eager chief leaped up the lofty side of the ship, followed by several of his crew. Before the remainder could join him, their vessel was separated from the ship, and a small band alone were left fighting, hard pressed by the Spanish crew. Quarter was neither asked for nor given; and, one by one, the pirates were cut down or driven into the sea.

Again the schooner made a desperate attempt to run alongside; but water-logged, and sinking fast, she was unmanageable. A wild, despairing shriek arose to heaven. The combatants for an instant suspended their upraised weapons, and the still surviving pirates beheld with dismay the waves closing over their vessel, and the fate which she had brought on so many others was now hers. Hope abandoned them; they fought more like demons than men. But their valour availed them not; and ere many minutes had passed, but one alone remained alive on the blood-stained deck. It was their chief, Alfonso.

Proudly he stood at bay, and even his enemies admired his undaunted courage; but, pressed on by numbers, at length his sword fell powerless by his side. His life was spared, and he was reserved to suffer the fate of a malefactor.

Several days had passed by, and Alfonso lay in the hold of the ship. Chains were on his limbs—bread and water had been his only food—and he was in darkness. His thoughts were full of anguish—the past afforded no consolation—the future was hopeless. By the motion of the ship, the straining of the timbers, and the loud noises overhead, and the cries of the people, he knew that an awful storm was raging.

In vain he strove to free himself from his chains. With all the feeling of a seaman, he longed to be on deck to face the fury of the elements; but to die thus like a slave was doubly bitter. With anguish he cursed his fate.

Already a sound, whose import he well knew, struck his ear; it was that of water forcing its way into the hold. The pumps were manned; but their efforts were in vain—the water gained rapidly upon them—the ship then would founder, and he, without one struggle for life, must die.

The bitterness of death was on him, when his eyes beheld the dim light of a lantern approaching the spot where he lay. A human voice struck his ear:

"You may not remember one who once served with you; but even in the heat of the fight I recognised you, Alfonso," it said, and whispered a word in a lower tone. "The ship is dismasted, and will probably founder; but I would not leave you thus to die without an attempt to save you."

"Thanks, friend, for the boon," answered the pirate; "a wretch like me has naught else to give; yet, quick!—release me from these fetters, and I shall be grateful."

A file and hammer did the work required, and the stranger, without another word, disappeared. The pirate stretched his benumbed limbs.

"I shall at least die like a man!" he cried, as he prepared to ascend to the upper decks.

Unquailing, yet unrepentant, he still remained. As he explored his way to the after-part of the ship, he passed the open door of a cabin. He listened, for the tones of a soft and feminine voice, raised in earnest prayer, reached his ear. He heard his own name pronounced.

"For the gentle Virgin's—for my sainted mother's sake—oh! remove the heavy curse pronounced by my grand-sire on his head! Oh! merciful Heaven! hear then my last prayers; with my dying breath let me beseech thee to pardon the unhappy Alfonso!"

He listened, his heart softened within him, and the fierce pirate dropped on his knees to pray, to ask pardon for his dark sins, his crimes unnumbered. He lay prostrate on the deck: how long he remained thus he knew not; he poured out his soul to God, he melted into tears; a supernatural influence was over him. He raised his head, and the image of his lost Isidora knelt by his side, pale as she was wont to be, but lovely and young as when first they met.

"Isidora!" he said.

"Who calls me by my name?" said the kneeling female.

"Isidora! Know you not the hapless Alfonso?" he asked.

"My prayers then are heard; merciful Heaven—it is, it is my father!"

As the beautiful being uttered these words, she threw herself into the arms of the repentant pirate. A father's heart told him it was his long-lost daughter. For some time they thus stood, forgetful of the dangers which surrounded them—all thought of external things lost in the ecstasy of the meeting. At last, the increasing roar of the elements, and the rush of water into the lower part of the ship, still more dreadful to a seaman's ear, warned the father to seek the upper deck, if he would endeavour to preserve his newly-found child. Not a moment more must be lost, and lifting her in his arms he bore her upon deck. What a sight then met his view. The masts were gone by the board; the deck was covered with the wreck of the spars and rigging; the dark waves, with crests of white foam, danced madly round the devoted ship, while lowering clouds hung, like a funeral pall, over head; but this alone would not have daunted the pirate's bold heart.

The ship was deserted; not another human being remained to aid him in his efforts to preserve his child's life. In the far distance some black specks appeared ever and anon on the summit of the foaming billows. If they were the boats, they were beyond recall from any signal he could make, had they even the power to return. The pirate clasped his daughter with one arm, while with the other he held on by the companion-hatch, for the slippery deck afforded no footing, and the dismasted ship laboured fearfully in the heavy sea which broke over her, deluging her fore and aft, and threatening every instant to ingulf her. Thus he stood a picture of dauntless courage. He pressed his child closer to his heart.

"My Isidora," he cried, "the severest punishment Heaven could have stored for me, was to give you to me, to tear you again from me. For myself, I am doomed to wander ever over the ocean, the curse of all who admit me among them."

"Say not thus, my father," answered his daughter, throwing her arms round his neck. "Heaven has heard the prayers of your child."

As she spoke, a strain of music, like an angel's song, sounded in the air, and before them appeared the same majestic and lovely form Alfonso had before beheld. The face, no longer downcast, was radiant with happiness; and as she floated above the white spray of the ocean, she beckoned them on, and pointed encouragingly in the direction the ship was driving.

"See, see, my father," cried Isidora, exultingly; "that angel spirit, which from my earliest days has watched over me, assures us that safety is at hand."

"It is no mocking phantom, then," said the pirate, in a deep voice. "And Heaven, who deigns to send celestial messengers from above, may still pardon my transgressions. Isidora, my child, thy prayers may yet preserve thy guilty father's soul."

The lovely girl turned her countenance, full of love and gratitude, on her father, and as her heart thrilled with pious joy at the thoughts of preserving him, she forgot the terrors of the surrounding scene. At the same instant another strain of joyous music floated through the air; the wind, calmed by the presence of heavenly influences, gradually decreased, the sea went down, the dark clouds dispersed, the blue sky appeared, the glorious sun came forth, and the ship, though water-logged and unmanageable, floated calmly on the bosom of the deep.

Onward was borne the ship, her course pointed out by the beautiful phantom, who seemed, as before, to grow less and less distinct to the eyes of Alfonso and his daughter, till, as they gazed at her, regardless of all else, before them appeared a lovely island, rising out of the waves, with a soft and sandy shore, and green trees of many varied tints. Still pointing to the land, the ethereal being vanished from their sight.

Scarcely had she disappeared, when the ship took the shore without shock or noise, and a raft, easily constructed, transported Alfonso and his daughter to the dry land, on which the pirate's foot had not trod for many a long year. By his child's side, her hand in his, he knelt and prayed. The old man's curse was removed from his head.

My tale might tell how, ere long, a noble youth, the betrothed of Isidora, in a gallant bark, came to search for her amid these rude seas—how, guided by the bright star of pure love, he found her in that lonely isle, and, with her father's blessing, bore her away as his bride to other lands—how the repentant pirate there dwelt for many years, a solitary hermit, in expiation of his sins, his occupation to succour the shipwrecked mariner, and, with contrite heart, to offer up his orisons to heaven, and to teach the heathen who came to him the way of truth. Years passed away, and a ship touched at that shore. Her crew wandered into the woods, and, before a humble cottage, they beheld the form of an aged man, the wreck of strength and beauty, a few white locks on his head, streaming in the breeze. He reclined against a tree as if he slept. His eyes were closed—he was dead. In his hands he held a scroll; it contained the tale of "The Father's Curse," and at the bottom was inscribed the name of Alfonso, the pirate.

"A long time ago, you, sir, were good enough to promise to give us some of your adventures," said Upton, turning to the captain, who was present. "We hope that you will not disappoint us this afternoon."

"I have been thinking of a commencement to my story, which you shall have forthwith," returned Captain Dainmore. "But I am obliged to be careful what I say when a fellow like Fairfield is ready to log down my words. You all remember the song,—

> " 'Come, all ye jolly sailors bold,
> Whose hearts are cast in honour's mould,
> While English glory I unfold;
> Huzza to the Arethusa.'

The gallant Arethusa played a prominent part in the affair I am about to describe. She was a noble frigate, and nobly commanded. You may head my yarn, if you like, Fairfield, 'The Taking of Curaçao.'"

Our good captain deserves a chapter to himself.

CHAPTER XXVI.

CAPTAIN DAINMORE'S STORY—THE TAKING OF CURAÇAO.

"HUZZA! my fine boys, I've glorious news for you," exclaimed Pat O'Sulivan, throwing up his cap, and catching it again several times, as he rushed into the gun-room of his Majesty's frigate

———, where I, with the rest of his brother-officers, except the one who had just relieved him on deck, were seated round the mess-table, discussing our wine and fruit at the conclusion of dinner. O'Sulivan, as his name betokens, was from green Erin's Isle, and as good a seaman and honest a fellow as ever stepped a plank; notwithstanding that he possessed not a few of the peculiarities of his countrymen. "Now, don't be in a hurry, or you'll never be able to comprehend what I've got to communicate," he continued, taking his seat on a vacant chair. "Steward, a clean glass, and Galt, my boy, pass the wine, for, till I've wet my lips, I shall not be in fit trim to say my say."

"Well, bear a hand, and out with it!" cried several of the mess together.

O'Sulivan tossed off the glass of Madeira to which he had helped himself, and rapidly proceeded in his communication.

"Well, then, my boys, not to keep you longer in suspense, our skipper has just hinted to me, that we are likely to have some sharp fighting before the world is many days older, with the Mynheers; for that our gallant commodore, Charlie Brisbane, instead of diplomatizing, and memorializing, and procrastinating, and negotiating, and all that sort of botheration, has determined to sail right into the harbour of St. Ann, and take Curaçao by a *coup de main.*"

"Come, now, O'Sulivan, you are wishing to try the metal of some of the youngsters," said the master, quietly sipping his wine. "We shall have to wait long enough before we get in there, except we can first heave all the Dutchman's guns into the sea, you may depend upon it. Why, the place is impregnable; though, if the commodore thinks fit to lead us against stone walls, I'm ready enough to follow—mark that!—only, I don't think he will attempt it."

"All I know is, that the captain told me; he said he would be master of Curaçao before the year was a day old; and he is not a man to break his word," answered O'Sulivan. "So, master, I'm going to fortify myself for the best that may happen. I only can tell you, that I fully believe we shall attempt it; and, if the place is impregnable, that's no fault of anybody's but the Dutch, so we must make them pay for the trouble they give us. If you wish to know more, you must go on deck, where, I dare say, you will find the skipper, and, I doubt not, if he happens to be in the humour, he will tell you all about the affair."

Leaving O'Sulivan to finish his dinner in quiet, the remainder of the gun-room officers quickly assembled on the quarter-deck; but for some time longer our curiosity was doomed to be unsatisfied, for, when we came from below, the captain had already retired to his cabin; so we continued pacing up and down, discussing the probability of the report we had heard being true or not. I believe that there was not a man among us who did not wish it might be so, in spite of the danger to be incurred.

In those days I had high health and buoyant spirits—nothing came amiss to me,—I was ready to fight an enemy, or to make love to a pretty girl,—to be tossed by the waves, or to dance on shore. How rapidly has the time flown by since then! yet, although nearly forty years have passed since the period of which I am speaking, so vivid was the impression which the events I am relating made on my mind, that I remember them as clearly as if they occurred but yesterday. "Here to-day and gone to-morrow," as Corporal Trim observes, and he was not a bad moralist. "Time flies with a quick foot," and so in truth I have found; for I can scarcely persuade myself, as I speak to you of these circumstances, that so great a length of time has elapsed since they occurred. However, a truce with moralizing, or I shall never finish the long story I have to tell you. Our business is with the past; and if some of my observations prove useful to the present generation of Benbows, if they excite their naval ardour, and warm up the love of their country, if they persuade them to perseverance, and a determination to overcome difficulties, I shall be content.

Napoleon having driven the Dutch into a war with us, it had become our business to destroy their commerce, to deprive them of their colonies, and to injure them in every way to the utmost of our power, just to bring them to their senses; and it was considered that we could not do so more effectually than by the capture of the rich and fertile island of Curaçao, the most valuable of their possessions in the West Indies.

Admiral Dacres was then commander-in-chief on the West India station, and had his flag flying on board the Shark at Port Royal, from which harbour we sailed at the latter end of November, 1806, in company with two other frigates, with orders from him to cruise off the island of Curaçao, to reconnoitre it well, and to land whenever we had an opportunity, in order to ascertain the feelings of the inhabitants with regard to placing themselves under the protection of Great Britain. A year or so before, an expedition had been sent against the island, but had totally failed, the troops being driven back to their ships with considerable loss; but not having been out there at the time, I do not recollect the particulars. We were now anchored off a small island called Oruba, to the westward of Curaçao, having reached the spot only the previous day, owing to a powerful current setting against us, and a strong gale from the south-east, the trade-wind, indeed, against which we had been beating for the last three weeks. The other two ships of the squadron were at no great distance from us.

Those who have been in the tropics know how hot it can be on occasion, and so we found it on that same 23rd of December, the fierce rays of the burning sun making the pitch bubble and boil up from between the planks of our decks, cracking the wood, and turning the countenances of those exposed to it to many tints, varying, according to their previous complexions, from a bright sienna to a dark sepia.

Although an awning was stretched over part of the deck, it served but to temper in a slight degree the excessive fury of the sun's rays: the hot atmosphere being cooled, however, at times by the sea-breeze, which ever and anon came in from the offing, and conquered the land wind which had hitherto been blowing: the ships all the time rolling their yard-arms almost in the water, as the smooth glassy swell rose sullenly from beneath their keels.

Our walk had gradually been growing slower and slower as our muscles felt the relaxing influence of the heat, when the look-out hailed the deck to say that a strange sail had just hove in sight from the eastward. The other frigates saw her at the same time, and signalized to that effect. An officer having descended to give the captain the information, we were all on the tiptoe of expectation, both to learn the truth of O'Sulivan's report from our chief, when he should come on deck, and to ascertain the character of the approaching stranger.

Our commander quickly made his appearance, nor did he keep us long in suspense before he gave us the intelligence, that Captain Brisbane had formed a plan to take Curaçao by surprise, as soon as the squadron was joined by another frigate, the Fisgard, which he expected daily to fall in with. Scarcely had he spoken, when the Commodore signalized the other ships to be ready to make sail and slip in chase, should the stranger prove an enemy. The hands were accordingly turned up, and men were at their stations ready to act as might be required, every eye being turned towards the approaching ship, some with the pious hope that she might prove a foe, on the principle that one bird in the hand is worth two in the bush, as we should probably capture her; others trusting that she might be the Fisgard, that we might the sooner start on our expedition. I being as anxious as anybody, slung my spyglass across my shoulder, and in spite of the broiling I was doomed to bear, went aloft the sooner to make her out. Gradually her topgallant-sails and top-sails rose from out of the bright sparkling surface, behind which they were hid, and at last her courses and hull appeared.

"What do you make her out to be, Mr. Dainmore?" hailed the skipper from the deck.

"A large frigate, sir, with the look of a British ship," I answered from my lofty perch. "She is signalizing, but I cannot yet make out the colour of her buntin."

While we kept a sharp look-out on the stranger, an eye was turned to the Commodore, should he think fit to make sail, in case she should prove an enemy. There was soon no doubt that the stranger saw us, but still she boldly continued her course, and our surmises were quickly set at rest, by her hoisting the number of the Fisgard, we showing ours in return; and in a quarter of an hour, bringing up a fine breeze, she dropped her anchor within two cables' length of us.

Captain Brisbane forthwith summoning the three other captains on board the Arethusa, so famed in song and story for her dashing exploits, he there finally explained to them the daring scheme he had formed for capturing the island, and which was detailed to us on the return of our skipper on board.

It appears, you must know, that the Dutch inhabitants of Curaçao have, or rather had, a regular custom of drinking the old year out and the new year in. I should think the lesson we gave them would have made them change it! but nothing is so inveterate as habit, and the Mynheers are not fond of changing even the cut or proportions of their unmentionables. On the last evening of the old year, every man, woman, and child in the island gets drunk, more or less, from the highest to the lowest. Father Mathew would be in despair. Not a tee-totaller is to be found in the place, and as to M. Priestnitz, they would as soon follow his prescriptions as drink up the water from the sea. I was afterwards credibly informed, by no less a personage than my washerwoman, a most excellent and veracious specimen of her sex, that the daughter of one of the chief merchants of Amsterdam went about the streets on the morning of that very 31st of December, 1806, with a bottle and glass in her hand, offering schnaps to all she encountered, and that all the young ladies and gentlemen did the same; the latter, however, soon becoming too drunk to perform any long peregrinations. I afterwards became acquainted with the said Miss Vanvoorst, and a very charming, well-informed, elegant young lady I found her. She sang sweetly, danced to perfection, and was amiable in the extreme, but she did not appear to consider it in the least derogatory to her character to indulge, on that particular occasion, in the fascinating liquid. She was then fair and blooming, numbering scarce twenty summers; but forty winters have passed since then over her head, and she now, if still the good soul lives, is in all probability round and red, comforting her heart with draughts of the soothing liquid, "deep as the rolling Zuyder Zee," instead of the moderate libations in which she then occasionally indulged.

The chances are, therefore, if she were to hear the tales I tell of her, instead of being offended, she would clap her hands to her fat sides, and laugh at them as jokes of exceeding raciness. Sweet girl! I think I see her now as she then was, a regular-built Hebe, swimming before my eyes on the light fantastic toe, or presiding, as the divinity she was like, at her most estimable father's well supplied supper-table, mixing the sangaree and passing round the glasses of schnaps. Such was the young lady of whom my excellent washerwoman, Frau Vanfromp, spoke as inciting the population of Amsterdam to inebriation, and I must again assure you that old Nelly Vanfromp was not a person to tell a falsehood. She was a good woman, and to her I firmly believe I am indebted for the preservation of my life, as I will some day tell you; but, by the by, I am getting altogether out of my latitude.

I am going to describe to you the plan Captain Brisbane formed for attacking Amsterdam. Curaçao is a long thin island, generally low and level, except round Amsterdam, which is at the south-west end, and there is also another elevation about six miles further to the east, on which a strong fort was situated.

The fortifications round the harbour of St. Ann's are of immense strength, and such as, if defended with courage and ability, a fleet of line-of-battle ships could scarcely silence. The entrance, something like the mouth of Portsmouth harbour, is not more than fifty fathoms wide, with Fort Amsterdam, mounting sixty-six pieces of cannon, in two tiers, on the right-hand side, and on the left a battery with three tiers, and a chain of forts extending for a considerable way along the heights of Misselburg above it, while an almost impregnable fortress, called Fort Republique, at the bottom of the harbour, within a sufficient distance to throw out showers of grape-shot, enfiladed the whole harbour, which is nowhere more than a quarter of a mile in width.

So much our gallant Commodore knew from the charts and the descriptions of the place with which he was furnished; but besides these fortifications, he had every reason to expect to find some ships of war moored in the harbour to dispute our entrance. Nothing daunted by these impediments, he determined, should the wind prove favourable, to take advantage of the probable inebriated state of the soldiers, and the inhabitants of the island, to make a dash with his four frigates right into the mouth of the harbour, on the morning of the 1st, and to storm the forts with his ships' companies and marines.

No sooner was the determination known throughout the fleet than every man belonging to it set enthusiastically to work to make the necessary preparations. The better to deceive the Dutch, and to make them believe that we had a large body of troops on board, the seamen were rigged out in uniforms; our men having white jackets with blue facings and black cross-belts, and when paraded on deck with muskets on their shoulders, they made a very respectable soldier-like appearance. Part of each crew was then told off into storming companies under the command of the Lieutenants, and others were formed into parties headed by boatswains of their respective ships, with ladders to place against the walls, and crowbars to break open the gates.

At an early hour on the morning of the 24th of December, our Commodore gave the signal for the fleet to weigh anchor and make sail to the eastward. With more than usual alacrity the capstan bars were manned, the jig played, the people went round with a merry tramp, a loud cheer was given as the anchor was away; it was soon run up to our bows, and with every stitch of canvass we stood out to sea with the rest of the fleet. Everything augured well for the success of our enterprise: the weather promised to be favourable, the crews were in high spirits and good health; they were eager to fight, and they had confidence in their officers, for they will always rather follow those who prefer fighting to diplomatizing.

Had Captain Brisbane, on the contrary, instead of poking the muzzles of the guns into the windows and doors of the honest burghers, remained with his small fleet idly off the port, displaying his weakness, and waiting while the Dutch Governor and his Council slumbered through the forms of a negotiation, and the Dutch forts were put in a better state of defence, and the soldiers took in a large stock of courage, the chances are that by the time their pipes were out, they would have come to the conclusion that they would rather not capitulate at all.

War, bloodshed, and all their dark attendants are very dreadful things; but when such work is to be done, the sooner it is begun and the sooner it is over the better. I do not recollect much about our passage from Oruba, except that we had a dead beat most of the time against an easterly wind, and that we were fully occupied in making ladders, sharpening cutlasses, cutting out coats and belts, and drilling the men.

The stars were shining forth bright and lustrous, from the intensely dark blue sky, their light playing on the dancing waves, whence, from the darker portions, issued forth phosphorescent flashes with such rapidity that the whole ocean appeared at times composed of a sheet of luminous matter. A fresh breeze filled our whitened canvass as we ploughed the deep, while ahead and astern of us appeared the lofty sails of our three consorts, towering up darkly in the sky, against which every rope and spar appeared clearly defined.

"What a lovely night is this!" said St. John, who was somewhat fond of indulging in romance. "How tranquil and soft! It would almost make one fancy that this world was formed for peace and tranquillity, instead of war and bloodshed. I wonder where you or I shall be to-morrow, Dainmore?"

"In Fort Amsterdam, or else in those regions where many a brave fellow has gone before us," I answered, laughing. "Why do you ask the question?"

"Because I cannot help thinking, my dear fellow, that I shall be to-morrow in the latter place you speak of," replied he. "I do not know why, but the idea has got hold of me, and I cannot shake it off. It does not make me unhappy, and I hope I shall not do my duty the worse for it. However, if I fall, write home about it; break the news as gently as you can to my mother, and give my best, my devoted affection to Julia."

I tried to combat my friend's forebodings, and with some success; at all events, his spirits did not appear to flag. Whether they proved true or not will be afterwards seen.

Our conversation was interrupted by the intelligence that land was seen on the starboard bow; and as we eagerly looked out, the high land of St. Barbary rose gradually before us. Thus commenced the memorable 1st of January. We had been compelled to work thus far to the eastward to catch the south-east trade, in order to stand directly up for the harbour of St. Ann's. We now continued standing on for the remainder of the night, with the dark line of the coast full in view; and, as morning broke, we found ourselves directly off the mouth of that port. The Commodore now ordered us to heave-to, and to get our boats into the water, which being done, we towed them after us, when we again made sail. A line of battle being next formed, the Arethusa leading, followed by the Latona, Anson, and Fisgard, in the order I mention them, the fleet stood boldly on, reaching close up to the forts before they attracted any attention from the drowsy garrison.

The Arethusa was the first to enter the harbour, with a flag of truce flying at the fore, in case the inhabitants, on the sight of so daring an armament, should be induced to capitulate without offering any resistance. We watched her progress with deep anxiety, for certainly the descriptions of the fortifications had in no way been exaggerated. The white stone forts, bristling with cannon, seen through the grey light of morn, seemed sufficient to destroy us in a moment, by sending their shot right down through our decks, besides which, a little way up the harbour, and moored directly athwart it, we made out the masts and hulls of several vessels, which we judged rightly to be ships of war. On stood the saucy Arethusa, however; her sails were full, with a fine north-easterly breeze, and for some minutes not a sound disturbed the serenity of the scene. The harbour, I must observe, runs in length nearly north and south, so that a slight change of the wind more from the north would have prevented our entering, and of this we had good reason to be afraid, as it had already been veering about from point to point during the morning, and might head us as we got between the forts.

The early morning air was pure and cool, the bright tints of the tropics were now softened and mellowed in that subdued light, the mists which hung over the land in the interior gave a great apparent extent to the view, the sea looked transparent and clear, while astern, the sky glowed with a roseate tinge, which, gradually increasing, reflected its glowing hues on the heights above us. Suddenly, as the Arethusa got abreast of the forts, a column of smoke ascended to the sky in a blue towering wreath—the deep silence was broken by the loud report of a gun, followed in quick succession by several others from the different forts.

This was the signal for us to stand in after our leader; the flag of truce was disregarded, and fighting was to be the order of the day.

We were not the lads to disappoint our friends. The drums along all the forts beat to arms, calling the sleepy, half-drunken burghers from their beds; the soldiers rushed to their posts, the seamen hurried on board their ships, and the most indescribable confusion prevailed among all the rest of the inhabitants.

Meanwhile, our little squadron steadily continued their course, close-hauled on the starboard tack, disregarding the random shots discharged at us, and which fortunately committed no material damage, either to the rigging or hulls. Every moment was, however, precious, for the Dutch artillerymen were fast assembling at their guns, and we could see the officers and men of the ships in the harbour pulling on board their respective craft as fast as the drunken crews could handle their oars.

We now made out a thirty-six-gun frigate, which we afterwards found to be the Keenan Haslar, commanded by a very brave fellow, Captain Cornelius Evertz, and a large corvette, mounting twenty guns, called the Surinam, whose captain rejoiced in the name of Jan Van Ness; besides which, there were two armed schooners of considerable size.

Onward we proudly sailed, the crew at their quarters—some with the lanyards of their guns in their hands, others standing by the braces, the tacks, and sheets—the captain in the weather mizen rigging, conning the ship—the marines and idlers drawn up on the quarter-deck and forecastle, the latter rigged in uniform, with muskets shouldered, doing duty as military—trusty hands were in the chains—signal midshipmen with their glasses at their eyes—the anchors unstopped and ready to let go—the magazines were open—shots were piled up on the decks—in a word, we were in as perfect a state of preparation as possible for whatever might occur.

I already well knew what fighting was, in its varied forms of horror, and so did most of my shipmates. In those stirring times, few had to wait long without encountering it. I had served under our great Naval Chief in some of his most glorious and bloody engagements; I had seen hostile fleets engage, when, shrouded in smoke, and surrounded by fire, shot and shell were issuing from many thousand guns; I had seen hundreds of brave men fall to rise no more, amid the roar of cannon, the shrieks and groans of the wounded, the cries of despair, and the shouts of victory; but never had I engaged in a more daring undertaking, and never did I feel more excitement than at that moment.

What, then, was our disappointment and vexation when, the wind suddenly shifting round to the north, we beheld the sails of the Arethusa taken aback, and our farther progress stopped. There lay the gallant frigate, exposed to the fire of the enemy, which was, as I before observed, fortunately not very well directed, while every man in the ships astern of her was anxious to be allowed to jump into the boats and pull to her assistance.

Such appeared the sad end of our hopes of victory. Our skipper stamped with very vexation of spirit, and whistled audibly for another shift of wind.

"By J——s!" exclaimed O'Sulivan, "I'd give all the dirty acres my dad possesses in Tipperary just for a capful of the soft balmy breezes of the south which blow over my native bogs."

"And I ten of the best years of my life," added St. John, enthusiastically.

"I said we should never take that place," muttered the master; "it's known to be impregnable."

Just then a shout of joy escaped the lips of every one of our crew, for, with a sudden squall, the wavering wind shifted back to the north-east, filling the Arethusa's sails, and, followed closely by the rest of the squadron, she boldly stood up the harbour. Unfortunately, the Fisgard, to the extreme vexation of her brave captain and crew, having kept too much to the westward, owing to the wind heading her, took the ground, though in a position where she was not much annoyed by the fire from the enemy's forts; her boats' crews, however, did good service in the ensuing engagement.

Captain Brisbane, having now brought the Arethusa's broadsides to bear, one upon the Dutch frigate, the other upon the town, with his jib-boom over the walls, dropped his anchor, and made the signal to the other ships to do the same as they got into their positions. As yet we had not fired a shot, for the flag of truce was still flying at the Arethusa's fore, and Captain Brisbane, humanely anxious to prevent the unnecessary effusion of blood, wrote, on the capstern-head of his frigate, the following summons to the inhabitants:—

"The British squadron are here to protect, and not to conquer you—to preserve to you your lives, liberty, and property. If a shot is fired at any one of my squadron after this summons, I shall immediately storm your batteries. You have five minutes to accede to this determination. I have the honour to be," &c. &c.

This laconic, but forcible epistle was forthwith dispatched by a boat to the Governor, and for some minutes longer we were doomed to remain in uncertainty as to what the result of the summons might be. Some thought the Mynheers would yield—others, who knew their stubborn natures better, insisted that they would fight it out to the last. In the meantime, the ships of the enemy were preparing for action, the tipsy crews were driven to their quarters, and their guns were loaded. When I speak of the drunkenness of the enemy, I do not mean in any way to detract from the credit due to our exploit; but had it not been for this circumstance, we should have had much harder work to undergo, or probably the expedition would not have been undertaken at all.

At length our doubts were put an end to, and His Excellency, Pierre Jean Chanquion, not thinking fit to send any polite acknowledgment of the receipt of the note within the specified time, the flag of truce was hauled down, and we began blazing away with our guns as fast as we could load them. This compliment was warmly returned from the Dutchmen's ships and forts, one of the latter, on the top of the hill, throwing red-hot shot down upon our decks, but fortunately without doing us any material damage. The Haslar made a gallant resistance, under her brave Commander, Cornelius Evertz, the Commodore on the station; but Captain Brisbane, determining to silence her guns, ordered his boats to be manned, and leaping into his gig, made a bold dash at her. With a shout of encouragement, he bravely led on his boarders; the Dutch received him with thrusts of pikes and pistol-shots, but, nothing daunted, after a severe tussle he gained possession of their decks. Meanwhile, Captain Lydiard, of the Anson, with a party of his crew, had in a like manner attacked the Surinam corvette, when her commander and several of her officers being badly wounded, her flag was struck, and she was taken possession of.

On Captain Brisbane hauling down the flag of the Haslar, he ordered the Latona to warp alongside, and secure her. This was quickly accomplished, and when the officer who took possession stepped upon her decks, he found several of her people lying dead or badly wounded, and among the former was her brave captain. The captain of the British frigate had asked for him to receive his sword.

His first lieutenant shook his head: "He is there," he said, pointing to a flag thrown over a body stretched along the quarter deck; "he will never fight more." He lifted the flag—there lay the Dutch Commodore, his countenance blanched by death, though calm and composed, as if he slept: yet a cannon-shot had taken off the entire back part of his head, and he must have died instantaneously. He reverently again covered up the body. He was a determined, energetic man, who, had he lived, would have fought his ship to the last, and never consented to the capitulation of the town. The people and military looked up to him far more than they did to the Civil Governor, who appeared to have been an opposite character in some respects, though not destitute of loyalty to the power he served. There was not much time, you may be sure, either for meditation, or to regret the death of our brave enemy.

As soon as the prisoners from the frigate, as well as those of the corvette, had been secured, and also of two schooners, which quietly struck their flags, we were ordered into the boats to commence our operations on shore. I ought to have said that we saw a strong body of troops marching down on the western shore, with the evident intention of crossing over to the town, but our guns opened so warm a fire on them that they were glad to beat a retreat, leaving their friends to fight it out as best they could. As soon as the ships were taken possession of, the Commodore and Captain Lydiard, at the head of the boats of their two ships, pulled directly under the walls of Fort Amsterdam. This was the most exciting business of all. With loud huzzas the soldier-seamen leaped on shore, led on by their brave chiefs. The ladders were placed against the walls, and up they swarmed, like active seamen as they were, to the no small astonishment of the Mynheers, who took them of course for soldiers. The vigour of the assault was irresistible, the cutlass did its work well, and line after line of the fortifications was won, while another party with crowbars were battering away at a gate, which opened towards the sea. This at length gave way, and the marines and seamen rushed in. The Dutchmen, finding themselves assailed on every side, through the walls and over the walls, begged for quarter, and hauled down their flags, and that of Britain flew in its stead, though the fort contained nearly three hundred regular troops. It is difficult to describe the various events which were taking place in so many different spots. During this time the other ships' companies were busily employed in storming the fortifications on the west side of the harbour, leaving men on board barely sufficient to guard the prisoners, and make some show from the shore, lest the true numbers of our little force might be suspected, for the Dutchmen fully believed that we had come with a large body of troops. It is extraordinary with what rapidity we stormed fort after fort, shouting, and slashing, and leaping as we fought our onward way. Not the least energetic was my friend St. John, whose melancholy forebodings on the previous night I have already mentioned. Finding him by my side on one occasion, I congratulated him on this not having hitherto proved true.

"The ides of March are not over yet," he answered: and just then a shot whizzed past our heads. "An inch or two more and I should have been settled for," he said, dashing aside a Dutchman's musket.

"And so should I with the same on the other side, and yet I had no forebodings," I replied; and after that we were separated.

I had soon the pleasure of meeting St. John on the deck of our frigate, safe in life and limb, and he is now well up on the list of Post Captains.

I am always wandering from my main subject. Though the forts on each side of the harbour were in our possession, we had still the strongest of all, Fort Republique, to silence. This was a work of no slight difficulty, for it alone was fully capable of blowing us out of the water, if its guns had been properly served. For some time we all blazed away at it, a compliment its garrison returned to the best of their ability, without appearing at all inclined to yield; so at last our military proceedings having hitherto proved successful, three hundred seamen and marines were landed and marched inland, so as to go round and attack it in the rear. Jack likes soldiering once in a way, provided he has not much drilling to go through, and our men appeared to enjoy it amazingly. Away they marched at a double-quick pace, and in spite of all impediments, and notwithstanding some severe fighting, managed, by ten o'clock, to scramble over the intrenchments in the rear, and to hoist the British flag on the walls of Fort Republique. Thus in about four hours, to the very great astonishment of our master, no less, probably, than to that of the Mynheers, this impregnable position was in our possession.

The fat burghers, as they recovered their senses, rubbed their eyes, and could not make out the change of flags, so they lighted their pipes, and sat down to cogitate on the matter, and endeavour to discover the cause of the noise and tumult which had disturbed their slumbers.

That same 1st of January will not be forgotten by them or their sons in a hurry. We have just reason to be proud of it, for it was in truth as gallant an action as was ever fought, planned daringly and ably executed.

Our labours were not, however, over, for though the fortifications round Amsterdam were ours, there was still another castle in the island, about six miles along the coast, to the eastward, to be reduced. Thither I was immediately despatched, with a strong force, with guides and a flag of truce, to summon the garrison to surrender. I found it a very strong position, on a lofty eminence, with a round tower in the centre, mounting eight guns, and surrounded with lines of more modern date. Its garrison, however, though doubtless brave as lions on occasion, hearing that the Governor was a prisoner, and that the principal fortifications in the island were in our possession, wisely considered that they were not called on to risk their lives, when they should probably have, in the end, to yield; and, therefore, following the example set them, hauled down the Dutch colours, and allowed those of England to be hoisted in their stead. The other strongholds in the island, behaving in the same judicious way, by 12 o'clock the whole of Curaçao was in our power. We had, however, abundance of work on our hands, for we now found ourselves possessed of an island containing, it was said, forty-five thousand inhabitants, while the utmost force we could number could not amount to more than twelve hundred people to man the ships, to take care of the prisoners, and to garrison the forts.

Captain Brisbane, as you see, was not a man to be daunted by difficulties. His great care was to conceal the paucity of our numbers by making a parade both of the seamen on the decks of the ships, and of the newly clothed soldiers on shore. He also divided the island into eight districts, and summoned all the inhabitants to bring in their arms to certain posts, while he secured any person likely to be troublesome, politely providing them with better quarters on board the ships. The articles of capitulation had been at once drawn up and agreed upon between Captain Brisbane, the senior Captain of His Majesty's ships, and His Excellency Pierre Jean Chanquion, Governor of the Island of Curaçao and its dependencies, to the effect that the said island was to be delivered into the hands of the British; the garrison, as well as the officers and crews of the captured ships, sent to Holland at the expense of the victors, not to serve again during the war, before they were regularly exchanged. All the civil officers were to retain their respective appointments; and the persons and property of the burghers, merchants, planters, and other inhabitants, without difference of colour or opinion, were to be respected, provided they took the oath of allegiance to His Britannic Majesty. The Dutch Governor wanted to do us out of a part of our prize-money, by insisting that the merchant-vessels and their cargoes in the harbour should remain in the possession of their former owners, but to this the Commodore would not agree, and Mynheer Chanquion was obliged to yield.

A day was next appointed on which the oath of allegiance to His Britannic Majesty was to be taken by all the principal civil officers, the captains of the Militia Companies, and the chief inhabitants; and when, to his credit, the Governor and Commander-in-chief of the island, his Excellency Lieutenant-General Pierre Jean Chanquion refused so to do, Captain Brisbane gave himself forthwith an acting order to rule in his stead, which circumstances he took care should be well notified all over the island. Thus, with four frigates, and their ships' companies, an island containing upwards of thirty thousand inhabitants, rich and fertile in the extreme, was captured by the British, a feat of which as many line-of-battle ships, and a dozen transports, full of troops, might have good reason to boast.

The new governor was a fine, tall, handsome man, courteous in his manner, and affable to all, so that he quickly gained the esteem and affection of his subjects. He was seen everywhere, galloping about the country with an eye all round him, visiting the forts and conversing with the people. He was also not a little fond of pomp, and did his best to display it, or probably he did not value it so much for itself as for the useful effect it produced on others. This reminds me that it was here I first saw a class of soldiers whose existence many people discredit, but of which you have doubtless often heard, called Horse Marines. Governor Brisbane, however, literally called them into existence, for requiring a guard to attend him on his excursions, he mounted such of the marines as could ride on horseback, dispensing with the usual cavalry accoutrements, and certainly to a military eye they did cut rather an odd appearance; that he cared little for: they served his purpose, and kept the people in awe. He had before this raised a body of men from among his own crew, to whom he gave the appellation of Determinés, which they bore in gold letters in front of their hats. They were picked men, every one of them dashing, bold fellows, ready to execute any daring exploit he might propose, and it was considered a high honour to belong to them. They were his bodyguard, his sacred band; and I truly believe nothing was too difficult for them to undertake. I was, I confess, very partial to Sir Charles Brisbane (he was knighted for this exploit), for I received many marks of kindness from him; but without prejudice in his favour, I think his example might well be followed on similar occasions. He was afterwards appointed to the government of St. Vincent's, and of other important islands in the West Indies, and was, I believe, one of the oldest governors in those colonies.

But to return to Curaçao. Among others who had to do duty on shore, I was appointed commandant of the strong fort of which I have already spoken, about six miles along the coast, to the eastward of Amsterdam, with a body of seamen to hold it. As it was in an elevated position, it was considered of great importance, commanding a view of the plantations spread out on the low lands, on the one side, and the wide extending ocean on the other. There I took up my quarters for a considerable time.

CHAPTER XXVII.

CAPTAIN DAINMORE'S STORY CONTINUED—THE TAKING OF CURAÇAO.

THE post I held required my utmost vigilance; for not only might the inhabitants of the island be induced to revolt, but we might expect a visit of the enemy from the Spanish main, as soon as they heard that Curaçao had fallen into our power, before we could possibly receive reinforcements from Jamaica or elsewhere. I therefore was constantly on the watch, going my rounds at all times of the night, to see that the sentinels were alert at their posts, and that my subordinates were doing their duty. One night, soon after we had taken possession, the mate, who acted as my lieutenant, roused me from my short slumbers to say, that he had just seen a number of fires blazing up in various directions, and that he could not make out what they meant.

Throwing on my cloak in a moment, I rushed out to the ramparts, and through the darkness of night, beheld on the land side a line of bright fires; it seemed glowing in the distance and almost surrounding us.

"The Spaniards or French have doubtless landed on the north coast, and have lighted these fires as they advance across the island, to distract our attention," I cried. "Beat to quarters!" The men were in admirable discipline; and as the first tap of the drum sounded, hurried to their posts. The garrison were all under arms; the outposts remained unmolested; not a sound disturbed the silence of night; yet still the fires continued blazing up in the distance, and rather increasing in numbers than diminishing, although they did not approach nearer. "Can it be that incendiaries are at work, and that the sugar-houses and plantations are being destroyed?" I observed to my sub.

"I should think not, sir," he answered; "they are too close together for that."

"You are right," I replied; "yet I can scarcely believe the conflagration is caused by an invading force: they would rather endeavour to catch us napping."

"Then what can they be?" asked the youth, with some vexation in his tone, at not being able to solve the difficulty.

I must confess that I felt no little anxiety on the subject; for with the mere handful of men I had with me I could scarcely hope to offer a successful resistance should any large force be brought against us, though I felt confident my fellows would stand by their colours as long as they had legs to stand on. At last my young sub asked leave to take two or three of the people with him, and to sally forth to reconnoitre the supposed enemy. To this proposal I at length consented, for I had every confidence in his courage and judgment. Having selected three of our best hands, and promising to return in an hour at the furthest, he set forth on his expedition.

As I stood on the ramparts, I watched the dark forms of the party as they silently descended the hill, and cautiously took their way along the plain below. Oh, what a lovely night that was! I could not help ever and anon turning my gaze from the world below me to the pure sky above me. How different it appeared to the solid canopy of a northern clime, the stars palely shining like dim lamps from amid the dark mass. Here the clear soft atmosphere seemed composed of a transparent sea of liquid azure, in which floated thousands of gloriously bright lights, unobscured by a single wreath of vapour, while other and lesser luminaries filled up the intervals of incalculable space. Turning seaward, I beheld the ocean sleeping in tranquil splendour, reflecting in long lines of glittering brightness the larger stars in the sky above, while on one side a dark headland formed a boundary to my view, and on the other, the woods and fertile fields sloped gradually down to the sandy beech.

How long I had been indulging in the sensations to which this enchanting scene gave rise I scarcely knew, when I was aroused from my reverie by the challenge of the sentries, the watch-word given in return followed by a long, loud laugh, and the merry tones of young Dixon's voice.

"Well, what news of the enemy?" I asked, as he approached.

"They throng the island, sir," he answered, laughing; "they swarm round the fires in thousands—ha, ha, ha! But I never knew before that the Dutchmen were cannibals—ha, ha, ha! We found that, instead of joining them to destroy us, they were busily employed in catching and eating them—ha, ha, ha! All those fires were lighted to catch the land-crabs."

A few mornings after this event, as I was standing on the top of my look-out tower, sweeping the horizon with my glass, I observed a horseman galloping towards the fort; and as he came nearer, I made him out to be one of the Governor's Horse Marines. As he doubtlessly came with a despatch for me, I descended to meet him, when he put into my hands a note from the Governor, ordering me to hurry down to him with all the men I could possibly spare from the fort; as, from information he had just received, he had reason to expect a sudden attack from the Spaniards. Accordingly, leaving young Dixon as commandant, with a few men to do duty as sentries, and urging on them the necessity of vigilance and caution, I marched out with the remainder of my garrison to the support of the governor.

We did not spare ourselves; for when fighting was in prospect, all were eager to arrive in time; and a hot run we had of it, at double-quick time, along the dusty road.

When we arrived, no enemy had as yet appeared; and after waiting some hours without a sign of their approach, Captain Brisbane began to suspect that he had been imposed on, which was in truth the case.

It was impossible to say, however, when the Spaniards might make their appearance; and there were many chances that they might make a landing at the end of the island where my fort was situated, particularly if they should receive information, that it had been left without a sufficient defence. Accordingly the Governor ordered me to make the best of my way with my men back to my post. "Stay," he observed, "you are already weary and knocked up with the heat, and will not be fit for work when you get to your journey's end, it will therefore be much better for you to go by sea, and you will find a large schooner in the harbour which you can take for that purpose; but remember, that it is of the utmost importance that you should arrive there before nightfall. You have two hours to spare, and a fresh breeze, and in little more than an hour you can be there. Good by, Mr. Dainmore.". I accordingly made my *congé*, and, with my men, hurried down to the harbour, where I found the schooner moored a few fathoms from the shore. As soon as possible, we got on board, unmoored ship and loosened sails; but when we came to hoist the mainsail, we found that the gaff had been shot away. As we could not sail with it in this state, we were obliged to get it repaired, which work took up a considerable time. I forgot to say, that I had asked my friend, Mr. Hermes, to dine with me; and on my way down, I sent word to invite him to come on board, in order to accompany me. There had before been a strong breeze, but during this unavoidable delay, the wind freshened up considerably, and headed us completely. On seeing this, Hermes excused himself from accompanying me, saying he should prefer galloping over by land, as he should be there as soon as we could. It was providential for him that he did so. The events of that day made a deep impression on my mind, which can never be erased from my memory. It would be black ingratitude to the great Dispenser and Preserver of life, did I forget them, or cease to be thankful for his providential care of me. Most men have during their lifetime gone through dangers of some sort or another, but few have been exposed to greater peril than I was on that day, as I am about to relate to you.

At last the gaff was substantially repaired, and with storm-jib set, and a reef in our mainsail, we stood out of the harbour of St. Ann's. As soon as we got clear of the land, the vessel felt the full force of the wind, and heeled over to her scuppers at every blast. She was rather a crank vessel, and had besides a long 18-pounder swivel gun on deck mounted on a high carriage, and a quantity of shot and iron ballast stowed away below, which made her far from a lively craft. The sea ran high, and, in white foam, broke over our bows; but my orders were imperative, and I saw that it was only by carrying on I could hope to obey them, particularly as the wind was dead on end along shore. It was thus tack and tack the whole way. Sometimes I stood off a considerable way, in the hope of getting a more favourable slant of wind, but I was often baffled in my calculations.

In the tropics the ocean slumbers for a while, and seems so gentle and tranquil, that one almost fancies that it must thus rest for ever; but a change quickly comes over it, and when once aroused, there are no bounds to its fury. In the same way, so soft are the balmy zephyrs which are wafted from the spicy shore, that one is apt to forget that there are such things as squalls, tempests, and hurricanes. The wind and ocean were now broad awake, as onward we ploughed our way, leaving a quickly-dispersed track of boiling foam astern of us, while billow upon billow rose up ahead, threatening every instant to break on board us. I had, with my own hands, taken a turn of the fore-sheet round the belaying-pin, and stationed a man to hold it between his finger and thumb, with orders to him to keep his eye upon me, and to let it go as I should make the signal. I then took my station near the helm at the weather-bulwark, to con the vessel. Onward we held our course; now the dark line of the shore was on our lee-bow, now on our weather-quarter, the dark leaden waves fringed with foam dancing and bubbling around us, the clouds rapidly chasing each other over the sky in a way which gave every indication of an increase of wind.

"I don't think the craft likes quite so much canvass on her, sir," observed a seaman, who, acting as quarter-master, now stood near me. "These schooners is ticklish things in these seas."

"I know it," I answered; "but the commodore's orders must be obeyed; and if we were to lay her to to reef sails, we should lose so much time we should never be up to the fort before dark. No higher, my man," I sang out to the man at the helm. "Keep her full!—now, meet her—meet her," I added, as a huge wave came tumbling towards us. The vessel dipped her head into it, deluging the decks and half-scaring the man at the fore-sheets; but she rose again and bounded onward.

Thus we continued beating up till we had got about six miles to windward of the harbour. We were standing off shore, and near, as I could guess, about two miles distant from it, when, as I was keeping a sharp look-out to windward, I saw a heavier squall than any we had encountered rushing towards us. Down it came like a whirlwind, with the rapidity of lightning. "Let go!" I sang out to the man at the fore-sheets, "Let go!" But he stared at me with idiotical gaze, scared and terrified, and held on. The vessel felt the fury of the blast—down, down she bent before it. "Let go!" I again shrieked out, but the wretched man seemed turned to stone; and had I held a pistol in my hand, I would have shot him to preserve the rest, for it was impossible at that moment to reach him.

The wind swept over the dark sides of the schooner, and her canvass lay flat upon the waves. A wild cry of terror escaped the hapless wretch who had been the cause of the catastrophe; it was the last sound we heard from his lips, for the next surge swept him away. The rest of the crew sprang to the weather-rigging and bulwarks, as the foaming sea rushed up the now perpendicular decks, and washing away the hatches, poured down the hold in furious torrents. All hopes of righting the vessel were in a moment gone; the dreadful conviction forcing itself with terrible certainty on my mind that she was sinking, and that we must be left to float alone on the wild waves. Had I known, as I afterwards did, that the sea was swarming with sharks, I should, I think, have given way to despair, but, as it was, my confidence never forsook me; my first thought was to preserve the people under my care.

"Can you all swim?" I sang out, as I hung on to the weather bulwarks, near which I had before been standing.

All the men answered, "Yes," but two, who, with voices of terror, declared their inability to save themselves.

"Well then, do you two, each of you, catch hold of those two gratings near the fore-bits there, see them clear of everything, keep your arms well extended, your heads up—don't attempt to struggle—and put your trust in Providence. The rest of you get hold of anything that will float to assist you; off with your jackets and shoes, and be prepared to withstand the influx of the water as the vessel goes down."

Having rapidly given these orders, I climbed to the main-rigging, where I took off my own coat, in the pocket of which were some valuable papers, and made it fast to the pennant-halliards, in the hopes of thus being able to preserve it, forgetting at the time the immense depth of the sea round the coast. I had it still in my hand when the vessel suddenly righted, the sea made a clean breach over her deck, a wild cry escaped some of the people, answered by a groan from the submerging hull, and I felt her sinking beneath my feet. I sprang off from her side into the boiling sea, and then first recollected that I had neglected to secure for myself anything to assist me to keep afloat, so completely had my thoughts been engaged in endeavouring to preserve my crew. It is now nearly forty years ago, and I may say what was really the case. Down went the vessel, her masts and spars gradually disappearing beneath the waves. It was like a dreadful dream. I even then could scarcely persuade myself of the reality of what had occurred, as I lay tossed about on the wide world of waters, without a plank on which to rest my foot. I looked anxiously around as I rose to the top of a wave, and saw the two men who could not swim floating safely on the gratings; the rest of the people were keeping themselves up by means of spars, hencoops, oars, and chests, which had burst out from below, but nothing could I see near me to lay hold of. At last I recognised one of the best men in the ship, named Pierson, holding on by the end of an oar, at a short distance from me.

"Pierson," I cried, as I swam towards him, "I don't think I shall be able to hold on long without something to keep me up, but if you will let me take hold of the other end of your oar, and follow my advice, we may both be saved; for as it is, you now only use half of it."

"Is that you, sir?" he answered, when he heard me. "Lord

bless me, sir, of course; catch hold at once, sir. I am glad you have escaped; I was afraid you had gone down with the craft."

"No, I hope we may both survive to reach the shore," I replied, as I caught hold of the end of the oar. "They must have seen the schooner capsize, and will put off in boats to our assistance, so keep a good heart."

"Oh, no fear of that, sir," was the answer, but just then a sea washed over his head, and filled his mouth with salt water; indeed, between the intervals of speaking, I had been much inconvenienced in the same way; nor must you suppose that I spoke as much as I did without considerable difficulty, and at long intervals.

"This will never do," I observed; "do you, Pierson, lie flat along the water, and I will steer the oar with my legs, so as to keep directly to windward of you, and we shall thus ride much more easily."

I forthwith did as I said, although every wave washed clean over my head, and then over Pierson's, when we were obliged to shut our mouths; we had sufficiently long intervals, as we rose again, to breathe freely, and look about us. We were, as I may say, on a see-saw—now he was up in the air, and then I rose high enough to get a glimpse of the distant shore, and the mouth of St. Ann's harbour, which we had just opened as the schooner capsized.

It was a melancholy prospect, the wild boiling sea around us, and the dark line of coast, with its fringe of white breakers, which we could not possibly hope to reach without other assistance than our own strength afforded us. We put our trust for help in Him from whom alone help can come in all our difficulties and dangers. I encouraged Pierson, and his good spirits kept up mine, and as I caught a sight at intervals of any of the rest of my men, I sang out to them to be of good cheer, for help would assuredly come. They answered my hail with an encouraging "Ay, ay, sir, we'll hold on to the last, never fear." I must confess, however, that though I felt assured we should be saved, I could not tell by what means. The schooner had probably been observed to go down from the harbour, but as that was six miles distant, a boat would take a long time to pull up to us against a head wind, and we might be food for fishes before she could arrive; their canoes might possibly come off to us from the shore, but there was a heavy surf, and not many of them along that part of the coast.

It is very extraordinary that all this time it never occurred to me that our chief danger lay from the sharks; indeed I never once thought of them, though they were swarming thickly around us, far down in their liquid homes; had I done so, I think my courage would have failed, for I possessed all a sailor's horror of those voracious animals, whether belonging to sea or land. How long we had continued thus I cannot tell, when, as I rose to the top of a wave, I saw a black object breaking through the white line of foam which fringed the shore. For some time I said nothing, for I thought I might be disappointed, but I soon saw it followed by another similar object, and I then felt confident that I was not mistaken, and that they were canoes coming to our assistance. This joyful intelligence I communicated to some of those near me, and it served to keep up their spirits, which with one or two had begun to fail.

On similar occasions you will observe that it is not so much physical strength as mental which serves to preserve people, or rather that the strongest man is but as an infant when his strength avails him nought. A lesson of deep import might be learnt from it. There we were, weak mortals, floating on the bosom of the wide ocean, without a spot on which to rest our foot, such as we had been accustomed to. We felt palpably and sensibly our own complete helplessness. A cramp might seize the limbs of the strongest, a shark might grasp us in his mighty jaws, and then what would become of that power of which strong men on shore delight to boast? We should have been more powerless than a sparrow in the beak of a noble eagle, a worm beneath the foot of man.

Bravely the headmost canoe dashed through the foaming sea, and rapidly advanced towards us, and as she neared us, I blessed the eager faces of the two black men who paddled her, but she was of small size, and could at the utmost only carry two additional people. A considerable portion of my men were some way in shore of me, and towards these she first approached, with proper caution, taking in one over the bow and another over the stern. As soon as she had got them safely on board, away the blacks paddled with all their might and main, leaving the remainder with a sensation of forlornness still floating alone. Before long, however, another canoe came up, and two more were taken on board, the courageous blacks, in like manner as the former ones, pulling as fast as they could back to the shore. They were not ignorant, it must be remembered, as we were, of the numbers of sharks in the neighbourhood, and were fully aware of the danger they incurred if the canoes were capsized. At last a third canoe was launched by some people who saw the success of the former ones, and who now, with cries of encouragement, pulled towards us. It was much more trying work, I can assure you, to those who remained, than if we had all been longer in the water, and saved together, for it was very tantalizing to our human natures, however we might reason ourselves out of the feeling, to see our companions carried off to a place of safety, while we were left to buffet the waves alone. I felt, however, that I had but one line of duty to follow, and that was to remain in the water as long as any of my people were in danger, however much my love of life might tempt me to endeavour to preserve myself before them. The third canoe had already got her proper cargo on board, when a third man grasped hold of her stern, and with loud cries and oaths insisted on being taken in. Had the blacks yielded to his demands, the boat would probably have been capsized, and all hands lost, so they were compelled to strike at his hands, and compel him to let go. With a look of despair the poor wretch swam back to the plank to which he had been floating, and which was some way from us, so that his strength was much exhausted by the time he reached it; had he performed his duty, it would have been much better for him.

The two first canoes now again returned, and took on board four more of the people; and as they were pulling away, they pointed towards the harbour, and made signs to us to look that way. As

P

the next wave lifted us high enough to enjoy a wider range of horizon, I beheld, to my infinite satisfaction, a large boat pulling towards us from the harbour; but she was still at a considerable distance, and hard work her crew had to make head against the sea and wind. So long, indeed, was she coming up, that the canoes were able to take nearly all the people on shore before she was within hail.

At last a canoe pulled up to where Pierson and I were floating. I had, I forgot to say, kept on my cocked hat all the time, for I thought the gold lace would be more easily seen at a distance; indeed, it served considerably to protect my head and eyes from the spray.

"Jump on board, bukra captain, jump on board; we no see you before," cried the blacks, as they caught sight of me.

"The other man will get on board first," I answered. "Pierson, do you get hold of the bows, while I swim round to the stern. Now, in with us," and lifting ourselves steadily up, we crawled in at the same moment.

I uttered an ejaculation of thankfulness for our preservation—a person has little time for more on such occasions—when looking round, I beheld the two men who had hold of the gratings, keeping exactly as I had told them, and floating close to us, and the man who had attempted to get on board the canoe at some distance off to windward.

The first two, when they saw me, exclaimed with feeble voices,—
"Oh, save us!—save us!—we cannot hold out any longer; indeed, indeed we cannot."

I saw that what they said was true, though not so much from want of strength as of courage.

"Pierson," I said, turning to my brave companion, "it will never do to let those poor men perish when we might save them. You are a good swimmer, and can well keep afloat till the boat from the harbour picks us up. Will you jump in again? I must."

"I will do as you do, sir."

"Well, then—one, two, three, 'over;'" and standing up as I uttered the words, he leapt over the bows and I over the stern of the canoe, and were once more buffeting the waves. The blacks looked astonished; but comprehending my intentions, instantly took on board the two men who could not swim, and made off with them towards the shore, the poor fellows being too much exhausted to express the gratitude which I fully believe they felt.

"We have done what is right," I said to Pierson, as he swam by my side towards the gratings the others had quitted, and which we soon reached without much difficulty. We found them more buoyant support than our oar had been.

The boat from the harbour was now within thirty fathoms of us, and I could see my friend, Lieut. H——y, of the ——, standing up in the stern sheets, and urging on the crew, who cheered as the tough oars bent with their sturdy strokes.

"Gracious Heavens!" exclaimed Pierson, with a cry of horror. "What is that large black thing moving near us? A shark, sir! a shark! I see his pointed fin "

"In case it should be," I replied, though I had little doubt he was correct, " keep your feet moving about, and sing out at the top of your voice. It may serve to scare him away. Let us be thankful the monsters did not scent us at first, or we should all, long ere this, have been their food."

"A shark, a shark! O God, it is, sir!" he cried. "I see him swimming closer and closer round us."

H——y heard our cries and knew the cause. The men redoubled their exertions, and joined us in our shouts. The boat flew towards us; we were alongside. H——y and the stroke-oar bent over the gunwale; they seized my collar; they dragged me on board, as the tyrant of the deep, turning up his white belly, made a grab at my legs. Pierson was in like manner hauled on board, over the bows, and the disappointed monster swam off to windward.

He was not, however, to be baulked of his prey. The crew saw his black back gliding towards the man yet floating a-head of us, and again bent to their oars to save him, but the shark swam faster than they could pull. The hapless wretch saw his destroyer approaching at the moment his preservation seemed sure. The dreaded monster rushed greedily at him; with a terrific shriek of horror and despair he threw up his hands, as if supplicating for mercy, and was dragged far down beneath the foaming waves. He and the man by whose madness the accident had been caused were, I knew, both lost, but how many more might have been taken off by the sharks, I could not then say. The idea filled me with grief.

"He was the last," said Pierson, who had seen the catastrophe, which I had not; and the crew, pulling the boat round, ran down before the wind for the harbour, much more quickly than they had come up.

No sooner had H——y hauled me on board, than his excited feelings gave way. He burst into tears. " My good, good fellow, I am so glad you are safe!" he exclaimed, as he pulled off his uniform coat, and putting it on me, buttoned it so closely round that he almost throttled me. " You will catch cold; I am sure you will. What an escape you have had!"

"Oh, never fear," I answered. "I do not feel at all the worse for it. But can you tell me if my poor fellows have escaped?"

H——y made the inquiry of the men, which Pierson answered, by assuring me that he had counted the men as they were taken up by the canoes, and that all were preserved. This information set my heart at rest; and I was able, as the boat pulled back to the harbour, to describe to H——y how the accident happened.

The first person I met on landing was Mr. Hermes, who had been engaged to dine with me, but who had—through some strange presentiment of evil, as he said, probably from not liking the looks of the weather—excused himself from accompanying me. I was warmly congratulated on my escape by my numerous friends, and kindly treated by all, being fully exonerated by the Governor from any blame in the loss of the vessel.

Hermes insisted on my accompanying him to his house, where he wanted me to go to bed, and take sundry draughts, hot and strong. The first part of his advice I declined—though the latter I partially followed, while I was donning dry habiliments, and his dinner was preparing. The next morning I got back to my fort, where I found that all my men had arrived, without suffering any serious effects from their long submersion in the water.

It has always struck me as a singular dispensation, that the only two men who were lost were the one who caused the accident, and the other, who, from his impatience and want of trust in Providence, had attempted to save himself at the risk of destroying others.

It was some days after the dreadful accident which had occurred, before I got rid of the sensations produced by it, and for long after, if I were at all ill from fever, I used to fancy myself floating on the wild world of waters, now surrounded by shrieking wretches; then a shoal of huge sharks would play their part upon the scene, and carry off my companions one after another; and then I would be left alone in darkness and silence, the wild billows tossing me helplessly to and fro. Sometimes I would see H——y and his boat's crew pulling towards me, and then the boat would turn into a huge monster about to swallow me up. At other times, he would pass close to me without seeing me, the oars splashing the water over my face, and do all I could, I was unable to make myself heard for help. Then perhaps he would stand up in his boat, and, as he pulled away, turn into a grinning skeleton. At length other events banished such phantasies for ever.

I have said that the Governor used constantly to ride about the island, and to ingratiate himself with all classes. Sometimes he would stop at a Dutch farmer's house, enter into conversation with him, pay a compliment to his wife, praise his children, and ask for a luncheon. At other times he would stop and take a friendly dinner with one of the richer proprietors; and he more than once honoured me with his company at the fort. I was one forenoon walking on the ramparts of my castle, like any feudal lord of old, only my power was rather more limited, when I saw a horseman galloping towards the fort. He seemed to be in a desperate hurry, for he rode along at a most Jehu-like pace—(I suppose Jehu rode as furiously as he drove),—so I descended to meet him. As far as I could make out his costume from a distance, it was not this time one of the Governor's Horse Marines. I therefore concluded that he came on a mission of peace, whoever he might be; and as I reached the gate of the fort I at once recognised the messenger as belonging to the Governor's suite in the multifarious capacities of coxswain, steward, butler, trumpeter to his troop, and factotum-general, his dress partaking slightly of the characteristics of all offices. He was not a bad horseman—at least he could always stick on; and what is more, make the most obstinate beast go a-head, and was in every other respect a most valuable attendant. Tumbling off his steed, in true sailor-like style, he doffed his hat, hitched up his trowsers, and delivered himself of the following message, which caused me not a little perplexity:—

"Please, sir, his Excellency the Captain ordered me to come on here as fast as my four legs would carry me, to say that, if you had no objection, he, with some of the gentlemen from the town, and some of the officers, would come out and dine with you at three o'clock.

A Lieutenant does not generally make any objection to what the Governor of a province proposes, not to say the Senior Captain of a squadron, but I felt very much inclined so to do at that minute, for the simple reason that I had nothing to give my guests to eat. I cogitated for some time, whether I should commence the intended feast with peas-porridge and boiled pork, washed down with porter, of which I thought I might possibly muster a sufficient quantity to take the edge off their appetites, and prevent them from being anxious for much more; when I remembered that it would be necessary to make some answer to the message.

"Tell his Excellency," I replied, "that I shall be very happy to see him, and as many friends as he likes to bring. But, I say, Tomkins, just hint that they must expect to be on rather short commons as far as delicacies are concerned, though I can give them ship's beef and pork."

"Oh, sir, you need not trouble yourself about all that," answered Tomkins, to my great joy. "The Captain—I means his Excellency, thought you would not have much overplus of grub, so he sent some provisions on before him. I passed them on my way."

This information was most satisfactory, and relieved my mind from all care on the subject of provender, particularly when several niggers soon afterwards arrived, carrying baskets on their heads, full of fowl, fish, and meat, fruit, vegetables, and sundry bottles of generous liquids, to cheer the hearts of the coming party. Besides these things, there arrived at the same time Captain Brisbane's black cook to dress them. This he accomplished in the most artistical and satisfactory manner; and by the time the feast was prepared the Governor and his friends arrived. A very capital dinner we had; and I can only say I much admire that manner of giving a feed.

As you may suppose, I had plenty of idle time on my hands, much of which, however, I passed most agreeably with the numerous friends I formed among the Dutch inhabitants of the neighbourhood. I also took it into my head to study the native language of the country, from one of the aborigines or red men, as they are called, who used daily to come into the fort with water. Some writers of great credit affirm that no descendants of the inhabitants of the Antilles, when discovered by Columbus, now exist, and that the whole race have become extinct. This is certainly a mistake, as red men are to be found in nearly all the West India Islands, though their numbers have wofully decreased. If the man I speak of were not descended from them, I know not from what race he and his companions could have sprung. He was short in stature, scarcely five feet and a half, of a reddish-yellow complexion, with dark eyes, and long lank and glossy hair, of ebon hue, and a countenance betokening apathy as well as mildness. His shoulders were broad, and bust massive, though his hands and feet were small and delicate. Though they are generally considered an idle, unenergetic, and apathetic race, my friend was always ready to work, and gain an honest livelihood, and by conversing constantly with him I completely won his affection and confidence. The language he spoke was, I soon discovered, a very mongrel composition of the different races which had inhabited his country. The groundwork was doubtless the language of his forefathers. I thus found that the names of all things used by civilized men, for some centuries past, were Spanish, and that those of articles of luxury, or new inventions, were Dutch, thus giving a history, as it were, of the various invasions his island had undergone.

One of the nearest neighbours I had to the fort was a Mr. L——, a very hospitable, kind-hearted man, with whom I very frequently used to dine, and jovial merry parties we had at his well-spread board.

I must now narrate an event which caused me great grief. I had a servant, whom I had brought from England with me, a very honest good fellow, and much attached to me. The gun-room steward having fallen ill, my messmates asked my leave to allow him, as he was a clever servant, to take the place of the other man till he recovered. One day I had gone on board the frigate to pay my friends a visit, and, while I was lunching with them in the gun-room, I observed that I was almost eaten up at night in the fort by the scorpions, centipedes, and other noxious animals which swarmed there, but that if I had a canopy over my bed I should be safe from them. My faithful servant heard what I had said, and on the following day he asked leave to be allowed to pay me a visit, and to carry up several things I required. This request was granted, and having made up a large bundle with various articles of my property, and the canopy of my bed-place, he set off from the ship.

Two days after this I was dining with my friend Mr. L——, at his house near the fort, with several Dutch gentlemen, and one or two brother officers, when, the first course having just been removed, another guest dismounted in the court-yard in front of the house, and made his appearance among us. After hurriedly apologizing for being too late, he took his seat near me, and commenced making amends for lost time. When he had satisfied the first cravings of hunger he began to be more communicative than at the beginning, and observed that he had been infinitely shocked at a discovery he had made as he rode along, by rather an unfrequented path from the town. He said that he was accompanied by a very sagacious dog, and that as he was about half way to the fort, the animal, who had been ranging on each side of the road, suddenly rushed out from a narrow pathway, which led among the wood on one side, barking and whining, and making evident signs for him to follow him. He accordingly did so, when what was his horror to find a man lying dead across the path. He said that on examining the body he had discovered undoubted signs of his having met with a violent end, and that, from his appearance, he was much afraid he was an Englishman.

While he was speaking, a presentiment came over my mind that the murdered man was my faithful servant, whom I had been expecting all the previous day. I laid down my knife and fork, without being able to touch another mouthful, and on making some more minute inquiries respecting the appearance of the man, I had little doubt that it was he.

So anxious did I feel, that, apologizing to Mr. L—— for quitting his table, I entreated him to allow me to mount one of his horses, in order to ride off and ascertain the truth.

"I then must beg leave to accompany you, to show you the spot," said the gentleman who had brought the account; "I can never allow you to go alone."

"And I," exclaimed another, "I will go also."

"And I—and I," added others.

So it ended by the whole of the party leaving their half-consumed dinner, and getting on horseback to accompany me. We had a hot ride over rather a rough road, though the scenery on each side was rich and beautiful; but I was too much occupied to pay it much attention. I only know that we passed fields of sugar-canes and tobacco, indigo, maize, and cassava, among groves of oranges and citrons.

As we were riding rapidly along, my Dutch friend pointing to a spot on one side of the road, exclaimed, "There you will find him." Pulling up, I leaped from my horse, and with a sickening sensation of the heart I cannot well describe, I approached the spot. My worst anticipations were fully realized, for there lay my poor servant, his head dreadfully fractured by blows from a club, and the canopy of my cot wrapped round his body in a way which clearly showed that he had died while endeavouring to defend it. The bundle of other things was taken, but as this was covered with his blood, the murderers had probably been afraid to carry it off. The Governor offered a reward of 50*l*. to whoever would discover the murderers, but they escaped detection. The Whites accused the Blacks, the latter the Red men of the deed. It was supposed, indeed, from various circumstances, that the lowest class, the degraded aborigines, were the guilty parties.

It was sad news I had to send home to the mother of the poor fellow who had thus, in his last moments, given such proof of his devoted affection.

I could go on all day giving you accounts of my friends and my adventures in Curaçao, and I must not forget, among other persons, my good friend, old Nelly, my washerwoman. I had received a bite from a musquito on my leg, which caused so much inflammation and pain, that at last I was compelled to go on board to let the doctor look at it, and prescribe for me. This, of course, he did, but to so little effect, or rather with such bad success, that it grew worse and worse, till at last I was completely laid up in my berth. There I remained, till one day old Nelly came on board with my clean clothes, and, finding me in this state, asked to look at the wound. Shaking her head, she asked if the doctor were within hearing.

"No," I answered, "if you speak low."

"Well, then," she said, "follow my advice, instead of his, or you will to a certainty lose your leg, if not your life. Such things are not to be trifled with in this climate."

"But cannot you recommend the doctor what to do, and see if he approve of your prescription?" I asked.

"No," she answered, "either give me up your leg entirely, or I will have nothing whatever to do with it. He would never agree to what I propose."

"Well," I observed, "I will hear what he has to say on the subject. Doctor," I sang out, as I knew he was in his cabin, "Frau Vanfromp here says that if I will give her my leg, she will set me up on it in quicker time than you can. Will you let her have it?"

I heard the Doctor growling and muttering for some time from the inward recesses of his berth; for there is nothing medical men dislike so much as to have their patients interfered with. Many would rather send an unfortunate wretch to his grave than let anybody else lift him out of it. It is human nature, and noble is the man who conquers the feeling. At length our honest Medico growled out,—

"Your leg is your own to do what you like with, so you may give it to old Nelly or the d—l, if you please!"

"Thank you for your generosity, Doctor," I replied, laughing. "Frau Vanfromp, the leg is yours."

"Well, then," she said, "you show your sense and confidence in me, and I will not disappoint you; only follow my directions exactly. I will now go on shore to get the necessary remedies, and return in an hour."

She was as good as her word; and in less time than she mentioned she returned on board, with a large monkey full of cold water—one of those red earthen and porous jars to cool water in. The air passing through this, when it is hung up in a draft, cools the water most deliciously. Having taken off all the Doctor's bandages, and washed my leg, she poured the cold water over it, telling me to let her know when I felt any great pain. This at last I did, when she expressed herself satisfied that no mortification had commenced, and then took out of her basket some leaves of the calabash, which she put into her mouth, and chewed into a complete paste. With this mixture she covered over the sore, and then bound it carefully up, charging me to allow no one, as I valued my life, to touch it.

While this operation was going forward, I asked her if she could not manage to beat up the leaves in a mortar, instead of chewing them.

"You know nothing on the subject," she answered. "Let me follow my own method, or I will leave you to your friend the Doctor."

I did so, and in the course of a few days, after she had regularly every day repeated the same operation, I was perfectly well, and able to resume my duties at the fort.

We seamen held the island for six months, when we were relieved by troops from Jamaica. I quitted it with regret, for I left many kind friends behind me.

"There, gentlemen, I have talked enough at one spell to make amends for my previous silence, I hope, though I might go on all night describing the scenes which occurred while I was on the island, so rapidly does my memory recall them."

We all warmly expressed our thanks for his interesting narrative.

"Sir Charles Brisbane was a gallant officer," I observed.

"He was, in every respect, a first-rate officer," said the captain.

'He was not only a brave man, but he had a clever head on his shoulders. His attack on Curaçao was one of the best planned and executed exploits during the war. Fifty other men, brave as he was, might have wished to take the place, but would not have succeeded. It is a pity young men are so little apt to remember that they may some day become chiefs, and thus forget to prepare themselves for the post of responsibility. All wish and hope to rise, yet how many neglect the very means by which that object may be attained. Once upon a time, the dunce of the family was considered good enough for the navy, but parents must now understand that, if they wish their sons to succeed in the service, they must select the cleverest and finest-spirited of the lot. But I do not think that any of you require a lecture on the subject."

CHAPTER XXVIII.

THE MERCHANT SKIPPER'S STORY.

WE lay off St. Helena several days, and were once more on our course back to the coast. We found ourselves one day, some little time before we came in sight of land, becalmed close to an outward-bound merchant ship. I boarded her to gain information from home; and the master very civilly supplied us with newspapers and several little luxuries for our table.

Finding Captain Andrews a very respectable old man, I invited him on board to dine in the gun-room. Hearing me talk about my collection of sea-stories, he offered to add to them, if we wished, by narrating an occurrence which happened to him in his youth; and from his evident respectability and gravity of manner I have no reason to doubt his belief in its truth—though of its probability I will allow my readers to judge for themselves. He called it—

THE DEMON PILOT.

"I was just out of my apprenticeship when I was appointed, by a friend of my father's, a merchant in Liverpool, Mr. Damer by name, as third-mate of a fine large brig he had just launched at that port, and called after his wife, 'The Mary Damer.'

"Well, as it happened, a week or ten days before we were ready for sea, the master Mr. Damer had selected to command the brig was taken very ill, and was utterly unable to proceed on the voyage. A day or so after the owner had been informed of this, a young man presented himself with a letter from his correspondents in London, stating that he had been for some years in their employ as mate and master, and that he had always afforded them the greatest satisfaction; so that they regretted being unable to provide him at once with a ship, but that if Mr. Damer could give him the command of one of his for a voyage, they should feel much obliged. I was in his office at the time, waiting for orders.

"'You have arrived very opportunely, captain—I beg your pardon—what is your name?' said Mr. Damer.

"'Penrose, sir—William Penrose,' replied the stranger.

"'Oh, yes, I see,' looking at the letter. 'Captain Penrose, I am happy to be able to forward your wishes. I have a vessel just about to sail, and you shall have the command of her, if you please. She is the Mary Damer. Go on board; and then if you like the look of her, come and tell me your opinion—after that we can settle the matter.'

"'It is not necessary,' answered Captain Penrose. 'I saw that very brig alongside the quay as I was strolling down to the river, and could never wish for a finer craft.'

"'Well, then, we will consider the affair settled,' said the merchant. 'When did you arrive in Liverpool, Captain Penrose?'

"'Only last night, sir,' answered the captain; 'I hurried down from London as fast as a horse would carry me, for I hate idleness, and am no sooner on shore than I wish to be at sea again.'

"'I like your spirit, captain—it will much assist your success in the world,' observed Mr. Damer. 'The Mary Damer is bound for Port Royal in Jamaica, and will return with a cargo of sugar. By-the-bye, have you ever been before to the West Indies?'

"'Know every creek and key among the islands,' answered Captain Penrose, quickly. 'Wherever you may wish your ship to go, depend upon it I can take her.'

"'So far so good,' observed the kind-hearted gentleman. 'You can sign your agreement to-day, and go on board and take command; you will be able to expedite affairs, which the illness of poor Captain Jones has much delayed. Before you go, I will make known to you a young man who is to act as your third mate.' And he beckoned me to come forward, for I had been standing during this conversation at the farther end of his office.

"After I had been introduced, and Captain Penrose, as he called himself, had expressed his confidence that we should pull well together, he took his leave, promising to return in an hour, when the papers were to be ready. Mr. Damer was an acute man, and a great observer of men's characters. He was, however, sometimes mistaken.

"'I like your new master, Andrews,' he remarked, as soon as Captain Penrose had quitted the room; 'he appears a very honest, intelligent man, and I think you will find him a pleasant person to sail with.'

"'Yes, sir,' I answered mechanically, for I had no reason to offer for an opposite opinion; yet somehow or other I could not cordially agree with him.

"There are some men who appear like very saints on shore, yet the moment they get into blue water, show themselves in their true colours, as very devils incarnate; and such an one, by the glance of his eye, as I felt it for a moment fixed on me, did I suspect was my new captain; but of course I could not say this to our owner. After I had taken my leave, Captain Penrose returned, was formally invested with the command of the Mary Damer, and soon afterwards returned on board and took charge of her. We were at that time still rather short of hands, but in the course of two or three days, six stout, active fellows presented themselves, who were instantly entered by the captain, and our complement was soon complete.

"I had never met any of the new men before, nor had any of the rest of the crew; but there was nothing strange in that. They were obedient and orderly, and prime seamen, as I could judge by the way they worked at setting up the rigging and bending sails. The expression of their countenances was certainly not prepossessing, I thought; and what struck me as odd was, that though they apparently had never met each other before, they at once kept entirely together, speaking very little to the rest of the crew. I must confess, though not of a suspicious disposition, I was not altogether easy in my mind about our new captain and the seamen he had entered; yet there was nothing tangible to lay hold of, and I feared either to wrong him, or to appear a mischief-maker to our owners, should I whisper my suspicions, so I kept them to myself, and determined to hold a strict watch on all that was going forward. In truth, Captain Penrose had the manners of a very agreeable gentleman, and contrived quickly to ingratiate himself both with Mr. Damer and his family, and with his mates and all his crew; indeed, before we sailed, I began to laugh at the thoughts I had at first entertained.

"He certainly, by his exertions and resources, got the ship in a very short space of time ready for sea; and the day before we sailed, Mr. and Mrs. Damer, and a party of friends, came on board and drank success to our voyage, when Captain Penrose stood up, and in a neat speech expressed his thanks for their good wishes, and promised to return as quickly as possible with a rich freight.

"That evening we hauled out into the stream, and the next forenoon, with a fine breeze, we were standing out of the Mersey, and before dark we were fairly on our voyage running down the Irish channel.

"I must not forget to tell you, that we had two cabin passengers, one a married lady, going out to join her husband at Port Royal. She was still young, and very handsome, but she had charge of a young lady, scarcely seventeen years old, whose father was in the West Indies. She was the sweetest rose-bud ever seen, charming in her manners, and delightful in her disposition; so that, though I did not actually fall in love with her at first sight, I felt ready to die to serve her.

"In those days it was not safe to navigate the Caribbean Sea without being armed; for although the old pirates of the Blackbeard race had long before been extirpated, there were still a number of picarooning villains cruising about ready to pounce upon any craft unable to protect herself. England was also at war with France, and with the revolted States of America, who sent out shoals of privateers to destroy her commerce; so that plenty of enemies were to be found in every direction.

"The Mary Damer, therefore, was supplied with letters of marque; carried six guns, two long nines and four carronades, with plenty of muskets and cutlasses for all the crew, of whom, including officers, there were five-and-thirty; so that we were well able to bid defiance to most vessels of our size, although we were strictly charged by Mr. Damer, who did not approve of privateering, not on any account to go out of our way to make prizes, but to avoid all contests, and merely to defend ourselves if attacked.

"She was also a very fast craft; indeed, in no way did she disappoint our expectations. She was a good sea-boat, as stiff as a church under canvass, and possessed as nimble a pair of heels and as much beauty as any young lady in the three kingdoms.

"Now I am going to tell you a very extraordinary circumstance which happened on the evening of the very day we sailed, though of course, I did not know it till long afterwards. Mr. Damer was sitting in his counting-house congratulating himself on the prospect of a favourable voyage for his brig, when a person presented himself, looking very pale and haggard, who stated that his name was Penrose: that he was travelling from London on horseback with a letter from his correspondents, when he had been attacked by robbers, who took everything from him, and left him for dead; and that as soon as he was sufficiently recovered, he had hurried on to Liverpool, as he was anxious to get to sea to make up his losses.

For some time Mr. Damer would not believe the story, treating the poor man as an impostor; and at last, though he thought he might be speaking the truth, he was still convinced that there must be, though a curious coincidence, two Captain Penroses, and that he could not have given the command of his fine new brig to an impostor, and something worse. Of course he wrote to his friends in London to ascertain the truth—what that was I shall by and by tell you.

"Everything went on well on board the Mary Damer. With a brisk north-easterly breeze, for many days, we kept a direct course for Madeira.

"Though the wind headed us till we were within about sixty miles of that island, the fine weather continued, the blue waves dancing gaily in the sunbeams which darted forth from an unclouded sky. The ladies were constantly on deck; indeed, Miss Arden—for that was the name of the youngest—spent most of her time beneath the shade of an awning we used to spread, to protect them from the burning rays of the sun. In those days, as was to be expected from my age, I was rather sensitive to the tender passion, and it was not long before the charms of Miss Arden made a deep impression on my heart, nor was the poor girl insensible to my attentions, though they were bestowed in rather a boyish manner. The other mates were blunt, honest fellows, who never thought of interfering with what they considered my nonsense; indeed, it rather amused them, so that the captain was the only person likely to prove my rival,—but he flew at other and less lawful game, but of that by and by.

"Well, one night the second mate being ill, I took the middle watch, it being his turn off duty. The watch were snoozing away between the guns, except a look-out man forward, and the man at the wheel, and I was taking my solitary walk on the quarter-deck, whistling for want of thought or company, when, as I stopped for a moment, as I reached the waist, to take a glance along the horizon, over the starboard bulwarks, I felt a hand laid upon my shoulder. I knew not why, a cold shudder ran through my veins.

I fancied that no human being was near me. For a moment I dared not move, when a low, quiet laugh recalled me to my senses, and turning suddenly round, I beheld the captain.

"'What! indulging in a reverie, Andrews?' he observed. 'I fear that I must have interrupted it; but, truth to say, I could not sleep, so have come to take a turn on deck.'

"'It's a night fine enough to tempt any man from his hammock, I answered, for want of something better to say.

"'Fine enough, yes; but tame and dull.' He spoke as if musing to himself, rather than addressing me. 'For my part, I prefer the tempest and the fight to idleness and a calm. What say you, Andrews—would you not rather be pursuing a richly-freighted enemy—a heavy Spanish galleon, for instance—than sailing on in a steady course as we are doing?'

"'I should not mind a fight, if it were necessary, but I find no fault with the weather we have at present,' I replied.

"'Well, it will be strange if we cross the broad sea without some change, and I hope we shall have luck enough to fall in with an enemy of our own size, without going out of the way to look for her. Do you think the men are stanch?' he asked.

"I said that I thought they were, and ready to fight any Frenchman, Dutchman, Don, or American we were likely to meet. For more than an hour he continued the conversation while pacing the deck, though it was some time before I discovered its drift. He spoke of the pleasures of a privateer's life, the large fortune to be rapidly acquired, and the contemptible dulness of a mere trader's existence. While we were conversing, the wind gradually fell, and, in a short time, the loud flapping of the sails against the masts showed that we were almost becalmed. The captain took a look round the horizon.

"'Rouse up the watch on deck, Mr. Andrews, and hand the topgallant sails,' he sang out sharply. 'We shall have a stiff breeze before morning.'

"The order was quickly obeyed; the rest of the lighter canvass was then furled, and the now useless courses clewed up. The captain, instead of going below, kept the deck, watching with a seaman's eye the signs of the heavens. He was not deceived. Before the end of the morning watch, dark masses of clouds came rolling on from the south-west, and the ship was already beginning to feel the heavy swell which precedes a storm, although as yet there was little wind. The topsails were now closely reefed, and everything made snug. Fortunate, indeed, was it for us that it was so, for, just as day was breaking, a squall struck the brig, laying her almost on her beam-ends, and carrying away the gaff of the mainsail by the jaws.

"At that instant I heard the cry of a man overboard, and turning round, I observed that the captain was no longer where I had just before seen him standing. Running aft, I saw an object in the water close astern of us, for the brig had not gathered way, and without a moment's consideration, being an admirable swimmer, I slipped out of my shoes and jacket, and plunged overboard. At first I sank, but rising again, I found myself close to the figure of a human being, and on swimming up to it I discovered that it was the captain, but insensible from a blow he had received on his head. It was surprising that he did not sink at once. Having grappled him by the collar, I looked round for the ship, when what was my horror, to see her, through the faint light of the morning, apparently driving away from us before the gale. The foaming, bubbling waves were around me, the dark clouds overhead, the hissing of the waters in my ear; I was giving way to despair when I saw a broken spar floating close to me, and pushing the captain towards it, I managed to get hold of it, and to secure him to it likewise.

"At first I thought we were to be abandoned to our fate, and while under this impression, the captain's senses returned.

"He appeared as if just waking from a deep sleep, and while mechanically grasping the spar he looked round to see where he was. Instantly comprehending our awful situation, and seeing who had preserved him, he exclaimed,

"'By Jove, Andrews, you are a gallant fellow! I meant you wrong, but if we live, I will die sooner than harm you.'

"I thought he was raving as he spoke, so paid little attention to his words; indeed, I was rather thinking of preparing for another world, where I felt that both of us must soon be sent. The white foam, driven by the furious wind, dashed over my head, almost blinding and suffocating me; and every instant I feared the captain would be washed from his hold. I had given all up for lost when, as we mounted to the top of a wave, I saw through the gray dawn the brig heave-to, and directly afterwards a boat pulled round from under her stern.

As yet the sea had not got up very much, though it was rapidly rising, and every instant was of importance. The men in the boat bent bravely to their oars, but they had hard work to pull up against the gale, which sent the white foam flying in sheets over them. They cheered as they came near us, and I grasped still tighter hold of the captain, who could do little to assist himself, his arm I found having been injured by the blow which knocked him overboard.

At last the boat reached us, but there was no little difficulty in approaching the spar without risk of staving in the bows of the boat, or giving either of us a knock on the head, which would inevitably have sent us to the bottom. The bowman, however, contrived to seize hold of the captain's collar, and with the aid of the rest hauled him on board, while I was still hanging on to the spar. At that moment I observed that the crew who manned the boat were those who had been last shipped by the captain, the next instant the send of the sea separated her from me, as I was about to grasp hold of an oar.

"'Let the young coxcomb drown, and be d—d! We've no time to waste in hauling him on board,' I heard one of the men exclaim in a loud tone.

"Life, however, was not to be abandoned without a struggle, and making a desperate effort, I grasped hold of an oar, but the villain, pulling it, would have shaken me off, had not the captain, seeing the treachery of the men, ordered them with a terrible threat to take me on board. The intervening moments while I held on the oar were those of dreadful suspense, for my strength was too much exhausted to enable me to swim another stroke. Indeed, I scarcely knew what occurred till I found myself in the boat pulling towards the brig. I was close to the captain.

"'Utter not a word on board of what has just occurred, and you are safe,' he whispered, putting his fingers to my lips. 'If not, I have no power to protect you.'

"I had little time to meditate on the meaning of these strange expressions before we were alongside the brig, and, with considerable difficulty, got on board. Scarcely was the boat hoisted up when the gale came down upon us with fresh fury, and the ship being once more got before it, away we scudded under bare poles. It did not, however, last many hours, though we were several days retracing our course before we reached Madeira.

Our lady passengers were very much alarmed at the storm; of the accident they knew nothing till the captain and I were safe on board again, and with the return of fine weather their spirits revived. With me, on the contrary, it was a time of anxious suspense, yet though my suspicions were aroused that all was not as it should be, with all my vigilance I could find nothing definite to communicate to my brother-officers. I felt, at the same time, that I also was narrowly watched by the captain and the men I have spoken of, though I was scarcely prepared for the dreadful catastrophe which was about to occur.

After taking in wood and water, and fresh provisions at Madeira, we again sailed, shaping our course for the West Indies. Everything went on favourably for some days, with a fair wind and a smooth sea; the ladies were constantly on deck, and I, as before, continued my attentions to Miss Arden, which she received with apparent pleasure. We sighted several sail during the passage, and more than once were pursued, but always had the heels of our enemy. Another point I did not like was, that the captain insisted on keeping a more southerly course then the two senior mates approved of, he alleging that we should thus more easily make Jamaica, which was not the case, we all well knew. At last we found ourselves running in through the broad passage between Grenada and Trinidad, when, the wind falling during the night, we lay completely becalmed.

At the dawn of the following morning a sail was perceived about four miles to the southward of us, which we were not long in making out to be a sloop of war under British colours. We accordingly hoisted our ensign, and in a short time perceived a boat pulling towards us, which, as she approached, we saw contained an officer and ten men, fully armed. A dark frown came over the captain's brow at sight of this, and mustering the men on deck, he told them that some of them would to a certainty be impressed on board the man-of-war; that if they chose to be made slaves of they might, but that if they resisted he would protect them. Saying this, he threw open the arm-chest, and stuck a brace of pistols in his belt, the greater number of the men following his example, so that when a lieutenant from the ship of war with his men stepped on board, he found a determined band ready to encounter him. Undaunted, however, by our hostile appearance, he went about the performance of his duty in a quiet, firm manner, selecting me and seven more of the crew to serve His Majesty. Not only was I not armed, but I was prepared with a heavy heart to yield to my fate, when I heard the captain exclaim in a voice of thunder—

"'Take my men if you like, but do so at your own peril!'

"'We shall see,' replied the lieutenant, seizing one of the men (five of them were the volunteers of whom I had the doubts I spoke of).

"'There's a breeze coming down to us from the nor'ard, my boys,' sang out the captain.

"The man took the hint, and with the butt-end of his pistol felled the young officer to the deck. It was the signal for a general slaughter.

"The man-of-war's men fought with desperation, for they saw that they had little hope of quarter after the outrage which had been committed. A shot from one of their pistols brought me on the deck, as I was rushing forward to preserve their lives; and at the same moment, the captain, not knowing my intentions, but seeing me fall, vowed he would avenge me; and drawing his cutlass, like a madman, gnashing his teeth with fury, he cut down the man-of-war's men on every side. Not one of them escaped. I heard a loud cry as a cannon-shot was thrown into the boat alongside, and the man remaining in her felt himself left floating on the wide waters. The still breathing body of the lieutenant was thrown overboard, followed by those of his slaughtered and dying crew.

"A fresh breeze filled our sails; and as we flew from the scene of destruction, I heard some of the savages jeering at the hapless wretches still struggling in the water, and soon to become the prey of the voracious sharks, which were sure before long to assemble round them.

"I knew not what happened for some hours, for I fainted from loss of blood, till I found myself on a sofa in the cabin, with Miss Arden sitting by my side, and bathed in tears.

"'What has occurred?' I asked, lifting myself up on my arm, after having somewhat recovered my senses and strength, and looking wildly around me.

"Miss Arden uttered a faint cry as she saw me come to myself.

"'Thank Heaven that you have recovered, Mr. Andrews!' she exclaimed. 'But, oh! do not ask me what has occurred, for I scarcely dare to utter the dreadful suspicions which have risen in my mind. There have been bloodshed and murder, and I much fear that it is not yet over.'

"'I will go on deck and ascertain the truth,' I answered. 'Oh! I recollect—the officer and boat's-crew of the man-of-war were basely murdered, and I had no power to save them. Alas! Miss Arden, I fear your worst suspicions are correct; but, believe me, whatever happens, I will protect you to the last.'

"'I trust to you, Mr. Andrews; and, should all else fail me, that must be my last resource.'

"As she spoke, she pointed to the now foaming ocean, seen through the stern-ports, or rather scuttles. She endeavoured to prevent me rising, entreating me to remain quiet; but assuring her that, for her sake, I would be careful how I behaved, I succeeded in getting on my feet, and gaining the deck. My worst anticipations were realized. Complete was the change which had occurred since I was carried below. A heavy gale had arisen, dark clouds were chasing each other over the sky, and a high broken sea was running, through which the ship was working her way, close-hauled, the water washing over her decks in clear sheets, almost burying her bows beneath its weight; while, far away to leeward, appeared the man-of-war in hot pursuit, with as much canvass set as she could venture to carry.

"On board, the signs of recent strife were still visible. Three of our own crew lay wounded on the deck, while the two mates, with their hands behind them, were lashed to the main-mast, and four more, forward, were evidently prisoners. The captain stood aft, with a spy-glass under his arm, with which, every now and then, he turned a glance at the man-of-war, but seemed to be paying little attention to the sailing of the brig. Two men were at the wheel, and near them appeared a swarthy man, with an eye piercing as an eagle's, who was conning the ship, and acting as one accustomed to command. I regarded him attentively, and was soon convinced that he was a perfect stranger, though *how* he had come on board it was impossible to say.

"The longer I looked at him the greater difficulty I found in withdrawing my eyes from him. I felt myself fascinated, like the bird hovering over the jaws of the snake. There was something indescribably dreadful in his aspect; his bronze-like, passionless countenance, his eyes glowing like hot coals; his tall, undefined figure; the involuntary shudder which ran over me as I first beheld him, gave me the idea that he was a being not of this world. I had heard that the evil one had been known to come on board ships to pilot them to destruction, but did not believe the tales. 'Could they then be true? Can such things be?' I asked myself. I looked again at the dark stranger, and felt convinced that they might. A rapid survey showed me what I have taken much longer to describe. I was hesitating how to act, when Captain Penrose, seeing me, advanced to where I was standing, near the companion-hatch.

"'Andrews,' he exclaimed, 'you are not in a fit state to be on deck. Remain below, and you are safe,' he whispered. 'If you draw the attention of the men on you, your life is not worth a moment's purchase; but I promised to protect you, and will do so if you follow my directions.'

"'I do not understand you, Captain Penrose,' I replied; 'what is the meaning of all I see?'

"'That the Mary Damer has changed owners, and that all who refuse to obey my orders are likely to find themselves without a plank to stand on,' was the answer.

"'All hands about-ship,' cried out a hoarse, unearthly voice.

"The men, obedient to the call, flew to their stations, the helm was put a-lee, the yards were braced round, and the brig was darting away on the other tack, quickly weathering on her pursuer. While this operation was going forward, I again asked the captain the meaning of what I saw, but instead of answering me, he took my arm and led me below. As I passed Mrs. Lawley's cabin, I heard her sobbing violently, and her female attendant endeavouring to comfort her, but the captain paid no attention to it, and leading me up to Miss Arden, desired her to watch that I did not again venture on deck. Having done this, he hurried from the cabin. As soon as he was gone, the young lady entreated me to tell her the worst, and though I would willingly have calmed her apprehensions, I felt that it would be impossible so to do; and I confessed that my conviction was, that the captain, having once set the laws at defiance, was about to commence the accursed calling of a pirate, though I did not venture to whisper my suspicions of the terrific character of the dark stranger.

"'Great Heaven! and what will be our fate?' cried the poor girl, wringing her hands.

"'I feel that had the captain intended you any injury, he would not have waited till now,' I answered. 'He evidently also means me well; so that we must place our trust in Providence, and hope for the best.'

"I continued talking to her for some time, though nothing I could say served to soothe her alarm. Our conversation was at last interrupted by a wild shriek, which came from above, and my curiosity getting the better of my discretion, I again sought the deck. Had I remained below I might have saved myself from being witness to the scene of murder which met my sight, and in which everybody was too much engaged to observe me at first. The first mate was nowhere to be seen, and the fate prepared for the second showed what his had been. He was at that moment standing at the end of a plank projecting over the bulwarks, near the main rigging, with his arms lashed behind him, and his eyes blindfolded.

"'Will you sign the articles?' I heard the dark stranger exclaim.

"'Never!' cried the mate, firmly.

"'Then walk him forward,' shouted the stranger; and a shriek of despair escaped the unhappy youth, as the board on which he stood being tilted up, he felt himself plunged beneath the boiling waves.

"Two of the petty officers were next led aft, and remaining faithful to their trust, were likewise made to walk the plank, while the wounded seamen, lashed back to back, were hove overboard, and the wild tempest howled above their lifeless forms.

"This work of death being concluded, I expected that my turn would come next, but neither the captain nor any of the crew appeared to pay me any attention, and I was allowed to wander about the decks as I pleased, he asserting that I was mad, which was, I believe, not very far from the truth; the supposition, at all events, saved my life with the superstitious sailors.

"The evening was now approaching, and the gale every instant growing more furious; but still the brig continued to beat against it, for the avenger of blood was seen to leeward, hovering, like the white wing of a sea-bird, on the dark mass of waters. At last darkness came on; but away, away we flew, with unabated speed, into the black obscurity, the tall masts bending like reeds, the rigging straining, the white sails ready to burst from their bolt-ropes, the wind howling, the sea roaring, the waves dashing over us, loud thunder rolling through the sky above, and vivid lightning, serving only to show the horrors of the scene, darting ever and anon from the opaque clouds, and casting a blue, unearthly hue over the faces of the crew and the swarthy stranger. If I were to live a hundred years never should I forget that night; it was one fit for demons to hold their revels in, and an appropriate accompaniment to the work of murder which had been just accomplished. But neither the captain nor his crew seemed to heed the fury of the gale, though never before was mortal bark pressed as was ours, but they knew *whom* they had got on board, and placed reliance on his mysterious skill and power. Every order which was issued came from his mouth, in the same deep, unnatural tones I had before heard, and promptly, too, were they obeyed.

Horror-stricken at all I saw, I could not tear myself from the deck, my anxiety to see what might next occur conquering all other feelings; indeed, I expected every instant to find the masts go by the board, and to feel the ship striking on some coral reef or rock, and her timbers parting beneath our feet; still, on we tore into the black, unexplored space of darkness rising before us, like suicides rushing into an unknown eternity. At last, a still more heavy squall than usual struck the ship, and away flew her mainsail into a thousand shreds. Her head, deprived of its balancing power, no longer kept up close to the wind, but, falling off from the seas, she drifted rapidly to leeward. A momentary lull followed.

"'Square away the main-yards, and up with the helm,' cried the stranger, in his terrific voice.

"The fore-yards were next squared, and away flew the brig before the wind. The crew were then ordered to their quarters, and the guns were loaded and run out, while the men stood with their matches in their hands ready to fire, the swarthy stranger going round and pointing each with his own hands. I was not left long in doubt as to what was to happen. Onward we rushed before the gale, when, directly ahead of us, I beheld the white canvass of the corvette, just then made visible by a vivid flash of blue lightning. I thought we should have run into her, as our bows almost grazed her spanker boom.

"Fire!" shouted the stranger.

"Gun after gun, pointed with a demon's power, discharged a deadly shower into the hapless bark. Loud fearful shrieks arose and filled the night air, drowning the sound of the tempest, and, as it seemed, echoed by the mocking laughter of a thousand evil spirits.

"Not a shot struck us in return—there was a fearful pause—then a deafening report was heard, and bright flames burst forth—the tall masts with their canvass spread shot upwards to the sky, the dark hull itself seemed to rise above the waves, human forms appeared by the bright lurid light amid the wild confusion, then in another instant all vanished as a dream from sight—a solemn silence followed—and we bounded onward in our demon-directed course.

"Daylight at length appeared, but it served alone to reveal the horrors of the scene; the storm raged as furiously as ever, the seas ran mountains high, and away we wildly careered before it, as if flying from some unseen foe. When the gale abated we were close in with the Spanish main, and hauling our wind we stood to the westward till we reached one of the numerous islets which abound on that coast, with deep bays in them, where a vessel may lie securely concealed, even from any craft expressly looking for her. Into one of these we hauled the brig to water and wood, and while here I entertained thoughts of escaping from her, but though I enjoyed apparent liberty, I felt that I was narrowly watched, nor could I leave the unhappy young lady, Miss Arden, to her fate, without attempting her rescue. I consequently remained on board the brig, entertaining, however, but slight hopes of escaping with my fair companion in captivity.

"Thrown together as we now were, every day she wound herself more closely round my heart. I was all in all to her, for unhappily her friend Mrs. Lawley could render her no consolation or advice. I need not describe how we spent our time at the island; our stay was brief, for the pirates were eager to be off to commence the life of plunder and dissipation, which they contemplated for themselves. How Miss Arden escaped other annoyance than such as her imprisonment entailed, I know not; unless it was by the influence of the captain, who took every opportunity of showing his gratitude to me. It was the redeeming trait in his character.

"What may seem extraordinary, all the time we lay there, the mysterious pilot did not once appear; indeed, from the moment we left the open sea I did not observe him. What had become of him I could not tell, nor did the men seem to know more than I did. Some affirmed that he came on board in a canoe after the massacre of the king's officer and boat's crew; but others again denied this statement, and declared no boat of any sort had come alongside; indeed, at the distance we were from the land, such was not probable, if she were indeed a bark built by human hands, and he a human being. Of that I had strong reasons at the time for doubting. Afterwards the certainty forced itself on me, that a spirit of darkness and evil had come among the devoted crew to urge them on to destruction.

"At last we sailed, and, as the canvass was loosened, a coal-black ensign was run up at our peak, a broadside was fired, and three loud cheers from the maddened crew saluted the pirate flag.

"Away we flew on our course of havoc and destruction, and many a richly laden bark we met never entered her destined port. I am not going to give a detailed description of all the atrocities committed by that accursed crew; indeed, my recollection of those dreadful events is far from distinct, except that the mysterious pilot was always the chief instigator and leader. No sooner had we quitted the harbour, where we watered, and got into the open sea, than he appeared at his post on deck. He never entered the cabin, he never spoke to the men, but, when the tempest raged the loudest, and the fight grew the hottest, his voice was heard above the howling of the wind, or the shrieks and groans of the dying· and the shouts of the victorious, encouraging the pirate band, or urging them on to fresh deeds of violence.

"Sailing northward, our course marked by plunder and destruction, we reached the coast of Cuba. It was towards the evening when we stood in near one of the Keys at the back of that island, when a signal was hoisted at the fore, and before dark we again stood off the land. During the night, we tacked and beat back towards a fire we saw burning close down to the water. We then fired a gun and hove-to. Not long afterwards the splash of oars was heard, and through the darkness I discovered two large boats approaching the vessel. Captain Penrose hailed them, and the answer appeared satisfactory, for they were allowed to come alongside.

"Immediately a number of dark forms swarmed up the side of the vessel. I scarcely thought the boats could have contained so many of them. Whoever they were, they were warmly greeted by our crew. They were savage-looking beings, habited in every sort of costume, and, apparently, of every clime and nation under the sun. As soon as they were on board, the boats which brought them pulled back again to the shore. All that night there was a wild carousal among the newly-met comrades, and, had they been attacked, they would have fallen an easy prey to an enemy. Drunkenness and brawls were the consequence—daggers and knives were drawn, and more than one fell beneath the steel of a shipmate.

"Twice I heard the sullen splash of a heavy body thrown overboard; the dark water was the only grave, an obscene jest the only obsequies the murdered pirate received. During this time, Captain Penrose continued moodily pacing the deck, keeping a few of the people to attend to the necessary duties of the ship, but not attempting to interfere with the rest. He evidently felt that his authority over them was gone, while the mysterious pilot was moving among the excited crew the whole time, encouraging them to increase their debauch, and fomenting fresh disputes and quarrels.

"We now again stood southward towards the Spanish main, and, though before we had captured many defenceless vessels, we now attacked any we encountered of equal force with ourselves, and always came off victorious. Some, after plundering, the pirates set on fire, with all their people on board; the crews of others were made to walk the plank; some were sunk; and none escaped to betray the perpetrators of these atrocities.

"With a ship loaded with plunder, we then repaired to a Spanish port, where the pirates were received by the inhabitants with open arms. Here they soon spent their ill-gotten gains in debauchery and excess of every kind; and, not till they had no means left of purchasing these gratifications, could they be induced to make any preparations for putting to sea in search of more plunder. During this time I remained a close prisoner on board; nor could I account for the anxiety of the captain to detain me, till he one day came to me, and told me that he purposed landing me and Miss Arden, on the first opportunity, at Jamaica, or on one of the nearest islands belonging to the English, concluding, by saying,—

"'I shall then, Andrews, have fulfilled my promise to you: for your sake, also, I have preserved Miss Arden, and you thus have no cause to say, that among my other crimes ingratitude is one.'

"I expressed my thanks for his intentions and the favour he had already shown to my unfortunate companion and to me.

"'Speak not of it,' he answered; 'I do not willingly part with you, for you are the only man on board this accursed craft with whom I can have any sympathy, and yet I have made most of them what they are. I would have made you also a comrade, but you were not to be tempted. Well, I cannot find fault with you; mine is not, perhaps, the most enviable career, but I have pursued it too long to dream of turning back; my soul is already lost without hope—lost, lost, lost!'

"He was silent for a moment.

"'What nonsense I was speaking!' he exclaimed, suddenly, a ghastly smile lighting up his features. 'We shall part soon, Andrews, and shall never meet again; for my time is nearly up, and there is one waiting for me who never allows his bondsmen to escape.'

"He again checked himself.

"'More folly!' he suddenly exclaimed, breaking into a loud, wild laugh. 'I have been apt lately to talk in a rambling way. What did I say? Well, no matter. I was telling you I would land you and Miss Arden, as soon as possible.'

"And why not quit this dreadful life yourself, Captain Penrose, before it is too late? I uttered, hastily.

"The same ghastly smile, as before, passed over his features.

"'The advice of a boy, Andrews!' he replied. 'Because I am wedded to it, and it to me, with bonds stronger than the church ever bound man to woman.'

"'All hands unmoor ship!'

"These words were uttered in the unearthly voice of the dark stranger, yet no one was aware that he was on board.

"'My last cruise!' exclaimed the captain, springing from his seat, and rushing on deck. 'All hands unmoor ship!' he repeated, and in a moment he was all life and energy. 'Huzza, my boys! the wealth which floats on the wide sea shall be our reward!' he shouted, to encourage the men as they ran the anchor up to the bows.

"'The wide sea shall be your reward!' cried the mysterious voice.

"'Ha, ha, ha!' rang through the ship.

"The seamen for a moment stood aghast, but they were not to be daunted; they persuaded themselves it was the voice of the captain; but that night they had terrible cause to think differently. The sails were loosened, the tacks hauled on board, the sheets aft, and once more the doomed brig flew seaward to her accursed work; tempest and lightning accompanying her on her course.

"No sooner were we clear of the land, than the sky, hitherto of azure hue, became overcast with clouds; the wind increased to a furious gale, the sea rose with wild foaming crests, and away we drove before the blast; the lightning flashing vividly, the thunder roaring, and the waves in deluges breaking over our decks. Whenever I went on deck, there I saw standing, near the helm, the mysterious stranger. He might have been taken for a statue, so calm and unmoved he stood; not a word did he utter, his dark, bronze-coloured countenance alone exhibiting marks of satisfaction, as the storm raged more fiercely, and any of the seamen showed signs of fear at the awful strife of the elements. There was something peculiarly terrific in the stern glance of his dark eye, and the sarcastic curl of his otherwise immovable lip. As spell-bound I gazed on him, my limbs shook, till I sank senseless on the deck.

"On, on we flew towards the north, day after day, when a sail was made out right ahead.

"'A prize! a prize!' was the cry on board.

"We neared her fast, nor did she attempt to escape us. We seemed to fly over the waters, at such a rate did the gale drive us onward; and the pirates little thought what demon power blew those furious blasts, urging them on to destruction. The stranger was soon made out to be a large ship, and the pirates, eager for plunder, insisted that she was a richly-laden merchantman. Every preparation was, however, made for a fight, should she prove, as she probably was, well armed. The black flag was hoisted to intimidate the enemy, and before long we brought her within range of our guns. As we were about to run alongside, she suddenly hauled her wind, and before we had time to luff likewise, she poured in from a broadside of ten guns a heavy fire, raking us fore and aft, and then keeping away again, allowed us to range up on her beam, giving us a taste of her quality on that side also.

"Never shall I forget the shrieks, the cries, and the groans of the enraged pirates, or their fearful denunciations of vengeance. They stormed and swore in vain; their oaths and cries echoed with mocking laughter by the same mysterious voice as before; and *this time* the seamen guessed from whence it came. Every shot from the enemy had told with awful effect, while we had done but little damage in return. Numbers lay dead, others dying or dreadfully wounded, some of the guns were dismounted, the bulwarks torn and decks ploughed up, slippery with gore, and encumbered with the wreck of the shattered spars and rigging, while the mainmast, struck just above the deck, looked as if ready every instant to fall.

"Above all the noise and confusion, the voice of the dark stranger was now heard with terrific tones, encouraging the pirate crew to renewed exertions. Their only chance of victory was to run alongside, and try a hand-to-hand struggle, but scarcely could they hope for success against a well-armed king's ship. The attempt, however, was made, the pirate captain lashing the fluke of the bow-anchor into the fore-rigging of the enemy. Then came the fiercest strife. Three times did the pirates gain a footing on the deck of the king's ship, and as often were they driven back, and boarded in return, each time with much diminished numbers; but they fought for life and liberty, and well knew that quarter would neither be asked nor given.

"Among the first who boarded us, from the king's ship, was a gentleman in plain clothes, who fought with the greatest desperation. Even the fiercest held back till he crossed swords with the captain. At that moment the unhappy Mrs. Lawley, instigated by what motive I know not, rushed on deck, and no sooner did her glance fall on the brave man who was defending himself against such fearful odds, than she uttered a piercing shriek, which sounded above the din of battle and the roaring of the wind.

"'My husband! my husband!' she exclaimed; but scarcely had she uttered the words, when the sword of the pirate pierced him to the heart. She rushed forward to stay the murderer's hand, but it was too late; and as she beheld the lifeless body of her husband, she clasped her hands with an expression of hopeless agony on her countenance, which I shall never forget, exclaiming,

"'And was it thus for one abandoned like me you died? Oh, Henry! how unworthy was I of you, but I will not survive you.'

"As she uttered these words, she threw herself on the body. She took the hand on which the chill of death was already stealing; she gazed into the eyes of the corpse now glazed and senseless. She assured herself that her husband was indeed dead; then, imparting a kiss upon the cold brow, she sprang on her feet, and before any of the pirates could stay her, she threw herself, with a shriek of convulsive laughter, into the raging ocean. The sound was echoed in yet wilder strains, by a thousand mocking voices, which seemed to issue from the dark clouds, hanging like a funeral-pall overhead.

"Even the bold pirates stood aghast, but the captain ordered a boat to be instantly lowered. The command was obeyed, and the boat was swamped alongside, while three of the crew were swept away by the sea; indeed the attempt was useless, for the moment the unhappy lady plunged into the water, she sank beneath its surface, nor was the slightest trace of her again visible.

"During every action I had been on deck, standing near the mainmast, but taking no part in the fray, and caring little whether a shot knocked me over or not. Had it not been for Miss Arden, I should have welcomed death, as a release from the life of thraldom I was doomed to bear, and the horrors to which I was daily a witness; but to protect her I wished to live, only I was determined that the pirates should not say that I held back from joining them through cowardice.

"It might seem extraordinary that I should care for the opinion of such reprobates, but I believe my behaviour in this respect mainly assisted the captain in preserving me from their fury. While I was standing as I have described, the shot and splinters flying harmlessly about my head, thrice did the Demon Pilot pass close to me, a gleam of malignant satisfaction on his bronze-like countenance, for he knew full well that the souls he had lured to destruction were about to become his prey. The guns roared louder than ever, the shot crashed through the sides of the brig, the yells of the combatants grew fiercer and fiercer, when it struck me that the ship was settling deeper in the water.

"The thought that Miss Arden would be left to perish rushed into my mind, and I sprang below. I found her stretched on the sofa fainting from terror, and the water already washing the deck of the cabin. Lifting her senseless form in my arms, I hurried again on deck, when seizing a cutlass, I struck a pirate dead who attempted to oppose me, and at that instant the quarters of the two vessels meeting, I sprang over the hammock nettings on board the king's ship. The last act had been witnessed by one of the officers, or I should have been cut down immediately, for the seamen thinking that they were about to be boarded in that direction, came aft to repulse the enemy, but the fresh air recovering Miss Arden, she instantly perceived what had occurred, and throwing herself before me, exclaimed,

"'He is no pirate! oh, do not injure him!'

"At these words the men restrained their hands, and the next moment their attention was called off to witness the awful fate of the pirate ship. During the action the storm had much increased, and the crew of the corvette, seeing her condition, contrived to cut her clear of their own ship, just as I was leaping on board. To the last, although the water was almost awash with the deck, the pirates continued firing their guns, uttering fearful yells, shrieks, and curses.

"As I gazed at her with staring eyes, I beheld the terrific form of the dark stranger, standing upright amid the bodies of the dying and the dead, and the wreck of spars and rigging which cumbered the deck. Gradually his figure expanded into gigantic proportions, growing every instant more hideous and awful. His bronze-like countenance, with his eyes glowing like furnaces, reached the topmast-head as he stood between the two masts of the brig, grasping one in each hand, the vivid lightning playing round his stern features, while the roar of the thunder and the cannon, the crashing of spars and timbers, the wild tumult of human voices, and the shouts of the mocking laughter of the invisible spirits who surrounded us, made a wilder din than is heard in the fiercest fight.

Furiously he stamped his feet; the wild sea rushed over the deck of the pirate ship: again he stamped with greater fury than before, and the waters dashed upwards from the stroke, the thick spray flying in showers over our mast-heads; a third time he stamped, and down, down, down went the accursed brig to the unfathomed depths of the ocean, the despairing shrieks of the crew ringing in our ears ere they were ingulfed beneath the foaming waves, the last object seen being the tremendous countenance of the demon, lighted up with a gleam of satisfaction at having thus secured his prey. That also grew gradually fainter and fainter, till it totally disappeared, and not a trace was left of the doomed bark.

"No sooner had this dreadful event occurred, than the wind subsided, the sea went down, the clouds were dissipated, and the bright sun shone forth from the blue sky. What may seem extraordinary is, that not a man, a spar, or a sail of the royal cruiser had been injured. I was immediately led up to the captain, who, hearing the account of the officer who witnessed my killing the pirate, believed my rather incredible story (which I hope, by the by, you will do), and every attention which courtesy and humanity could dictate was paid to Miss Arden and myself. We soon reached Port Royal, in Jamaica, where Mr. Arden, who had given his daughter up as lost, was so overjoyed at her recovery, that he could deny her no request she made. One of the first was, that she might bestow her hand upon me.

"On my return to England I called on Mr. Damer, who of course thought that I must have been lost in his brig. He expressed himself much pleased at seeing me safe, and satisfied with my conduct throughout, though he did not appear quite to comprehend the account I gave him of the Demon Pilot. I afterwards met the real Captain Penrose, who happened just then to be in Liverpool, and he narrated to me how he had been robbed by a man who had assumed his name, and run away with the brig; but to this day no one has been able to discover the true name of the pirate chief."

We thanked Captain Andrews for his yarn, and he having made himself, as he said, perfectly comfortable, returned to his own ship, which, on the following morning, made sail to the southward, and we saw no more of him.

I have strong suspicions that at the time he referred to, he was out of his mind, and that the Demon Pilot was the phantom of a heated brain.

CHAPTER XXIX.

IT is impossible to describe all the adventures I encountered, both by sea and land, during the two years and a half I remained on that detestable coast. Night after night have I spent with my gallant men in open boats, while searching for slave vessels up the rivers, without any shelter to guard us from the noxious exhalations which rose from the black muddy banks, and from the vast accumulation of decayed matter created by the luxuriant vegetation which surrounded us, when we should have been thankful for a spot no better than the darkest cellar in London to lay our heads in. Constantly we were engaged in mortal strife with Spaniards, Portuguese, French, and with the most desperate reprobates of all nations employed in that diabolical traffic—sometimes, even, we were attacked, when on shore, by the blacks themselves, whom we were endeavouring to protect. Sometimes we had gales which lasted for several days together, or the ship was struck by sudden squalls, which carried the sails out of the bolt-ropes, or nearly threw her on her beam-ends—so that what with dangers of shipwreck and drowning; with hot burning suns, and damp fevergiving fogs; with alligators up the rivers, and sharks at sea, should one chance to get into the water; with slavers' bullets and cold steel in every direction; with disagreeables and hardships of every description; the life of a naval officer on the coast of Africa is not quite so luxuriously idle as some worthy gentlemen in England would wish to make the public believe. We chased upwards of a hundred suspicious-looking vessels, and captured twenty, which were condemned, and it is impossible to say the number we boarded of all descriptions, to ascertain their character, often, from the heavy sea running, at no little risk of our lives. We made some little prize-money, certainly; but can any one with the feelings of a gentleman dare to assert that this was an incentive to action? I do not mean to say that such prize-money is not acceptable, especially to those who have wives and families. It serves to form a fund, perhaps the slight pittance which is to support the dear ones they leave behind, when noxious climes or foemen's swords have done their work—a fund for which they can save nothing out of the magnificent salary it is asserted they receive for idling in Malta harbour, from the hard-taxed population of Great Britain. But a defence of the service is unnecessary, for I feel assured, as will all thinking men, that the honour, the safety, and prosperity of England, depend on her maintaining a large and efficient navy; and that, as it has hitherto warded off the greatest curse which can afflict a nation—an invasion of the country, so will it in future, if properly supported, be the means of keeping the horrors of war from our island shores.* But I must return to my narrative.

After some weeks' cruising off the River Bonny, we took another prize, the Teresa, which was sent under charge of Seaton to Sierra Leone, and her crew were taken on board the Albatross, and landed a few days afterwards at the Island of Anabona, where they were left to shift for themselves. For several weeks after that we had little success, except so far as in driving slavers off the coast, and in preventing their taking slaves on board. At last we fell in with the commodore, and our captain went on board his ship. He returned with a gleam of satisfaction on his countenance.

"I am happy to tell you, gentlemen, that we are soon to leave this part of the coast for the southward," he observed, as we stood round him on the quarter-deck. "Seaton and the Teresa's prize crew are to return in the Sparrow, and, as soon as we get them on board, we are to sail for the Cape."

We had still long to wait, and I remembered Don Diego Lopez de Mendoza's observation, "That there's many a slip between the cup and the lip;" though he, by the by, found that he could not slip his neck out of the rope spun to hang him.

Seaton and the Teresa's prize crew had rejoined us, and we were

* While the preceding sheets were going through the press, a work was sent me, with which I have been so much pleased that I am glad to have an early opportunity, as I have departed from the thread of my story, of bringing it before the notice of such of the service as may read these pages. It is written by Lieutenant A. F. Kynaston, Royal Navy, late of H.M.S. Rodney, and is entitled, "Casualties Afloat, with Practical Suggestions for their Prevention and Remedy," published by Trelawny Saunders, 6, Charing-cross. When a man devotes his attention to the means of saving the lives of his fellow-creatures, he at least merits their affection and gratitude. I feel it my duty to recommend Mr. Kynaston's work to all officers, whether of the royal navy or mercantile marine, on account of the very valuable suggestions he offers as to the best means of rounding to a ship, and lowering a boat when a man falls overboard, under the various circumstances of a moderate, fresh, or strong breeze, or a strong gale. He also gives plans for improved life-buoys, and a life-boat, as also for a cradle for lowering a boat into the water; indeed I consider the book in question as an important "voice from the ocean," and one which I hope may be heard far and wide. I at least may claim to be unprejudiced in favour of the author, for I have no personal acquaintance whatever with him. The book is not only nicely got up with very pretty illustrations, but is full of amusing anecdotes, which will make it prized by all lovers of romantic stories.

only waiting to communicate once more with the commodore, to sail for the Cape of Good Hope, when, as we were reaching off the land with a strong wind from the southward and westward, a sail hove in sight standing in for the land. She approached us till we were about three miles apart, when we had little doubt, from her appearance, that she was a slaver; and she, not liking our look, disguised as we were, tacked, and stood off close hauled on the wind.

A heavy sea was running, and the breeze was freshening, but we packed on every stitch of canvass the Albatross could carry, to come up with her. Our respective rates of sailing were nearly equal at first; though the stronger it blew the faster we overhauled her, and the more we were incited to maintain the pursuit. The master watched his masts and spars with an anxious eye, for they cracked and bent under the unusual pressure, but Captain Dainmore had no thoughts of taking in canvass. At last we got the chase within range of our guns, and several shots were sent after her from our bow chasers; as long as none took effect, she continued her course, in the hope that we might carry away some of our spars, but when two hit her hull in succession and a third wounded her mainmast, her crew hauled down her colours and hove her to. I was accordingly sent on board to take possession, which, with some difficulty, I accomplished, and found her fitted with a slave deck and watercasks, and irons on board. Her crew were a villanous-looking set of fellows, and I saw at once that the utmost precaution would be necessary on our parts to guard our lives from them. I would gladly have dispensed with their society altogether, but scarcely had I got on board than a heavy squall came on, and so increased the sea that there would have been much risk in passing from one vessel to the other. Having informed Captain Dainmore of the character of the prize, he signalized me to secure my prisoners, and to make the best of my way to Sierra Leone. I thus found myself in command of the San José, Portuguese schooner of two hundred and fifty tons, last from Bahia, and bound for Loanda.

Seaton had fortunately accompanied me as my second in command, so I had an active and intelligent companion. While we were still under the guns of the brig, I made the Portuguese crew go aloft and shorten sail, and during that time I sent Seaton below to examine the vessel, and to secure all the arms he could find. This done, as soon as we had got everything snug, I ordered the Portuguese down into the fore peak, and placed sentries over them, well armed, with directions to shoot the first man who attempted to come on deck without leave. The captain and mates I confined by themselves, and allowed only one to come on deck by himself at a time. It must be remembered that we had only eight men to keep thirty fellows in check. At night we lost sight of the Albatross, when it came on to blow harder than ever, and before morning a very heavy gale had sprung up. It continued all day increasing in violence, till we were obliged to heave the schooner to. She proved herself a very fine sea boat, and as she was in good condition, I had no fears on the score of her safety. Seaton and I were on deck together, just as he had relieved me in the morning watch, when, as we were anxiously looking out for a change in the weather, we fancied we perceived through the mist what appeared a large ship dismasted, and driving before the gale. Our glasses told us that it was so. Just then we apparently were perceived by her, for the report of a gun came booming over the waters—another and another followed at a minute's interval, speaking a tale of distress in a language a seaman well knows.

"Seaton," I said, "that ship requires our aid. We must run down to her at all risks, and keep near her till we can get on board. I think there is less sea than there was. What say you?"

"We can do it, sir. There's risk, certainly; but the object is worthy of it," he replied.

"Very well," I answered. "Call six of the Portuguese on deck—we shall want their assistance in getting the boat out, but tell our men to keep an eye on each."

Watching for a favourable opportunity we got the schooner before the wind, one sea breaking on board of us, but doing little damage, and we bore down to the ship, now to the north-west of us. As we neared the ship, we saw that she laboured very much, and that the seas occasionally broke over her and swept her decks, while the British ensign was hoisted half-way up the stump of her mizen-mast. Her crew had rigged a jury foremast, which kept her before the wind, but her rudder was gone; and though some spars were towing astern, to aid in steering her, they answered their purpose badly. Her crew also were at the pumps; and from the fresh streams of water which spouted from her sides, she had evidently sprung a serious leak. As we passed close to her a voice hailed,—

"The water gains on us: in mercy don't desert us."

"We'll assist you, if possible," I exclaimed, as we swept by, and a loud cheer from the ship was the answer.

We now clewed up everything but a close-reefed topsail, and though we had passed ahead of the ship, I had little fear of being able to heave the schooner to, till she again drove down to us. As the day wore on the sea went down, and the wind decreased, and providentially it was so, for, notwithstanding this, the leak increased rapidly on the ship. I accordingly prepared to send a boat on board, for she had lost all hers, and for this purpose it was necessary that she also should heave-to. This she accomplished by hoisting a topsail on the stump of her mizen-mast, lowering the sail forward, and suddenly hauling in forward, on a spring made fast to the spars she had been towing aft. We then hove-to under her lee, and I sent Seaton on board, with directions to return with some of the crew to aid in working the schooner. He did so immediately, with the first mate and eight men, and we then set to work, and got the remainder of our boats into the water. The mate told me she was an outward-bound Indiaman, and had numerous passengers on board.

Seaton had hurt his leg in the first trip, and an unaccountable desire seizing me to go on board, I manned one of the boats with the Portuguese, who behaved well, and ordered him to take charge of the schooner. There was considerable risk in getting alongside, but I reached the ship's deck in safety. The passengers were crowding up from below, for the report had got abroad that she was sinking fast. Her master, a noble-looking old man, stood near the gangway, his white locks streaming in the wind.

"The ladies—the females first, as you are men!" he exclaimed.

Several were already being lowered into the mate's boat. I rushed aft. I descried a female form on the deck, which my heart would have recognised among a thousand.

She was seated on a bench on deck, calmly waiting her turn to be summoned to the gangway to be lowered into the boat. Her feelings had told her who was approaching as she first saw me in the boat, but she could not believe her senses. As I sprang on to the poop she looked up; she knew me. It was my own Edith! She rose to meet me, but fell fainting in my arms. In a few moments she recovered, and I bore her to the boat; I would intrust her to no one else as I lowered myself down, holding her round the waist with one arm, while with the other I grasped a rope and kept her with my foot from touching the side of the ship. Several other ladies and children were next lowered into the boat, and I received them in my arms and placed them carefully on the seats, but I could not bring myself to quit my prize. My boat was soon loaded with as many persons as it was safe to carry, and shoving off from the side of the ship, I steered towards the schooner.

I had little time to question my Edith as to what unlooked-for circumstance had brought her on board the ship, but the few words she spoke made me supremely happy. As she reclined in the stern-sheets, wrapped up in a boat-cloak which I had folded round her, to shelter her somewhat from the sea which broke over us, she looked up in my face while I was steering, and smiling, said,—

"I would rather that you had preserved me, Walter, than any other human being."

We soon reached the deck of the schooner, and, with joy at my heart, I placed Edith in safety on the deck, surrounded with the other ladies I had been the means of preserving. Talk of wealth or luxury creating happiness—that day of tempest, peril, and exertion was, I believe, the happiest, or one of the happiest, in my life. I scarcely remained a moment on board the schooner, but was soon again alongside the ship. I clambered up on deck, where I met the master, who was calmly telling the people off into the boats.

"We have no time to lose, sir," he whispered. "By the peculiar motion of the ship, and the low groans I hear issuing from her hold, I suspect that she is settling down fast."

I listened.

"It is so, I fear," I answered. "Our most expeditious method of getting the people on board the schooner will be to carry ropes to her, and they must haul themselves on board."

No sooner said than done. While the boats conveyed the less active persons, the soldiers and other landsmen, the seamen made their transit to the schooner by the flying bridge we had constructed. I had returned on board to receive the people, and to give the order to cut away the ropes, should the ship give signs of going down. It was nervous work to watch the men swinging over the boiling waters, and now and then submerged in them, as the ropes twisted and surged in their grasp, in a manner which would have allowed none but seamen to hold on. The old master was still standing on the deck of the ship, when the last boat-load came on board. His hat was off, and his white hair was streaming in the wind.

"He refuses to quit her, sir, till everybody is out of her," cried the mate. "He says he will get on board by the warp."

"That must not be," I exclaimed. "Go back for him and insist on his coming."

"He will not move for me, sir," returned the mate.

"Then I must try and prevail on him," I cried, and leaping into the boat, the men gave way towards the ship.

The sea was already rushing into the lower ports of the Indiaman. As I got alongside, the remainder of the crew made a rush into the boat, and almost swamped her. Several, however, when they saw the danger, returned, and got along by the ropes. I had just time to seize the old master by the arm, and to hurry him to the boat, when the ship gave some heavy rolls, which seemed like her dying struggles.

As we passed the short space to the schooner, he turned round to gaze at the ship; and now, that all responsibility was removed from his shoulders, he appeared quite bewildered at what had occurred.

I leaped on the schooner's deck—

"Cast off everything—cut away!" I cried. "Up with the helm."

Not an instant had we to spare. We were scarcely clear of the ship, when she once more rolled heavily, and instead of rising, her bulwarks sunk down, and the waves danced over the spot where she had been. The wind now came round and blew a steady breeze from the northward. With the number of passengers I had on board, it was, of course, important that we should reach a port without delay: and as they were bound to the Cape of Good Hope, I determined to shape a course for Cape Town. The schooner was fortunately well supplied with provisions and water, and we had a remarkably quick run, so that, except that the people were very much crowded, no one had much cause to complain.

I will not dwell on the delight with which I watched over my Edith, and how supremely proud and happy she made me, by assuring me that she would never be faithless to me. Her father, she told me, had lately been appointed to the command of a regiment at the Cape, and had sent for her to join him, as the surest means of breaking off the match with me. There is an old saying, that "Man proposes, but God disposes," and I also verily believe that happy marriages are arranged in heaven, and ill-assorted unions in the abode of evil spirits; for here were two people, against all probabilities, thrown together in the very position of all others they might have wished for, to bring about a result, to prevent which another was taking every precaution in his power.

We arrived some time before the Albatross, and surprised, indeed, were our shipmates to find us there. I got great credit for the manner in which I rescued the people from the wreck of the Indiaman, and on being introduced to Colonel Mowbray, he received me very cordially, and I was not denied when I called the following morning to inquire for Edith. I got transferred to the flag-ship at the Cape, and Seaton received an acting commission on board the Albatross in my room. I am proud to say that my messmates parted with me with regret. They sent me a large bundle of papers endorsed, "Voices from the Ocean," which I intend some day to give to the public under that or another title.

Captain Dainmore and Upton are both most deservedly promoted, and I am happy to say the first made a good deal of prize-money, which will aid somewhat in supporting his family. My excellent friend Green has proved a father indeed to the little Eva, but has been unable to discover her kindred and friends. Perhaps he would rather not.

My commission as a commander not long after arriving, thanks to the exertions of certain friends who shall be nameless, Colonel Mowbray at length relented, and I have now every right to call Edith my own. I learned a lesson by these events which I wish to teach others—Never despair when the prospect looks the blackest, but trust that a kind Heaven will soon brighten it again.

THE END.

www.ingramcontent.com/pod-product-compliance
Lightning Source LLC
Chambersburg PA
CBHW021355230426

43666CB00006B/531